Meditation in Buddhist-Ch
A Critical Anal
edited by
Elizabeth J. Harris and John O'Grady

Meditation
in Buddhist-Christian
Encounter

A Critical Analysis

edited by
Elizabeth J. Harris and John O'Grady

Cover design: Orinta Rötting, Munich

First impression 2019
ISBN 978-3-8306-7954-7
Copyright © EOS – Editions of Sankt Ottilien

All rights reserved. No part of this publication may be
reproduced, stored in a retrieval system, or transmitted,
in any form or by any means, electronic, mechanical,
photocopying, or otherwise, without the prior permission
of the Publisher

A catalogue record for this book is available
from the German Library
http://dnb.ddb.de

EOS – Editions of Sankt Ottilien
www.eos-books.com | mail@eos-books.com
Printed in Germany

This book is dedicated
to all those who work
for understanding
between the different
religious traditions of our world
especially in locations of conflict

ACKNOWLEDGEMENTS

The contributions to this book arose from the twelfth conference of the European Network of Buddhist-Christian Studies (EN-BCS), which was held at Montserrat, near Barcelona, in 2017, in partnership with the Universitat Pompeu Fabra. The title of this book replicates the theme: Meditation in Buddhist-Christian Encounter: A Critical Analysis. We are grateful to all the speakers for their willingness to revise their papers for publication and to respond to editorial queries.

We are also grateful for our collaboration with the Universitat Pompeu Fabra. Particular thanks must go to Prof Raquel Bouso García and her team of helpers, who liaised with the staff at the monastery at Montserrat and worked tirelessly during the conference to ensure everything went smoothly. We thank the community of Montserrat Abbey, who hosted our conference. Thanks must also go to the following donors without which the conference would not have been possible: the Association of Protestant Churches and Missions in Germany (Evangelisches Missionswerk in Deutschland), EKD (Protestant Churches in Germany), the Protestant Church of Hessen Nassau, the Lund Mission, the Spalding Trust and research funds secured by Prof Bouso García.

All members of the Management Board of the ENBCS contributed to the success of the conference. Particular thanks must go to Prof Perry Schmidt-Leukel, the Acting Treasurer, and Dr Martin Rötting, the Network's Secretary.

The publication of this book would not have been possible without the help of EOS Publishing House, with which we have had a productive relationship for many years. We are particularly grateful for the advice and assistance of Fr Dr Cyrill Schäfer OSB.

This is the seventh volume that EOS has published in cooperation with ENBCS and we hope that there will be more.

Our hope is that this work will contribute to understanding and cooperation between Buddhists and Christians.

March 2019   *Elizabeth J. Harris and John O'Grady*

TABLE OF CONTENTS

THEME 5:
MEDITATION AND ACTION IN BUDDHISM
AND CHRISTIANITY

INTRODUCTION

Elizabeth J. Harris

The term 'meditation', as it is used in contemporary English-speaking western societies, popularly denotes a spiritual practice that involves sitting in silence, perhaps in the lotus posture, with closed eyes. It is linked with peace and calmness, and, more often than not, with Hinduism or Buddhism rather than Christianity. The term itself, however, as Karl Baier explains in this volume, originated in Greek culture with the words *melétē* and *meletáō* and was translated into Latin as *meditatio*. When the term was appropriated by Christians, they used it to translate a Hebrew term that had nothing to do with silence but rather conveyed a murmuring of or pondering on texts. It was the term 'contemplation', from the Latin *contemplatio*, which came to denote silent, non-conceptual practices aimed at union or direct encounter with the love of God. Only in a process of reduction did the two terms eventually become almost interchangeable for western Christians within modernity. When the word 'meditation' was then appropriated to translate some Buddhist technical terms, a consequence of the encounter between Buddhism and western societies in the context of colonialism, there was an ongoing process of reductionism. For instance, in the Pāli tradition, terms as various as *samādhi* (concentration), *bhāvanā* (becoming or mental development through practices aimed at calm or insight), *jhāna* (absorption or a higher state of consciousness gained through concentrating on an object), *kammaṭṭhāna* (lit: working ground, traditionally exercises using an object for concentration under the guidance of a teacher), *samatha* (tranquillity) and *vipassanā* (insight) were translated as 'meditation'. For this reason, Sarah Shaw, in this volume, prefers to concentrate on one Pāli term in her survey of 'meditation' in Buddhism – *bhāvanā*, a term that embraces practices that are much wider than the popular representation of 'meditation' as a 'sitting' practice.

The term 'meditation', therefore, as used today in western societies is highly reductive, when viewed from a historical perspective. Yet, it has been adopted by both Buddhists and Christians, across the globe, bringing practitioners of the two traditions together in inter-monastic exchange, joint meditation retreats, dialogues concerning the relationship between meditation and social action, cross-tradition pupil/teacher relationships and joint academic explorations into the parallels between Buddhist and Christian meditative/contemplative practice. Admittedly, within the last fifty years, there has been an experiential asymmetry in this, with Christians benefitting more from encounters with Buddhist meditation than Buddhists have benefitted from encounter with Christian contemplative practice. Nevertheless, the practice of meditation has become one of the most significant 'grounds for meeting' within contemporary Buddhist-Christian relationships.

Within this context, an academic collection that critically analyses the role in Buddhist-Christian encounter of the variety of practices embraced by the term 'meditation' is timely. The contributors to this book use the academic tools of historical inquiry, sociology, cultural studies, philosophy and comparative textual study. The result is an interdisciplinary contribution, which takes the religious experience of those involved in Buddhist-Christian encounter seriously, without reifying it above its cultural and socio-political contexts.

The collection is structured around four case studies: Christian-Buddhist encounter through Zen practice; Christian-Buddhist encounter through mindfulness; the Hesychast tradition and its affinities to Buddhism; and meditation and action in Buddhism and Christianity. Each contains contributions from both Buddhist and Christian perspectives. Prefacing these case studies, however, are three additional contributions, which landscape the topic by offering surveys of: (1) key moments in history, when meditation featured in the encounter between Buddhists and Christians;

(2) the presence and role of 'meditation' and 'contemplation' in Christian history; (3) the presence and role of *bhāvanā,* one of the terms translated into English as 'meditation', in the Southern or Theravāda tradition of Buddhism.

Summary of Chapters

Elizabeth Harris, in her introductory chapter, surveys the history of meditation in Buddhist-Christian encounter, through focussing on a series of 'moments', beginning with the Italian missionary priest, Ippolito Desideri, who travelled to Tibet in the early eighteenth century, and ending with an initiative of the US-based Society for Buddhist-Christian Studies in the late twentieth century, when five Christians were asked to reflect on Buddhist meditation and five Buddhists, to reflect on Christian prayer. Some of these 'moments', on both the Christian and Buddhist side, were characterized by incomprehension, hostility or dogmatism and some, by a serious wish to understand the other tradition. Particular emphasis is given to the historical factors that conditioned these positive and negative encounters. For instance, the chapter illustrates that, in the context of the power relationships of imperialism and the missionary zeal of an evangelical Protestantism, the possibility of mutual understanding between Christian and Buddhist practitioners about meditative/contemplative practice was extremely low.

Karl Baier offers an extensive, detailed history of the role of 'contemplation' and 'meditation' within Christianity, which breaks new ground. Beginning with pre-Christian ancient Greece, his focus is primarily but not exclusively the Roman Catholic tradition. 'Meditation', he explains, was originally used within Christianity to translate the Hebrew word, *hagah,* meaning to murmur, to recite or to ponder. It came to mean an intellectual or imaginative pondering on a theological concept or a biblical narrative to enable a deeper bond of love between the Christian and God. Contemplation, on the other hand, traditionally concerned preparing the mind and heart for a non-conceptual encounter with God with a loss of the egocentric self. Some forms, he explains, retained a distinction between creator and creature, whilst others anticipated a 'union of indistinction' between humanity and God. He then charts the turbulent history of competition between the two practices, culminating, at the end of the seventeenth century, with the persecution of the practice of contemplation by the Roman Catholic hierarchy, because it focussed on inner experience rather than the sacraments and the teachings of the Church. Lastly, Baier turns to the revival of contemplative prayer within modernity, first expressed in a renewed theology of mysticism from 1900 onwards and then, after 1960, in movements that sought to spread contemplative practice. Throughout the chapter, Baier illustrates his account with people, from Anselm of Canterbury to St Ignatius of Loyola, from George Fox to Augustin-François Poulain, from Evelyn Underhill to John Main and Thomas Keating.

Sarah Shaw, in her survey of the role of meditation in Buddhism, focusses on the concept of *bhāvanā* in the Southern Buddhist tradition (Theravāda Buddhism). In a wide-ranging chapter that covers the Pāli Canon, traditional lay and monastic practice, and contemporary developments, she argues that the modern characterization of Buddhist meditation as a solitary, sitting, insight-orientated practice is a reduction of the complexity and richness of *bhāvanā* within the Southern tradition, within which *samatha* (practices arousing calm) and *vipassanā* (practices arousing insight) were inter-dependent and equally valued. She draws particular attention to contemporary research into *samatha* practice in countries such as Cambodia, Sri Lanka and Thailand, where the use of mantras and body-centred visualization techniques were common. Her chapter, therefore, addresses the level of reductionism within western representations of 'meditation', through a historical and contextual examination of lived practice in what is considered to be the oldest Buddhist tradition.

Within the first case study, Christian-Buddhist encounter through Zen practice, Ursula Baatz uses historical, sociological and biographical tools to argue that the practice of Zen by Christians arose within a multi-layered context, in an increasingly globalized world. She reflects first on the concept of 'religion', arguing that both its socio-political dimensions and its orientation towards self-cultivation and transcendence must be taken into account. Turning to Japanese Christians in the late nineteenth and early twentieth centuries, she charts their willingness to harmonize their Christianity with Zen Buddhism as a way of asserting their patriotism and nationalism, paving the way for western Christians. Only then does she turn to the two Christian figures that form the focus of her chapter: Hugo M. Enomiya-Lassalle and Thomas Merton. Each is placed in his postcolonial historical context, Lassalle as the socially active Jesuit in Japan, critical of western-style Christianity and survivor of the Hiroshima bomb, and Merton, the archetypal spiritual seeker who becomes a Trappist monk and is then drawn to Asian spirituality. Both encounter prominent teachers of Zen, Merton with D.T. Suzuki and Lassalle with Harada Sōgaku Roshi of the Sanbōkyōdan (Three Treasures Association) with Baatz agreeing with Sharf, in the next chapter, that Yamada's appointment of Lassalle as a Zen teacher was 'illegitimate'. She then assesses what Zen meant for both before, again, placing this in the historical context of the victory within Christianity of the conceptual and verbal *meditatio* over the non-verbal *contemplatio* from the late seventeenth century to the mid-twentieth century. In this context, Zen was, therefore, seen by Christians such as Merton and Enomiya-Lassalle as a practice that complemented and enriched their Christian belonging.

Robert Sharf, in a critically significant study of why some Buddhists in Japan were willing to teach Zen to Christians, begins by contrasting the methods of the traditional Japanese Rinzai teacher, Sasaki Jōshū (1907-2014), with those of reformers within the previously mentioned Sanbōkyōdan, which was founded in 1957. The former, when teaching Christians at St Joseph's Abbey in Massachusetts, sought conversions to Zen and a willingness in his listeners to engage with the totality of Zen textual and liturgical practices. In his entire time in the West, he ordained no western Zen masters. The Sanbōkyōdan, on the other hand, was willing to adapt Zen teachings to the spirituality of Christians, not insisting that Christians should reject their religion in order to practice Zen and considerably reducing traditional kōan training. The result was that many Roman Catholics were recognized by the Sanbōkyōdan as Zen masters. Sharf points out that these methods were not endorsed by the majority of Zen practitioners in Japan and had affinities with those of a New Religious Movement. He creates an intriguing parallel with an imaginary group devoted solely to spreading Thomas Keating's Centring Prayer. Without formal links to the Roman Catholic Church and wider Christian practice, this imaginary group nurtures practitioners who consider themselves more Roman Catholic because of their contemplative achievement than those formally within the Church. The implicit question he raises is whether the Christians who drew Zen into their practice through the influence of the Sanbōkyōdan truly experienced the Zen tradition in its complexity and fullness or only a reified version, crafted for a western Christian constituency.

The second case study, Christian-Buddhist encounter through mindfulness, is introduced by Andreas Nehring, who offers a cultural studies perspective on the popularity of the essentially Buddhist concept of mindfulness in western societies. He argues that the near-normative status of the concept in psychotherapy, medicine, education, the prison system and discourses surrounding the avoidance of burn-out in stressful workplaces holds up a mirror to the socio-cultural factors underpinning western spirituality and, by implication, changes in spiritual practice among Christians. With reference to Jon Kabat-Zinn's Mindfulness-based Stress Reduction courses and Nyanaponika Thera's advocacy of 'bare attention', he points to the way 'mindfulness' is shaping popular discourse on the nature of religion and the nature of Buddhism, threatening to reduce the latter to a philosophy for the self-inspection of one's own consciousness. Without questioning the benefits of the practice of mindfulness for individuals, he nevertheless calls for a critical appraisal of its role in society, of the representation of Buddhism it encourages and, by extension, of its place in Buddhist-Christian encounter. Parallel to Sharf, the implicit question Nehring raises is: if Christian encounter with

Buddhism is informed only by the popularity of mindfulness in western societies, how authentic is that encounter?

In a further chapter that breaks new ground, Elise DeVido examines the role of Thích Nhất Hạnh in publicizing, shaping and embodying the global mindfulness movement. As a monk in Vietnam, he was at first known as a poet and a proponent of engaged Buddhism, not primarily as a teacher of Zen or mindfulness. These latter emphases, she argues, arose mainly through inter-cultural and inter-religious interactions in western contexts, including encounters with Christians. Thích Nhất Hạnh's fashioning of himself as a Vietnamese Zen monk, whose focus was both socially engaged and meditative, therefore, was conditioned by the particular context within which he found himself in the United States and Europe. DeVido then surveys the methods used by Thích Nhất Hạnh and his colleagues to create a popular western mindfulness culture that has influenced Christians and Buddhists, as well as those without any religious belonging, and also draws attention to an overlooked side of Thích Nhất Hạnh's contribution: his work on the textual foundations of mindfulness. The implicit question behind the chapter is again similar to that behind the contributions of both Sharf and Nehring: has the prioritizing of mindfulness in western discourse about Buddhism reduced awareness of complexity within Buddhist spiritual practice?

Sybille Fritsch-Oppermann, in contrast to both Nehring and DeVido, offers a philosophical perspective on both the meeting between Christianity and the Buddhist practice of mindfulness, and the wider meeting between Buddhism and the West. Preferring to see 'mindfulness' in Buddhism as the active practice of awareness and drawing on the Zen tradition, she examines the western appropriation of mindfulness in therapies such as Mindfulness-based Cognitive Therapy. She then seeks for analogies between Buddhist mindfulness meditation and Christian contemplation, noting the development of a Christian concept of mindfulness. Drawing the reader into an intercultural and comparative philosophy of emptiness and fullness, she suggests that the concept of mindfulness could form a starting point for an understanding of both ecology and Emotional Intelligence.

Nicholas Alan Worssam offers the first perspective within the next case study on the Hesychast tradition of Eastern Christianity and its affinities to Buddhism, offering a wide-ranging comparative textual study of Pāli sources and hesychastic writings. His aim is to explore 'the echoes of Buddhist categories of meditation practice to be found in the Christian tradition of hesychastic prayer'. He finds many such 'echoes', whilst accepting that 'at the end of the path the final metaphors may seem to divide'. He concentrates particularly on the Jesus prayer and the practice of 'watchfulness' in hesychasm, comparing the latter to Buddhist concepts such as *sati* (commonly translated as mindfulness), *indriya saṁvara* (guarding the doors of the senses) and *appamāda* (usually translated as earnestness or diligence). Towards the end, he touches on the experience of light in the *jhāna*s and hesychastic prayer. In spite of his awareness of difference, his conclusion is that 'there is a significant degree of contact between the two traditions', on the basis of textual evidence.

Elizabete Taivane, in a complementary, largely textual study, offers a comparative examination of hesychasm and the tantric elements of Buddhism in Tibet. Justifying her exercise in 'comparative mysticism', she appeals to the concept of 'universal patterns of human experience'. As Worssam, she is aware of difference between the two traditions. Mantra practice and the Jesus prayer are not the same, she insists, and tantric 'psychotechniques' are 'unique and do not have parallels in hesychast traditions'. At the same time, drawing on Russian writers, she demonstrates that both traditions speak of pacification of the body, thoughts and passions. Both 'deal with the same psychic phenomena' when they turn consciousness inwards. Both speak of a liberative vision of light – 'uncreated light' within Hesychasm and 'the clear light of bliss' in Tibetan Buddhism – and, for both, this is an experience that is transcendent, and linked to love and compassion. Her conclusion is that, in spite of difference between the two traditions, there are more convergences than divergences when it comes to the detail and consummation of spiritual practice.

Lastly, within this case study, Thomas Cattoi examines the concepts of *ālaya-vijñāna* (storehouse consciousness where impressions of past actions are stored as seeds for future experience) and *āśrayaparāvṛtti* (the manifestation or overturning of the basis whereby the storehouse is purified of defilements) in selected Yogācāra texts, and the notions of *nous* (the mind or intellect which receives imprints of actions) and *apatheia* (dispassion) in the writings of Evagrios Pontikos (late fourth century BCE). Cattoi first examines the concepts separately with particular reference to cognitive purification and the attainment of a tranquillity characterized by the absence of passionate attachment. He then brings them together in a dialogue that recognizes difference in cosmology, anthropology and the nature of ultimate reality but also 'intriguing points of contact'. The three contributors to this case study, therefore, on the evidence of textual study, point to the potential within Buddhist-Christian encounter of this area of exploration, as the points of contact between the hesychastic tradition of contemplation in Eastern Christianity and Buddhist meditation practices are examined more fully.

The final case study concerns the intersection between meditation and action in Buddhism and Christianity, particularly the way in which Buddhists and Christians have influenced one another at this intersection. John Makransky, writing from a Buddhist perspective, argues that effective compassionate action to alleviate suffering should integrate Buddhist insights into the misperception and reduction of the Other that spring from delusion, greed and ill-will, and Christian insights from liberation, Asian, African, feminist and womanist theologies into the need for social analysis to uncover the nature of oppressive structures present. In other words, if social action is to be marked by 'fierce compassion rather than dysfunctional forms of anger', then contemplative practice to uncover our delusive thinking is necessary, enriched by an awareness that deluded perceptions take shape in economic and political structures, an insight particularly present in the prophetic tradition of Christianity. His argument, therefore, is that insights from both traditions are needed for truly effective social action.

Leo Lefebure offers a Christian perspective on this case study, focussing on the Christian monastic motto *ora et labora* (pray and work) and its expression in different monastic Orders, beginning with the Benedictines and then moving to the Franciscans, the Dominicans, the Carmelites and the Jesuits, whose modes of being included variously: radical hospitality, the embrace of societal outcasts, the critique of the Spanish treatment of indigenous peoples in the Americas, the mystical paths of Teresa of Avila and St John of the Cross, the *Spiritual Exercises* of Ignatius of Loyola, and Pope Francis's 2015 encyclical on the environment, *Laudato Si'*. Throughout, he offers insights into how contemporary followers of these practices have engaged with Buddhists, citing the Buddhist-Christian encounters at Gethsemani Abbey (United States) in the late twentieth and early twenty-first centuries, Jesuit encounters with Zen and Theravāda Buddhism, and a Buddhist-Roman Catholic dialogue at Castel Gandolfo in Rome in 2015.

In the last chapter, Thao Nyugen offers a succinct and significant comparative study of the Six-Period Rituals of Repentance developed by Tran Thai Long of the Vietnamese Truc Lam Zen tradition and the daily examination of conscience developed by St Ignatius of Loyola. Whilst not overlooking differences, Nyugen draws attention to remarkable parallels between the two, for instance in the use of the senses, the development of self-awareness, the recognition of human weakness and the emphasis on action, namely the cultivation of discernment for more effective living in the world. The chapter ends with the potential for interreligious learning and mutual enrichment within both Christian and Buddhist communities if the two practices could be brought together in dialogue.

In Conclusion

Within any process of inter-religious encounter or learning, a spectrum of attitudes is present. At one end is assertion of irreducible difference between the traditions concerned and, at the other, the assertion of identity between them. The danger of the former is that similarities are hidden by an inflexible ideological or doctrinal dogmatism. The danger of the latter is that the wish to find identity between religious traditions leads to reducing one or all of the religious traditions in the encounter. This collection critically illustrates this spectrum, from historical examples of doctrinal dogmatism within the first chapter to the tendency to reduce the complexities of traditional spiritual practice in the case study concerning the communication of Zen to Christians. Nevertheless, the collection also illustrates the middle range of the spectrum, where differences and similarities between traditions are acknowledged and made the ground for reciprocal learning through dialogue and encounter. The result, as indicated by several chapters, can be transformative, illustrating that religious practice, and religion itself, is dynamic, developing and changing through encounter and dialogue.

INTRODUCTORY ADDRESS

MEDITATION
IN BUDDHIST-CHRISTIAN ENCOUNTER:
A CRITICAL ANALYSIS

Elizabeth Harris

Abstract

In this chapter, I examine key 'moments' in the history of Christian encounter with Buddhist meditation, and Buddhist encounter with Christian contemplation and meditation. I begin with the accounts of two Roman Catholic priests: Ippolito Desideri, who visited Tibet in the eighteenth century, and Vicentius Sangermano, whose account of Burmese practice was utilized by Francis Buchanan in 1799. I then pass to nineteenth century Sri Lanka and the lack of mutual understanding present in the writings of the evangelical missionaries and a key Buddhist revivalist, Anagārika Dharmapāla, the former influencing the latter. My twentieth and early twenty-first century 'moments' include Thomas Merton's championing of an inter-monastic dialogue of meditation and contemplation, Lance Cousin's Study of St Teresa of Avila and Buddhaghosa, an address given to the Eckhart Society by Ven. Ayya Khema, and the publication of Christians Talk about Buddhist Meditation; Buddhists Talk about Christian Prayer *in 2003, by the US-based, Society of Buddhist-Christian Studies. Through this historical examination, I will reflect on the contexts that have conditioned different levels of understanding of meditation and/ or contemplation in the two traditions, from incomprehension and hostility to rigorous dialogue, academic exploration and transformed spiritual practice.*

Keywords: Buddhism, Christianity, meditation, contemplation, *samatha, vipassanā*, Buddhist-Christian encounter

Introduction

My aim in this paper is to offer a not-too heavy survey of some 'moments' in the Christian encounter with Buddhist meditation, and the Buddhist encounter with Christian contemplation and meditation. I place within the category of Buddhist 'meditation', activities that 'arouse both calm (*samatha*) and insight (*vipassanā*)', to use Sarah Shaw's definition of *bhāvanā* in this volume. These activities include not only silent, sitting meditation but also devotional practices and chanting. Within Christian 'meditation', I place both contemplation and meditation, as defined and expanded by Karl Baier in this volume. In neither tradition are the terms used to describe these forms of practice unproblematic, as the introduction to this volume explains. The term 'meditation' is, in reality, a form of short-hand that covers diverse sets of practices, in both religious traditions.

My main interest is what conditioned my 'moments' of encounter, which produced judgements that ranged from incomprehension and hostility to deep engagement and transformed spiritual practice. Place and context are, therefore, important in my survey. I do not claim comprehensiveness. My choice of 'moments' is subjective, conditioned by my personal experience and research interests. Many others could be taken. Using a narrative technique, I begin with the Roman Catholic missionary priest, Ippolito Desideri, in eighteenth century Tibet, and end with a project of the US-based Society of Buddhist-Christian Studies.

Ippolito Desideri

Ippolito Desideri (1684-1733), an Italian Jesuit, arrived in Lhasa in 1716 as a missionary, after a period in Ladakh, where he had his first encounter with Tibetan Buddhists (Bray 2018, 23). In line with established Jesuit practice, he made contact with the court in Lhasa and began to learn Tibetan (Filibeck 2018, 64). He sought to remain independent, not wishing to receive alms, and employed local staff (Sweet 2018, 121). Within a few years, he was writing treatises in Tibetan on Christianity and extensive 'Notices' of his experience for public consumption (Sweet 2018, 119). From the latter, we know that he studied Buddhist texts under Tibetans and stayed at more than one Buddhist monastery (Sweet 2010). We know also that Buddhists allowed him to say Mass and that he debated with Tibetan Buddhist leaders. Further information about his life in Tibet, more honestly portrayed than in his 'Notices', can be found in his Account Books (Sweet 2018; Zwilling 2018).

Desideri visited Tibet when Chinese feudal overlordship was replacing that of the Mongols. It was a period of political turbulence, Desideri having to buy himself out of being conscripted into a militia in 1720, a feat that left him with few financial resources and that could have hastened his departure (Sweet 2018, 119). Before Desideri arrived, there had been a Capuchin presence between 1707 and 1711.

Desideri was a missionary priest, using the methods that the Jesuits had used in China and Japan, making high level contacts and studying the texts of Buddhism in order to refute them. Nevertheless, his presence was not connected with an imperial or colonizing project, which meant that Tibetan Buddhists did not necessarily see him as a threat. This context allowed a more reciprocal relationship between Desideri and Tibetan Buddhists than if Desideri had arrived under the mantle of an Italian expansionist imperialism. In addition, Desideri, as a Jesuit, was schooled in the philosophical thought of Thomas Aquinas (Pomplun 2018) and was heir to Ignatian spiritual practice, with its emphasis on the 'examination of conscience', a form of meditation.

There is evidence in Desideri's 'Notices' that he listened, observed Buddhist practice and read Buddhist texts with sensitivity and diligence, with a wish to truly understand the Other that was Buddhism, qualities which led Gasbarro to consider him an anthropologist (Gasbarro 2018). With reference to meditation, Desideri was fascinated by Tibetan treatises on 'the passions' and the Tibetan way to conquer them:

> The Tibetans have very beautiful treatises on this subject that with the finest moral philosophy explain the nature of each of the passions individually, the way that the actions that proceed from them are born in us, the evils and harms that come from them, and finally the way to conquer them, with the remedies for each one and its countervailing virtue. (Sweet 2010, 367)

He continued by stressing the Tibetan belief that the best way of conquering the 'passions' was to 'abandon the world and enter the religious life' but was aware that, for the one who had liberated himself from these 'passions', there was a further aim: 'to lead innumerable beings, to the best of his ability, to the same final and total escape and the achievement of eternal salvation' (Sweet 2010, 368). He then elaborated on this embryonic description of the Bodhisattva Vow, drawing on the texts, beginning with what he called 'the principal virtues', namely:

> patience, contemplation, diligence, fervor, and precise perfection in all things, complete impartiality toward all living beings without exception, great benevolence and love for all, a most affectionate and tender compassion, and finally, loving-kindness and compassion that is both affective and effective. By virtue of these a true *jangchup sempa*, or soul perfect in itself and zealous for others' salvation, not only shares and feels the pain of others and intensely desires to free them from suffering and evil, and lead them to rest and the good, but also, having exchanged himself with others, he no longer has any concern for himself but devotes himself entirely to others. He is like a loving mother who has seen the son she loves most tenderly fall into the depths of a most foul and dangerous ravine; she is not satisfied with just crying, screaming and sighing but descends into the depth herself. (Sweet 2010, 369)

Most significantly for this chapter, Desideri was aware that the path towards this attainment involved reflecting on such things as impermanence (*anicca*), contemplating 'the infinite afflictions of transmigration' and making 'solemn vows' (Sweet 2010, 366-368), all of which could fall under the term 'meditation'. Later Desideri amplified what he called 'contemplation' in the Tibetan system, describing three levels of practice directed towards 'the conquest of one's own passions', from the more focussed to the abstract (Sweet 2010, 388-389). Sitting meditation in a solitary place was also mentioned by Desideri, together with the visualization of the 'saints' and their 'virtues', which involved 'stimulating in oneself a great love for those virtues and setting them before oneself as the only objects worthy of one's affections' (Sweet 2010, 390). Earlier in his account he had recognized the role of retreat in monastic discipline:

> Some of the more observant monks will occasionally, with their lama's permission, retire for at least a month to one of the hermitages belonging to the monasteries in various places, to make a retreat and devote themselves to solitude, meditation, and fervent prayer. During this retreat they do not engage in any conversation or have any other thoughts or distractions, and they observe great poverty and austerity. Some monks are so enamored with the sweetness of contemplation that they ask for and obtain permission to live permanently in one of these hermitages, where they lead lives of great austerity, continual prayer and meditation. (Sweet 2010, 333)

Desideri's intense listening and observation understandably led him to comparisons that identified touching points and divergences between Tibetan Buddhist and Christian meditative/contemplative practice. He saw touching points particularly in the Tibetan concern that defilements or 'passions' should be destroyed. He also claimed that when Tibetans talked of five vices, these, in effect, embodied the seven deadly sins of Christianity. According to Pomplun, he also interpreted 'emptiness' in a positive way (Pomplun 2018, 110). In a pattern that would be repeated in later centuries in Christian representations of Buddhism, however, he detected within this the development of indifference to feelings and objects of sense. So, he wrote:

> Even though in this highest level of contemplation they are aim-
> ing at the same goal as we Christians, and they similarly aim
> to lead others there and to get there themselves, the Tibetans
> distance themselves greatly from us in their choice of means
> through which a person can easily reach his longed-for goal of a
> perfect, calm, and blissful transcendence of himself and all per-
> ceptible things. They take as their means and solution the guiding
> of their will to a state of impassability and abstraction from every
> feeling and every conception of any object, without the slightest
> inclination towards anything, remaining completely in a state of
> equilibrium or rather in a complete suspension. (Desideri 2010,
> 390)

This led him to the greatest difference of all: belief in God. Although Cattoi argues convincingly for an embryonic fulfilment
theory in Desideri's critique of Buddhist terms such as karma
and *pratītyasamutpāda* (Cattoi 2018), throughout his account of
the Tibetan Buddhism he witnessed, positive description is inter-
weaved with evocation of the diabolical. Ultimately the Buddha,
whom he termed the 'lawgiver', drew his followers away from
the conception of God and, for Desideri, in spite of the good he
had witnessed in the tradition, which could indeed by fulfilled by
Christianity, this 'fact' indicated the work of the devil. So, after
describing the bodhisattva path, he wrote:

> Having established such a fine beginning, their infernal lawgiver
> proceeds to search for what that root cause can be, and with dia-
> bolic artifice, under the pretext of completely eradicating the root
> cause of all the passions from the heart of his followers, totally
> extirpates from their minds the true, legitimate, and primary root
> for the cognition of God. (Sweet 2010, 370)

Therefore, in spite of Desideri's appreciation of certain aspects
of Buddhist practice and belief and his willingness to see Christianity as fulfilling rather than condemning these, Desideri shared
with some other Roman Catholic missionaries of his day the view
that even similarities between other religions and Christianity
were part of the devil's plan to draw people away from true faith
in God. Nevertheless, at this stage in the Christian encounter with

Buddhist meditation, principally because of Desideri's Jesuit and Thomist formation, there is more understanding of the purpose of meditation than in the following two centuries, when Buddhist meditation came under the gaze of Protestant Christians.

Francis Buchanan in Eighteenth Century Burma (Myanmar)

My next 'moment' is eighteenth century Burma, now Myanmar, and the compilation of Buddhist doctrine made by Francis Buchanan (1762-1829), a British civil servant in India, who spent time in Myanmar. In 1799, in the sixth volume of *Asiatick Researches*, the orientalist journal of The Asiatic Society of Bengal, founded by William Jones (1746-1794) in 1784, he published a lengthy account of Buddhism in Myanmar, 'On the Religion and Literature of the Burmas' (Buchanan 1799). This was not entirely his own work. It centred around three treatises that another contributor to *Asiatick Researches*, Lieutenant Colonel Symes, had gained from an Italian priest, Vincentius Sangermano, who had translated them into Latin: a 'cosmography' that Sangermano had 'extracted' from Burmese writings; a treatise by a 'king's confessor' 'with an intention of converting the *Christians*' and 'a translation of the book of ordination' (Buchanan 1799, 166). Buchanan translated these into English and united them 'into one connected account' (Buchanan 1799, 166) 'intermixing' them with his own reflections, drawn from observation and conversations with Buddhists.

Buchanan published at a time when British power in India was still relatively young and its influence in Myanmar was embryonic. Outright British rule in Myanmar arrived only after Buchanan's publication, with the annexation of land in the 'extreme southeast and southwest in 1826' (Turner 2014, 1), including Arakan (Rakkhine). British imperial power in the area, therefore, was not yet a certainty. It was the potential for power that the British anticipated and this led to a drive to understand, categorize and label what they experienced on the Indian subcontinent and Myanmar. Buchanan represents this ethos, without a missionary agenda. On the Burmese side, at this point, neither British civil servants nor the European missionaries who had been present in the country for some time were seen as a threat to the existence of Buddhism in the country.

Buchanan's compilation focussed on Buddhist belief rather than practice, particularly on Sangermano's Buddhist cosmology, which included representations of the constellations, the planes of existence, the geography of the world, the different nations with which the Burmese were acquainted, and convictions about the destruction and re-formation of world systems. Within this, however, Buchanan included other aspects of belief. Buchanan/ Sangermano were among the first Europeans to record, for instance, that Buddhism did not speak of the transmigration of a soul, but of a different kind of continuity across births based on good and bad actions (Buchanan 1799, 179; quoted in Harris 2006, 18), and Buchanan, in his commentary on Sangermano, contested the missionary view, including that of Sangermano, that *nibbāna* was annihilation or a kind of annihilation (Buchanan 1799, 180; quoted in Harris 2006, 18-19).

The most detailed information about practice was given when Buchanan drew on the short treatise written by the 'king's confessor', which included a description of a traditional model of Buddhist lay practice: morality (*sīla*), generosity (*dāna*) and 'Bavana' (*bhāvanā*). The latter was described in the treatise in the following way:

> It consists in thoughtfully pronouncing these three words, *Aneizza* [*anicca*], *Doccha* [*dukkha*], and *Anatta* [*anattā*]. By the word *Aneizza* is understood, that he who pronounces it, recollects, that by his particular situation he is liable to vicissitudes; by the word *Docca* is understood, that by the same situation he is liable to misfortune; and by the word *Anatta*, that it is not in his power to exempt himself from being liable to change and misfortune. Whoever dies without having observed the *Sila, Dana*, and *Bavana*, will certainly pass into one of the infernal states, and will become a *Nirea* [Pāli: *Niraya* – the hells], a *Prietta* [Pāli: *peta* – a hungry ghost], or some animal. (Buchanan 1799, 272)

Buchanan's own reflections came mainly at the end of the compilation and they were largely directed towards what would now be called 'lived religion'. For instance, he mentioned personal devotion, using the word 'prayer' to describe this: 'Every true worshipper of GODAMA prays before he goes to sleep, and before he rises in the morning, which is generally the dawn of the day' (Buchanan 1799, 296). He surmised that these prayers were in Pāli. Making offerings to the 'temple' and the devotional activities surrounding the main festivals were also mentioned by Buchanan, including 'gilding a patch' of the 'temple' (Buchanan 1799, 298). He did not mention sitting meditation, probably because he did not witness this.

Within Buchanan's compilation, therefore, meditation in the narrower sense of sitting meditation is absent. Nevertheless, the mental culture normatively linked with meditation is evoked in the treatise written by a 'king's confessor' in its description of bringing *anicca*, *dukkha* and *anattā* to mind. Buchanan did not comment on this practice either positively or negatively, probably because he was familiar with similar mental practices in Christianity. When he himself described the wider field of Buddhist practice that Shaw places under the concept of *bhāvanā* in this volume, his stance was neutral and praise was given to Buddhist morals (Buchanan 1799, 255). For him, these were the less contentious parts of Buddhism. He was far more negative about Buddhist cosmology as presented by Sangermano, claiming that it involved 'the most puerile and absurd fables' (Buchanan 1799, 255). He also noted the lack of a belief in 'a Supreme Being, the creator and preserver of the universe' but, unlike Desideri, does not link this with the diabolical (Buchanan 1799, 255).

Nineteenth Century Missionaries in Ceylon (Sri Lanka) from the 1840s

My next 'moment' occurred in mid-nineteenth century Sri Lanka. British imperial power in Asia was on a much firmer footing than at the beginning of the century. British administrators in India and

Sri Lanka, therefore, spoke more about achievement than potential. In addition, Christian missionaries, most of them products of the Evangelical Revival in Britain that had begun in the late eighteenth century, were representing the emerging British Empire as a God-given opportunity to christianize and civilize the religious Other.

These Christian missionaries, whether they were from the evangelical tradition or High Church Anglicanism, drew exclusivist conceptual and spatial boundaries between the Christian and the non-Christian, between christianized space and 'heathen' space (Harris 2018, 25-42). Although some could praise Buddhist ethics, as Buchanan had done, most undermined Buddhism, even when they attempted to be fair to it. When it came to understanding Buddhist meditation, they were at their weakest. They would have been familiar with the use of the term 'meditation' in the King James version of the Bible, for instance in the Psalms, where the term is used to describe 'meditating on' something (Harris 2019). They would have perhaps used the term themselves to describe their reflections on the goodness and promises of God. Yet, they would probably not have been familiar with the whole Christian contemplative tradition, or if they were, their reaction might have been negative because of its link with Roman Catholicism. Wesleyan Methodist missionary in Sri Lanka, Robert Spence Hardy (1803-1868), for instance, was harder on Roman Catholic monasticism than Buddhist monasticism in his first book on Buddhism, *Eastern Monachism* (Spence Hardy 1850). However, especially after the mid-point in the century, the Christian missionaries would have been aware of the growth of interest in spiritualism, the esoteric and mesmerism in Britain, which gave them a vivid vocabulary bank linked with 'trance' and the supernatural to describe Buddhist meditation (Harris 2019). This 'moment', therefore, is conditioned by a Christian ethos that was very different from that which informed Desideri. I take Daniel John Gogerly (1792-1862) and Bishop Reginald Stephen Copleston (1845-1925) as representative examples.

Daniel John Gogerly

Gogerly was a scholar missionary. He arrived in Sri Lanka in 1818 as the lay person responsible for the Wesleyan missionary press in Colombo. He was ordained in 1823 and began studying Pāli and collecting Pāli texts in the 1830s, when he was stationed in Buddhist majority Dondra, in the south of the island. In the late 1830s, he started to publish translations from the Pāli texts, one of the first British people to do so, a fact masked in Europe because he published in Sri Lanka (Harris 2010; Harris 2018b).

Gogerly's publications consisted of translations from the Pāli texts, versions of papers given on Buddhism in Sri Lanka and works of Christian apologetics, mostly in Sinhala, such as *Kristiyāni Prajñapti* (1849).[1] In one of his early papers on Buddhism, published as 'An Introductory Sketch of Buddhism' in 1847 (Bishop 1908 I, 1-14), Gogerly included the term 'meditation' when describing the 'respect and homage' given by lay people to a member of the monastic Sangha, who had 'devoted himself to meditation and self-control for the purpose of purifying his own heart and who instructs others in the path of virtue' (Bishop 1908 I, 3). The term, however, was not explained further and was linked only with the practice of those who had renounced lay life.

Gogerly's translations show that he had little problem with the idea of 'meditating on' something, since this resonated with Christian models, and could relate to the idea of controlling or subjecting the mind, as shown in the quote above and in his translations from the *Dhammapada* (Harris 2010, 191-192; Harris 2019). He had more difficulty with the idea of diligently heeding the mind, as is conveyed, for instance, by the Pāli word, *appamāda*. And when faced with the *jhāna*s, he drew on the vocabulary of trance and

---

1   *Kristiyāni Prajñapti*, which can loosely be translated as 'The Evidences and Doctrines of the Christian Religion' argued for the superiority of Christianity using Buddhist textual evidence. It was instrumental in causing a new phase in Buddhist revivalism in Sri Lanka. See Malagoda 1976, 217-219, Young and Somaratne 1996, 80-102.

insensibility. For instance, in a presentation given to the Colombo YMCA in 1861, he mentioned them within his Buddha biography. The Buddha on the night of enlightenment, he explained, 'bent his mind to intense meditation' adding:

> This profound meditation is termed *jhána*, and while the devotee is engaged in these exercises he becomes insensible to all external things; he can neither see, hear, nor feel, but is in a state something similar to that which is called the mesmeric trance, and no means exist by which he can be aroused from this state until the meditation is ended. (Bishop 1908 I, 17; Harris 2019)

He then described the *jhāna*s briefly, implying that the Buddha's enlightenment followed in a direct progression from the fourth *jhāna* (Bishop 1908 I, 18; Harris 2019).

Gogerly's encounter with meditation or mental culture in Buddhism, therefore, was mediated both through his western preconception that 'meditation' was an intellectual activity, a 'meditating on' something, and the vocabulary of trance. Although he recognized that 'meditation' was a necessary precondition of the Buddha's enlightenment and that the monastic Sangha meditated, he failed to see it as an integral component of the Buddhist path. One reason for this was that it did not touch his own preconceptions about the nature of religious practice.

Reginald Stephen Copleston

Bishop Reginald Stephen Copleston (1845-1925) was a High Church Anglican with a training in classics, who arrived in Sri Lanka in 1875 at the age of 30 to be Bishop of the Colombo Diocese. For him, the roots of civilization lay in Greece and Rome. His default position, therefore, was to compare what he experienced within Sri Lankan religion to this precedent. In an 1888 publication, he stated that he had read some Pāli texts but also stressed that the main reason he was entitled to speak of them was because he had been guided by 'those who have been familiar all their lives with the traditional interpretation' (Copleston 1888,

113; Harris 2006, 68). Copleston's appreciation of meditation in Buddhism, however, went little further than Gogerly's.

Key to Copleston's position was that the heart of the Buddhist path involved developing a distaste for life. When describing the ethos of this path for the ordinary Buddhist, he stated, 'He must not love life; but must fix his mind on the idea of dissolution, transitoriness; and convince himself that he now need not, and in fact does not, now exist' (Copleston 1892, 115; Harris 2006, 130-131). When he first mentioned meditation, he recognized that it performed two roles: to bring knowledge to bear on conduct and to arrive at truth (Copleston 1892, 89, Harris 2006, 134). Since the Buddhist path, for Copleston, involved both a killing of the intellect and of 'desire', even of consciousness itself (Harris 2006, 133), he could only make sense of this by holding that meditation contributed towards indifference, non-involvement and distaste for life. Meditation involved withdrawing 'the faculties from all exercise whatever' (Copleston 1892, 89). When he attempted to describe the *jhāna*s and the *arūpa* states in the context of the Buddha's achievement and monastic practice (Copleston 1892, 89 & 130-131), he stated that the fourth *jhāna* led to 'supernatural capacities (iddhi)' and 'it is pretended, the power of working miracles' such as flying through the air (Copleston 1892, 131). He added, however, that the Buddha himself 'despised' *iddhi* (Copleston 1892, 131). Significantly, he was also aware of the commentarial term, *kammaṭṭhāna*, and *kasina* practice as a component of this.[2] He judged *kammaṭṭhāna*, to be 'elaborate systems of what may be called mechanical meditation or self-mesmerism by mechanical processes' (Copleston 1892, 130). The term 'mesmerism' appeared again when he touched on the *Satipaṭṭhāna Sutta* (*Majjhima Nikāya* I 55-63), where he again judged the process to be mechanical 'akin, I suppose, to mesmerism, by which peculiar conditions are induced' (Copleston 1892, 220).

---

2   *Kammaṭṭhāna* literally means 'place of work' and is used in commentaries such as the *Visuddhimagga* to cover a range of meditation practices using an object, under the guidance of a meditation teacher or preceptor.

In Copleston's work, therefore, there is evidence of textual knowledge, both of the canonical books and the commentarial tradition. At a technical level, he was aware of where meditation fitted into the Buddhist path, namely, that it was connected with insight into truth. His working model of that truth, however, was so negative that meditation also became a negative practice for him, one which involved a movement towards abstraction, indifference and unconsciousness.

Anagārika Dharmapāla

My next 'moment' moves to a Buddhist representation of Christianity within the British colonial period in Sri Lanka, namely, that of David Hewavitharana, a prominent Buddhist revivalist, who chose the name Anagārika Dharmapāla (1864-1933) to denote an ascetic state in between that of a lay person and a monastic. Dharmapāla attended Christian schools and, therefore, became familiar with biblical vocabulary. The main influences in his early years, however, were revivalist Buddhist monks, such as the Ven. Mohoṭṭiwattē Guṇānanda, and western theosophists, most particularly Henry Steel Olcott (1832-1907), who arrived in Sri Lanka in 1880 to aid the Buddhist revival. Dharmapāla worked closely with him from 1886 until about 1905 (Prothero 1996, 165-69). Dharmapāla internalized from both of these influences an anti-Christian rhetoric that he consequently developed. Christian missionaries, for instance, became 'the foil for Dharmapāla's representation of Buddhism as rational, scientific and ethical' (Harris 2013b, 719). Dharmapāla's published writings and his personal diaries, therefore, were conditioned by the experience of British imperialism, the negative representation of Buddhism held by Christian missionaries and a Buddhist revival predicated on anti-Christian sentiment. I wrote in 2013:

> When his diaries are compared with his writings, a considered position arises: that the god of Judaism and Christianity was violent and capricious (e.g. unpublished diary 4th December 1891); that an exclusivist theology of atonement, hell and heaven was

unmerciful and uncivilized; that the lives of contemporary missionaries were unethical; that the life of the mendicant Jesus, particularly his asceticism, contained the worthy. (Harris 2013b, 721)

In 1929, for instance, he published the following about the teachings of Jesus:

Take away the sermon on the mount [which AD thought was influenced by Buddhism] from the gospel, and you have the pronouncements of a theological dogmatist breathing vengeance without any hope. For a calm philosophic thinker dogmatic Christianity appears gruesome and morbid. It leads to partial insanity, and to the Buddhist Christian theologians appear as if they were half insane. (*Maha Bodhi Journal* 37, March 1929; Guruge 1981, 286)

Dharmapāla was aware, however, that a form of prayer linked with a 'well-disciplined mind' was part of Judaism, Christianity and Islam, as the following extract demonstrates, taken from a treatise he wrote in 1917:

Jesus with his little flock of disciples preached a doctrine which spread after his death rapidly in many lands. Judaism, Islam of Mahammad and Christianity are Semitic religions. The credulity of the human mind is remarkable. A mere sound is enough to change the views of a human being. Fasting and prayer had been always popular with religious minded people, and a moderate course of asceticism and a well disciplined mind with a desire to live the purified life help man to gain mystic insight into the penetralia of mysteries. (Guruge 1991, 270)

His attitude towards it, however, was dismissive. He added, mimicking the exclusivism of the missionaries, 'The only religion with a complete psychology from beginning to end is the Arya Dharma enunciated by the Lord of Mercy, Sakya Muni, the Tathagata Buddha' (Guruge 1981, 271). Nevertheless, his unpublished diaries demonstrate that vocabulary from his Christian education came readily to his mind. For instance, on 17 February 1891, he wrote, 'Prayer to a God won't relieve the man of the miseries of

Existence, rites and ceremonies won't do. Purity of life is needed. This night at 12 for the first time in my life I experienced "that peace that passeth all understanding".' Was he aware that he was drawing on Christian contemplative tradition?

Anagarika Dharmapāla's writings, therefore, are an example of a 'moment' when power-infused imperialism and the anti-Buddhist activities of Christian missionaries prevented many Buddhists from seeing any similarities between Buddhist mental culture, and Christian prayer or spiritual practice.

Twentieth Century Moments of Buddhist-Christian Encounter

I now leap to the mid-twentieth century when European imperialism was waning, western converts to Buddhism were a feature of Europe's increasingly plural religious landscapes, the term interfaith dialogue was entering Christian vocabulary and some Christians were drawing from the spiritual wisdom of other religious traditions in their own practice. In addition, the term 'mysticism' and the insights of Christian mystics such as St Teresa of Avila, Richard Rolle and St John of the Cross were being rehabilitated within Protestant Christianity, for instance, through Evelyn Underhill (Underhill 1995 (1911); Underhill 1960). In 1936, Underhill wrote, contesting the stereotypes of her time, 'A mystic is not a person who has queer experiences; but a person for whom God is the one reality of life, the supreme Object of Love' (Underhill 1960, 231). All this created a new context for more positive encounters between Buddhist and Christian meditation and contemplation. Robert Sharf, in this volume, examines Christian encounters with Zen meditation. Elise DeVido and Andreas Nehring explore the engagement of Christian cultures with the essentially Buddhist concept of 'mindfulness'. I begin with Thomas Merton (1915-1968) in the United States, who is also examined by Baatz in this volume, and then pass to the British Buddhist academic, Lance Cousins (1942-2015), the German Buddhist nun, Ayya Khema (1923-1997), and an exercise within the US-based

Society for Buddhist-Christian Studies, in which Christians reflected on Buddhist meditation and Buddhists reflected on Christian prayer.

Thomas Merton (1915-1968)

Thomas Merton's autobiographical 1948 book, *The Seven Storey Mountain*, an account of his journey towards Gethsemani Abbey and ordination as a Trappist monk, became popular reading and contributed to a growth of interest in monasticism informed by Christian contemplation (Merton 1981 (1948)). The ethos of the book was strongly Roman Catholic but it was a Roman Catholicism that was conversant with the Christian mystical tradition. In 1949, Merton was already using a vocabulary of 'emptiness' in his writing on contemplation, the 'emptiness' that arises after the tenacity of self-centredness had been uprooted, writing, 'The contemplative, nourished by emptiness, endowed with poverty and liberated from all sorrow by simple obedience, drinks fortitude and joy from the will of God in all things' (Merton 1960 (1949), 106). In 1955, developing his 1949 book, he again stressed the concept with reference to God's presence in the life of a Christian:

> There, rest and action, will not alternate, they will be one. Everything will be at once empty and full. But only if we have discovered how to combine emptiness and fullness, good will and indifferent results, mistakes and successes, work and rest, suffering and joy, in such a way that all things work together for our good and for the glory of God. (Merton 1977 (1955), 114)

It was only after these publications that Merton truly journeyed towards other religious traditions, and an important part of this was, in Shannon's words, 'a journey to the East' (Shannon 1993, 271-284). At first this was through books but, in March 1959, he made contact with D.T. Suzuki and a rich correspondence followed (Pramuk 2008, 68). The two met in 1964. In the 1960s, he wrote *Mystics and the Zen Masters* (Merton 1999), which ended with a call to engage with more than 'Christian and European cultural traditions' (Shannon 1993, 282). Before his tragic death in Bangkok in 1968, he became convinced of the need for an inter-monastic dialogue that stretched over the western/eastern divide, becoming the father of contemporary inter-monastic dialogue and exchange, and setting an example through encounters with Suzuki, the Dalai Lama, Thích Nhất Hạnh in 1966 (Downey 2017, 82) and, in 1968, Chogyam Trungpa (Downey 2017, 75). His 'Notes' for a paper to be delivered in Calcutta at the Temple of Understanding in October 1968 contained these impassioned words, 'I am convinced that communication in depth, across the lines that have hitherto divided religious and monastic traditions, is now not only possible and desirable, but most important for the destinies of Twentieth-Century Man' (Burton, Hart & Laughlin 1973, 313). He saw this task as particularly appropriate 'for those who have been seriously disciplined by years of silence and by a long habit of meditation' and as concentrated on 'what is really essential to the monastic quest; this, I think, is to be sought in the area of true transcendence and enlightenment' (Burton, Hart & Laughlin 1973 (1968), 316).

By this time, Merton was conversant with Buddhist and indeed Hindu meditation. He had had a deep encounter with Zen, which Pramuk argues turned him towards the 'Sophia tradition of Russian Orthodoxy', and had developed a theology that was able to accept Suzuki 'on his own terms' (Pramuk 2008, 67 & 82). He had also encountered Tibetan Buddhists (Downey 2017, 86) and had visited Theravāda Sri Lanka.

Those who have studied Merton's 'Asian Journal' have often made much of his experience at the Gal Vihāra in Polonnaruva in Sri Lanka, when, after gazing at the majestic images carved into rock there, one of the Buddha in meditation, one of him in death and one of Ānanda standing in grief, he wrote:

> All problems are resolved and everything is clear, simply because what matters is clear. The rock, all matter, all life, is charged with dharmakaya...everything is emptiness and everything is compassion. (Burton, Hart & Laughlin 1973 (1968), 235)

Shannon has argued that this lay in a direct line with other similar experiences (Shannon 1993, 278-279) and Pramuk, that echoes of Russian theology and Gerald Manley Hopkins can be detected in it (Pramuk 2008, 80). Downey has placed it in the context of his being the 'perennially restless pilgrim' (Downey 2017, 88) and Keenan has argued that Merton's understanding of 'emptiness' in the Buddhist tradition was incomplete (Keenan 2017, 116). All this may be accurate. I would argue, however, that, in terms of his understanding of the points at which Buddhism and Christianity touched, it was a supreme moment of spiritual awareness. The theme of 'emptiness', which had been present from the beginning of his monastic life in a Christian context, was now articulated with emotive force in the context of an overpowering encounter with Buddhism. For Merton, at this point, in spite of the stress in his notes for the Calcutta talk that 'there must be a scrupulous respect for important differences' (Burton, Hart & Laughlin 1973 (1968), 316), there was a unity, a non-duality that transcended religious boundaries. Merton, therefore, illustrates the 'moment' when Buddhist insights, particularly those linked with meditation, began to inform Christian spirituality and enrich it.

Lance Cousins (1942-2015)

Lance Cousins was both an academic, and a Buddhist practitioner and teacher of meditation. After academic research in Cambridge, he was appointed Lecturer in Comparative Religion at the University of Manchester in 1970. Here he concentrated on the teaching of Indic religions, Pāli and Sanskrit. In 1973, he became the founding Chairman of the Samatha Trust, formed to encourage the practice of *samatha* meditation; he taught meditation for the Trust until his death. He gained a reputation throughout his life for meticulous scholarship, particularly in connection with Pāli textual sources. However, he was also interested in comparative mysticism. He taught a course on this at Manchester (Gethin 2015) and also wrote a seminal article in 1989, 'The Stages of

Christian Mysticism and Buddhist Purification: *Interior Castle* of St Teresa of Avila and the *Path of Purification* of Buddhaghosa.' I will concentrate on this article to describe this 'moment'.

In this article, Cousins was unwilling to create easy equivalences between Buddhist and Christian meditative experience, claiming that, 'in certain respects', it would be misleading to 'think of a single transcendental mystical experience' within different religious traditions (Cousins 1994 (1989), 103). His preference was to see 'the phenomena of mysticism' as a 'mystical way, involving a series of experiences, some quite distinct from others' (Cousins 1994 (1989), 103). So, he continued, 'What I wish to argue is that there is considerable *similarity* in the structure and stages of the mystical way as conceived in different traditions' (Cousins 1994 (1989), 103). With particular reference to his two points of comparison, he stated at one point that:

> It should occasion no surprise if we find that it is not possible to match concepts on a one-for-one basis. Indeed it would be very surprising if we could. What we may, and I believe do, find is parallel clusters of concepts functionally similar in their psychological effects. (Cousins 1994 (1989), 108)

He presented Teresa of Avila as 'an extremely fine observational psychologist' (Cousins 1994 (1989), 104), a teacher and counsellor of others, whose 'genuineness' of experience should not be disputed, even if 'one may not agree with her cosmology' (Cousins 1994 (1989), 115). In contrast, he recognized that the writer of the *Visuddhimagga* offered a 'systematization and reorganization' of materials available to him about the path rather than an account of his direct experience of it or his teaching (Cousins 1994 (1989), 104). It is from this base that he explores with a remarkable thoroughness, given the restrictions of a single chapter, what I would call the 'touching points' between St Teresa's experiential account of seven 'Mansions' and the 'Spiritual Marriage' that lay beyond this, and Buddhaghosa's account of the path towards enlightenment. His very mode of writing assumes that he is dealing with two religious giants, whose accounts could not but contain similarities. So, the fact that both started with the foundation of morality and that this foundation was similar did not surprise him. That both recognized the need for 'purification' before achieving 'any kind of higher state' was almost too obvious to stress (Cousins 1994 (1989), 109). When it came to Teresa's 'Prayer of Quiet' and 'Prayer of Union', he drew direct experiential correspondences with '*jhāna* factors', seeing the former as similar to the concentration that comes before the *jhāna*s, namely, access concentration (*upacāra samādhi*) (Cousins 1994 (1989), 113). Similarly, in connection with Teresa's 'Prayer of Union', he wrote, 'One might perhaps sum up by saying that *jhāna* is certainly what St Teresa would call union, but whether she would call it union with God is perhaps another matter' (Cousins 1994 (1989), 114).

Significantly, he went beyond this in his analysis, fully aware that both of his 'giants' saw that there was further work to be done after 'union' or *jhāna*, namely, an 'extraordinary leap':

> St Teresa's Sixth Mansion and the account given by Buddhaghosa of the sixth purification have at least this much in common; both describe an acute rejection of ordinary worldly life in order to make a further extraordinary leap. (Cousins 1994 (1989), 117)

For Teresa, this was a leap towards a revelation of the Trinity and Cousins describes this sensitively. The parallel in Buddhaghosa was that, in the seventh purification, there was also 'an experiential realization of fundamental doctrine', namely the Four Noble Truths (Cousins 1994 (1989), 118). Both experiences, he stated, whilst doctrinally and cosmologically different, were 'functionally similar' as 'statements of the relationship between the ultimate and the temporal' (Cousins 1994 (1989), 119). He then moved to the 'effect' of both, seeing a direct correspondence in Teresa's 'forgetfulness of the self which really seems no longer to exist' and the eradication of 'personality belief' in the stream-enterer within Buddhism (Cousins 1994 (1989), 119). It is worth giving Cousins's conclusion in full:

What I would wish to argue in this context is that there are between the accounts of St Teresa and Buddhaghosa a whole series of similarities. In particular the models of the path which both of them give run parallel. Each begins with purification, each moves on to states of interiorization, joy and peace, then to trance phenomena, then to rejection of the world combined with non-normal acquisitions of knowledge and each finishes with a transformatory knowledge which remains permanently accessible. Although there are many differences of detail and a very different context, the general structure is remarkably similar. (Cousins 1994 (1989), 120)

Cousins's piece, I would argue, is representative of the 'moment' in the mid-twentieth century when Buddhist academics and meditation practitioners – Cousins combined both – were able to engage with the Christian contemplative tradition with deep respect and an open attitude of inquiry, although it is worth noting that the attainment of 'stream enterer' is still rather distant from enlightenment itself. My next 'moment' goes a little further.

Ayya Khema (1923-1997)

Ayya Khema was born in Berlin into a Jewish family. She left Germany in 1938 and was taken to Scotland, later joining her parents in Shanghai, where the family, during World War II, were placed in a Japanese prisoner of war camp. To cut a long story short, she married and had two children, and after encountering meditation in Asia, began to teach it. This eventually led, in 1979, to her taking the robes of a contemporary Buddhist nun in Sri Lanka, following ten rules of discipline. She later received higher ordination (*upasampadā*) in the United States. After her first ordination, she spent a number of years in Sri Lanka. She founded Parappaduwa Nuns' Island, near Dodanduva in the south of the country, and became a popular teacher of meditation, gaining a devoted following of English-speaking Buddhist women. I first met her then. She was one of my meditation teachers but I found her rather hostile to Christianity. However, after she returned to

Germany and established a Buddhist centre there, *Buddha Haus*, she wrote two positive books on biblical themes (Harris 2013a, 110). The 'moment' I choose, however, is her address to the Eckhart Society in September 1995, *Mysticism is no Mystery*, published in the following year. In it, she asserted her conviction that Christian contemplatives such as Meister Eckhart and the Buddha shared 'what all mystics have in common', namely, that 'their teaching was directed towards the fact that we are operating under an illusion; that the idea of "I", "me" and "mine" is a fallacy and not a reality and that we should get rid of it' (Ayya Khema 1996, 45). She continued:

> In the course of talking on the comparisons between Christianity and Buddhism and engaging in ecumenical dialogue, I have come to the conclusion that God (or Godhead) and Nibbāna are identical – that they cannot be anything else. (Ayya Khema 1996, 45)

They were identical because they both embodied the truth that happiness or inner peace could only arise for sentient beings if the emphasis on 'me' had been eradicated.

The rest of her address expanded on this point with reference to Meister Eckhart's forty-fifth sermon, *In omnibus requiem quaesivi*, and Buddhist meditation, particularly the *jhānas*, *samatha* and *vipassanā*. She equated *nibbāna*, for instance, with the 'rest' that ensued, for Eckhart, when God drew people back 'with Him into their first beginning' (Ayya Khema 1996, 49), a beginning in which the individual self was 'done'.

The whole talk was a remarkable example of a Buddhist monastic practitioner of meditation not avoiding the language of 'God' to draw parallels between Buddhist and Christian meditative experience. Her focus, however, was not cosmology or metaphysics. If it had been, she would have had to engage with difference. It was experience and philosophy. At the end she stated:

> It is very interesting that Meister Eckhart says there is no true being except in God. There is not true being anywhere in absolute truth, all creatures are strictly speaking nothing. In fact, he also

> says, somewhere else, that God is nothing. It sounds shocking.
> But we say Nibbāna is nothing that can be described, nothing
> that can be felt, nothing that can actually be had. It is that which
> is the total dissolution of everything in heart and mind. I have
> argued in this talk that this is what Eckhart is saying too. (Ayya
> Khema 1996, 57)

This 'moment' at the end of the twentieth century, when a western
Buddhist nun creates an experiential and philosophical equiva-
lence between the ultimate in Buddhism and Christianity, namely,
Godhead and *nibbāna*, and then proceeds to deconstruct both,
does not arise through academic textual study. It was the fruit
of a life of meditative experience to which was added Buddhist-
Christian encounter in a European context.

Christians Talk about Buddhist Meditation: Buddhists Talk about Christian Prayer

The Society for Buddhist-Christian Studies (SBCS) emerged out
of the East-West Project of the University of Hawai'i in 1987, at
a Buddhist-Christian conference in Berkeley. *Buddhist-Christian
Studies* then became the SBCS journal. The journal pioneered
new models of formal Buddhist-Christian dialogue and a handful of edited books emerged from journal papers. For volumes 21
and 22, five Christians were asked to reflect on Buddhist meditation and five Buddhists to reflect on Christian prayer, with two
members from the other religious practice responding to each set
of reflections. In 2003, this interchange became a book, edited by
a Buddhist and a Christian, Rita Gross and Terry Muck, office-
bearers of the Society (Gross & Muck 2003). It is significant that
there was an asymmetry between the Christian and Buddhist reflections, in that the Christian contributors spoke either from the
experience of drawing Buddhist meditation methods into their
Christian practice or from a deep learning from Buddhism, and
the Buddhist contributors engaged in more detached comparative
exercises. As Rita Gross wrote in her 'Conclusion':

> Most Christians report on how they have incorporated Buddhist meditation into their spiritual disciplines, whereas most Buddhists attempt to show that, despite its non-theism, Buddhist practice includes many 'prayer-like' utterances. (Gross & Muck 2003, 150)

I will give two examples from both sides of the dialogue. Frances Adeney, a Christian, wrote of being introduced to what she called 'entering silence' by her spiritual director and only later learning that it was 'indeed a form of Buddhist sitting' (Gross & Muck 2003, 17). She continued to explain that she used the method alongside 'other forms of Christian prayer and meditation, seeing it as complementary rather than contradictory to practices of verbal prayer, meditative Bible reading, and community liturgies'. She understood it as: 'a preparation for an encounter with the Divine'; 'a way of fostering self-understanding'; 'a form of discipline that puts into perspective individual transience and smallness in relation to the universe and the Divine' (Gross & Muck 2003). She said little in her contribution about the Buddhist worldview; she was perhaps the supreme example of what Buddhist respondent, Grace Burford, described, without censure, as valuing Buddhist methods as 'alternative ways to accomplish Christian goals' (Gross & Muck 2003, 58).

Christian academic and chaplain, Terry Muck, in contrast, speaking from a deep encounter with Theravāda Buddhism rather than the practice of Buddhist meditation, focussed mainly on the doctrine behind meditative practice, stating that he had learnt from it 'the lesson of readiness as the foundational step on any religion's spiritual path' (Gross & Muck 2003, 37). The Theravāda Buddhist emphasis that a foundation in morality (*sīla*), energy and confidence was a 'preparation for *samadhi* and *panna*' (Gross & Muck 2003, 58), he explained, caused him a 'crisis' because he had been accustomed to seeing morality as the fruit of the spiritual path. This crisis, in turn, led to a deep learning that entered his own Christian spiritual life as the realization that morality had 'a dual role – as fruit *and* root of the spiritual life' (Gross & Muck 2003, 41).

To turn to my representative examples from the Buddhist side, Robert Aitken, writing from a Mahāyāna perspective, described seven Buddhist practices that he believed 'may be analogous' to Christian practices, including the *nembutsu* (recalling Buddha), *zazen* and 'sutras and sutra services' (Gross & Muck 2003, 69-70). With sensitivity and respect for both traditions, he drew parallels between each and Christian practice, for instance, between the *nembutsu* and the Jesus Prayer, between the sitting meditation practice of *zazen* and the Desert Fathers, and between the 'sutra services' and the effect of singing and chanting in the Roman Catholic mass (Gross & Muck 2003, 70-83). In effect, he argued that Buddhist and Christian meditative practices moved in the same spiritual landscape.

Mahinda Deegalle, academic and Theravāda Buddhist monk, on the other hand, sought for prayer-like activities in non-theistic Buddhism and found numerous examples, from the four mindfulness recollections of a Theravāda Buddhist monk (on their robes, almsfood, lodgings and medicine), 'meal prayers' in the Zen monastic tradition, 'the liberating prayer' of the New Kadampa Tradition in the West and 'prayer' to the goddess Pattini in Sri Lanka (Gross & Muck 2003, 121-130). He concluded that the functional notion of prayer was very present in Buddhism. He did not, however, touch on any parallels between sitting meditation and Christianity.

The chapters of this volume expand on a number of themes that were present in this early twenty-first century dialogue. In the western context, it was a pioneering exercise, an expression of the respect, honesty, rigour and trust that can be present in contemporary Buddhist-Christian encounter. However, as the Buddhist participants were not slow to recognize, it also highlighted the asymmetry between Buddhist and Christian responses to the question of meditation and prayer in the two traditions, with the Christian participants having gained more from Buddhist meditation in terms of transformative experience than the Buddhists had gained in their encounter with Christian prayer.

Concluding Thoughts

My focus in this chapter has been the differing conditioning contexts of Buddhist encounter with Christian contemplation and meditation, and Christian encounter with Buddhist meditation. I have argued that the level of understanding within this encounter has been dependent on factors such as attitudes towards and knowledge of the Christian contemplative tradition within both Buddhist and Christian communities, preconceptions about the nature of religious practice in both traditions, and the extent to which the power relationships of imperialism or convictions of Christian or Buddhist superiority were present in the encounter. Until the middle of the twentieth century, it would be fair to say that Buddhist-Christian understanding was low when it came to this area of practice. From this point onwards, however, meditation became a positive focus within Christian explorations of Buddhism and awareness among Buddhists of a Christian contemplative tradition increased. Formal Buddhist-Christian encounter and dialogue facilitated this. The 'moments' I have chosen to illustrate these differing contexts will, I hope, provide a foundation for the critical analysis that follows in the chapters of this volume.

Bibliography

Ayya Khema, 1996. 'Mysticism is no Mystery'. *Eckhart Review*, Spring: 44-57.

Bishop, A.S., ed., 1908. *Ceylon Buddhism: Being the Collected Works Writings of Daniel John Gogerly* 2 Vols. Colombo: The Wesleyan Methodist Bookroom; London: W.H. Allen and Co.

Bray, John, 2018 'Ippolito Desideri and his Muslim Guides in the Buddhist Kingdom of Ladakh'. *Buddhist-Christian Studies* 38: 15-30.

Buchanan, Francis, 1799. 'On the Religion and Literature of the Burmas'. *Asiatick Researches* VI: 136-308.

Burton, Naomi, Patrick Hart & James Laughlin, eds., 1973 (1968). *The Asian Journal of Thomas Merton*. New York: New Directions.

Cattoi, Thomas, 2018. 'Ippolito Desideri and the Universitality of Aristotelian Rationality: A Model or a Hindrance'. *Buddhist-Christian Studies* 38: 69-82.

Copleston Reginald S., 1888. 'Buddhism in Ceylon', reprinted in 1953 in *Studies in Buddhism*. New Delhi: Asian Educational Services: 113-133.

Copleston, Reginald S., 1892. *Buddhism Primitive and Present in Magadha and Ceylon*. London: Longmans, Green and Co.

Cousins, Lance, 1994 (1989). 'The Stages of Christian Mysticism and Buddhist Purification: *Interior Castle* of St Teresa of Avila and the *Path of Purification* of Buddhaghosa'. In *The Yogi and the Mystic: Studies in Indian and Comparative Mysticism*, ed. Karel Werner. Richmond, Surrey: Curzon: 103-120.

De Rossi Filibeck, Elena, 2018. 'Luciano Petech and Desideri'. *Buddhist-Christian Studies* 38: 61-68.

Downey, Jack, 2017. '"We Drank Many Gin and Tonics": Desire and Enchantment in Merton's Buddhist Pilgrimage'. *Buddhist-Christian Studies* 37: 73-92.

Gasbarro, Nicola, 2018. 'Ippolito Desideri: Anthropologist of Modernity'. *Buddhist-Christian Studies* 38: 83-95.

Gethin, Rupert, 2015. 'Obituary Tribute to Lance Cousins', written for the International Association of Buddhist Studies: http://iabsinfo.net/2015/05/obituary-tribute-to- lance-cousins/ (last accessed 28.11.2018).

Gross, Rita M. & Terry C. Muck, eds., 2003. *Christians Talk about Buddhist Meditation: Buddhists Talk about Christian Prayer*. New York & London: Continuum.

Guruge, Ananda, ed., 1991. *Return to Righteousness: A Collection of the Speeches, Essays and Letters of the Anagarika Dharmapala*. Colombo: Ministry of Cultural Affairs and Information.

Harris, Elizabeth, 2006. *Theravāda Buddhism and the British Encounter: Religious, Missionary and Colonial Experience in*

Nineteenth Century Sri Lanka. London & New York: Routledge.

Harris, Elizabeth, 2010. 'Manipulating Meaning: Daniel John
Gogerly's Nineteenth Century Translations of the Theravāda
Texts'. *Buddhist Studies Review* 27.2: 177-195.

Harris, Elizabeth, 2013a. 'Buddhism and the Religious Other'. In
Understanding Interreligious Relations, eds. David Cheetham,
Douglas Pratt & David Thomas, Oxford: Oxford University
Press: 88-117.

Harris, Elizabeth, 2013b. 'Dharmapala, Anagarika'. In *Encyclopedia of the Bible and its Reception* vol. 6. Berlin & Boston:
De Gruyter: 719-721.

Harris, Elizabeth, 2018. *Religion, Space and Conflict in Sri Lanka: colonial and postcolonial contexts.* London: Routledge.

Harris, Elizabeth, 2019. 'Buddhist Meditation and the British Colonial Gaze in Nineteenth Century Sri Lanka'. *Contemporary
Buddhism* 20.1 (forthcoming)

Keenan, John P., 2017. 'Thomas Merton's Unfinished Journey in Dialogue with Buddhism'. *Buddhist-Christian Studies* 37: 103-128.

Malalgoda, Kitsiri, 1976. *Buddhism in Sinhalese Society 1750-
1800: A Study of Religious Revival and Change.* Berkeley &
Los Angeles, California: University of California Press.

Merton, Thomas, 1960 (1949). *Seeds of Contemplation.* London:
Burns & Oates.

Merton, Thomas, 1977 (1955). *No Man is an Island.* London:
Burns & Oates.

Merton, Thomas, 1981 (1948). *The Seven Storey Mountain.* London: Sheldon.

Merton, Thomas, 1999 (reissued edition). *Mystics and the Zen
Masters.* New York: Farrar, Straus & Giroux.

Pomplun, Trent, 2018. 'Ippolito Desideri and Madhyamaka: On
the Interpretation of Giuseppe Toscano'. *Buddhist-Christian
Studies* 38: 109-117.

Pramuk, Christopher, 2008. '"Something Breaks Through a Little": The Marriage of Zen and Sophia in the Life of Thomas
Merton'. *Buddhist-Christian Studies* 28: 67-89.

Prothero, Stephen, 2010. *The White Buddhist: The Asian Odyssey of Henry Steel Olcott.* Bloomington, IN: Indiana University Press.

Shannon, William H., 1993. *The Silent Lamp: The Thomas Merton Story.* London: SCM.

Spence Hardy, R., 1850. *Eastern Monachism: An Account of the Origin, Laws, Discipline, Sacred Writings, Mysterious Rites, Religious Ceremonies, and Present Circumstances of the Order of Mendicants Founded by Gotama Budha, From Singhalese MSS. and other Original Sources of Information.* London & Edinburgh: Williams and Norgate.

Sweet, Michael, J. transl. & ed., 2010. *Mission to Tibet: The Extraordinary Eighteenth Century Account of Father Ippolito Desideri, S.J.* Somerville, MA: Wisdom.

Sweet, Michael J., 2018. 'Gleanings from Desideri's *Account Book* 1: New Light on Some Episodes of His Life in Tibet'. *Buddhist-Christian Studies* 38: 119-123.

Tiso, Francis V., 2018. 'Ippolito Desideri: An Experience of Theological and Psychological Transformation'. *Buddhist-Christian Studies* 38: 125-137.

Turner, Alicia, 2014. *Saving Buddhism: The Impermanence of Religion in Colonial Burma.* Honolulu: University of Hawai'i Press.

Underhill, Evelyn, 1911. *Mysticism: The Development of Humankind's Spiritual Consciousness.* London: Methuen & Co.

Underhill, Evelyn, 1960. *The Mount of Purification with Meditations and Prayers, 1949 and Collected Papers, 1946.* London: Longmans, Green & Co.

Young, Richard F. & G.P.V. Somaratne, 1996. *Vain Debates: The Buddhist-Christian Controversies in Nineteenth Century Ceylon.* Vienna: Publications of the De Nobili Research Library Vol 23.

Zwilling, Leonard, 2018. 'Gleanings from Desideri's *Account Book* 2: The Teacher, the Servant, and the Cook'. *Buddhist-Christian Studies* 38: 139-146.

THEME 1:

MEDITATION / CONTEMPLATION IN TRADITIONAL BUDDHISM AND CHRISTIANITY

MEDITATION AND CONTEMPLATION: TWO BASIC TYPES OF SPIRITUAL EXERCISES WITHIN WESTERN EUROPEAN CHRISTIANITY

Karl Baier

Abstract

The paper begins with terminological clarifications that are followed by an investigation of the ancient roots of Christian meditation and contemplation and the main strands of their development within Western Europe until the end of the Quietist controversy. Special emphasis is laid on the changing meanings of these terms in various periods, the growing differentiation between meditation and contemplation, and the ways in which they were correlated to each other. The role of meditative and contemplative exercises within different Christian groups and churches as well as their respective cultural and theological contexts are highlighted. The concluding part of the paper investigates the renaissance of contemplation that took place in two waves, the first one from around 1900 until the 1930s, and a second one from the late 1960s until the present day.

Keywords: Catholic spirituality, *oratio*, *Devotio Moderna*, Victorines, Quietism, mysticism, infused contemplation, Evelyn Underhill, John Main, centring prayer, Thomas Keating, *lectio divina*

Introduction

This paper deals with two forms of Christian practice that emerged in the Greco-Roman world and have survived up to the present day, undergoing many transformations. During the last century, the term 'meditation' (and to a lesser degree also 'contemplation') became part of the vocabulary of comparative religious studies.[1] Moreover, both are used within religious communities and currents all over the world insofar as they are using European languages to articulate themselves. For these reasons it may be interesting to take a look at the historical roots of these concepts—and not only with regard to the history of Christian spirituality.

In the first part of the paper, Christian terminology concerning prayer, meditation and contemplation will be clarified. Thereafter, the origins of meditation and contemplation in the patristic period and their development until the end of the seventeenth century will be examined. Meditation and contemplation will be carved out as ideal types of religious practice and different ways to relate the two will be described. The Quietist controversy (1675-1700) that ended with the suppression of contemplative forms of prayer within the Catholic Church also merits some discussion. The closing section thematizes the renaissance of contemplation from the end of the nineteenth century onwards.

My home base, as it were, is the history of Catholic spirituality. But I am, of course, aware of the fact that Western European spirituality from the sixteenth century onwards has been an ecumenical phenomenon. The role of meditation and contemplation within the Protestant Churches has to be considered as part of this entangled history. As both the Hesychast tradition of the Eastern churches and meditation/contemplation as a medium of the Buddhist-Christian encounter are treated within other chapters of this volume, these topics are left aside.

---

1   For this see the respective entries in dictionaries like *The Encyclopedia of Religion* (1987) or the German *Handbuch religionswissenschaftlicher Grundbegriffe* (1998).

Terminological Clarifications

Since the times of the Church fathers, the term 'prayer' in its most basic sense denotes an existential opening towards the ultimate reality that Christians call God. As John of Damascus (d. 754 CE) put it: *Oratio est ascensus mentis in Deum* (prayer is the elevation of the mind towards God).[2] Accordingly, every inner attitude, thought, decision, emotion, verbal utterance or deed deliberately or subconsciously oriented towards a greater proximity to or union with God can be called prayer. A modern representative of this view is Karl Rahner. 'But what is prayer actually?', he asks and continues: 'First, let's say something quite simple about prayer, something very self-evident which is at the very beginning of prayer and which we usually overlook: in prayer we *open* our hearts to God' (1997, 2-3, Rahner's emphasis). Within Christian theology, prayer as this kind of initial opening and the whole range of specifications that derive from it are usually understood as a response to the self-disclosure of the mysterious ultimate reality that Christians call God.

In the narrow sense of the word, the term 'prayer' stands for a verbal addressing of God (may it be inaudible or spoken aloud) in different speech-acts such as greeting, thanksgiving, petitioning, paying homage to God, vowing, praise, lament, blessing, intercession, consecration and invocation. This rich variety of articulated ways of prayer mirrors the diversity of situations in which the opening towards ultimate reality takes place.

The understanding of prayer as a speech-act also dates back to patristic texts. According to a frequently quoted passage from Augustine's interpretations of the psalms, *oratio est locutio ad Deum* (prayer is talking to God),[3] which contrasts with reading the Bible understood as listening to what God has to say to the reader. Cassiodorus (d. ca. 585) substantiated this understanding

---

2   John of Damascus, *De fide orthodoxa* 3.24. An example for the reception of this definition within medieval theology is Thomas Aquinas, *Summa theologiae*, 2a 2ae, q. 83, a. 1, 3: 1841b.

3   St. Augustine, *Ennaratio in Psalmos*, 85, 7 (CCL 39, 1182).

with an (incorrect) etymological interpretation. For him prayer (*oratio*) is spoken reason (*oris ratio*).[4] Prayer in the sense of a speech-act has often been narrowed down further by assessing petition as the paradigmatic form of prayer in the strict sense.[5]

Although Christian meditation and contemplation often include prayers in the strict and strictest sense, they should be distinguished from them. What makes the difference? Meditation and contemplation are ritualized, methodical exercises of self-cultivation aiming at transforming the practitioner's mind to deepen the relationship with God. They are thus specifications of prayer in the broader sense. Traditionally, they have often been labelled as 'mental' or 'interior' prayer. However, these designations are not very useful as every kind of silent prayer could be called 'mental' or 'interior'.

In the course of history, many philosophers, monastics and theologians did not draw a rigorous distinction between meditation and contemplation. Time and again they were (and still are) used interchangeably. Based on patristic theology, from the twelfth century onwards, increased attempts have been made to distinguish the two and to define them in a more systematic manner. With only few exceptions, contemplation has been seen as the superior form, with meditation being a kind of preparation for it. Only in modern times has the term 'meditation' become a synonym for what, in earlier ages, was conceived of as 'contemplation', or is used as an umbrella term for both meditation and contemplation in the traditional sense.

---

4   See Cassiodorus, *In Psalterium Expositio*, 38, 14 (PL 70, col. 285).

5   The English 'prayer' and the French 'prière' as well as the Italian 'precario/ preghiera' are derived from Latin *precari* (ask, beg, entreat). A major reason for the importance of petition within Western European Christian conceptions of prayer is the outstanding role it plays in the Bible. The Lord's Prayer, which to the present day is considered to be the Christian prayer par excellence as, according to the New Testament, it has been taught by Jesus Christ himself, is a supplication.

Roots and Ramifications

1. Meditation

The contemporary English terms 'meditation' and 'to meditate' are derived from the Latin *meditatio* (care, attention, exercise, practice, study, consideration, rehearsal) and *meditare* or *meditari* (to consider, to ponder, to exercise), words that were used as translation of the Greek *melétē* and *meletáō*. In the Greek and Latin translations of the Bible, the Septuagint and Vulgate, the verbs *meletáō/meditare* are used as translation of the Hebrew *hagah* (to murmur, to speak, to recite and to ponder). The most famous and influential example of this is Psalm 1:2: 'Blessed is the one [...] who meditates on his [the Lord's] law day and night.'[6]

Hagah in this context denotes the practice of murmuring texts (Stordalen 2013). Accordingly, in the days of the early Christian ascetics one of the foremost meanings of *melétē/meditatio* was the loud or half-loud chanting of the Bible and of other spiritual teachings as well as the constant repetition of short *sententiae* (sayings of the fathers, key sentences) or prayers like 'Son of God, have mercy on me' that recall the later Jesus prayer. Thus, the practice of *ruminatio* (repeated reading or recitation) was one of the main meanings of *meditatio* (Ruppert 1977). The original sense of *ruminatio* is 'digesting food through repeated chewing'. Its metaphorical use indicates a process of personal interiorization of the read or recited subject matter.

The Greek and Latin terms for *hagah* add the emphasis on exercise and learning to the original meaning. Additionally, under the heading of *melétē/meditatio*, several other spiritual exercises were taken from the Greco-Roman philosophical culture. As Pierre Hadot has demonstrated, the Stoa, neo-Platonism and the Epicurean school had a therapeutic dimension and developed a wide range of practices for the cure of their followers' souls.

---

6   Translation according to the New International Version (NIV) of the Bible. The Vulgate translates *Beatus vir qui...in lege [Domini] meditabitur die ac nocte.*

Taken from these sources, the methodical practice of 'paying attention, taking care about oneself' (*prosochē*) became particularly significant for Christian monasticism (Hadot 1995, 126-144). It included the regular *praemeditatio mortis*, the meditative realization of one's own death and mortality as well as the examination of conscience at the beginning and/or end of each day.

Within the Hellenistic schools of philosophy and rhetoric as well as within Christian asceticism, the training of memory (*mneme, memoria*) in the sense of the ability to recall the learnt and accepted philosophical and religious principles within the times of spiritual practice and the changing situations of daily life was of crucial importance. 'The purpose of the verbal *melétē/meditatio* is to make the *sententia* a constant habit of mind, or to implant the precepts into one's self, so as to have them constantly at hand. The aim is a state of "preparedness", when confronting impressions and future events' (Johnsén 2013, 103).

Philosophical and Christian meditation practices shared the interest in the cultivation of memory with the discipline of rhetoric, whose methods influenced European meditation from the very beginning (Carruthers 1998). Meditation methods and rhetoric often intermingled. From Late Antiquity to Ignatius of Loyola's famous *Spiritual Exercises*, rhetorical methods have been used to structure the thought processes within the practice of meditation and to deepen the impact of the meditated topics on the persons meditating.[7]

In medieval times the practice of meditation shifted from murmured rumination to methodical thinking.[8] *Meditatio* now stood for the interpretation of biblical and other authoritative texts and theological topics with exegetical and logical means,

---

7   The influence of rhetoric on Stoic, Epicurean and Christian methods of meditation as well as the continuity of this influence within the Christian era have been pointed out in the seminal study Rabbow 1954. For the relationship between rhetoric and meditation see also Butzer 2001.

8   See Guigo II. *Epistola de vita contemplativa* (Scala Claustralium) 84, 32-38: *Meditatio est studiosa mentis actio, occultae veritatis notitiam ductu propriae rationis investigans* (Meditation is the studious activity of the mind which searches for the hidden truth guided by its own reason).

and especially with the rhetorical techniques of *inventio* (methods to discover points and arguments) and *amplificatio* (techniques to heighten the cognitive, emotional and moral importance of a subject in order to motivate attitudinal and behavioural changes). Moreover, from Anselm of Canterbury (d. 1109) onward, the term '*meditationes*' was also used to denote a genre of devotional literature that dealt with emotional self-examination and introspection in the context of prayer (Bestul 2012, 158-160). Many books of this genre, influenced by the ancient *soliloquium* literature, were written to provide models for personal practice, although instructions by spiritual guides were considered to be indispensable.[9]

Within Hellenistic rhetoric, the visualization of certain situations was used for the preparation of speeches in order to intensify an orator's performance. The renaissance of rhetoric, and in particular the rhetorization of prayer within the monastic culture of the high and late medieval age, probably contributed to the booming of visualization in this period. The method of so-called affective meditation centred around the imagination of biblical scenes. 'The goal was to meditate the events of Christ's life, *sicut praesens*, as though one were actually present at the scene' (Bestul 2012, 162). The imaginations not only consisted of visual elements, but included all senses. They aimed at the creation of pious emotions and the cultivation of virtues.

In order to elicit compassion and love for the suffering son of God, the imagination of the passion of Christ became especially widespread.[10] Historical research has shown that mainly women were drawn to this practice and that the male theologians who wrote about it, and thus promoted the spread of affective meditation throughout Western Europe, were influenced by female piety. Caroline Walker Bynum explained this by referring to late medieval gender ideology (Bynum 1986). Women were considered to

---

9   A related type of literature that has existed since antiquity and is also connected to the tradition of the *soliloquium* but in a less devotional way is the philosophical *meditatio*. Within the scope of this article it is not possible to treat this interesting genre and its relation to the devotional *meditationes*.

10   For the early stage of this development see Fulton 2002.

be more 'carnal' than men and therefore were expected to focus their meditations on the incarnated Christ. Moreover, on a symbolical level the suffering body of Christ was thought of as feminine and this could have also motivated women to identify with it. Referring to the legal concept of 'marital affection' (*maritalis affectio*), Sarah McNamer has convincingly argued that an even stronger motive for nuns and female recluses to cultivate compassion with Christ via visualization practices has been to become a 'true' spouse of Christ—in this life and for all eternity (McNamer 2010). In accordance with the appreciation of visual elements, the use of devotional images to support this dimension of meditation became quite common.

From the late fourteenth to the early sixteenth century, the reform movement Devotio Moderna (New Devotion) triggered an advanced systematization of practice. The steps to be taken within each meditation became more differentiated and were put in a methodologically reflected order that should one by one activate the Augustinian faculties of the soul, namely *memoria* (memory), *intelligentia* (intellect) and *voluntas* (will and emotion).[11] Additionally, training programmes *(exercitia)* were developed that covered larger spans of time in which a sequence of topics should be meditated. During this period of spiritual reform, many religious orders introduced daily meditation to their schedule. Influenced by the methods of Devotio Moderna, Ignatius of Loyola (1491-1556) finally combined several forms of meditation in his *Exercitia Spiritualia* (1548), which in their long version last for one month. Ignatius's spiritual exercises became a paradigm of Catholic retreat culture and meditation practice. In the context of this paper, I would only like to mention his 'meditation with the three faculties' (*meditación con las tres potencias*). Since the late sixteenth century, this form has become the most prominent and influential Jesuit method of meditation. The more contemplative ways of meditation that Ignatius had integrated into his *Exercitia* have been downplayed or even forbidden, mainly because of the

---

11 For meditation practices within the Devotio Moderna see Baier 2009a, 58-70; Staubach 2011.

persecution of the *alumbrados* and the Quietism debate (see below). The scheme of this kind of meditation goes as follows:

Preparatory Prayer

Prelude 1: visualization of a biblical scene or of a scene with symbolic meaning fitting to the topic of the meditation

Prelude 2: asking of God what one wishes in this exercise

Points: 1. memorizing central points concerning the topic

2. pondering them

3. moving emotions and will according to the results of point 2

Colloqui: conversing with Jesus Christ, Mother Mary (both visualized), or God

Concluding prayer

During the seventeenth century, a widespread interest in meditation manifested itself in a growing number of devotional books that explained meditation methods and gave examples that should inspire readers. Within the Catholic Church, the practice of meditation was propagated for all Christian estates (monastics, priests, lay people)—not least as a counter-reformatory weapon against the spread of the new Churches. Concurrently, Protestant theologians adopted Catholic meditation techniques as a means to reform the religious life within their own communities (Sträter 1995). Half a century after Luther's death, a growing number of critical theologians called for a renewal of the Protestant denominations. They integrated meditation and contemplation in their reform programmes. A main reason for the new emphasis on meditation was the 'crisis of the sermon'. Many Lutherans expressed serious doubts about the effectivity of preaching with regard to the transmission of faith. Meditation as a way of intellectual as well as emotional interiorization of the word of God seemed to offer a solution to this problem.

In 1606, the leading Lutheran theologian, Johann Gerhard, published the *Meditationes sacrae*, a bestseller among the devotional books of the seventeenth century that has been reprinted in more than two hundred editions in at least twelve languages, thus becoming the most successful Protestant meditation manual ever (Sträter 1995, 43). The Latin version was used as a handbook within academic theological studies.

In the preface to his book, Gerhard uses the language of spiritual alchemy by comparing Jesus with the philosopher's stone and the medical processes within the physical body with the purification of the spiritual body. Due to this, the *Meditationes sacrae* were appreciated by Paracelsists and had some influence within alchemical circles (Steiger 2000, 50). The meditative and contemplative exercises of spiritual alchemists, Rosicrucians and radical pietists, who were sometimes also influenced by Kabbalist practices, are a highly interesting strand of Western European spirituality and would deserve further investigations that cannot be undertaken here.

In Gerhard's *Schola Pietatis* (1622), meditation again was of central importance as a tool prescribed by the Holy Spirit to gain, retain and enhance the true Christian life (Sträter 1995, 49-52). Another tradition of Protestant meditation was established in England. There, at the beginning of the seventeenth century, the interest in meditation was growing as in many other European countries. The first available meditation handbooks were translations of Catholic sources. Joseph Hall, bishop of Exeter and later of Norwich, pioneered the fusing of Catholic meditation techniques with Calvinist theology. He published two important books on meditation: *Art of Divine Meditation* (1606) and *Occasional Meditations* (1633). One of Hall's innovations was the distinction between deliberate meditation (of the Bible) and spontaneous occasional meditation that emerges at different occasions, such as listening to the singing of a bird, smelling the scent of a rose, or the encounter with a crying child.[12] His occasional meditations are structured according to what was then the common scheme of meditation. The perception of the object of meditation is followed by an analytical part with pondering. The exercise is completed with an emotional prayer or exhortation.

---

12 For Hall's writings on meditation see Frank Livingstone Huntley 1981.

In the second half of the seventeenth century, translations of English literature on meditation (Joseph Hall, Lewis Bayly) influenced Lutheran practice and contributed to the emergence of the German Pietist movement that emphasized spiritual practice (Taubner 2014). With the decline of Pietism in the nineteenth century, the practice of meditation became almost forgotten within the Lutheran Church and the same seemingly happened within other major Protestant churches.[13] It was the US-American Mind-Cure movement (also known as New Thought) that reintroduced meditation practices together with contemplation into Protestantism at the end of the nineteenth century.[14] Independent of New Thought approaches, in the mid-1930s, Dietrich Bonhoeffer tried to revitalize Martin Luther's meditation of the Bible within his underground seminary for the Confessing Church at Finkenwalde that was closed down by the Nazis in 1937. He created a ritual of meditative reading and pondering the meaning of biblical texts with regard to their significance to the readers' lives in the style of the old *lectio divina* (Baier 2009, 672-673).[15]

---

13 In the mid-nineteenth century, the Lutheran theologian Löhe wrote: 'Eine Übung und Aeußerung des inwendigen Lebens ist bei uns ganz verloren gegangen, nämlich die *Meditation*...' (There is a certain exercise and expression of the inner life that has become completely lost among us, namely *meditation*) (Löhe 1852, 122; Löhe's emphasis).

14 It was William James who first highlighted the key role of the Mind-Cure movement for the renaissance of Protestant meditation and contemplation. See James 1902, 406: 'It is odd that Protestantism, especially evangelical Protestantism should seemingly have abandoned everything methodical in this time...It has been left to our mind-curers to reintroduce methodical meditation into our religious life.' In a typical modern way, James uses 'meditation' as an umbrella term for what was traditionally distinguished as meditation and (acquired) contemplation.

15 In a letter written in 1936, Karl Barth criticized Bonhoeffer for his attempt to establish meditation as a separate discipline distinct from scientific theological reflection. He felt disgusted by the 'flair of monastic eros and pathos' of Bonhoeffer's experiment. Obviously, Barth had been ignorant of the long tradition of Bible meditation within the Protestant churches and only repeated obsolete anti-monastic and anti-Catholic prejudices (see Bonhoeffer 1996, 945).

During the interwar period, the physician, psychotherapist and spiritual director, Carl Happich, from Darmstadt, Germany, introduced new methods to meditate on and contemplate visual symbols and imaginary scenes for the members of the protestant reform movement, Berneuchener Bewegung, and the Michaelsbruderschaft, a brotherhood, which eventually emerged from this movement. After the war Happich's methods influenced the therapeutic use of meditation and contemplation within humanistic and transpersonal psychology. They were practised within the Michaelsbruderschaft at least until the 1960s (Baier 2013).

In the Catholic Church, traditional meditation survived albeit in rather formalized and petrified ways (compared with the creativity of the seventeenth century) and had a final heyday within the context of the so-called retreat movement from the beginning of the twentieth century until World War II.

2. Contemplation

The English term 'contemplation' is a loan from the Latin *contemplatio* (the act of looking, gazing attentively, consideration) that was used as a translation of the Greek *theōría* (watching, beholding). *Theōría* has had different meanings that derived from the basic sense of 'beholding'.[16] In ancient Greece, it denoted a civic institution: the pilgrimage of someone (the *theōrós*) to a religious festival or an oracle to witness sacred events and spectacles (Nightingale 2004). 'This sacralized mode of spectating was a central element of traditional *theoria*, and offered a powerful model for the philosophic notion of "seeing" divine truths' (Nightingale 2004, 4). In Greek philosophy, *theōría* could also mean the investigation of truth for its own sake in a more general, not only a religious sense; and last but not least, a way of life dedicated to these meanings of *theōría*: the *bíos theōretikós* (*vita*

---

16 An overview of the different meanings of contemplation in Greek philosophy and Christian theology is given by Nef, 2005. For the pre-Christian Greek tradition of contemplation see McGinn 1992, 24-62.

contemplativa) as opposed to *bíos praktikós* (*vita activa*).[17] Josef
Pieper summarized the major meanings of *theōría* and *contemplatio* in a lucid way:

> *Theoria* and *contemplatio* devote their full energy to revealing,
> clarifying, and making manifest the reality which [sic] has been
> sighted; they aim at truth and nothing else. This is the first ele-
> ment of the concept of contemplation: silent perception of reality.
> A second is the following: Contemplation is a form of knowing
> arrived at not by thinking but by seeing, intuition. It is not co-
> ordinate with the *ratio*, but with the *intellectus*, with the capacity
> for 'simple intuition'. (Pieper 1998, 73-74; Pieper's emphases)[18]

Pursuing the second element that Pieper mentions, medieval epistemological texts connect the studying of texts and meditation in
the sense of methodical discursive thought with tedious labour
whereas contemplation is seen as an effortless and joyful consummation of what reading and meditation are searching for:

> Thinking [*cogitatio*], [scattered thought driven by passions and
> mostly based on phantasies, KB] crawls; meditation marches and
> often runs; contemplation flies around everywhere and when it
> wishes suspends itself in the heights. Thinking is without labor
> and fruit; in meditation there is labor and fruit; contemplation
> continues without labor but with fruit.[19]

Along the lines of this tradition, referring to Sirach 32:15-
16 in the prologue to his early commentary on Boethius's *Heb-*

---

17 For the different concepts of the relationship between active and contemplative life from early Greek philosophy to the Church father see Vogl 2002 and
   Bénatouïl, Bonazzi 2012.

18 For the distinction between *ratio* and *intellectus* that can be traced back to
   Aristotle see Thomas Aquinas *Summa Theologiae* 1, q. 59, a. 1, ad 1: Sed
   intellectus et ratio different quantum ad modum cognoscendi, quia scili-
   cet intellectus cognoscit simplici intuitu, ratio vero discurrendo de uno in
   aliud (Intuitive insight and discursive thought are different according to
   their modes of knowing; because intuitive insight knows by a simple gaze,
   whereas discursive thought has to run to and fro from one to another).

19 Richard of St. Victor, *Benjamin Maior* (*De arca mystica*), Ch. III, quoted
   according to Richard of St. Victor 1979, 155-156.

domads, Thomas Aquinas recognizes an essential relationship between the delight of contemplating divine wisdom and play (*ludus*). As Mary Carruthers already has pointed out, the meaning of the term *ludus* is not identical with the usual monastic leisure, *otium*, but adds some aspects to it, namely, uselessness and delight (Carruthers 2014, 76-77). Why does he consider *contemplatio* to be a kind of play? 'First, because play is delightful and the contemplation of Wisdom possesses maximum delight…Second, because things done in play are not ordered to anything else, but are thought for their own sake, and this same trait belongs to the delights of Wisdom' (Aquinas 2001, 5).

For Neoplatonic authors like Plotinus (205-270), whose religious philosophy heavily influenced Christian concepts of *theoría/contemplatio*, contemplation culminates in a unitive experiential knowledge of the divine source of all being, an experience that transcends the usual seeing of someone or something:

> No doubt, we should not speak of seeing; but we cannot help talking in dualities, seen and seer, instead of, boldly, the achievement of unity. In this seeing, we neither hold an object nor trace distinction; there are no two. The man is changed, no longer himself nor self-belonging; he is merged with the Supreme, sunken into it, one with it: centre coincides with centre. (Plotinus, *Ennead* VI, 9.10, trans. by Stephen MacKenna and B.S. Page)

Explaining the ascent to 'mystical contemplation', the Christian theologian, Pseudo-Dionysius (fifth-sixth century), adopted Plotinus's advice to let go of everything (*aphele panta*; see Plotinus, *Ennead* V, 3, 17, 38) in order to unify the soul and the Divine One.[20] 'For, by the unceasing and absolute renunciation of thyself and all things, thou shalt in pureness cast all things aside, and be released from all, and so shalt be led upwards to the ray of that divine darkness that exceedeth all existence' (Pseudo-Dionysius, *De Mystica Theologia* I, 1000A, trans. by C.E. Rolt).

---

20 According to Bouyer 2004, 177-78, the term 'mystical contemplation' (*mystikè theoría*) was already used before Pseudo-Dionysius by Gregory of Nyssa (335-394).

Following Bernard McGinn, two conceptions of contemplative union exist, broadly speaking, within the Christian traditions: union with God through a bond of love that emphasizes the distinction of creator and creature, and a union of indistinction in which God and man merge into a simple oneness. 'There was a considerable variety of ways of conceiving these modes of union, and many mystics used language and images expressing both forms' (McGinn 2012, 204).

Similar to the case of *hagah*/*melétē*/*meditatio*, the Greco-Roman semantics of *theoríā*/*contemplatio* interacted with biblical vocabulary:

> A whole assembly of biblical words whose root meanings center on the notion of resting in God – *quies, otium, vacatio, sabbatum* – constitute the second linguistic field. These terms were often employed synonymously with contemplatio and its cognates, though each word also has its own semantic resonance. (McGinn 2004, 139)

Contemplation became a term for 1) states of mind that transcend all words, rational discernments and images and 2) practices that were meant to bring about these states. Different names were given to the *locus*, the 'place' of contemplative encounter and union with God beyond the ordinary faculties of body and soul: *acies mentis* (edge, sharpness of the mind, keen gaze), *apex mentis* (peak of the mind), *apex affectus* (peak of love), *abditum mentis* (hidden depth of the mind), *scintilla animae* (sparkle of the soul) or *radix animae* (root of the soul).[21]

John Cassian (360-435) who pioneered the transfer of early Christian monasticism from Palestine and Egypt to Western Europe explains in his famous tenth *conlatio* (*Conlationes* 10, 10-11) how one should perform the continual recollection of God that leads to contemplation. As synonyms for *contemplatio* he uses 'purified prayer', 'perfect prayer', or 'glowing prayer'. Cassian recommends the steady repetition of the *spiritalis theoriae*

---

21 The historical background and dissemination of these terms are investigated by Ivánka 1990, 315-385 and Reiter 1992, 84-282.

formula (formula of spiritual contemplation): 'God, come to my rescue. Lord, hurry to help me' (Psalm 70:1, ISV). The continuous recitation of this formula should culminate in a prayer beyond images and words. The mind's attentiveness should be set ablaze and called forth in an 'unspeakable ecstasy of the heart' that transcends 'all feelings and visible matter'.

Here we have the case of a very short and simple standardized prayer used to develop a contemplative state of mind. After Cassian, this kind of practice of preparing the mind for a non-conceptual encounter with God became a widespread exercise among monastics and recluses. Under the name 'prayer of the heart' or 'Jesus prayer' it is often thought of as an exclusive heritage of the Orthodox Churches but it has been also practised throughout the history of Western European Christianity.

One example for this is the well-known *The Cloude of Unknowyng*, written in the late fourteenth century.[22] The anonymous author of this treatise describes contemplation as a 'special prayer' that exceeds all other forms of praying. To contemplate would mean to cultivate a wordless inner silence filled with the love of God. In order to unfold inner calmness, the author recommends an undivided attention on single monosyllabic words, especially 'sin' and 'God', without any discursive mental acts.[23] With the concentration on these words, two major topics of meditation are transferred to a higher level of understanding. Intellectual reflections and other activities of the soul except a pure selfless love of God are left behind in a 'cloud of forgetting' and with his or her 'point of spirit' (*apex mentis*) the practitioner enters the 'cloud of unknowing'. One becomes immersed in 'a nothing' that is 'all' because within this cloud one learns to comprehend all things at once without discriminative knowledge.[24] Within this nothingness, God and the soul are revealed in their oneness.

---

22 In the following I refer to the critical edition of the text provided by Hodgson 1982. For a more detailed analysis of practices described in the *Cloud of Unknowing* and their historical context, see Baier 2009, 101-109.

23 See *Cloud* 40,15-44,14.

24 See *Cloud* 67,37-68,21.

Some teachers like Teresa of Ávila or Miguel de Molinos recommended reduced forms of concentration on Jesus Christ to bridge the gap between the usually Christocentric meditations and the complete emptying of the mind in contemplation. After having been trained in meditating on the details of Christ's life and death, one should switch to see his humanity 'by a simple act of faith [i.e. without imaginations and discursive thoughts, KB], loving it, and remembering that he is the tabernacle of divinity, the beginning and end of our salvation…' (Molinos 2010, 97).

Another exercise to develop inner silence and a non-conceptual opening towards God was the practice of Pseudo-Dionysian negative theology as spiritual exercise. Referring to Pseudo-Dionysius, the anonymous *Tratado de oración y contemplation* that dates back to the beginning of the seventeenth century and was attributed to the Carmelite Tómas á Jesu (1564-1627), explains two kinds of knowledge of God on which two ways of contemplation are based, the affirmative and the negative.[25] Affirmative contemplation considers God as wise, powerful, good, etc. The negative way is described as follows:

> The soul, placed in prayer,…after it is habituated to know God in the contemplation of the attributes and divine perfections…it raises itself to God saying interiorly, 'God bless me! God is more than being, more than substance, more than goodness, more than wisdom, more than everything we can understand; then what is God? God bless me! What will be this God who is so great?' And searching here for what He is, it finds nothing that is comparable to God. It finds itself placed in an abyss where it loses its footing, grows weak, and is submerged, and the will [in the sense of love, KB] is enkindled and is inflamed, and the affect holds vigil,

---

25 Actually, all forms of Christian contemplation finally come down to the practice of apophatic theology as spiritual exercise. Nevertheless, contemplation guides do not often refer to Pseudo-Dionysius as master of the *via negativa* as explicitly and theoretically reflected as in the case of Tómas á Jesu. In popular instructions to the prayer of silence one often finds the simple advice that one should trust in the presence of God, surrender to his will, and stay in silence without thinking anything special; just upholding pure faith and love.

although the understanding shuts itself off; and the soul loves
what it does not know with particular and distinct knowledge.
(Biblioteca Nacional de Madrid, ms. 12398. Book 1, Chapter 4,
f. 64^r – 64^v, translation quoted from Arraj 1999, 63)[26]

Apart from this kind of exercise, Tomás á Jesu is more known for
having introduced the term 'acquired contemplation' into the vocabulary of Catholic spirituality. It was used for all exercises that
skip the schemes of meditation in order to prepare the practitioner
for the higher states of union caused by infusion of Divine grace
(passive, infused contemplation). Additionally, acquired contemplation was the name for the states of inner calmness, emptiness
and loving attentiveness to the divine presence that are produced
by these practices and therefore were not considered to be the
results of extraordinary Divine grace.[27]

The attitude towards disturbances and temptations during
contemplation differs from meditation. A long line of spiritual
teachers that ended with Miguel de Molinos and Madame Guyon
taught that no active fight against evil thoughts, demonic temptations and carnal desires should take place in contemplation:

When dealing with impertinent, importunate, and lewd thoughts
in the time of recollection, know that God values the peace and
resignation of your soul more than good propositions and grand
sentiments. The very force you use to resist these thoughts is an
impediment and will leave the soul more unquiet. What is impor-

---

26 From the last important Victorine theologian, Thomas Gallus (1190-1246),
onwards, the Pseudo-Dionysian distinction between affirmative and negative theology has often been related to the polarity of *intellectus* in the sense
of rational understanding and *voluntas/affectus*, i.e. love that alone would
lead to to the superintellectual union with God. Tomás follows this current.

27 The centuries-long discussion on the validity of acquired contemplation and
its relation to infused contemplation can be broken down to the question
whether or not silent non-discursive awareness in general and especially the
contemplative openness towards God is a human capacity, a skill that can be
trained by certain practices. See Sherman 2014, 12. Like Sherman, I would
argue that besides theological and philosophical arguments, our knowledge
of the history of religions as well as modern empirical research provide a
strong evidence base for conceiving acquired contemplation as a skill.

tant is to scorn them gently, to know your misery, and to offer the disturbance to God. (Molinos 2010, 82)

Among other points that will be mentioned in the next section, this attitude became a problem, especially when contemplation started to spread outside the monasteries and became a popular practice.

The Democratization of Contemplation and its Suppression

Similarly to meditation, but to an even greater degree, for almost one and a half millennia contemplation has been the privilege of monastics and hermits, and at least a few aristocrats or other members of the upper classes who had the interest and leisure to engage in spiritual exercises. Starting from the fifteenth century, monastic reform circles (often associated with groups of lay people) in Spain, Italy, the Low Lands and finally in France propagated contemplation as something that every Christian should practise rather than religious specialists alone (Sluhovsky 2007, 97-137). Devotional books started to praise contemplation as an art easy to learn and more suitable for accelerating spiritual progress than any other practice. Uneducated believers were now praised for being more gifted for contemplation than the arrogant academic theologians. Subsequently, different forms of contemplative prayer became relatively widespread Sluhovsky 2007, 100). Comparatively, the democratization of meditation practice has been rarely attacked, as it basically complemented quite well the usual forms of prayer, the Christian rites including confession and the messages conveyed in the sermons of the priests. By contrast the dissemination of contemplation soon became highly controversial.[28]

---

28 Nevertheless, the spread of meditation techniques also had to face attacks from Catholic theologians and church officials who connected it with a dangerous upgrading of individual experience (especially of lay persons) over against the salvific value of the sacraments, the official teachings and the hierarchical order of the Church. See Sluhovsky 2007, 100. I will come back to these points below. Because of their individualistic approach, even the

The persecution of the increasingly popular contemplative practices and the groups whose spirituality focussed on them started with a reformist movement that later was called *alumbradismo* (illuminism) by its adversaries. It arose among Franciscan circles in Castile, Spain in the 1510s. *Alumbradismo* was based on the cultivation of *dejamiento*, the total abandonment to the love of God. This kind of radical non-discursive opening was not dependent on sitting silently at a calm place. The *alumbrados* (i.e. 'women and men illuminated by the Holy Spirit') taught that *dejamiento* could and should be performed everywhere, at all times, and by all people (Hamilton 1992, 30-31). This claim refers to an important form of contemplation that has not yet been touched – one that is worth dwelling on briefly.

Contemplation has been often conceptualized as a retreat from worldly affairs, the closing of the corporeal and exterior senses and a turning inwards to focus on God who dwells within the depths of the soul. According to this understanding, a tension between contemplation and action exists that can at most be overcome by very advanced practitioners who have already experienced an ecstatic union with God and are capable of keeping a steady attention towards him while also being actively engaged within the world. On the contrary, *dejamiento* and similar models conceive contemplation from the very start as a mode of everyday existence that should be cultivated as such. The central exercise then is to radically let go of one's self-centredness and submit oneself to God irrespective of whatever one does during the day. Longer sessions of silent, motionless contemplative prayer are replaced by this form of radicalized everydayness or are used as supplement and source of inspiration for it.

Day-to-day contemplation, the exercise to search and find God in all things, thus becoming a contemplative in action as the Jesuit Jéronimo Nadal (1507-1580) took it, time and again had its devot-

---

Ignatian exercises were sometimes accused of being crypto-Protestant. On the other hand, the Protestant opponents of meditation understood it as a typically Catholic practice based on a theological synergism that would undermine the principles of *sola gratia* and *sola fide*. See Sträter 1995, 29, 52.

ed proponents and charismatic teachers within the history of Western European spirituality. In medieval times, Master Eckhart was a strong advocate of the unity between contemplation and action. One of the most remarkable masters of this path in early modern times was Brother Lawrence of the Resurrection (c. 1614-1691), a cook and shoemaker who worked as a lay brother (i.e. servant) in a Carmelite monastery in Paris and taught the practice of being aware of the presence of God within each and every moment. He instructed his followers to do whatever they would do with diligence and care. 'We must perform all our actions carefully and deliberately, not impulsively or hurried, for such would characterize a distracted mind' (Brother Lawrence of the Resurrection 1994, 38). Additionally, he recommended small exercises to support the awareness of divine presence: short spontaneous prayers during the day and the practice of stopping whatever one is actually doing for a few moments to reconnect with the God within: 'During our work and other activities…— and I emphasize, even during our religious exercises and vocal prayers – we must stop for a moment, as often as possible, to adore God in the depth of our hearts, to savor him, even though in passing and stealthily' (Brother Lawrence of the Resurrection 1994, 38 -39). In a similar way, the *Treatise on Abandonment to Divine Providence*, written by an unknown eighteenth century author and erroneously attributed to Jean-Pierre Caussade (1675-1751), develops a spirituality of abandonment to the divine providence within each present situation.[29]

Returning to *alumbradismo*, the movement attracted Franciscans and other clerics, educated and semi-educated laity, and especially women, some of whom held leading positions (Montoya 2010, 13). Many of its members descended from second-generation *conversos* (Jewish converts). This made the *alumbrados* even more suspicious. With its doctrine still in the making, *alum-*

---

29 Both Brother Lawrence and the *Treatise on Abandonment* were steeped in the Quietist tradition. The twentieth century renaissance of their kind of contemplative awareness via philosophers and theologians like Martin Buber, Gabriel Marcel, Romano Guardini, and Simone Weil is treated in Baier 2009, 695-813.

bradismo was first detected by the Inquisition in 1519. In 1524, its leaders were imprisoned. In the following year, the inquisitors published an edict in Toledo that condemned forty-seven propositions attributed to the *alumbrados*. Several propositions explicitly refer to questions of prayer. The inquisitors rejected the claim that mental prayer should replace vocal prayer and that meditation was of no use as it depended on sentiments and thoughts that would cause undesirable effects, whereas contemplation was wholesome (Sluhovsky 2007, 107). The central Proposition 12 asserted:

> Alumbrados: Having abandoned themselves to God, such people did not have to work, in order not to block whatever God wished to accomplish. They could withdraw themselves from all created things. Even to meditate upon the humanity of Christ hindered abandonment to God (*dejamiento en Dios*). And such people could refuse all thoughts that occurred to them, even if the thoughts were good, because they should look to God alone. They thought refusing such thoughts was virtuous. Being in that spiritual state of quietude (*estando en aquella quietud*), they even thought it was a temptation to remember God in order not to be distracted.
> Inquisitors: This proposition is false, erroneous, scandalous, and heretical. (Quoted from Montoya 2010, 87)

In the next century, other edicts followed against groups that the inquisitors identified as *alumbrados* in various parts of Spain. Until the beginning of the eighteenth century, the term *alumbradismo* and its derivatives (like 'illuminism') were used here and there across Western Europe as an accusation by theologians and the Inquisition, whereas on the other hand, contemplative groups felt the need to distance themselves from it. Nevertheless, in the second half of the seventeenth century, yet another heresy became the major target of the opponents of the contemplative current within Catholicism.

During this period, the dissemination of contemplation gained momentum again through reformist groups and spiritual guides in Italy and France. Their thoughts and practices now were labelled 'quietism' (from 'prayer of quiet', a then well-known synonym of contemplation). The Spanish Jesuit, Miguel de Molinos (1628-

1696), who was a very famous priest and spiritual director in Rome—well connected with the Roman nobility and the highest levels within the Vatican's hierarchy—became the leading representative of the movement. Together with other works from Quietist authors, his *Guia espiritual* (The Spiritual Guide), a widely read manual of meditation and contemplation published in 1675, sparked a controversy about the doctrinal validity of the Quietist practice that had become a kind of religious fashion:

> The theological question at the heart of the debate concerned the proper place of meditation in the spiritual life. For Molinos, meditation was a necessary and important practice for spiritual beginners, but it was ultimately incompatible with the immediate practice of 'pure faith' that he prescribed for those advanced on the spiritual path. (Baird 2010, 9)

The critics of Molinos, especially a group of Jesuits led by Paolo Segneri (1624-1694), in his time the most celebrated Jesuit preacher in Italy, understood his teachings as an attack against the usual meditation techniques centred on the humanity of Christ (Baird 2010, 9). He was accused of being theologically too innovative and of following the heretical tradition of *alumbradismo*. In 1687, the papal bull *Coelestis Pastor* condemned the *Guia espiritual*. The condemnation not only referred to his published work but also to manuscripts and letters that were found in Molinos's house and to his verbal teachings. He was sentenced to life and died in prison in 1696. Compared to earlier works on contemplation, Molinos does not offer great surprises. Nor did the sixty-eight propositions of the bull reveal anything new about the views of those who acted as the defenders of orthodoxy against contemplative groups. But the long-term effects of his condemnation surpassed earlier prosecutions of contemplative practice.

Three years before Molinos's death, the infamous French Quietist controversy began, the last theological debate that aroused great public interest within Western Europe.[30] It ended in 1698

---

30 For the history of this debate, see Heppe 1875. The theological significance of Fénelon's thought is investigated by Spaemann 1963.

with the condemnation of François Fénelon's *Explication des maximes de saints*. In this popular book, Fénelon (1651-1715) defended Quietism and Jeanne Marie Guyon du Chesnoy (1648-1717) – the already mentioned Madame Guyon, a charismatic quietist, spiritual guide and writer whom he admired and who influenced his theological thought. Between 1695 and 1703, Madame Guyon was imprisoned in the Bastille. She spent the last years of her life in a village near Blois, surrounded by a small ecumenical contemplative community of disciples from different countries and Christian denominations.

One could sum up the arguments that were articulated against Quietism as follows. Because of their focus on inner experience, the Quietists would neglect Christian doctrine as taught by the Magisterium and reject the hierarchy of the Church as well as its redemptive rites, i.e. the sacraments. The passivity of contemplation would downplay the importance of works of charity and other good deeds thus undermining the cultivation of Christian virtues. It would furthermore invite attacks of demons in the form of delusions and evil phantasies. The practitioners would be inclined to think that whatever comes into their minds in the state of contemplation is inspired by God and therefore good, even if it would be against the moral rules proclaimed by the Church (Sluhovsky 2007, 116). Consequentially, the Quietists would use contemplation to justify sin and especially sexual immorality. The practice of pure love of God for God's own sake, rather than out of fear of punishment or hope for rewards, would disarm fear as a means to leading a pious and virtuous life (Bruneau 1998, 143-144). Additionally, from the angle of pure love, common religious practices like prayers of petition and methodical meditation would be discredited as mere expressions of selfish love (Sluhovsky 2007, 131).

Some of these arguments may have been valid with regard to isolated cases of abuse and separatism. Others simply mirrored the power interests of the Catholic Church apparatus *in toto*, as well as of special groups within it. They seemed to be afraid of the subversive potential of contemplation. Although contemplation has never been totally rejected as a legitimate Catholic practice, it ceased being a recognized form of prayer due to the oppression and final collapse of the Quietist movement. Even within contemplative orders like the Carmelites the respective writings of their founders were censored. Public expressions of Quietist thought and practice became almost impossible. A long-lasting phobia of contemplative prayer emerged. Its practice survived only in small, mainly monastic circles. It took two hundred years until a revival of contemplation occurred from the end of the nineteenth century onwards.

The Protestant Reception of Quietism

The suppression of Quietism and particularly the fate of Miguel de Molinos, as well as the controversy about Fénelon, inflamed the interest of German Lutherans. In 1687, the year of Molinos's condemnation, August Hermann Francke published a Latin translation of the *Guía espiritual*. A German edition by the radical Pietist, Gottfried Arnold, followed in 1699. Arnold also dedicated a chapter of his *Unpartheyische Kirchen= und Ketzer=Historie* (1729) to the Quietists.[31] In 1704, the Huguenot pastor, philosopher and theologian, Pierre Poiret (1646-1719), published an anthology of the writings of Madame Guyon called *Opuscules spirituels* that additionally comprised several other Qietist writings.

A good example of the influence of Quietist contemplative spirituality within Protestantism is the aforementioned Brother Lawrence.[32] Already in 1701, his works had been translated into German together with those of Madame Guyon and with a preface written by Gottfried Arnold. The writings of Brother Lawrence exercised decisive influence on Gerhard Tersteegen, the famous Pietist theologian and poet, whose major theological topic, the presence of God, was inspired by the Carmelite lay brother.

---

31 Arnold's relationship to Quietist contemplative spirituality is treated by Marti 2002.

32 For Brother Lawrence's international influence, see Salvatore Sciurba 1994, xxxiv-xxxvi.

Tersteegen probably came to know Brother Lawrence through the edition of his works published by Pierre Poiret in 1710 under the title *La Théologie de la Présence a Dieu*. In the second volume of his *Außerlesene Lebensbeschreibungen Heiliger Seelen* (Selected Biographies of Holy Souls) from 1785, Tersteegen devoted a comprehensive chapter to Brother Lawrence and thus made him known in Germany and the Low Countries. Gottfried Arnold later published a biography of Brother Lawrence.

John Wesley (1703-1791), the founder of Methodism, made him known in the English-speaking world. In more recent times, William James (1842-1910) rediscovered Brother Lawrence and quoted him at length in an article on *The Gospel of Relaxation* (1899), thus connecting the emerging modern culture of relaxation with Quietist everyday contemplation. 'The simple-heartedness of Brother Lawrence', he writes, 'and the relaxation of all unnecessary solicitudes and anxieties in him, is a refreshing spectacle' (Jams 1911, 77). In today's globalized contemplative culture, an edition of Brother Lawrence presents him as a 'Christian Zen master' and publishes his sayings along with quotations from different famous Buddhist teachers.[33]

Similarities between the Quaker Movement and Quietism existed from its very beginning, as the founder, George Fox, underlined the importance of approaching the Godhead in silent contemplation. Historians of Quakerism pointed to parallels between the early Quaker theologian, Robert Barclay (1648-1690), and Quietist positions. Their historical relationship has not been sufficiently clarified yet. The third period of Quakerism, which lasted from the end of seventeenth until the first years of the nineteenth century, is usually called Quietist Quakerism because of

---

33 See Brother Lawrence 2011, 11: 'In this book, you will find modern-language paraphrases from *The Practice of the Presence of God*, paired with writings from many different Buddhist teachers, divided into sections based on common themes. These couplings are not meant to demonstrate a one-to-one correspondence, nor are they intended to prove that Zen Buddhism and Christianity (or at least Brother Lawrence's version of it) are one and the same. They are not. But one can shine light on the other' (emphases in the original text).

the strong influence of continental Quietism and especially the writings of Molinos, Fénelon and Madame Guyon.[34]

Meditation and Contemplation as Opposite Types of Practice

According to the 'classical' Western European conceptualization of spiritual exercises that began to emerge in antiquity, became established in the medieval age, and survived until modern times, the term 'meditation' relates to practices for the development of self-knowledge and the knowledge of God that engage ritualized reading or reciting, thought, imagination, emotions, willpower and sometimes bodily gestures as well. These elements are used to deepen the understanding of the redeeming relationship to God via Jesus Christ, overcome vices and attain the virtues necessary to move forward on the Christian path. A major point in meditation is the analysis of one's own sins, to regret them, to activate the will to minimize them and to ask God or Jesus Christ for mercy. A second major point is to develop insights into the message of the gospel, with a focus on the realization of God's love and compassion through meditation on the life and death of Jesus Christ. Meditation is used as a means to create and deepen the bond of love between the practitioner and Jesus Christ.

The term 'contemplation', on the other hand, is used for forms of prayer in which the activities of the faculties of the soul are soothed or even transcended—and also the body is quietened. To practise contemplation means to cultivate inner calmness and recollection that should lead to the experience of a void or nothingness, an annihilation of the egocentric self through which the awareness of the presence of God arises. Accordingly, the attitude towards disturbances, temptations and one's own sins differs from meditation. The active aiming for self-improvement is superseded by a gentle detachment from importunate thoughts. Higher stages of contemplation are thought of as graces that one cannot deliberately achieve.

---

34 For Quietist Quakerism, see Healey 2013.

The polarity between the two paths of practice can be typologized in the following way:

MEDITATION	CONTEMPLATION
Practices that activate and direct the faculties of the human being (the senses, gestures, discursive thought, imagination, emotion, will) to serve religious purposes	Practices that calm down the activities of the different faculties, recollect the mind and open the practitioner to a non-conceptual awareness of the presence of God (acquired contemplation) and union with him (infused contemplation)
Focus on 1. The human nature of Jesus Christ, his life, suffering and death. 2. Arousal of pious emotions, insights and moral acts through discursive reflections and visualizations 3. Fight against temptations, evil thoughts and vices	*Focus on* 1. The divine nature of Jesus Christ. 2. Cultivation of inner calm and recollection, the pure love of God without selfish interests 3. Passive detachment from temptations, evil thoughts and vices 4. Deeper levels of union with God that are not achievable deliberately (infused contemplation)
Trend towards differentiated methods, multiple topics and lengthy programmes	Trend towards simplified methods or even the negation of methodical practice except the maintenance of inner silence and a simple non-discriminative awareness of the formless and imageless God
Usually thought of as stabilizing and strengthening the established religious regime	Time and again thought of as subverting the established religious regime

Ways to Correlate the Two

As already indicated at the beginning of this paper, from the High Middle Ages onwards, attempts were made to clarify the relationship between meditation and contemplation. In the twelfth century, the Carthusian abbot, Guigo II, developed a hierarchical system of spiritual exercise (*spirituale exercitium*).[35] According to his influential *Scala Claustralium* (The Ladder of Monastics, i.e. the ladder whose rungs lead from earth towards heaven), the individual spiritual practice of monastics should start with careful ritual reading or listening to the recited texts of the Bible and supplementary scriptures (*lectio*). Meditation then focusses on certain passages or sentences, particularly those that impress the reader. One reflects upon their meaning with special regard to one's own life (*meditatio*). Afterwards, one turns to and asks God to remove what is evil and to grant what is good *(oratio)* according to the results of meditation. The highest level of practice is reached when God interrupts the flow of prayer to reveal Godself. The practitioner's mind is then elevated above itself to enjoy a foretaste of the joys of eternity (*contemplatio*). *Contemplatio* here is understood as a state of mind that spontaneously arises caused by God's grace (infused contemplation according to the terminology of later centuries) not as a form of practice.

Guigo II interlocks these stages in a systematic manner. He points out that meditation needs to be directed by reading to avoid errors, whereas reading without meditation remains fruitless. Prayer would be too lax without meditation. Conversely, meditation would only in exceptional cases be able to lift the mind to the heights of contemplation. Whenever the prayer that builds upon meditation is really devout, contemplation would

---

35 Guigo II 1970. For a detailed analysis and comparison with Buddhist practices see Baier 2013a. From the late medieval times onwards the *Scala Claustralium* has been translated into vernaculars. It ceased to function as exclusive manual for monastics and became a spiritual guideline for lay people as well.

happen quite regularly and with ease. Guigo II concedes that the different steps may not always be taken in the proposed order, and that, according to the situation and level of the practitioner, their significance may change.

As has been showed above, in the following centuries, meditation and contemplation became two independent forms of mental prayer. Thus, the question of how they should be related to each other assumed new urgency. In the following I will sketch some typical answers.

In most of the treatises I am familiar with, meditation is thought of as preparation for contemplation. The intensity of practice and the value given to meditation differ, and certain groups or spiritual guides may have even thought that sometimes it would not be necessary to practice meditation before one starts with contemplation. However, I could not find any evidence of a complete rejection of meditation. At the other end of the scale, scepticism towards contemplation, as well as systems of practice that at least implicitly exclude contemplation, can be easily found.

The author of the *Cloud of Unknowing* considers long-time meditation practice as essential for achieving the perfection of religious practice, namely contemplation. He appreciates the potential of meditation to reshape emotional life and the faculty of imagination that have been distorted through sin. On the other hand, he warns against the dangers of meditation, such as deceptive visions and overblown emotions, which cause exaggerated forms of pious behaviour. One should start with contemplation as soon as meditation becomes dry and one feels drawn towards contemplative states, either spontaneously or inspired by books or spiritual guides.

In later times, refined sets of criteria were elaborated to enable practitioners and their spiritual guides to evaluate if the time was ripe to proceed from meditation to contemplation. The theory of the three signs created by Juan de la Cruz (1542-1591) probably became the most influential of these attempts. His criteria for starting with contemplation are:

1. The practitioner is no longer able to gain satisfaction from meditation, as no new insights and inspirations appear
2. Nevertheless, there is no desire to fix attention on non-religious matters
3. The practitioner experiences an inner silence and rest during practice that he/she feels inclined to, even if there is still a wish to stick to the familiar meditation techniques.

With criteria two and three, Juan de la Cruz wants to rule out the inability to meditate being caused by the craving for earthly things or by a pathological disinterest that we today would call depression. He emphasizes the danger of overlooking these three signs and encourages his readers to follow the call to contemplation. If the signs appear, then one should end meditation and instead spend the time in mental prayer by simply abiding in quietness and loving attentiveness for the presence of God without active imagination or thought (see St. John of the Cross 2017, 189-191).

Some important authors within this discourse look at the correlation between meditation and contemplation from a Christological point of view. This line of thought is represented in Chapter 49 of the classic *Ejercitatorio de la vida espiritual* (Manual of exercises for the spiritual life) compiled and partially written by García de Cisneros and published in Montserrat, Spain, in 1500. The chapter is taken almost verbatim from Gerard Zerbold van Zutphen's *De spiritualibus ascensionibus* (On the spiritual ascensions), a major work of one of the leading theologians of the Devotio Moderna (Terence O'Reilly 1973, 316-321). In line with Zutphen (1367-1398), Cisneros distinguishes three ways of contemplation. The word 'contemplation' here is used as an umbrella term for exercises that function as stages on the mystical ascension towards union with God. The Christological argument runs as follows: Because Jesus Christ shares two natures, the human and the divine, he is able to mediate between the ultimate reality, namely God, and the world of human beings. Taken step by step, three levels of spiritual practice reveal Jesus Christ as the doorway towards the experience of God:

1. Ruminating on the earthly life and death of Jesus Christ to learn from his virtues and to intensify one's admiration, love, and devotion for him as an exemplary man (meditation on Jesus as a human being).
2. Learning to conceive the life and death of Jesus as disclosure of God (meditation on Jesus as human being and God).
3. Developing a loving knowledge of the ever-lasting light of the Godhead (contemplation in the strict sense focussing on the Divinity of Jesus Christ, i.e. the loving God that he reveals through his life and death).

In this way, a theocentric Christology is used to differentiate and relate different forms of mental prayer and to substantiate the superiority of contemplation. In a similar vein, Miguel de Molinos argues that although the humanity of Jesus Christ is the most perfect means to reach God and the ultimate channel by which the faithful receive all the good they hope for,

> nevertheless humanity is not the summit of goodness, which consists of seeing God. And just as Jesus Christ is greater according to his divinity than according to his humanity, so he who always thinks of and looks at God always thinks of and looks at Jesus Christ (since in Christ divinity is united to humanity). This is especially true of the contemplative, in whom faith is the most simple, pure, and practiced. Means always cease when one reaches the end. (Molinos 2010, 58)

Naturally, those who supported the absolute superiority of meditation on the life and death of Jesus Christ took a different stance. With his *Vita Christi* (after 1348), one of the most widespread devotional books of the late medieval ages, Ludolph of Saxony became one of the foremost teachers of imaginative meditation. Although he was unable to give rational reasons for the superiority of this kind of practice over imageless contemplation, he preferred it because of the pleasurable emotions raised by the devotion to Jesus Christ's humanity:

> Oh good Jesus, how sweet you are in the heart of one who thinks upon you and loves you...I know not for sure, I am not able fully to understand, how it is that you are sweeter in the heart of one who loves you in the form of flesh than as the word, sweeter in that which is humble than in that which is exalted...It is sweeter to view you as dying before the Jews on the tree, than as holding sway over the angels in Heaven; to see you as a man bearing every aspect of human nature to the end, than as God manifesting divine nature, to see you as the dying Redeemer than as the invisible Creator. (Quoted from Duffy 2005, 237)

After the suppression of Quietism, discursive meditation became the unquestioned summit of mental prayer in Catholic spirituality. Contemplative forms of meditation that would encourage the transition from meditation to contemplation still had a place within theories of prayer, but they had been downplayed as transient side effects of practice. It was considered to be presumptuous to strive for the higher stages of contemplation. Meditation became increasingly formalized and it was functionalized in order to support the official trend within Catholic spirituality to focus on the emotional devotion of Jesus Christ as sent from God to suffer for the sins of mankind, as well as on the moral conclusions that one could draw from his life and death.

The Renaissance of Contemplation

Over the last century a revival of contemplative prayer within and without the Christian churches took place in two waves (Arraj 1999, 185-229). The first one started around 1900 and was in full swing during the interwar period. It prepared the ground for the second wave that gained momentum in the late 1960s (Baier 2009, 543-583, 909-941). The reappraisal of contemplative prayer and its history has been connected with new insights from comparative religion, psychological approaches and the influence of South- and East Asian forms of practice.[36] The first wave the-

---

36 The main representatives and currents of both waves are treated by Baier 2009, 543-941.

matized contemplation primarily within the context of a renewed theology of mysticism. Theoretical efforts to revive contemplative prayer dominated, although here and there also new forms of practice emerged. In the second wave the focus shifted towards the development and spread of contemplative exercises.

The reasons for the modern interest in mysticism are manifold. A widespread consciousness of the 'crisis of Western culture' and a critical look at the negative effects of industrialization and the modernization of society in general led to increased scepticism with regard to materialistic worldviews and the belief that modern science, technology and social change would lead humankind straight away into a golden future. World War I, of course, deepened this consciousness of crisis. At the same time, the hegemonic Christian Churches lost their self-evident and undisputed credibility—at least among the educated classes and the members of Marxist and socialist movements that differed from the older Christian forms of socialism and communism (Strube 2016).

The revival of mysticism was far from being a mere nostalgic traditionalist reaction against the modern times or an elitist response to the mediocre mainstream religiosity within the Churches. It shaped modern culture and the arts in a creative way, connected theology and religious studies with the latest achievements within psychology and philosophy, and inspired new developments within the broader religious field.

Many spiritual seekers looked for religious experiences and practices that would help them in building up a new religious identity. Additionally, more and more information about non-Christian spiritualities became available and especially the 'mysticism of the East' gained appeal:

> The fin de siècle saw an upsurge of interest in elements that had all but disappeared from Christian orthodoxy and the development of an appetite for spiritual paths that were decidedly non-Christian. The new 'spiritual movement' looked instead to medieval and Renaissance Christian mysticism, heterodox inspirational neo-Christianity, and Eastern religions. (Owen 2004, 21)

In the course of the century, the number of teachers who disseminated meditative and contemplative practices with a Hindu or Buddhist background (usually under the umbrella term 'meditation') dramatically increased in the USA and in Europe. The Christian Churches perceived the growing interest in mysticism and contemplation and reacted critically or by reconsidering their own heritage in order to develop orthodox offers that would fit to the new religious needs and aspirations. Moreover, fascinating hybrids, like 'Christian Zen' or 'Christian Yoga', emerged within the second half of the century and brought with them controversies that are still ongoing today.

The revival of contemplation within the Catholic Church started in France with the publications of the Jesuit, Augustin-François Poulain (1836-1919), and Abbé Auguste Saudreau (1859-1946), a chaplain at the mother house of the Sisters of the Good Shepherd at Angers.[37] The books of these two founders of modern Catholic mystical theology were meant to be manuals for spiritual directors and practitioners but also became classics of the modern academic theology of mysticism. Both treated the traditional forms of meditation and contemplation in a historically well-informed and at the same time systematic way.[38] They rehabilitated the states of mystical union (passive, infused contemplation) and considered discursive meditation to be a prerequisite of contemplation.

According to Poulain, a profound gap exists between meditation as the most elaborate kind of ordinary prayer and infused contemplation. He compares ordinary prayer with the atmosphere that surrounds the earth. Thanks to it, the birds can rise above the earth:

> But this atmosphere has its limits. Above, lie those vast expanses that stretch away to the stars and beyond. Try as they may, they cannot penetrate thither, *even by redoubling their efforts*. The eagle is as powerless as the rest. God alone can transport them to

---

37 See Poulain1901 and Saudreau 1896, 1903. For a comparison between Poulain and Buddhist as well as Hindu sources, see Rose 2016.

38 They, however, still condemned the Quietist movement wholesale without any distinction.

this region; were He to do so, they would lie passive in His hand, there would be no further need to use their wings. They would have to discard their former methods of operation and adopt new ones. This upper region, where the wing no longer has any power, is a figure of the mystic state. It resembles it also by its peace, its silence. (Poulain 1928, 2; Poulain's emphases)

On its highest level, meditation becomes simplified to such a degree that 1) 'intuition to a great measure replaces reasoning' and 2) 'the affections and resolutions show little variety and are expressed in only few words' (Poulain 1928, 8). He calls this the 'prayer of simplicity' and identifies it with acquired contemplation (Poulain 1928, 11). According to Poulain, the prayer of simplicity tends to even further simplification:

The soul is then drawn to content herself with *thinking of God* or of *His presence* in a confused [i.e. non-discriminative, KB] and general manner. It is an affectionate remembrance of God. If this be consoling, the soul feels a sacred flame which burns on gently within her and takes the place of reasonings. (Poulain 1928, 13, Poulain's emphases)

This 'prayer of loving attention to God' or 'exercise of the presence of God' would be most recommended by all experts in the field of spiritual exercises (Poulain 1928, 13). For Poulain, it is closest to the states of infused contemplation. He thinks that many of those who practice mental prayer daily would arrive at this stage of practice, at least after some years, and that other people are from the very beginning of their practice more inclined to it than to discursive meditation, but does not give any detailed advice for its practice.

Saudreau, on the other hand, rejected the strict division between acquired and infused contemplation and emphasized that mystical contemplation is not a special grace but the common goal to which all Christians are called. He describes 'affective prayer' as an advanced form of meditation in which the emotional opening towards God becomes more important than discursive thought and moral introspection (Saudreau 1907, 249-265). He recommends periods of inner silence within meditation in line with Brother Lawrence and Caussaude, whom he actually quotes. This practice should serve as preparation for contemplation even before the signs for the call to contemplation have become apparent (Saudreau 1907, 308-309). Therefore, these pauses for Saudreau have almost the same function as the prayer of simplicity for Poulain.

The discrepancies between the two are based on their different concepts of spiritual development that have been intensively discussed in the Catholic theology of mysticism in the first half of the twentieth century. According to Poulain, the heights of the mystical states of contemplation are only reached by a rapture of the mind caused by a special divine grace that is only given to a limited number of people. For Saudreau, spiritual life is a gradual ascent from usual prayer to increasingly concentrated forms of meditation and finally infused contemplation. For him, in a certain way, the whole path is already present within the first step. Despite these differences, they were quite close to each other with regard to the practice of meditation and contemplation.

The Brother-Lawrence-type of contemplation in daily life was revitalized within a current that I have called the 'school of recollection'. One can find a very elaborate version of this kind of spirituality in the works of theologian and philosopher, Romano Guardini (Baier 2009, 695-813).

On the Protestant side, one should first mention Evelyn Underhill, an Anglican poet, lay theologian with strong Catholic leanings, a prominent spiritual director and leader of retreats within the Anglican Church. Underhill herself practised meditation and contemplation on a daily basis. Today she is venerated within the Anglican and Episcopal Church as a holy person, and she is liturgically commemorated on special feast days. In her most famous book, *Mysticism* (1911), she interpreted the Christian mystical tradition in light of modern psychological, philosophical and theological concepts (Underhill 1999). She also taught the practice of meditation and contemplation. In her *Practical Mysticism* (1915), she teaches a spiritual ascent that starts with recollection, in the sense of training the focussing of one's attention, and discursive meditation. The second step consists of a contemplation of the presence of God within God's creation and finally leads towards inner silence and the union with God through infused contemplation (Underhill 1915).

Besides the work of Underhill, the Protestant revival of mysticism was triggered by important liberal theologians of early twentieth century German Protestantism, such as Ernst Troeltsch, Friedrich Heiler and Paul Tillich.[39] In his *Die Soziallehren der christlichen Gruppen und Kirchen* (The Social Teachings of the Christian Groups and Churches), Ernst Troeltsch defines mysticism as a form of religion that focusses on the experience of the redeeming union between God and the individual. He distinguishes spontaneous mysticism from 'mysticism in the technical sense', the latter being an elaborate religious culture that combines theories about the path towards union with a system of religious practices. Mysticism in the technical sense comprises theoretical foundations, ethics of sanctification and perfection and 'techniques to gain and complete mystical experience' (Troeltsch 1912, 854-855).

According to Troeltsch, Christian mysticism found its most radical, individualistic expression within an early modern Protestant current known as 'Spiritualismus' (in the sense of 'spiritual religion') that he considered to be one of the historical roots of modern religiosity.[40] Romantic versions of this Protestant mysticism, which could be traced back to thinkers like the poet and philosopher Novalis and the theologian Schleiermacher, would be 'the secret religion of the educated people' of the present time

---

39 As one might expect the mystical turn within Protestantism unleashed intense debates. Karl Barth especially and other representatives of dialectic theology, like Emil Brunner, strongly criticised it.

40 'Spiritualismus' as Protestant historical current is not identical with spiritism or spiritualism as religious movements that claim to communicate with the deceased. According to Troeltsch, Sebastian Franck, Valentin Weigel, Dirck Coornheert, and John Salmartsch are the most important early modern spiritualists, followed by Karlstadt, Schwenkfeld, and others. See Troeltsch 1912, 862.

(Troeltsch 1912, 931). Troeltsch thought that the integration of this kind of Christian religiosity into Protestantism would be of crucial importance for its future existence. But he did not refer to any of the traditional techniques of contemplation nor did he discuss what contemporary practice might look like.

Friedrich Heiler (1892-1967) was an ecumenical Protestant theologian of Catholic origin, a scholar of religious studies, and leader of the High Church Movement in Germany. In 1918, he published his first major comparative study, *Das Gebet. Eine religionsgeschichtliche und religionspsychologische Untersuchung* (published in English as *Prayer: A Study in the History and Psychology of Religion*, 1932) based on his extensive doctoral thesis of 1917. Also in 1918, his important study on Buddhist meditation and contemplation, entitled *Die buddhistische Versenkung,* was released as a supplement to *Das Gebet.* In the latter, Heiler distinguishes several types of prayer within different religions (Heiler 1918). He generalizes the sequence of meditation–contemplation–mystical union by extending it to non-theistic mysticism:

> The passion of the theistic mystic [Gottesmystiker] expressed in prayer wells up spontaneously at times from the subconscious depths, but most often it derives its emotional intimacy and fervour from religious meditation. Even the deep absorption of the mystic of infinity [Unendlichkeitsmystiker] cannot dispense with preparatory meditation. All mystical prayer and contemplation is nourished by meditation, purposely cultivated and practiced... Meditation sometimes is predominantly logical-discursive, but more often it is of an intuitive-imaginative type. Pondered religious truths, the meditator envisions them as vivid as possible. (Heiler 1919, 287)

Heiler rehabilitates mysticism and praises contemplation as the most sublime form of prayer. On the other hand, he follows Nathan Söderblom's distinction between mystic and prophetic (i.e. biblical and Protestant religion) and applies it to his topic. Finally, he considers prophetic prayer as verbal addressing of God centred around petition and intercession as superior to contemplative mystical prayer (Heiler 1919, 409). In *Das Gebet,* this tension within his theology of prayer remains unresolved.

Heiler was not only a theoretician; he also experimented with liturgical worship, meditation and contemplation within the High Church movement. In 1933, he was one of the speakers at the first of the famous Eranos conferences in Ascona, Switzerland. The conference dealt with 'Yoga and Meditation in the East and the West' and Heiler presented several lectures on contemplation within Christian Mysticism (Eranos 1933). In addition to his talks, he conducted spiritual exercises for those in the Eranos audience who wished to engage practically in meditation and contemplation (Hakl 2013, 58-59).

In his Eranos lectures, Heiler no longer refers to the dichotomy of prophetic and mystical prayer. Instead, he emphasizes that, in spite of their prophetic-active character, already the Jewish roots of Christianity contained a strong contemplative element. Additionally, the contemplative dimension of Christian faith would have been strengthened by the influence of the Hellenistic mystery religions, Platonism and neo-Platonism. Heiler rejects the view of 'common Protestantism' that this kind of Hellenization has corrupted Christianity: 'The biblical-Christian and Hellenistic current merged and thus created the unprecedented richness of Christian-contemplative piety' (Heiler 1934, 254). The two main forms of this piety were the communal contemplation of the Christian cult and the individual contemplation that emerges from this spring. Very much like the innovative Catholic theologian, Romano Guardini, he connects the revival of individual contemplative prayer with the concerns of liturgical reform.

As already mentioned, the second wave of the revival of contemplation was more practically oriented than the first one. Unfortunately, the achievements of the earlier Catholic theology of mysticism, as well as the liberal Protestant approaches to mystical prayer, have more or less fallen into oblivion.[41] The intellectual level of the modern Christian contemplative movement suffered

---

41 With some remarkable exceptions like Hugo Enomiya-Lassalle and Thomas Keating.

from this amnesia. At the same time, two other significant changes have taken place. First, the traditional ways of meditation have lost their former importance and have been increasingly replaced or at least altered by more contemplative forms. Second, the distinction between contemplation and meditation has been removed, with the word 'meditation' becoming an umbrella term for both types of practices with an emphasis on contemplative exercises.

The final section of this paper deals with two similar, popular schools of contemplative prayer that emerged in the second half of the twentieth century: 'Christian meditation' developed by the Benedictine, John Main (1926-1982) and 'Centring Prayer', introduced by the Trappist, Thomas Keating (1923-2018) in collaboration with other members of his monastic community.

Neither monk founded a new contemplative order nor focussed on the contemplative renewal of their respective communities only. They chose international non-monastic organizations to spread their practices. Keating's Contemplative Outreach Ltd. and John Main's World Community of Christian Meditation draw mainly on lay practitioners, although the founders and a significant number of the teachers are still monastics and/or priests. The Catholic background of both schools is evident, but nevertheless they are ecumenically oriented. As shown in this article, an ecumenical character and a growing lay-orientation could already be observed in much earlier phases of the popularization of contemplation and meditation.

Main and Keating concede the influence that Eastern practices had on the genesis of their methods and position their schools as decidedly Christian responses to the challenge posed by them. John Main calls the contemplative practice he teaches 'saying the mantra', probably because it was Swami Satyānanda, a student of Swami Sīvānanda and founder of the Bihar School of Yoga, who first taught him how to contemplate. A second reason is probably the fact that, in the second half of the twentieth century, the term 'mantra' had become part of everyday language and Main might have thought that it would be more attractive for his target audience than 'prayer'.

As an abbot of St. Joseph's Abbey in Spencer, Massachusetts, Keating organized interreligious dialogue events with Christian, Buddhist and Hindu speakers. Additionally, Zen meditation took place in St. Joseph's Abbey. His experience with Asian practices motivated Keating to offer contemplative exercises as a way to prepare the mind for infused contemplation. He thus adds a new note to the old debate about acquainted contemplation:

> Contemplative prayer raises an important question: Is there something that we can do to prepare ourselves for the gift of contemplation instead of waiting for God to do everything? My acquaintance with Eastern methods of meditation has convinced me that there is. There are ways of calming down the mind in the spiritual disciplines of both East and West that can help to lay the groundwork for contemplative prayer. (Keating 2004, 29)

By introducing the practice of Centring Prayer, Keating and his associates deliberately formatted Christian practice in a way that was to be compelling for modern people with an interest in Asian forms of practice.

Main recommends concentrating on the Aramaic phrase *maranatha* that is mentioned in 1 Corinthians 16:22 and in the *Didachē*, an early Christian church constitution from around 100 CE. *Maranatha* can be read 'Our Lord has come', a formula to express the presence of Jesus Christ within the Christian community, or as 'Come Lord!', a call for Jesus Christ to become present. Like many other exegetes, Main adheres to the second option. Accordingly, the meaning of *maranatha*, as he understands it, is similar to the aforementioned *spiritalis theoriae* formula of John Cassian, to whom Main explicitly refers as source of his practice (Main 2017, 57-61).

The 'mantra' should be repeated silently in a calm and steady rhythm while sitting in an upright position. It should be accompanied by calm and rhythmic breathing. The aim of this practice is to reach an inner silence in which the mantra itself disappears, and the practitioner enters a 'cloud of unknowing' as Main says, paying tribute to the late medieval text on contemplation. In this cloud, the Holy Spirit would take over by speaking to the contemplating person from the depths of his or her heart. Main recommends a daily practice of about twenty to thirty minutes.

Centring Prayer is a kind of one-word contemplation that is even closer to the style of the *Cloud of Unknowing*. But in contrast to the old text, the practice of Centring Prayer is not bound to words that refer to traditional Christian meditation – and not even to a specific Christian tradition. The practitioners are free to choose their own 'sacred word'. Some words that Keating mentions as examples do have a strong Christian connotation like God, Jesus, Father, Spirit; but others, like Life, Peace, Love and Presence, do not. The 'sacred word' should in any case be a word one personally likes. Moreover, it should not only function as a tool for concentration but as a word that supports the intention of the practitioner of opening him or herself to the presence of God.

Like John Main, Keating recommends a regular practice of twenty to thirty minutes in a comfortable sitting position. He proposes starting with a few minutes of observing the breath to calm down the mental activities, but does not elaborate on the topic of breathing. Again, very similar to Main's method, the attention on the sacred word should lead to a 'resting in God' (a traditional term of Christian theology of mysticism) in which the word disappears and inner silence emerges. Referring to modern psychology, Keating argues that God dwells within the depths of the unconscious. The experience of his presence is buried under emotional entanglements that arise from early childhood onwards. He claims that Centring Prayer triggers a therapeutic process in which these affective patterns are disclosed and the practitioner is able to rediscover his or her divine source.

As has been shown in previous sections of this paper, the practice of concentrating on a single word or short phrase has been quite common throughout the history of Western European religion. Main and Keating are familiar with this tradition and draw primarily on the heritage of Christian practice with a clear focus on the Western European contemplation that they want to present in updated forms.

Contemplation is no longer bound to a preliminary stage of discursive meditation as it was in the first wave of the revival of contemplation at the beginning of the twentieth century, but has become a practice in its own right. Keating also introduces a contemplative form of *lectio divina* as a supplement to Centring Prayer, probably to connect the practitioners of Contemplative Prayer to a more bible-related spirituality. He reinterprets (and, from a historical point of view, misinterprets) the fourth stage of Guigo's *Scala claustralium* as methodical contemplative prayer (acquainted contemplation) and (historically correct) underlines its oppression in Catholic theology since the Quietist debate:

> In practice I think we can teach people to proceed in tandem toward contemplative prayer, that is, to read and reflect on the word of God in scripture, make aspirations inspired by these reflections, and then to rest in the presence of God. This is how lectio divina was practiced in the monasteries of the Middle Ages. The method of Centering Prayer emphasizes the final phase of lectio because it is the phase that has been most neglected in recent times. (Keating 2004, 28)[42]

The long and intertwined history of contemplation and meditation has finally reached a point in which, after a period in which it almost had died out, contemplative prayer can once again be learned and practised by every Christian who is interested in it. As the example of Keating's *lectio divina* shows, even if the different traditional kinds of meditation are a little out of fashion today, they still have good chances of not only surviving but of being renewed and reinvented in the spirit of contemplative silence.

---

42 Molinos, another protagonist of contemplation as methodical practice who tried to fit it into Guigo's scheme, historically wrongly identified the third stage (prayer) with acquainted contemplation and the fourth (historically rightly) with infused contemplation. See Molinos 2010, 187.

Bibliography

Aquinas, Thomas, 2008. *Summa Theologiae*. Latin-English edition. Scotts Valley, CA: NovAntiqua.

Aquinas, Thomas, 2001. *An Exposition of the 'On the Hebdomads' of Boethius (Expositio in librum Boethii De hebdomadibus)*. Washington, DC: The Catholic University of America Press.

Arraj, James, 1999. *From St. John of the Cross to Us: The Story of a 400 Year Long Misunderstanding and what it means for the Future of Christian Mysticism*. Chiloquin: Inner Growth Books.

Baier, Karl, 2009a. *Meditation und Moderne. Zur Genese eines Kernbereichs moderner Spiritualität in der Wechselwirkung zwischen Westeuropa, Nordamerika und Asien*. Würzburg: Königshausen und Neumann.

Baier, Karl, 2009b. 'Meditation and Contemplation from High to Late Medieval Europe'. In *Yogic Perception, Meditation and Altered States of Consciousness*, ed. Eli Franco. Wien: Austrian Academy of Sciences Press: 325-349.

Baier, Karl, 2013a. 'Lesen als spirituelle Praxis in christlicher und buddhistischer Tradition'. In *Text und Mystik. Zum Verhältnis von Schriftauslegung und kontemplativer Praxis*, ed. Karl, Baier, Regina Polak, Ludger Schwienhorst-Schönberger. Göttingen: Vienna University Press.

Baier, Karl, 2013b. 'Meditation im Schnittfeld von Psychotherapie, Hochgradfreimaurerei und Kirchenreform'. In *Paragrana. Internationale Zeitschrift für historische Anthropologie* 22.2: 51-75.

Baird, Robert P., 2010. 'Introduction. Part One: Miguel de Molinos: Live and Controversy'. In Miguel de Molinos, *The Spiritual Guide*, ed. and transl. Robert P. Baird. New York/Mahwah: Paulist Press: 1-20.

Bénatouïl, Thomas & Mauro Bonazzi, 2012. *Theoria, Praxis, and the Contemplative Life after Plato and Aristotle*. Leiden & Boston: Brill.

Bestul, Thomas H., 2012. '*Meditatio*/Meditation'. In *The Cambridge Companion to Christian Mysticism*, ed. Amy Hollywood & Patricia Z. Beckman. New York: Cambridge University Press: 200-210.

Bonhoeffer, Dietrich, 1996. 'Anleitung zur Schriftmeditation'. In Dietrich Bonhoeffer, *Illegale Theologen-Ausbildung: Finkenwalde 1935-1937*. Gesammelte Schriften, Bd. 14, Gütersloh: Gütersloher Verlagshaus: 945-950.

Bouyer, Louis, 2004 [1989]. *The Christian Mystery. From Pagan Myth to Christian Mysticism*. London: T&T Clark International.

Brother Lawrence of the Resurrection, 1994. *The Practice of the Presence of God: Critical Edition*. Washington, DC: ICS Publications.

Brother Lawrence, 2011. *A Christian Zen Master*. Vestal, New York: Anamchara Books.

Bruneau, Marie-Florine, 1998. *Women Mystics Confront the Modern World. Marie de l'Incarnation (1599-1672) and Madame Guyon (1648-1717)*. Albany: State University of New York Press.

Butzer, Günter, 2001. 'Meditation'. In *Historisches Wörterbuch der Rhetorik*, ed. Gert Ueding. Darmstadt: Wissenschaftliche Buchgesellschaft: 1016-1023.

Bynum, Caroline Walker, 1986. '...And Women His Humanity': Female Imagery in the Religious Writings of Later Medieval Ages'. In *Gender and Religion: On the Complexity of Symbols*, eds. Caroline Walker Bynum, Stevan Harrell & Paula Richman. Boston: Beacon Press.

Carruthers, Mary, 1998. *The Craft of Thought. Meditation, Rhetoric, and the Making of Images, 400-1200*. Cambridge: Cambridge University Press.

Carruthers, Mary, 2014. *Experience of Beauty in the Middle Ages*. Oxford: Oxford University.

Cassian, John, 1886. *Conlationes XXIIII*, ed. Michael Petschenig. CSEL 13. Vienna: Geroldus

Cisneros, Garcia, 1876. *A Book of Spiritual Exercises and a Directory for the Canonical Hours*. London: Burns and Oats.

Duffy, Eamon, 2005[2]. *The Stripping of the Altars: Traditional Religion in England 1400-1580*. New Haven, London: Yale University Press.

Eranos, 1933. *Eranos Jahrbuch 1933: Yoga und Meditation im Osten und im Westen*, ed. Olga Fröbe-Kapteyn. Zürich: Rhein-Verlag.

Fulton, Rachel, 2002. *From Judgment to Passion. Devotion to Christ and the Virgin Mary, 800-1200*. New York: Columbia University Press.

Guigo II, 1970. *Scala Claustralium: Lettre sur la Vie Contemplative (L'Échelle des Moines): Douze Méditations (SChr 163)*, eds. Edmund Colledge & James Walsh. Paris: Éditions du Cerf.

Hadot, Pierre, 1995. *Philosophy as a Way of Life: Spiritual Exercises from Socrates to Foucault*, transl. Michael Chase. Oxford: Blackwell.

Hakl, Thomas, 2013. *Eranos: An Alternative Intellectual History of the Twentieth Century*. Sheffield/Bristol: Equinox Publishing Ltd.

Healey, Robynne Rogers, 2013. 'Quietist Quakerism, 1692-c.1805'. In *Oxford Handbook of Quaker Studies*, eds. Stephen W. Angell & Pink Dandelion. Oxford: Oxford University Press: 47-63.

Heiler, Friedrich, 1918. *Die buddhistische Versenkung*. München: Reinhardt.

Heiler Friedrich, 1919. *Das Gebet. Eine religionsgeschichtliche und religionspsychologische Untersuchung*. München: Reinhardt.

Heiler, Friedrich, 1934. 'Die Kontemplation in der christlichen Mystik'. In *Eranos Jahrbuch 1933*, ed. Olga Fröbe-Kapteyn. Zürich: Rhein-Verlag: 245-326.

Heppe, Heinrich, 1875. *Geschichte der Quietistischen Mystik in der katholischen Kirche*. Berlin: Wilhelm Hertz.

Hodgson, Phyllis, 1982. *The Cloud of Unknowing, and Related Treatises*. (Analecta Cartusiana 3). Salzburg: Institut für Anglistik und Amerikanistik.

Huntley, Frank Livingstone, 1981. *Bishop Joseph Hall and Protestant Meditation in Seventeenth-Century England: A Study of the Art of divine meditation' (1606) and Occasional meditation (1633)*. Binghampton, NY: ACMRS Publications.

Ivánka, Endre von, 1990². *Plato Christianus. Übernahme und Umgestaltung des Platonismus durch die Väter*. Einsiedeln: Johannes Verlag.

James, William, 1902. *The Varieties of Religious Experience: A Study in Human Nature. Being the Gifford Lectures on Natural Religion Delivered at Edinburgh in 1901-1902*. New York: Longmans, Green and Co.

James, William, 1911. *On Vital Reserves: The Energies of Men. The Gospel of Relaxation*. New York: Henry Holt and Company.

Johnsén, Henrik Rydell, 2013. 'The Early Jesus Prayer and Meditation in Greco-Roman Philosophy'. In *Meditation in Judaism, Christianity and Islam. Cultural Histories*, ed. Halvor Eifring. London: Bloomsbury.

Keating, Thomas, 2004. *Foundations for Centering Prayer and the Christian Contemplative Life*. New York & London: Continuum.

Löhe, Wilhelm, 1852. *Der evangelische Geistliche*. Stuttgart: Samuel Gottlieb Liesching.

Main, John, 2017 [1980]. *Word Into Silence. A Manual for Christian Meditation*, ed. Laurence Freeman OSB. Seventh impression. Norwich: Canterbury Press.

Marti, Hanspeter, 2002. 'Der Seelenfriede der Stillen im Lande. Quietistische Mystik und radikaler Pietismus – das Beispiel Gottfried Arnolds'. In *Jansenismus, Quietismus, Pietismus*, eds. Hartmut Lehmann, Heinz Schilling & Hans-Jürgen Schrader. Göttingen: Vandenhoek & Ruprecht.

McGinn, Bernard, 1992. *The Foundations of Mysticism: Origins to the Fifth Century*. Vol. I of *The Presence of God: A History of Western Christian Mysticism*. London: SCM Press.

McGinn, Bernard, 2004 [1994]. *The Growth of Mysticism: Gregory the Great through the 12ᵗʰ Century*. Vol. II of *The Presence of God: A History of Western Christian Mysticism*. New York: Crossroad Publishing Company.

McGinn, Bernard, 2012. '*Unio mystica*/Mystical Union'. In *The Cambridge Companion to Christian Mysticism*, eds. Amy Hollywood & Patricia Z. Beckman. New York: Cambridge University Press: 200-210.

McNamer, Sarah, 2010. *Affective Meditation and the Invention of Medieval Compassion*. Philadelphia: University of Pennsylvania Press.

Molinos, Miguel de, 2010. *The Spiritual Guide*, ed. and transl. Robert P. Baird. New York/Mahwah: Paulist Press.

Montoya, Javier A., 2010. *El Sabor de Herejia: The Edict of 1525, the Alumbrados and the Inquisitors' Usage of Locura*. Unpublished thesis, University of Florida.

Nef, Frederic, 2005. 'Contemplation'. In *Encyclopedia of Christian Theology*, ed. Jean-Ives Lacoste. New York: Routledge: 353-361.

Nightingale, Andrea Wilson, 2004. *Spectacles of Truth in Classical Greek Philosophy:* Theoria *in Its Cultural Context*. Cambridge: Cambridge University Press.

O'Reilly, Terence, 1973. 'The Structural Unity of the *Exercitatorio de la Vida Spiritual*'. In *Studia Monastica* 15 [Barcelona: Abadia de Montserrat]: 287-324.

Owen, Alex. 2004. *The Place of Enchantment: British Occultism and the Culture of the Modern*. Chicago: University of Chicago Press.

Pieper, Josef, 1998. *Happiness and Contemplation*. South Bend, IN: St. Augustine's Press.

Poulain, Augustin-François, 1901. *Des grâces d'oraison: Traité de théologie mystique*. Paris: V. Retaux.

Poulain Augustin-François, 1928. *The Graces of Interior Prayer. A Treatise on Mystical Theology*. London: Kegan Paul, Trench, Trübner & Co.

Rabbow, Paul, 1954. *Seelenführung. Methodik der Exerzitien in der Antike*. München: Kösel.

Rahner, Karl, 1997. *The Need and the Blessing of Prayer*, transl. Bruce W. Gillette. Introduction Harvey D. Egan, SJ. Collegeville, Minnesota: The Liturgical Press.

Reiter, Peter, 1992. *Der Seele Grund. Meister Eckhart und die Tradition der Seelenlehre.* Würzburg: Königshausen und Neumann.

Richard of St. Victor, 1979. *The Twelve Patriarchs, the Mystical Ark & Book Three of the Trinity*, transl. and introduced Grover A. Zinn. Mahwah, New Jersey: Paulist Press.

Rönnegård, Per, 2013. 'Melētē in Early Christian Ascetic Texts'. In *Meditation in Judaism, Christianity and Islam. Cultural Histories*, ed. Halvor Eifring. London: Bloomsbury: 79-92.

Rose, Kenneth, 2016. *Yoga, Meditation and Mysticism: Contemplative Universals and Meditative Landmarks*. London et al.: Bloomsbury.

Ruppert, Fidelis, 1977. 'Meditatio – Ruminatio. Zu einem Grundbegriff christlicher Meditation'. *Erbe und Auftrag* 53: 83-93.

Saudreau, Auguste, 1896. *Les Degrés de la Vie Spirituelle: Méthode pour diriger les âmes suivant leurs progrès dans la vertu.* Angers: Germain et Grassin.

Saudreau, Auguste, 1903. *L'État Mystique: Sa nature – ses phases et les faits extraordinaires de la vie spirituelle.* Paris: Vic et Armat.

Saudreau, Auguste, 1907. *The Degrees of the Spiritual Life: A Method of Directing Souls According to their Progress in Virtue.* Vol. I. London & Glasgow: R. & T. Washbourne, Ltd.

Sciurba, Salvatore, 1994. 'General Introduction'. In *Brother Lawrence of the Resurrection. The Practice of the Presence of God: Critical Edition.* Washington, DC: ICS Publications: xvii-xlviii.

Sherman, Jacob Holsinger, 2014. *Partakers of the Divine: Contemplation and the Practice of Philosophy.* Minneapolis: Fortress Press.

Sluhovsky, Moshe, 2007. *Believe Not Every Spirit: Possession, Mysticism & Discernment in Early Modern Catholicism.* Chicago & London: The University of Chicago Press.

Spaemann, Robert, 1963. *Reflexion und Spontanität. Studien über Fénelon.* Stuttart: Kohlhammer.

St. John of the Cross, 2017[3]. *The Collected Works of St. John of the Cross.* Washington, DC: ICS Publications.

Staubach, Nikolaus, 2011. 'Die Meditation im spirituellen Reformprogramm der Devotio Moderna'. In *Meditatio – Refashioning the Self. Theory and Practice in Late Medieval and Early Modern Intellectual Culture,* eds. Karl Enenkel & Walter Melion. Leiden & Boston: Brill.

Steiger, Johann Anselm, 2000. '*Meditatio sacra.* Zur theologie-, frömmigkeits-, und theologiegeschichtlichen Relevanz der 'Meditationes Sacrae' (1606) Johann Gerhards'. In *Meditation und Erinnerung in der Frühen Neuzeit,* ed. Gerhard Kurz. Göttingen: Vandenhoek & Ruprecht.

Stordalen, Terje, 2013. 'Ancient Hebrew Meditative Recitation'. In *Meditation in Judaism, Christianity and Islam. Cultural Histories,* ed. Halvor Eifring. London: Bloomsbury: 79-92.

Sträter, Udo, 1995. *Meditation und Kirchenreform in der lutherischen Kirche des 17. Jahrhunderts.* Tübingen: J.C.B. Mohr (Paul Siebeck).

Strube, Julian, 2016. 'Socialist religion and the emergence of occultism: a genealogical approach to socialism and secularization in 18th century France'. *Religion* 46.3: 359-388.

Täubner, Tanja, 2014. '*Zum andern soltu meditirn'. Die Meditationspraktiken in der Pädagogik August Hermann Franckes.* Halle & Wiesbaden: Harrassowitz.

Troeltsch, Ernst, 1994. *Die Soziallehren der christlichen Kirchen und Gruppen.* Band 2. Neudruck der Ausgabe von 1912 in zwei Taschenbuchbänden. Tübingen: J.C.B. Mohr (Paul Siebeck).

Underhill Evelyn, 1999 [1911]. *Mysticism. The Nature and Development of Spiritual Consciousness.* Oxford: One World.

Underhill, Evelyn, 1915. *Practical Mysticism. A little Book for Normal People.* New York: E.P. Dutton & Company.

Vogl, Wolfgang, 2002. *Aktion und Kontemplation in der Antike. Die Entwicklung der praktischen und theoretischen Lebensauffassung bis Origenes.* Frankfurt/M.: Peter Lang.

Ward, Patricia A., 2009. *Experimental Theology in America: Madame Guyon, Fénelon and Their Readers*. Waco: Baylor University Press.

MEDITATION AND CONTEMPLATION IN THE BUDDHIST TRADITION

Sarah Shaw

Abstract

This chapter attempts to give an overview of the textual and recent history of what we like to call 'meditation', in the Southern Buddhist tradition. It argues that the Southern Buddhist tradition still maintains many of the tenets and guidelines recommended in the Pāli, our oldest complete canon within the Buddhist tradition. The paper also suggests that our classification of a certain activity as 'meditation', as an isolated activity, has meant some mild misunderstandings in our assessment of Southern Buddhism in practice. So, this paper explores the notion of bhāvanā, *which includes other activities that, in addition to sitting meditation, are also said to arouse both calm (*samatha*) and insight (*vipassanā*). Taking this as a basis, the two principal strands of meditative practice, calm and insight are examined, alongside their associated activity in the form of chants, communal as well as solitary practice, offerings, devotions and the discursive recollections, which in South and Southeast Asia almost always accompany the practices of either traditions. This paper explores some historical developments in the understanding of these two modes of practice, a trend reinforced by attempts to 'westernize' meditative procedures and theory. It also suggests that the recent movement towards mindfulness therapies in the global context have reawakened some interest in this ancient debate. The paper argues, however, that the two traditions really are 'yoked together', as the early texts suggest. In this regard the actual praxis and content of meditative and contemplative procedures are also explored, an* *area that has hitherto been somewhat less integrated into academic discourse and inter-faith discussion on the subject.*

Keywords: meditation, Buddhism, contemplation, *bhāvanā*, devotion, chant, *samatha*, *vipassanā*, Southeast Asia, South Asia

At dusk in Southeast or South Asian temples, people light butter lamps, make devotions, pay homage to shrines, offer lotuses to the Buddha figure, which is surrounded by candle-holders, drapings, incense bowls, and other Buddha figures in a rich range of postures, or figures of his *arahats* (awakened/enlightened followers): this is clearly not a lonely spot. Everywhere there are paintings, stucco figures, elaborate mouldings and decorations. People outside chant while circumambulating the stupa or tie auspicious flags on the Bodhi tree. Perhaps there is a talk going on in another part of the courtyard, and some are listening, or reflecting. Whole families, or groups of women dressed in white for the day, or working people just dropping in on their way home from work, chant, pay respects, walk, sit quietly, some in private meditation, and some just allowing the sense of peace to let things from the day fall aside. This is Buddhist *bhāvanā*, or practice, an activity that includes meditation and contemplation, but many other things too. When I first went to Sri Lanka in the early 1980s I was 'en-chanted' by the murmurings of so many *parittas* (texts believed to be protective) and chat, background sounds of cicadas and scooters on the road, the smell of the coconut-oil lamps and incense, as well as by the pools of soft lights in temples in dark forests and reed houses, on an island where electricity was still a rarity. The atmosphere was so calming and restorative, it felt at the time as if I would only need to do something like this once or twice a day, and I would feel completely revived. Dipping in and out of calm, mixing with others, listening to talks, chanting, companionability and different ages all around – yet the chance to practise meditation in solitude too - as this paper argues, this is all *bhāvanā*.

This chapter gives an overview of the textual and recent history of what we call 'meditation', in the Southern Buddhist tradition. It argues that the Southern Buddhist tradition still maintains many of the tenets and guidelines recommended in the Pāli canon, the oldest complete canon. But the broader practice of *bhāvanā* has often been overlooked by the Western classification of a certain, isolated activity as 'meditation', and this has meant a neglect of the practices of a far richer and more varied tradition of contemplation, chant, meditation, devotion and mindfulness than is sometimes supposed. The roots of this kind of practice, and its diverse manifestations, are found in the earliest texts.

Southern Buddhism

The text base used for this paper is the Pāli canon. It is not the only source of early material on meditation, but, as the earliest full collection of Buddhist texts, containing the Abhidhamma, Sutta and Vinaya, it indicates the way in which these sources on meditation work with one another in one early Buddhist tradition.

Buddha auto/biography – the context of 'meditation'

The spirit and structural ordering of Southern Buddhist meditation is embedded in the Buddha's biographical meditative path. The historical Buddha, Gotama, teaching in the fifth century BCE, worked in an atmosphere where meditative practice was usual, and debate about it widespread. From the evidence of the Buddhist suttas, there was experimentation, the challenging of views, and, in many cases, some extreme self-mortification (Bronkhorst 1993: 4-26). When Gotama renounced, he tried two formless meditations, that of neither-identification-nor-non-identification, and no-thingness, at which he apparently excelled. He gives the names of his teachers of these, suggestive of historical corroboration. He found, however, according to a rare, first-person autobiographical account, that on their own 'they did not lead to awakening and peace' (*Ariyapariyesanā-Sutta*: M I 166-167). He then attempted various extremes of self-mortification, and, according to some legends, nearly died. One day, however, he remembered a simple exercise he had tried once as a child, under the shade of the rose-apple tree, when his attendants left him alone for the first time in his life as his father instigated the earthy ploughing festival in nearby fields (*Mahāsaccaka-Sutta:* M I 246-247). At that time, watching the breath, according to the commentaries, he found a state of great unification and joy: the first *jhāna*, accompanied by thinking of (*vitakka*), exploring (*vicāra*), joy (*pīti*), happiness (*sukha*) and one-pointedness (*ekaggatā*, literally 'gone-to-oneness'). He asked himself why he was frightened of the happiness that was free from sensory attachment, and wondered if this could be a way both to peace and wisdom. In a context apparently governed by rigid dogmatism with regard to practice and an excessive asceticism, a rare use of an exploratory optative in an early Indian treatise is striking: it could, very loosely, be translated as 'Well, could this work instead?' (*Siyā nu kho aññomaggo bodhāyā 'ti*; literally: might there be another way to awakening?)[1] So he took food, went to the Bodhi tree and, through practising four *jhāna*s, found complete awakening, in liberation from suffering.

The premise was deceptively simple: that happiness, when free from attachment to senses, might itself be productive of liberation. It was crucial to his decision to use *jhāna* as the basis for finding the wisdom that confers freedom from suffering. This first *jhāna* is discussed further in this paper and formed the basis of his practice on the night of the awakening. Although the first discourse, the 'Wheel-turning discourse' the *Dhammacakkavattana-*

---

1   *Tassa mayhaṃ, Aggivessana, etadahosi: 'Kiṃ nukho ahaṃ tassa sukhassa bhāyāmi, yaṃ taṃ sukhaṃ aññatreva kāmehi aññatra akusalehi dhammehī 'ti? Tassa mayhaṃ, Aggivessana, etadahosi: 'Na kho ahaṃ tassa sukhassa bhāyāmi, yaṃ taṃ sukhaṃ aññatreva kāmehi aññatra akusalehi dhammehī 'ti*: 'And then, Aggivessana, it occurred to me, "So why am I frightened of this happiness, which is quite separate from sense-desires and unskilful states?" Then Aggivessana, it occurred to me, "I am not frightened of this happiness, which is separate from sense-desires and unskilful states."' (M I 247)

Sutta (S V 421-424), is not now taken as a historical account in its formulation of the middle way and the eightfold path, it does set the 'mythological' tenor of subsequent discussion and practice (Gethin 1992, 198), being delivered, it is said, to those practising ruthlessly austere asceticism (M I 246). This sense of a contented 'middle way' (*majjhimā paṭipadā*) between extremes (*anta*) permeates early texts. The 'middle way' is applied at various times to avoiding bodily torment or excessive sensory devotion (Vin I 10, S V 421, S IV 330-331), to avoiding indulgence (*āgāḷhā*) or burning (*nijjhāmā*: A II 156-162; Ne 21). It is applied to views, in avoiding the extremes 'all exists' and 'nothing exists', when the Buddha is said to teach his teaching 'by the middle' (*majjhena*; S II 17, 20, 75-77). In one context, it is applied to each one of thirty-seven factors contributing to awakening (A I 295-297). But it also applies to finding the right attitude, balance and preparation within meditation itself. Words associated with 'middle-ness' or the ability 'to be in the middle' permeate Buddhist meditative vocabulary, particularly in descriptions of the subtler levels of *jhāna*. A term that could be translated 'balance with regard to things' or, colloquially, as 'being right there in the middle of all this', *tatramajjhattatā*, is particularly associated with the equanimity of the higher meditation states (Items 5–8 in Table 1). It pertains to the manner of practice, the relationship between the meditator and the meditative object, and the state of balance required to sustain any given state, leave it at will and, crucially, recollect it afterwards. The fourth *jhāna* and formless meditations are said to have *majjhattatā cittassa*, a 'middleness' of the mind, equated to *tatramajjhattatā* (Vibh 271; Gunaratana 1980: 122). A Thai story tells of the king of the heavens, Sakka, playing a lute with three strings to Gotama before his awakening, to put him on the right path. One was too tight, one too lax, and one evenly tuned: the right note of balance found between the other two.[2]

---

2   This story is from the Pāli *Paṭhamasambodhi,* circulated widely in vernaculars in Thailand, Laos, Cambodia and other parts of Southeast Asia (Laulertvorakul 2003). This incident is depicted for instance, at Wat Ratchasittharam, Thonburi, Thailand, and is popular in manuscript art (Appleton, Shaw,

This sense of finding the evenly tuned sound, amongst the many and varied notes of a mix of often highly differentiated practices, characterizes the *samatha* (tranquillity) meditations of Southern Buddhism at every level.

Balance, diversity and an atmosphere of experimentation are considered central to the seven factors contributing to awakening (*bojjhaṅga*) and hence meditation: wisdom, mindfulness, investigation, vigour, joy, tranquillity, concentration and equanimity. In his teaching career, the Buddha integrated the meditations he learnt before from earlier teachers, with ones he may have developed himself, the form *jhāna*s, so that he offered a system of what becomes eight *jhāna*s: four 'form' and four 'formless'. But the spheres of no-thingness and neither-identification-nor-non-identification, learnt before the awakening, are taught in the *Nikāya*s only *after* the form *jhāna*s, and are eventually termed the third and fourth formless spheres, and then, sometimes, *jhāna*s. That he offered both form and formless meditations, and that those in the second category, the formless spheres, are taught only after the emotional cultivation and unifying peace of the first four *jhāna*s, as part of a graduated path, are a central feature to Gotama's contribution to Indian meditative practice at the time.

This table shows some ways the system developed:

First *jhāna*	Accompanied by thinking of, exploring, joy, happiness and one-pointedness	Experienced by the Buddha spontaneously as a child – recollected by him before the awakening and used as the basis of the practice of all of these meditations on the night of the awakening
Second *jhāna*	Accompanied by joy, happiness and one-pointedness	Said to be accompanied by 'internal peace' as various thinking processes are suspended

---

Unebe 2013, 56-50, 71-72). See also A III 374-376, for a counterpart in the Buddha's teaching to Soṇa.

Third *jhāna*	Accompanied by happiness and one-pointedness	Associated with an increase of mindfulness and clarity
Fourth *jhāna*	Accompanied by one-pointedness	This *jhāna* is particularly associated with the equanimity that arises after the emotional purification of the first three *jhānas*. All these first four *jhānas* are practised before the awakening
1st formless sphere (*arūpa*): 5th *jhāna*)	Sphere of infinite space	
2nd formless sphere (*arūpa*): (6th *jhāna*)	Sphere of infinite consciousness	
3rd formless sphere (*arūpa*) (7th *jhāna*)	Sphere of no-thingness	Practised by Gotama before the awakening, and subsequently integrated into his system as a *jhāna*
4th formless sphere (*arūpa*) (8th *jhāna*)	Sphere of neither identification nor non-identification	Practised by Gotama before the awakening, and subsequently integrated into his system as a *jhāna*

Table 1 The Buddhist *jhānas*

Abhidhamma has a ninefold system, whereby the first *jhāna* is split into two, the second having *vicāra* but not *vitakka*. So the second becomes the third, and so on.

Another state, *nirodha samāpatti*, is sometimes added to the list. It is accessible to those who have attained the third, and the fourth and final stage of the path, though little is said of this state.

Bhāvanā and meditation/contemplation

A cautious look at Christian terminology is helpful in appreciating the table. The word 'meditation' in English is derived from the word used by Richard of St Victor, to describe the discursive mind applying itself to a subject, with some salvific, devotional and sometimes joyful connotations. It has early associations with the Greek word 'practice' (μελέτη) (OED I, 297-298). So, in a Christian context, this is the repeating to oneself of formulae and observations concerned with the attributes of the divine (Standaert 2015). It is differentiated, by St Richard and by some subsequent Christian theological discourse, from 'cogitation', the usual applications of the mind in daily life. It is also distinct from 'contemplation', a state of, in the Christian context, deep prayer, where the mind rests upon the object without any verbal or ratiocinative faculties operating. St Richard defines this in *Benjamin Maior*:

> If the mind after a long time of searching finally finds the truth, then it usually happens that it receives a new insight with appetite, gazes at it with wonder and jubilation and stays in this amazement for a long time. This means to exceed meditation within meditation and to proceed from meditation to contemplation. Because the characteristic of contemplation is to dedicate itself to that which it sees full of joy and with astonishment/admiration. (*Benjamin Maior*, I, 4/Aris 9, 28-30)

In Table 1, the first *jhāna*, where the meditator is 'thinking' of and 'exploring' the object, there appears to be 'meditation' in St Richard's sense. All attention is brought to bear on the image in the mind's eye (*nimitta*) of the breath, the coloured *kasiṇa* device, or one of the four elements, objects taken to arouse calm – just as the mind at rest and in happiness can become absorbed, say, in a flower, or a vast view of the sea. The thinking mind is active, albeit fully and wholeheartedly engaged in a way absent in our usual mode of cogitation. The subsequent *jhāna*s, however, seem closer to what St Richard refers to as 'contemplation'. In the second *jhāna*, the meditator has an 'internal quiet' with the usual discursive thought processes suspended. In the third, joy is dropped, for a deeper contentment and intensification of alertness. After that, with yet more increased mindfulness, 'purified' by equanimity (*upekkhāsatipārisuddhim*), happiness gives way to unification and peace (Vib 271; Vism IV 194). In the formless spheres, these states themselves are examined; these develop unification, with the same accompanying factors as the fourth *jhāna*, in order to discern the very nature of 'subject-ness' and 'object-ness', and the discovery of an apprehension of an object, without attachment or 'I'-making. The Buddha had rejected formless meditation before the awakening, but re-integrates it into his system during his teaching career, as a specialist, optional form of *samatha* practice.

So, within Southern Buddhism, there are types of meditation/contemplation ranging from the discursive, where the mind is thinking, to the non-verbal and non-discursive, and, from there, to states where usual thought patterns are not only transcended, but examined in themselves, and the means whereby consciousness arises, and becomes associated with an object, is explored. All these states, however, depend upon one another. One should only follow the higher *jhāna* after an earlier one has been achieved, or one is like the 'foolish calf' that tries a too ambitious route up a mountain, and gets stuck (A IV 418-9; Vism IV 130).

In an article on St Teresa of Avila and the fifth-century commentator Buddhaghosa, L.S. Cousins says that he does not want to make things match between Christianity and Buddhism, but rather, 'I wish to argue there is a *similarity* in the structure and stages of the mystical way as conceived in different traditions.' Noting obvious differences between a theist model, and, say, a scientific analysis of different states, he says, 'we are dealing with a series of experiences or perhaps transformations which can, I think, be examined in their own right' (Cousins 1989, 103). He demonstrates important affinities between St Teresa's stages of prayer, outlined in her autobiography, and the first four *jhāna*s. Can we realistically explore such parallels in the more general context of Christian meditation? It seems we can, but first need broader explanation of what the word 'meditation' means in a Buddhist context, as this has led to some misunderstandings.

An important, and often unnoticed, distinguishing feature of the four noble truths is that a different verb is associated with each one, as the third element of something 'to be done', placed in the future passive participle: so suffering is to be understood, craving to be abandoned, the freedom from that is to be realized, while the path to freedom is to be cultivated, or 'called into existence' (*bhavetabba*) (S V 421-424). The Pāli word *bhāvanā* is the noun derived from the root of this word, *bhāveti*, the causative of *bhavati*, 'to become', and means literally, to 'make to become' or 'to cause to grow' (PED 503). So its domain is the cultivation of a very wide range of qualities that are required to be 'made to grow' on the Buddhist path. In practice, the term *bhāvanā* is usually taken as particularly associated with meditation, but inclusive also of many other kinds of 'practice' (Gethin 1992, 18, n.70). It often describes 'any type of meditational practice involving continuous attention by the mind' (Keown 2004): so it covers 'mental development' (*citta-bhāvanā*), 'development of tranquillity' (*samathabhāvanā*) and 'development of insight' (*vipassanā-bhāvanā*) (D III 219).

Yet, *bhāvanā* also includes other bodily and mental activities not usually classified as 'meditation': devotions, prostrations, circumambulations, flower-offerings, companionability, giving food to monks, chanting, and listening to talks: all the things, for instance, described in the beginning of this paper. These are all intended to arouse 'letting go' (*cāga*), happiness, health of mind, a sense of community and shared purpose with others (e.g. Ehara 1961/1995: 147-155). In the Buddhist meditative/contemplative tradition, while it is certainly important to develop a stillness of mind that suspends usual thinking, factors before and after the 'meditation' sitting practice are equally important, to keep the mind healthy, steer it in the right direction, and ensure that the basis of sīla, or morality, allows for some freedom from worry and care in the meditation (Harvey 1993; Palihawadana 1997; Shaw 2009, 92-110). These activities are also called *samatha* practices, or practices for calm. It is in this fertile ground that we find the most popular and abundant means to arouse calm and happiness in Southern Buddhism, a basis for further meditation or insight.

The ten mindfulnesses: Buddha, Dhamma, Saṅgha, Sīla, Cāga, Devas, Death, Body, Breath, and Peace

The first obvious thing about this list is its title – while said to arouse *samatha*, they are known as *sati*, or 'mindfulness', practices. Often translated as 'recollections', they are, literally, 'repeated mindfulnesses' (*anu* + *sati*). The commentaries stress the centrality and importance of these 'mindfulnesses' within Buddhist meditative practice (see, for instance, PF 148-179). They comprise ten of the forty meditation objects recommended for calm (*samatha*) by Buddhaghosa, and many are central to Buddhist daily practice, lay or monastic. Two, that of the breath and the body, lead to full *jhāna*, according to this system. The others are said by the commentaries to lead to a state defined by post-canonical literature as 'access concentration' (*upacāra-samādhi*), a meditation preceding *jhāna*, which lacks the support of the full development of the five faculties of confidence, vigour, mindfulness, concentration and wisdom. This is a commentarial rather than a canonical classification (Vism III 6). The first six of the ten, the *anussati*s, are concerned with bringing to mind the qualities of the awakened one, the Buddha, his teaching, his community, the good effects of practising morality and generosity, and the heavenly happiness possible through these activities. These six are central to Buddhist practice, both in the texts and throughout Buddhist history (Shaw 2006, 109-134).

Here is where we get an odd problem, in part created by Westerner commentators, for the meditations that do not lead to *jhāna* have historically sometimes not been seen as 'real' meditation, or even 'real' Buddhism, by various Western visitors, missionaries, aspirant meditators, scholars and observers, anxious to find within Buddhism what they feel it *ought* to have rather than what it actually does. The view recorded by the Countess of Jersey in 1884 persists in some scholarly quarters even now: 'Buddhism *as he* [Gotama Buddha] *taught it,* is not the religion of the five hundred millions who are said to reverence the shrines…Much of which its founder never dreamed was introduced into the system, and which, had he heard it, he would have treated as foolishness or presumption' (quoted in Almond 1988, 39). Indeed, there used to be, and still sometimes are, occasional attempts to find a 'true' or even 'pure' Buddhism, without such 'trappings'.

However, variations on the first six, the *anu-ssati*s or 'repeated mindfulnesses', where this charge is so often laid, are considered by South and Southeast Asian lay people and monastics essential as part of their daily round. Going to the temple, chanting, making offerings, giving food and taking solace in the fact that during that time one is keeping *sīla*, the five precepts, or sometimes eight, when white is worn all day, are core. These are felt to keep the mind on the right track, to offer protection from 'demons', inner and outer, and to sustain mindfulness and a kind of middle way of practice whatever the meditation, and whatever the activity in daily life (see Shaw 2006, 109-34). The *anussati*s, so closely linked to prostrations, making *añjali*s (literally an 'offering', this respectful greeting places the hands upright together with palms touching), and the rituals associated with offering flowers, butter lamps, incense and such like, are sometimes physically intricate, but not involved greatly with 'thinkings', and indeed, as so often with ritual, offer the mind something to engage with that is not the usual 'thinking' about things. Some, perhaps, lie at a halfway house between Richard of St Victor's cogitation and meditation, which involve both 'thinking about' things, and 'exploring' them, perhaps through repeated formulae, in the syllables '*buddho*', for instance, that can themselves be a meditation for sitting practice or during daily life. Some involve 'thinking about', in remembering different aspects of the Buddha, his teaching and his followers, and letting the mind go over events that bring reassurance and calm, as a way of ensuring health and resilience of mind. Such activities are considered essential for the deeper arousing of either insight or calm, *jhāna*, meditation and wisdom too. As Phra Maha Laow, an accredited Thai 'royal' exponent, has commented, 'Theravāda without chanting is a bit like if you cook but don't put in any ingredients.'[3] One could

---

3   During a conversation at Wat Mahathat Temple, King's Bromley, UK, September 2016.

say many of such chants are vocalized cogitations, encouraging factors needed in meditation, ensuring that any *jhāna* or moment of peace that arises is balanced, and then can form the basis for contemplation. They feature throughout the canon and in the *Visuddhimagga* as objects for mindful practice (e.g. Vism VII 2-67, 68-88, 89-100).

The *Iti pi so* (thus indeed) recollections are the formulae for the first three *anussatis*, the repeated mindfulness of the auspicious qualities associated with the Triple Gem of Buddha, dhamma and sangha.[4] They are practised in a chant that precedes meditations, in groups or alone, and are also walking practices, as in circumambulations around a stupa, or sitting. Chanting these, often with others, is so much part of the core of Buddhist practice that they are inextricably linked with other meditations.

Chanting, sitting and preaching are especially linked in Sri Lanka as *bhāvanā*. Modern forms of *baṇa* (usually translated as preach-

---

4   Found throughout the Pāli canon, these give full descriptions extolling the virtues and the strengths of the Buddha, the dhamma (the teaching) and the sangha (M I 38; A III 286): 1. *Iti pi so bhagavā arahaṃ sammāsaṃbuddho vijjācaraṇasampanno sugato lokavidu anuttarapurisadammasārathī satthā devamanussānaṃ buddho bhagavā ti*: 'The Lord is indeed thus: an arahant, completely self-awakened, perfect in knowing and doing, going along well, one who can see all worlds, an incomparable trainer of those ready for training, teacher of gods and men, awake, the Lord.' 2. *Svākkhāto Bhagavatā dhammo sandiṭṭhiko akāliko ehipassiko opanayiko paccattaṃ veditabbo viññūhī ti*: 'Wonderfully taught is the Lord's teaching: visible here and now, instantaneous, inviting, leading onwards, to be seen by the wise, each for him or herself.' 3. *Supaṭipanno Bhagavato sāvakasaṅgho ujupaṭipanno Bhagavato sāvakasaṅghosāvakasagho ñāyapaṭipanno Bhagavato sāvakasaṅghosānīcipaṭipanno Bhagavato sāvakasaṅgho yad idam cattāri purisayugāni aṭṭha purisapuggalā. Esa Bhagavato sāvakasaṅgho āhuneyyo pāhuneyyo dakkhiṇeyyo añjali karaṇeyyo anuttaraṃ puññakkhettaṃ lokassā ti*: 'Of good conduct is the community of hearers of the Lord, of straight conduct, of conduct conforming to the path, of right conduct. That is to say, the four pairs of men, the eight kinds of noble individuals (those attaining the four stages of path, and those experiencing the fruits of this). This indeed is the community of hearers of the Lord, worthy of veneration with offerings, worthy of hospitality, worthy of gifts, worthy of respectful greeting – an incomparable field in which merit grows for the whole world.'

ing) may include recitation of Pāli verses, the monastic speaking of scriptural passages in the vernacular and the melodious 'poetic preaching' consisting of the chanting of poems in Sinhala (*kavi baṇa*) (Deegalle 2007, 172-173). Throughout Burma and Thailand, chanting manuals (*samut khoi*), often beautifully illustrated, whose execution would also be seen as meritorious *bhāvanā*, are found and there are widespread local manuals in vernaculars (Appleton, Shaw & Unebe 2013). There is a whole mythology behind the chanting clubs for particular favourite chants throughout Thailand and Myanmar (McDaniel 2011), and, at shrines throughout Southeast Asia, such groups sit for many hours, chanting the longer chants, and working on them together as a group meditation, for they require real attentiveness to others, as well as to the movement of the chants throughout the body itself, sometimes linked to the breath. Chanting has its own often highly localized traditions and practices throughout Southern Buddhist regions. There are numerous different ways of chanting the *Namo Tassa* opening for the *Iti pi so* for specific occasions: the funerary is slow and melismatic, with special ornamentation and 'bent' notes for royal funerals; the ordination style is brisker, and the style used for the morning yet more awakening still.[5] One special practice chants the whole *Iti pi so* formula for the Buddha on one breath – a *tour de force* for real virtuoso chanters! All these chants and practices are associated with the active development of the five *jhāna* factors and the continued well-being of practitioners (Piyadassi 1999). The *Saṅgīti Sutta* lists five spheres of freedom: 'hearing the teaching from one who knows, hearing it from one who has heard it, chanting the texts, investigating them carefully, and grasping the sign (*nimitta*) of calm meditation' (D III 241). Trying to isolate these elements from one another as in some way more 'real' as Buddhist *bhāvanā* just does not work, in text or practice.

So, the word 'mindfulness' in these 'mindfulnesses' has a more active tone than some secular formulations. Practices included under the repeated mindfulnesses include chanting to the

---

5   Conversation with Ajahn Maha Laow, Wat Mahathat Temple, King's Bromley, UK, September 2016.

Triple Gem, practising and bearing in mind good ethics (*sīla*) and acts of generosity, and considering a divine happiness as the results of this. They are represented as helpful ways of directing the mind, with wise attention (*yonisa manasikāra*), so that its health, stability and cheerfulness are consistently maintained. Our popular understanding of mindfulness is simply a kind of awareness. According to the theory and practice, in text and modern application, one can initiate directions for mindfulness; it is clearly not just a simple watching, though may sometimes include that too.

The ten 'mindfulnesses' include practices that extend our understanding of mindfulness: as a creatively proactive as well as observational mental state. This is borne out by other canonical references to mindfulness, in Sutta and Abhidhamma. Within the Abhidhamma system, right mindfulness, a path factor so important within any meditative system, is a distinguishing feature of the healthy and skilful mind. According to the Abhidhamma, it is *always* said to arise in conjunction with other factors, such as balance, flexibility of mind and body, confidence, and, crucially, the ethical guards, self-respect (*hiri*) and regard for consequences (*ottappa*) (Rhys Davids 1900/1974, 14). As a concomitant of skilful or healthy (*kusala*) consciousness, mindfulness exercises intuitive discrimination: it steers the mind towards what is good for it and away from what is not (Soma 1981/2003, xv–xxvii). An innate sense of the ethical is present and behaviour on the basis of that is said to be 'happy', productive of good result, and a necessary accompaniment to all meditative practice (Harvey 2013, 264-286; M I 76, 483; M III 170-178). So mindfulness always works with accompanying factors. In Abhidhamma and commentaries, mindfulness is just one aspect of the awake and 'skilful' mind at every level of the path to awakening (*bodhi*) (see, for instance, Dhammasāmi 2000). At the deepest levels of meditation, it works as a refined awareness that is 'purified by equanimity' in the fourth *jhāna*, so becoming a meditative/contemplative factor of a particularly subtle and specialist kind.

Mention should also be made here of the practice of the divine abidings, of loving-kindness, compassion, sympathetic joy and equanimity: loving-kindness is described as a 'mindfulness' in the *Mettā Sutta*, perhaps the most popular Southern Buddhist text of all. This text is constantly chanted and used as the basis for practice, lay and monastic; loving-kindness is regarded as possible in daily life or in *jhāna*. One of the divine abidings is described as always present in all skilful consciousness in the Abhidhamma. Indeed it has been argued that in some suttas (SN 42) they are presented as salvific, a notion adopted by Sārvastavādin schools (Gombrich 1998; Cox 1992). Certainly they would be present in the practices of most of the major meditation traditions now.

We have quite a diverse picture of meditation here. In the twentieth century, the *popular* use of the word 'meditation' has evolved. As I have shown, it has come to denote a silent, solitary sitting practice, which people either 'do' or 'do not do'; so, it used to be said, lay people 'do not do' meditation' but monks 'do'. Isolated practices by monastics, while important, are, however, not the *only* way to practise 'meditation'; conversely, many monks do not practise this sort of sitting meditation, being more dedicated to chant and ritual. The devotional practices of lay people are fully validated as salvific by early texts and commentaries as calm practices. From the outset of the Southern Buddhist tradition, 'meditation' teaching was almost always embedded in teachings about other aspects of *bhāvanā*. Highly varied in local contexts, often stressing different elements with a particular force, chants, offerings, meditations, and the mindfulnesses, all *samatha/sīla* practices, move around in the place where ethics settles into an underlying confidence and peace of mind. One text says, 'There is a time for hearing *dhamma*, a time for discussing *dhamma*, a time for *samatha*, and a time for *vipassanā*' (A II 140). If each of these is practised from time to time, arahatship will surely be found — just as 'rains which fall on the mountains go surely and irrevocably to the ocean.'

So, the paradigm of the early texts, with some modifications within the Abhidhamma system, is a variety of what emerges as a threefold structure for the path itself, involving all three elements of *sīla*, *samādhi* and *paññā*. The one who has attained the first stage of the path has eradicated doubt and fulfilled the *sīla*s. The next two stages of the path involve the fulfilment of calm, as well as *sīla*, and the last, the attainment of arahatship, or awakening, the fulfilment of wisdom, as well as *samādhi* and *paññā*.

It should also be noted that the particular combination of meditations for any one person at any time, is, in early Buddhist texts, governed by what that person needs. So Meghiya, a monk who thinks he can go it alone, is advised, after his failures to practise both calm and insight: loving-kindness, breathing mindfulness, and some insight (Ud 34; Shaw 2006, 24-27); and the laywoman Vesakha is given most of the first six recollections, calm based practices (A I 206-211; Shaw 2006, 129-132). At different times, what various people are given for different stages also varies. The Buddha's son, at first not able to do some other meditations, is given the meditation on the four elements in one text, as a calm practice, and then other insight instructions at a later stage (M I 420-426; Shaw 2006, 189-193). Tissa, an accident-prone monk, is given different meditations and subjects to consider at various times, including both calm and insight as is needed, until he finally finds his difficult path to arahatship (see Shaw 2006, 53-56). In early texts, *samatha* tends to be given first; insight later, and ethics (*sīla*) constantly, throughout. In early texts, meditations are assigned to people, and tailored to the individual. This tends to be the practice of many modern meditative schools in South and Southeast Asia now. Other texts indicate the way the Buddha looked at the individual first – and then suggested a particular arrangement of meditations, often including these.

Modern practice – *Samatha* and *Vipassanā*

This brings me to the two main strands of meditative practice, *vipassanā* and *samatha*, and the recent history of Southern Buddhist practice over the last two hundred years. Whether or not practice has always followed canonical precedents is unclear, and it is rather unlikely that it always has. Monastic lines were lost in

Sri Lanka at certain times, suggestive that meditative traditions were too. Southern Buddhism perhaps gives us less information about this than other forms of Buddhism. Meditation practice is taught privately, and there is still a tradition of great personal reserve about discussion of such matters in public. Much of the teaching seems to have arisen in esoteric schools, whose techniques are less well known (Bizot 1992; Cousins 1997b; Crosby 1999; 2000; 2013; Crosby, Skilton & Gunasena 2012). Southern Buddhism also has none of the formal traditions of liberation narrative found in the Northern Buddhist schools, or the stress on extensive biographical and anecdotal accounts found in the Eastern, where a particular incumbent of a given lineage, as in Northern Buddhism, may be associated not only with formal hagiography but also informal and anecdotal record (Covill, Roesler & Shaw 2010). In Southern regions, the Vinaya ruling about not boasting about meditation states wrongfully has set a pattern of great reticence on the part of teachers to lay claim to any meditation state publicly, though auto/biographies from the mid-twentieth century in these regions have started to do so (Vin III 109).[6] But certainly over the last two hundred years, when we do start to have much more documentation, albeit in still untranslated vernacular manuals, the sort of mix described here seems to have been applied in most Southern Buddhist contexts.

There is, however, an ancient juxtaposition of *samatha* and *vipassanā*, perhaps a development of the pairing of *samādhi* and *sati*. Both sets of two are paired in the canon: amongst the list of twos, for instance, in the *Saṅgīti-Sutta* (D III 213).[7] There is some slight difference in approach between Sutta and the Abhidhamma systems, but, broadly speaking, both elements – that of meditation/contemplation and the work of insight, developing wisdom, are classically depicted as necessary for awakening. So, it is said,

---

6   This offence is one of the four *parājika*s that immediately exclude monastics from the order. The others are intentionally killing a human being, stealing and voluntary sexual intercourse.

7   See Cousins 1973, 1984 and 1997a. These articles have been so frequently consulted and used throughout this paper that they are not always cited.

development of *samatha* leads to developing *citta*, which leads to the abandoning of desire (*rāga*) by means of liberation of heart (*cetovimutti*). The route that follows this method rests largely on the practice of the first four *jhāna*s, and sometimes the formless ones too. Development of *vipassanā*, by contrast, leads to developing wisdom and then to the abandoning of ignorance and liberation of understanding (A I 61). Contemplation of the three 'signs': impermanence (*anicca*), suffering (*dukkha*) and non-self (*anattā*) is key. For this route there is some debate as to whether the first four *jhāna*s are needed, or even the first, but awakening is usually linked to the development of the *jhāna*, and then insight. One could say that the part of the dependent origination cycle that starts with feeling, is purified by *samatha*, and the part associated with ignorance to name and form, consciousness and *saṅkhara*s, with insight. Both need the other, in theory and in usual practice. So modern schools tend to work on one strand as the predominate one, but, in most reputable cases, do not exclude the other. Indeed, they are commonly described as 'yoked together'. One text describes four routes to awakening:

(a) …bringing into being insight preceded by peace
(b) …bringing into being peace preceded by insight
(c) …peace and insight yoked as a pair
(d) …the mind is gripped by *dhamma* excitement. 'On the occasion, sirs, when the mind stabilizes within, settles down, becomes one-pointed and enters concentration (*samādhiyati*), the path is born to him.' (A II 157)

The fourth method, associated with 'dry' insight, possibly without the *jhāna*s, has been the subject of debate in recent times; several modern insight movements can be seen to be associated with this.

The two approaches have quite different emphases in practice, and it is the latter, *vipassanā*, that has received more Western attention. *Samatha* schools, historically termed 'wet', place greater emphasis on mindfulness of feeling, and the development of the *jhāna*s, the meditations/contemplations described above, before insight. They usually have more complex instructions, often associated with some exercise of control of the breath as a means of permitting freedom of movement into and from the *jhāna* and stages of absorption. Mantra, ritual and visualization often play a key role, and a sense of versatility between various *jhāna*s, encouraged as a means of mastering attachment. From a historical point of view, these practices were certainly the most predominant in Southeast Asia until the mid-twentieth century, particularly in Thailand. Recent research by Kate Crosby, Andrew Skilton, Phibul Choompolpaisal, Amal Gunasena and other researchers at King's College, London, is revealing a whole sub-culture of meditation manuals, *nimitta* lists, and localized, adapted ways of categorizing various of the forty *samatha* objects, within manuscripts, notebooks, advice sheets and pamphlets of various kinds dating back to the eighteenth century, from throughout South and Southeast Asia, which are only recently becoming available and translated and circulated (Crosby 2000, 2013; Crosby, Skilton & Gunasena 2012; Choompolpaisal & Skilton 2014). Such *samatha* practices appear to be much older, and normative. While there have been royal and courtly practitioners in early centuries, they seem also to have strong local histories too in often non-literate, rural communities in Laos, Cambodia, Burma, Sri Lanka, Northeast Thailand and possibly Indonesia. *Vipassanā* schools, however, with the 'dry' method, stress more the refinement of identifications, or perception, for the cultivation of insight. Rendered particularly popular in the mid-twentieth century, these schools have middle-class, educated and often Anglophone supporters, attracted to what seems a scientific and even rationalistic ordering of experience. Where practised on their own, these derive from the late nineteenth century onwards. So, in the modern insight schools, there is less emphasis on the exploration of the breath, developing mental images (*nimitta*) or managing changes in its length, and more on, for instance, the area of physical contact with the breath, such as the abdomen, though this varies greatly from school to school (Nyanoponika 1992; Cousins 1996; 1997a;

Ledi 2007; Shaw 2012). Some differentiation between the 'feel' of these two styles dates from early texts, and represents a possible and continued development of an earlier axis of concentration and mindfulness.

However, it should be noted that all the traditions still usually place considerable emphasis on the practice of the divine abidings, the recollections, and the cultivation of serenity and peace. Calm and insight traditions also, in theory at any rate, place a great deal of emphasis on ethics, and, within those highly popular Burmese insight systems, where Abhidhamma is used as a meditative tool to aid understanding of the mind's working in daily life, investigation of the role of ethics in the skilful *citta* accompanies practice, analysis and discussion of ethics as an integral part of the system's understanding of human psychology and development in meditation/contemplation. Clearly the paths of these two traditions share many elements.

A Shift to *Vipassanā*?

The difference between the two approaches, which have their own correctives and supportive practices, has historical implications. In recent years, it would be fair to say that Southern Buddhism has been known for its insight, or *vipassanā* methods, now recognized worldwide and offering the sometimes hidden rationale behind much modern discourse concerning the secular mindfulness movements. But is this a fair representation of Southern Buddhist practice over the last two hundred years? This does not appear to have been the case until recently, and, as we have seen, the classical approaches to Buddhist meditation/contemplation have far more complexity and richness, as indeed, in practice, do the methods taught by insight schools, too. There are still people alive who remember the fifties and sixties of the twentieth century, at a time when, as Boonman Poonyathiro, a *samatha* meditation teacher in his eighties, says, 'I was a young novice in Thailand; everyone learnt *samatha* and then did *vipassanā*. This is what you did in rural monasteries everywhere.

You need to go to school before you can try university! Now everyone thinks they can go to university straight away.'[8]

Another dynamic is the extent to which lay people 'practise meditation'. This is a tricky one – traditionally, it is monks who are said to undertake meditation practice, but, as I hope this brief discussion has suggested, classifications of this kind are hazardous. As I hope I have indicated, many of the calm practices – of loving-kindness, the recollections or 'mindfulnesses' of the Triple gem, and the chanting and listening that accompany them, are so embedded in popular practice that it is impossible to say, as some do, that historically lay people 'have not practised meditation' and that it was 'only monastic'. Indicating the presence of earlier traditions, Kate Crosby and associates have found a manuscript made for one of the wives of the Kandyan king, Śri Rājasimha, on highly complex forms of *jhāna* meditation.[9] Chanting manuals, I have described, with texts, *yantras* (sacred diagrams) and pictures linked to other aspects of *bhāvanā*, attest to active traditions of chant, lay and monastic, again at least from the eighteenth century. Manuals, guide-books, celebratory leaflets, manuscripts, ola-leaf books and *samut khoi* from Sri Lanka, Thailand, Laos and Cambodia record many of these in great detail. Anecdotally, I found that forty years ago in Sri Lanka a number of lay people practised 'meditation/contemplation', but were reticent about discussing it with those who did not. Burma and Thailand have long public traditions of lay people practising meditation, possibly the result of the practice of so many adult males joining the sangha for short periods: while ordination is usually for life in Sri Lanka, Southeast Asia has historically encouraged short ordination periods for all young men. At times when the meditative tradition was active, this would mean in practice extensive introduction to *jhāna* practice. Many would have continued in daily life. Perhaps as a result of these factors, as recent research is demonstrating, *bhāvanā,* in its medita-

8   Interview at the Samatha Centre, Greenstreete, Llangunllo, Powys, UK, August 2016.
9   Work on this is ongoing and the findings not yet published.

tive/contemplative aspects, has clearly been practised widely in Southern Buddhism in the last two hundred years, amongst both lay and monastic practitioners.

So why is there so much insistence on insight methods amongst modern meditation teachers? The mild eclipse of *samatha* methods seems to have started in the early twentieth century, and has affected much practice and discourse on meditation as the twentieth century gave way to the twenty-first. The debate is ancient, as Gombrich notes, but the historical origins of this particular tide are difficult to assign to one cause, appearing rather to have multiple supporting factors (Gombrich 1996). The influence of sometimes Protestant based Western religious thought, a reforming movement of monk's Vinaya and the desire by some Southeast Asian countries to appear more 'scientific' and 'rationalist' have undoubtedly been key factors (Crosby 2013). In order to travel, monastic teachers must be *vipassanā*, and accredited as such, whatever their preference. A distrust of *samatha* manifests in other Southeast Asian contexts occasionally and is possibly the cause of, for instance, the suspicion that the primarily *samatha* based visualizations and practices of Wak Pak Nam and the Dhammakāya movement have aroused in Thailand in recent times. Early Burmese insight commentaries did not deny the importance of *samatha* practice, but rather emphasized other features: the possibility of attaining awakening 'in this very life', a stress on mindfulness and insight as being 'more suitable' for modern times, and a defence that such methods are more 'scientific' and thereby more creditable. In time, and in some few cases, an insistence developed that the practice of *jhāna* was not needed or desirable in the pursuit of a salvific path. Sometimes *jhāna* itself is presented as not involving mindfulness and wisdom, though all accounts, from Sutta, to the Abhidhamma, to modern-day practitioners, indicate that they are essential. Such discourse has in turn, incidentally and interestingly, provided many arguments that have supported the mindfulness movements of recent decades, which, sometimes unwittingly, employ tenets initiated by the writings in Pāli of the nineteenth century.

It would be possible from the effects of this to infer, as many scholars do, that the Buddhist meditative practice of Southern Buddhism is *vipassanā*. The picture before this time, however, in Southeast Asia and South Asia has, fortunately, been dramatically changed by so much recent research, which confirms what anecdotal evidence had already well known and asserted: that in practice monasteries around these regions would specialise in a number of practices, sometimes with local variations, drawn from indigenous *samatha* systems, rooted, however, on canonical precedent.[10] Francois Bizot provided ground-breaking material on this, after extensive fieldwork in rural Cambodia, which revealed mantra, visualization, *jhāna* practice and various teacher-based esoteric traditions deeply embedded in Cambodian life. The Cambodian traditions based on the fivefold combination of Na Mo Bu Ddha Ya, representing the five elements (four + space) and the five *jhāna* factors, place great emphasis on the factor of joy, circulation of the breath, the movement of focus through specific areas of the body, some visualization practice and balance (Bizot 1976; Crosby 2000). Much of this practice was rural, much lay, and a large part of it in vernaculars and hidden transmissions, hence there has been some difficulty in tracking sources. The origins of such practices, which appear to have been prevalent in other parts of South and Southeast Asia, are problematic, and a number of sources have been suggested. They do, however, accord with early Buddhist teachings.

The success of *vipassanā* amongst urban, middle-class inhabitants of Chiang Mai and Bangkok, as well as India, has certainly ensured that those who travelled and had contact with publishers and Buddhist groups abroad promoted such methods. The U Bha Khin groups, and the Goenka and Ledi Sayadaw methods are now widely accessible on a worldwide scale, and have met with

---

10 Ven Anandamaitreya discussed a number of his own *samatha* practices in conversations in the early 1980s at several visits to the Manchester Centre for Buddhist Meditation, as did Ven Piyatissa. L.S. Cousins and C.M.M. Shaw both made extended stays at the monastery devoted to traditional *samatha* meditation.

considerable success (Cousins 1996). The very presence of such movements certainly could be seen to imply some reaction to pre-existing modes of practice and the cultivation of *jhāna* as the basis, known loosely as the *Porāṇā* (ancient) meditative tradition. The *boran kammaṭṭhān* of the *samatha* schools, however, appears to have been the dominant tradition of South and Southeast Asia in the nineteenth century, and much of the twentieth.

Sri Lanka poses a different case, needing more research. Although Anagārika Dharmapāla claimed that *samatha* practice had died out in Sri Lanka by the beginning of the twentieth century, the untitled and unattributed work subsequently termed *The Yogāvacara's Manual of Indian Mysticism as practised by Buddhists*, brought by him for translation and publication by the newly formed Pali Text Society in 1896, suggests otherwise (Rhys Davids 1896). Anecdotal evidence at any rate testifies to the persistence of traditional *samatha* methods in Sri Lankan rural monasteries up to the time of the troubles in the 1980s. Sinhalese records suggest that many of these date from the Siam Nikāya movement in the eighteenth century, a revitalization project intended to restore Sri Lankan Buddhism, that included ordination lineages, artefacts, Buddha images, manuscripts and, it seems, some practice guidance too. The Siam Nikāya ordination is still one of the largest in Sri Lanka. This material for one eighteenth-century lay practitioner of *samatha* methods in Sri Lanka, presumably implies there were others too. Whatever its source, or date, the methods of the manual correspond to many found in Cambodia to the present day, and represent also an esoteric, teacher-based tradition. Breathing mindfulness is taught accompanied by mantra meditations on the syllables NA MO BU DDHA YA.

Concluding Thoughts

I have argued that the early canon sets a pattern of a great mix of practices, specifically assigned to people according to their needs and particular approach. Modern practice also suggests a complex picture. Modern *vipassanā* movements have become uniformly more highly regarded throughout South and Southeast Asia; they, however, employ many traditional *samatha* meditations routinely, such as the recollections and the divine abidings. Other, older methods, associated with *samatha*, devotional rituals and many other aspects of *bhāvanā*, also survive in many regions. Indicators so far are that *samatha* practices of great complexity, often lay, and often highly varied, have at least for the last two hundred years been widespread throughout South and Southeast Asia, as has the practice of *jhāna* for laity and monastics. Southern Buddhism, despite many attempts by 'reformers', anxious to make it appear more 'scientific' and 'rationalist', persists as satisfyingly difficult to categorise or regard as in any way uniform.

A Dominican friar, in a shared panel I was on recently, said, 'Western Christianity somehow forgot the body in the seventeenth century and afterwards. But the body and the breath are really the most important things about my practice (rosary). That is what grounds me, and sets me right'.[11] In so many traditions, it is a range of activities, from prostrating, kneeling, making ritual signs of respect like the añjali or the sign of the cross, and so many other chants, prayers and devotions, that steer and direct meditation/contemplation, even, in many cases being regarded as meditation/contemplation in their own right. In Southern Buddhism a spectrum of 'meditations' are seen as helpful, in text and modern praxis, both for laity and monastics. The traditions of meditation/contemplation in these regions are rich, and many need to be seen working together to be understood in perspective, both when we look at ancient texts and at the practices that are undertaken today.

---

11 Timothy Radcliffe OP, Blackfriars, Oxford during an interview with Neil McGregor recorded for BBC Radio 4, 13 June 2017.

Abbreviations of Pali Texts

A   *Aṅguttara-nikāya*
D   *Dīgha-nikāya*
M   *Majjhima-nikāya*
Ne   *Netti*
S   *Saṃyuttanikāya*
Ud   *Udāna*
Vibh *Vibhaṅga*
Vin   *Vinaya*
Vism *Visuddhimagga (The Path of Purification)* cited in Ñāṇamoli edition classification.
PF   *Path of Freedom (Vimuttimagga)*

Bibliography

Dictionaries

Oxford English Dictionary, Compact Edition, 2 vols., 1979, London: Book Club Associates = OED
Pāli-English Dictionary, T.W. Rhys Davids and William Stede, 1921/2008. New Delhi: Munshiram Manoharial Publishers.

Primary and Secondary Resources

Almond, Philip C., 1988. *The British Discovery of Buddhism.* Cambridge: Cambridge University Press.

Appleton, Naomi, Sarah Shaw & Toshiya Unebe, 2013. *Illuminating the Life of the Buddha: an Illustrated Chanting Book from Eighteenth-Century Siam.* Oxford: Bodleian Library publications.

Aris, Marc Aeilco, 1996. *Contemplatio. Philosophische Studien zum Traktat Benjamin Maior des Richard von St. Viktor. Mit einer verbesserten Edition des Textes.* Frankfurt/Main: Joseph Knecht.

Bizot, François, 1976. *Le figuier à cinq branches. Recherches sur le bouddhisme khmer* II, PEFEO CVII. Paris: L'École française d'Extrême-Orient.

Bizot, François, 1992. *Le Chemin de Laṅkā*. Paris, Chiang Mai, Phnom Penh: L'École française d'Extrême-Orient.

Bronkhorst, Johannes, 1993. *The Two Traditions of Meditation in Ancient India*. Delhi: Motilal Banarsidass.

Choompolpaisal, Phibul & Andrew Skilton, 2014. 'The Old Meditation (*boran kammatthan*), a pre-reform Theravāda meditation system, from Wat Ratchasittharam: the pīti section of the kammatthan matchima baeb lamdap.' *ASEANIE*. 33: 83-116.

Cousins, L.S., 1973. 'Buddhist *Jhāna*: Its Nature and Attainment according to the Pali Sources'. *Religion* 3.2: 115-31.

Cousins, L.S., 1983. 'Pali Oral Literature'. In *Buddhist Studies – Ancient and Modern* (London), eds. P. Denwood & T. Piatigorsky: 1-11.

Cousins, L.S., 1984. '*Samatha-yāna* and *vipassanā-yāna*'. In *Buddhist Studies in Honour of Hammalava Saddhātissa*, eds. G. Dhammapāla, Richard Gombrich, and K.R. Norman. Nugegoda, Sri Lanka: Hammalava Saddhātissa Felicitation Volume Committee: 55-68.

Cousins, L.S., 1989. 'The Stages of Christian mysticism and Buddhist Purification: *The Interior Castle* of St. Teresa of Ávila and *The Path of Purification* of Buddhaghosa'. In *The Yogi and the Mystic — Studies in Indian and Comparative Mysticism*, ed. Karel Werner. Richmond, Surry: Curzon: 103-120.

Cousins, L.S., 1996. 'The Origins of Insight Meditation'. In *Buddhist Forum IV*, ed. Tadeusz Skorupski. London: School of Oriental and African Studies: 35-58.

Cousins, L.S., 1997a. 'Buddhism'. In *A New handbook of Living Religions*, ed. John R. Hinnells. Oxford: Blackwell: 369-444.

Cousins, L.S., 1997b. 'Aspects of Esoteric Southern Buddhism'. In *Indian Insights; Buddhism, Brahmanism and Bhakti*, eds. Peter Connolly & Sue Hamilton. London: Luzac Oriental: 185-208.

Covill, Linda, Ulrike Roesler & Sarah Shaw, eds., 2010. *Lives Lived; Lives Imagined: Biographies of Awakening*. Boston, MA: Wisdom.

Cox, Collett, 1992. 'Attainment through Abandonment: The Sarvāstivādin Path of Removing Defilements'. In *Paths to Liberation. The Mārga and Its Transformations in Buddhist Thought,* eds. Robert E. Buswell, Jr & Robert M. Gimello, Studies in East Asian Buddhism 7. Honolulu: University of Hawai'i Press: 107-34.

Crosby, Kate, 1999. 'Studies in the medieval Pali literature of Sri Lanka with special reference to the esoteric Yogavacara tradition'. Unpublished DPhil thesis, Oxford.

Crosby, Kate, 2000. 'Tantric Theravāda: a bibliographic Essay on the writings of François Bizot and others on the Yogāvacara Tradition'. *Contemporary Buddhism. An Interdisciplinary Journal* 1.2: 141-93.

Crosby, Kate, 2013. *Traditional Theravada Meditation and its Modern-Era Suppression.* Hong Kong: Buddha Dharma Centre of Hong Kong.

Crosby, Kate, Andrew Skilton & Amal Gunasena, 2012. 'The *Sutta on Understanding Death* in the Transmission of Borān Meditation From Siam to the Kandyan Court'. *Journal of Indian Philosophy* 40.2: 177-98.

Deegalle, Mahinda, 2007. *Popularising Buddhism: Preaching as Performance in Sri Lanka.* New York: State University of New York Press.

Dhammasāmi, Khammai, 2000. *Different Aspects of Mindfulness.* Penang: Inward Path.

Ehara, The Rev. N.R.M., Soma Thera & Kheminda Thera, transls., 1995 (1961). *The Path of Freedom (Vimuttimagga) by Upatissa Thera.* Kandy: Buddhist Publication Society [= PF].

Gethin, R.M.L., 1992. *The Buddhist Path to Awakening: A Study of the Bodhipakkhiyā Dhammā.* Leiden: Brill.

Gombrich, Richard F., 1996. *How Buddhism Began: the Conditioned Genesis of the Early Teachings.* London: Athlone Press.

Gombrich, Richard F., 1998. *Kindness and Compassion as Means to Nirvana* (1997 Gonda Lecture). Amsterdam: Royal Netherlands Academy of Arts and Sciences.

Gunaratana, H., 1980. 'A Critical Analysis of the Jhānas in Theravāda Buddhist Meditation'. PhD dissertation for the American University, Washington DC, The American Library. Available online. www.buddhanet.net/pdf_file/scrnguna.pdf.

Harvey, Peter, 1993. 'The Dynamics of *Paritta* Chanting in Southern Buddhism'. In *Love Divine: Studies in 'Bhakti and Devotional Mysticism,* (Durham Indological Series, Vol. III), ed. Karel Werner. London: Curzon Press: 53-84.

Harvey, Peter, 2013². *An Introduction to Buddhism: Teachings, history and practice.* Cambridge: Cambridge University Press.

Laulertvorakul, Anant, 2003. '*Paṭhamasambodhi* in Nine Languages: Their Relation and Evolution'. *Manusya: Journal of Humanities* 6.1:11-34.

Ledi Sayadaw, 2007. *Ānāpāna-Dīpanī (The Light of Breathing).* Yangon: Promotion and Propagation of Ledi-Dīpanī Organization.

McDaniel, Justin, 2011. *The Lovelorn Ghost and the Magical Monk: Practicing Buddhism in Modern Thailand.* New York: Columbia University Press.

Ñāṇamoli, Bhikkhu, 2010⁴. *The Path of Purification Visuddhimagga.* Colombo: Buddhist Publication Society [= Vism].

Nyanaponika, Thera, 1992. *The Heart of Buddhist Meditation: A Handbook of Mental Training based on the Buddha's Way of Mindfulness.* Kandy, Sri Lanka: Buddhist Publication Society.

Palihawadana, M., 1997. 'Pali Sajjhaya and Sanskrit Svadhyaya: An Inquiry into the Historical Origins of Parittana Recitation'. In *Recent Researches in Buddhist Studies: Essays in Honour of Professor Y. Karunadasa,* eds. Kuala Lumpur Dhammajoti, Asanga Tilakaratne & Kapila Abhayawansa. Colombo, Sri Lanka; Hong Kong: Y. Karunadasa Felicitation Committee; Chi Ying Foundation: 493-515.

Piyadassi, Thera, 1999. *The Book of Protection.* With a foreword by V.F. Guneratna. Access to Insight website: https://www.accesstoinsight.org/lib/authors/piyadassi/protection.html#preface (Site accessed 23 November 2017).

Rhys Davids, Caroline A.F., trans., 1974[3] (1900). *A Buddhist Manual of Psychological Ethics: Being a Translation, now made for the First Time, from the Original Pali, of the First Book in the Abhidhamma Piṭaka entitled Dhamma-sangaṇi, compendium of states or phenomena.* London: Pali Text Society.

Rhys Davids, T.W. 1896. *The Yogāvacara's Manual of Indian Mysticism as Practised by Buddhists.* London: Pali Text Society.

Shaw, Sarah, 2006. *Buddhist Meditation: an Anthology of Texts.* Oxford Centre for Buddhist Studies Monograph Series. London: Routledge.

Shaw, Sarah, 2012. 'Breathing Mindfulness: Text and Practice'. In *Buddhist Philosophy and Meditation Praxis,* 2nd IABU Conference, ed. Ven. Dhammasāmi, [n.p.]: Mahachulalongkornrajavidyalana University Press: 378-390.

Shaw, Sarah, 2014. *The Spirit of Buddhist Meditation.* London: Yale University Press.

Soma, T., transl., 1981/2003. *The Way of Mindfulness* (5th rev. ed.). Kandy: Buddhist Publication Society.

Standaert, Nicolas, 2015. 'Ignatian Visual Meditation in Seventeenth-Century China'. In *Meditation and Culture: The Interplay of Practice and Context,* ed. Halvor Eifring. London: Bloomsbury: 24-35.

THEME 2:
CHRISTIAN-BUDDHIST ENCOUNTER THROUGH ZEN PRACTICE

WHY DO CHRISTIANS PRACTISE ZEN?

Ursula Baatz

Abstract

The participation of Christians in Zen practice is a rather recent phenomenon and the result of a multilayered process under the auspices of globalization: the colonial exchange which brought Buddhism to Europe and European missionaries to Asia as well as the signs of nationalism and imperialism under which Zen-Buddhism was understood as the core of all religions. At the same time, ideas of a 'perennial mystical stream' underlying all religions became popular in the West and there was an endeavour to de-westernize Christianity and inculturate it in Asian and Japanese culture respectively. Further, Vatican II opened the way to interreligious dialogue and a sharing of meaningful spiritual practice with non-Christians. In another layer, the history of Christian spirituality has to be taken into account, where for centuries a charged relationship existed between, on one side, the control of believers by collaborative efforts of church and state, and, on the other side, the freedom of deep spiritual practice conveyed by contemplation. The development of modernity coincided with the repression of contemplative practices within the church together with a growing interest in mysticism on the fringes. Following World War II, the practice of Zen became part of the counterculture, and thus Christians who practised Zen could see themselves as part of the cultural avant-garde. Whereas Hugo M. Enomiya-Lassalle SJ initially turned to Zen practice as a way of inculturation, the Trappist monk Thomas Merton saw mysticism in general and Asian practices like Zen in particular as a spiritual critique of consumerism. However, the question remains – and will be addressed here – how Zen practice may be communicated and translated in Christian theology.

Keywords: Zen-Buddhism, Christianity, mysticism, contemplation, meditation, Vatican II, Japan, inculturation, interreligious dialogue, globalization, theology of religions

For more or less fifty years, there has been quite a bunch of Christians who have studied Zen, as well as a handful of Christians who have taught Zen, not exclusively to Christians. There have also been Jews who have practised or even taught Zen Buddhism or other forms of Buddhism, while still maintaining their practice of Judaism (Grosshans et al. 2017; Kasimow et al. 2003). For many a Christian, who, due to historical reasons, cling more to dogmatic 'lock ups' than to personal practice, the idea of 'Christians who practise or study Zen' still invokes a taste of 'transgression'. It is because, to this very day, Christian denominations often continue to strongly discriminate against people of other religions or even other Christian denominations. To give a recent example of this: when, on the occasion of the 500 year anniversary of the Reformation, the present pope pointed out that there were bridges between Protestants and Roman Catholics, he was met with severe criticism by some Protestants as well as Catholics (e.g. Finger 2016, 2017). Thus, to study Zen, which is definitely not a Christian practice, arouses a lot of distrust in those who wish not to participate in such 'transgressions'.

The explicit use of 'transgression' in discussing the case of Christians practising Zen could signal a postmodern approach. However, it relates to the simple fact that there are religious, ethnic, linguistic and other kinds of boundaries involved which are 'passed over' (Dunne 1972) by those who practise Zen as Christians. It will be a topic of this paper to explore the boundaries involved, when, where and by whom they were crossed and whose identities were negated and/or affirmed in this process. In the following paragraphs I will concentrate on the quests of Thomas Merton and Fr. Hugo M. Enomiya-Lassalle, after discussing the endeavour of those Japanese Christians, who, at the end of the nineteenth century, turned to Zen in search of a Japanese Christianity.

Religion, a concept with complexity

Zen Buddhism and Christianity are labelled 'religions', and usually religions are seen as exclusive. 'Religion' is a European concept. It has no proper equivalents in Asian languages and its meaning is ambiguous. It comes from the Latin 'religio', a word that seems to have been current in the Roman Republic around 186 BCE. 'Religio' denoted a Bacchanal cult unapproved by the Roman Republic and seen as endangering the stability of the republic (Livius, 39, 8-20; Kippenberg and von Stuckrad, 103-104). 'Religio', therefore, was at first connected to the idea of public order and policy. Some six hundred years later, when Roman emperors Diocletian and Galerius attempted to return the Christians through persecution to the old religious order – the cult of the emperor thought to be vital for the coherence of the Empire – the Church father, Lactantius derived 'religio' from 'religare', intending to boost the status of Christians in the Empire.

He stated that humans are tied to God and bound by the bond of piety (Lactantius, *Divine Institutes*, IV, xxviii), which influenced the definition commonly accepted today. It was common sense in Rome and beyond that worship and piety had a foundational character for the identity of the polity (DePalma Digeser 2012, 74). Thus, Lactantius, who wrote his *Divinis Institutii* in the wake of persecution, wished to demonstrate that Christians were living under divine law as citizens of a divine polity (De Palma Digeser 2012, 75), which in turn seems to have inspired Constantine to adopt Christianity as a legitimate religion (De Palma Digeser, 2012, 82). Since then, to Europeans, the term 'religion' refers to sacred laws, the identity of local and regional communities (*Gemeinwesen*), and government, as well as to communal cohesion. Durkheim's famous definition of religion takes note of these dimensions. For the sake of this analysis, I will refer to the five dimensions of religion mentioned by the sociologist Linda Woodhead: religion as culture, identity, relationship, practice and power (Woodhead 2011).

There is also another trait of 'religion' in European heritage, which has not been mentioned yet and is rarely noticed by sociologists, namely, that of self-cultivation and orientation to transcendence. 'Religion' as a way of self-cultivation provides orientation: the framework to fulfil the urge to place one's life into a larger perspective and to develop and grow in accordance with it. Today this is mostly associated with Asian traditions, as self-cultivation is a major focus in Buddhism, as well as in Hindu traditions, Daoism and Confucianism. Nevertheless, self-cultivation is part of European philosophical and religious traditions as well. In late antiquity, the Epicureans and the Stoics had emerged from the Platonic academy as schools of self-cultivation, and Christians who were acquainted with these schools made use of their forms of mental training (Hadot 1999). During the persecution, at the end of the third century, some men and women withdrew into the desert to live a Christian life according to the scriptures. They also had knowledge of the philosophical schools of self-cultivation and their respective methods, which they found useful for their Christian practice. These 'desert-fathers' and 'desert-mothers' mark the beginning of Christian contemplative practice as a personal endeavour within the framework of 'religion' as a social and political entity. In the contemporary world, the concept of 'spirituality' is used to refer to the dimension of 'religion' that involves self-cultivation (Baatz 2017b; Schmücker & Heubel 2013).

Why do Christians study Zen? The question has to address religion not only in a Durkheimian sense – i.e. concerning identity, polity and communal coherence – but also with respect to self-cultivation, what is called 'the path' in Buddhism. Religion as a sociopolitical phenomenon and religion as a way of self-cultivation ('spirituality') are often seen as mutually exclusive, as if they were two different entities. Within the reality of religious practice, both are to a large extent interdependent, as recent research shows (Hense 2011). Spirituality as a way of self-cultivation and religion as a socio-political entity cannot be separated, as the latter provides the stage for the actors of religion as self- cultivation. In that sense it is not possible to exclude socio-political and historical perspectives from an exploration into a cross-religious and cross-cultural practice such as Christians studying Zen.

Stages and Actors

Nineteenth Century Japan: Samurai-Christians

After the arrival of US ships in Japan in 1857 and the Meiji emperor coming into power, Buddhism in Japan was influenced by the modernization of Japan. Buddhism, which had been connected with the regime of the samurai through the centuries, was criticized, and even persecuted. An anti-Buddhist movement had already developed during the late Tokugawa period and this gained momentum during the first decades of the Meiji era. Buddhist priests had been forced to defrock and Buddhist temples had been closed or destroyed. In 1870, an imperial prescript even announced the 'Great Doctrine' (*daikyō*), promoting Shinto as the national religion, radically separating the two traditions to oust Buddhism, which had been introduced to Japan in the sixth century. However, Japan was rapidly modernizing with Western experts setting up industries, building trains, training the military, and influencing the fine arts as well as schooling. Since 1613 Christianity had been proscribed in Japan, and only in 1873 was this anti-Christian policy abolished under diplomatic pressure, opening Japan up for Christian missionaries. Thus, Westernization and Christianization became two central aspects of the modernization of Japan, as Christianity at first was associated with scientific and technical progress by Japanese intellectuals. While Buddhists mobilized against Christianity, they were also stimulated to reform Buddhism, and this resulted in a renewal of Buddhism (*shin bukyō*), 'formed in an intellectual climate in which the West was recognized as both model and measure of modernity' (Snodgrass 2003, 115).

The accelerated introduction of Western knowledge and experts in the 1860s and 1870s was stopped by a comeback of Japanese values. As Thelle states, '[t]he trend towards Westernization in the mid-1880s which had brought about an almost wholesale rejection of Japanese traditions was inevitably followed by a nationalistic reaction favorable to Buddhism and indigenous religions and disastrous for Christianity' (Thelle 1987, 95-96). In this context, Christianity was now regarded as a foreign superstition and unpatriotic. Japanese Buddhists could rely on a long identification between the state and religion, and, after the end of the Tokugawa period and the rule of the samurai, they had transferred their loyalty to the Meiji state and its nationalism. Christians, most of whom had come from the samurai class, were loyal to the Japanese state, too, but had to fend off the smell of Western influence. After the change of attitude to Western ideas and knowledge, Japanese theologians – mostly Protestants – searched for ways of expressing Japanese Christianity and Japanese Theology independently from the West and in harmony with Japanese national values. At the same time, after the rejection by Christians of Buddhism in the 1860s and 1870s, together with a new sense of nationalism, a new interest in Buddhism also developed and led theologians to attempt to harmonize Christianity with Buddhism, in the sense of 'a Zen-flavoured Christianity' or 'an elegant Zen-like simplicity' (Thelle 1987, 176). According to Thelle, '[t]he interest in Zen was perhaps not surprising, considering that Christians of samurai background...were not entirely unfamiliar with Zen spirituality' (Thelle 1987, 176).

Very influential was Hoshino Tenchi (1862-1950, by birth Hoshino Shinnosuke), who first became a Calvinist Christian and, in his later life, a Roman Catholic. He was not only a writer and calligrapher, but also mastered martial arts. He underwent Zen training in Kenshoji in Kamakura and became a *koji* or lay supporter of Buddhism, by taking *jukai* lay vows or precepts. Lay

Buddhism and non-institutional lay practice (*zaike bukkyō*) was promoted in the Meiji period: 'It was not an unique phenomenon and did not seem to involve great problems, either among Buddhists or Christians' (Thelle 1987, 176). Hoshino recommended Zen training for Christians and especially for pastors. In 1898, another Christian and student of theology by the name of Yoshida Seitarō received three years of Zen training in the Tenryuji in Kyoto. He said he was 'called by God to do so' (Thelle 1987, 176) and later became a prominent pastor in the Protestant Church of Japan (Thelle 1987, 176.)

The relationship between Buddhism and Christianity in Japan of the Meiji era was tinged with political reasoning. In the beginning, the scale turned to Christianity as responsible Japanese citizens felt that, for the wellbeing of the state and its modernization, they had to become Christians (Snodgrass 2003, 123). The modernization of Japan was the agenda dear to their hearts. Japanese Christians, mostly Protestant, lacked sectarian zeal and cultivated a liberal attitude in doctrine (Snodgrass 2003, 193). Nevertheless, at first, missionaries and Japanese Christians used their knowledge of modern science to prove what they saw as the fallacies of the Buddhist worldview (Thelle 1987, 187), and Buddhists defended traditional Buddhist cosmology. But later, the emerging New Buddhism (*shin bukyō)* (Eiichi 2014) turned the tables on Christianity and used the new achievements of science, evolutionism and materialism, as well as arguments from the European enlightenment to criticize Christianity. But there was a kind of overarching framework, a common denominator between Buddhists and Christians: Japanese nationalism. In the 1890s, nationalism became a basis for cooperation for the sake of the nation and doctrinal divergences were radically de-emphasized (Thelle 1986, 172-173). Even at the World Parliament of Religions in 1893 in Chicago, Japanese Christians supported Japanese Buddhists for the sake of national unity (Snodgrass 2003, 191). The cooperation of Christians and Buddhists was based on the mutual conviction of the superiority of their own religion, namely, that their respective religion would finally conquer the other, and this gave each of them a confidence that made dialogue possible (Thelle 1986, 162). Although Japanese Christians were universalists, which should have contradicted nationalism of any kind, at the Chicago Parliament, Christians supported the idea of Japanese Buddhism as the highest development of Buddha's teaching, proof of the intellectual and spiritual superiority of the Japanese people (Snodgrass 2003, 191). The common denominator was the endorsement of Japanese spirit.

This applied especially to those Japanese Christians who practised Zen. Coming from samurai families to practise Zen was not only an appropriation of their inheritance, but also about affirming traditional communal identities: strong family identities, a strong ethnic identity and a nationalistic perspective which was connected with Buddhism. Their understanding of Christianity was a far cry from the orthodoxy of white American Christians, as can be seen in the talks of the Christian representatives at the Chicago Parliament (Snodgrass 2003, 193-194). Japanese Christianity was seen as a non-sectarian, non-heresy hunting culmination of Christianity, which would spread world-wide. At the same time, embracing Christianity in Japan opened up converts to Western values and included an assertion of modernity and the value of the individual. To convert to Christianity, and at the same time maintain family roots and practise Zen were not a given in society, but matters of personal choice and in that sense early types of spiritual wandering (Bochinger, Engelbrecht & Gebhardt 2009).

Twentieth Century Japan: a missionary goes native

As Japanese nationalism grew in the 1920s and 1930s, conflicts between Buddhism and Christianity resurfaced. In 1932, two Roman Catholic Sophia University students in Tokyo refused to participate in a memorial service for the spirits of soldiers killed in action at the Yasukuni Shrine, because they considered it *'communicatio in sacris'*. After an extensive discussion in the Japanese media and a diplomatic controversy, Rome declared that Catholics could participate in non-Christian rituals so long as they did so for reasons of piety rather than religion. Thus, Rome distinguished between acts of a communal nature and personal acts, between religion as a socio-political factor and an individual, spiritual act if you wish. Participation in non-catholic rituals would be considered as 'communicatio in sacris' only if it would be an act of personal spirituality, a decision by the Roman Curia which later became significant also for the young superior of the Jesuits in Japan, Hugo Lassalle.[1]

Lassalle, a descendant of German Huguenots, disembarked in Japan in October 1929. Wounded in World War I and disillusioned after the fall of the German empire, he decided to search for a deeper meaning in life. In 1919, he became a Jesuit. Soon he was appointed by the Superior General to Japan and so he studied Japanese and received a first introduction to Japan from Japanese fellow students at the Jesuit College in Valkenburg in the Netherlands. Arriving on October 3, 1929, he set up a large social project in the slums of Tokyo, and in 1935, at the age of 37, he became the superior of the Jesuits in Japan. Lassalle belonged to a faction in the Roman Catholic Church which was inspired by a rather unknown pope, by today's standards, Benedict XV, who, in his eight years of office (1914-1922), set markers for changes only realized decades afterwards. He appealed for a world-wide disarmament, and supported the League of Nations and the integration of Europe. Regarding church organization, in his Apostolic Letter, *Maximum Illud* (1919), dealing with Catholic mission after World War I, he was critical of nationalism and Eurocentrism and had a clearly antinationalist and anticolonial agenda. For missionaries, he recommended a lifestyle oriented to holiness.[2]

Complying with the papal requirements, Lassalle demanded from himself and his fellow Jesuit missionaries not only to strive for the *unio mystica* but also to become Japanese in mind (Baatz 1998, 111). Years before Vatican II, Lassalle wished to abolish Western-style Christianity for his faithful and instil a way

---

1   The chapters on Hugo M. Enomiya Lassalle draw on Baatz 1998.
2   *Maximum illud* is frequently quoted in *Ad Gentes*, the document of Vatican II about mission.

of Japanese Christianity. As superior of the Jesuits, he ordered the building of a new noviciate in Nagatsuka near Hiroshima in Japanese style. He met intense resistance from his fellow Jesuits and sometimes also from Japanese Christians who were keen on Westernization. Others, however, like Pedro Arrupe, the later Superior General of the Jesuits and at that time responsible for the formation of young Jesuits, were fully in accord with his ideas (Lamet 2014, 177-198). Lassalle's intentions also coincided with the prevalent and mostly Protestant effort to create a Japanese Buddhist-Christian Theology or a 'Christianity with a taste of Zen'. Since for Japanese Christians the Western verbalized style of prayer was not suitable, Lassalle searched for an appropriate way of prayer for his converts. His Japanese academic friends pointed him towards Zen Buddhism, as the nationalist Japanese Zeitgeist underscored the importance of Zen for Japanese culture, even as an incarnation of Japanese spirit.[3] In January 1943, in the midst of World War II, Lassalle participated in a Zen sesshin in Eimyoji, a temple near Hiroshima. He was impressed by the Zen monks' way of life, which resembled his own ascetic Jesuit lifestyle. His conclusion from this experience was that a similar lifestyle implied similar aims, although he was aware of the essential metaphysical differences.

On 6 August 1945, atomic bombing destroyed Hiroshima, where Lassalle had lived since 1939. He survived the attack, and, at the end of the war, initiated the construction of the Memorial Church despite many obstacles. During these stressful years, again and again he took up the impulse of the sesshin of 1943, which helped him to overcome the impact of his difficult situation and to find inner peace and deeper prayer.

On the evening of the inauguration of the church on 6 August 1954, he was told that somebody else besides him would become the new parish priest. Thus, unable to pursue his search for a Japanese Christianity as parish priest and pastor (*Seelsorg-*

---

3   According to Suzuki and the Kyoto school, Zen was 1) the essence of Japanese culture, 2) the essence of Buddhism and 3) at the heart of all religions (Sharf 1995).

er), he finally considered turning to Zen practice as a means for deepening the prayer of Japanese Christians. And so, in the fall of 1956, he became a student of Harada Sogaku Roshi, then one of the most renowned Zen roshis, and delved deeply into the practice of Zen, while also working as chaplain and teacher at Hiroshima Elisabeth College. In 1960, he published his first book with the title, *Zen – Way to Enlightenment*, in which he explained that Zen was a means for deepening Christian prayer. The book was well-received initially, but soon afterwards it was censored. Were it not for Vatican II, this would have been the end of Hugo M. Enomiya-Lassalle's attempts. However, the Council's declaration 'Nostra Aetate' opened the way for a deep encounter with other religions. After some small changes, therefore, a second edition of the book was printed and was translated into European and Asian languages. As early as April 1957, Lassalle had considered founding a catholic Zen monastery for Japanese Christians. This impulse was repeatedly modified and finally resulted in the retreat house, Shinmeikutsu, first established near Hiroshima and, in 1969, near Tokyo.

These years, however, were also repeatedly marked by his fellow Jesuits attempting to set firm boundaries against Lassalle's plans, for example, through arguing that Zen would risk a relapse into paganism among the Japanese Christians; and were it not for the support of Pedro Arrupe, his chaplain during the 1940s and now his superior, Lassalle would certainly not have been able to pursue his project.[4] In 1978, Lassalle was finally appointed as a Zen teacher by Yamada Kôun Roshi (1907-1989), the Zen-grandson of Harada Sogaku.

By this time, however, the stage had already shifted; by 1968 Lassalle was already spending more and more time in Europe teaching Zen to European Christians and former Christians in his notoriously overbooked sesshins.

---

4   For the relation of Lassalle and Arrupe, see also 'Enomiya-Lassalle SJ pionero del zen entre Christianos con el apoyo de Pedro Arrupe SJ'. In Enomiya-Lassalle 2015, 142.

Twentieth Century, Europe and USA: Merton, a spiritual wanderer

In February 1933, a young British student by the name of Thomas Merton, a professed agnostic, was travelling through Italy. When in a Trappist monastery in Rome, he suddenly experienced a deep moment of silence, which eventually would lead him to enter the order of Trappists. In 1937, Merton graduated from Columbia University and was fascinated by Aldous Huxley's *Of Ends and Means*, where Eastern mysticism is referred to as a solution for the ills of modern society. A year later, he was advised to study the Christian mystical tradition by Mahanambrata Brahmachari (1904-1999), a Hindu monk from Bengal. In the fall of that year, Merton received baptism and eventually, in 1942, became a Trappist monk at Gethsemani Abbey in the US state of Kentucky. A successful and prolific spiritual author, he had a great interest in other spiritual traditions, especially Eastern Christianity, and, in 1959, also engaged in dialogue with D.T. Suzuki (Daggy 1988). His 'Asian Journal' of 1968 further records his travels in Asia and even that he considered himself a Buddhist.

Although Merton belongs to the great-grandfather generation of today's young people – he was born in 1915 and died in 1968 – his journey from being agnostic to a Trappist monk to a Christian with a Buddhist leaning very much resembles the contemporary religious biographies of the spiritual wanderer, a type characteristic of contemporary religiosity, according to research from a large survey in Germany (Bochinger, Engelbrecht & Gebhardt 2009). Merton himself considered his life a spiritual journey in search of true identity or the true self, which according to him and in Christian terms was nothing other than God. As Carr stated, 'From the young, self-negating and world-denying monk of 1949 to the mature self-affirming and world-embracing Asian traveller and seeker of 1968, there is striking change as well as deep continuity in the search for the true self' (Carr 1988, 9). Merton considered his life as a journey into the unknown, a continuous conversion until the very end.

This search was inextricably linked to the practice and notion of contemplation, and by 'contemplation' Merton meant not *meditatio* but *contemplatio*, as he said, 'Contemplation goes beyond concepts and apprehends God not as a separate object but as the Reality within our reality, the Being within our being, the life of our life' (Merton 1962a, 19). Pointing out the difference between meditation and contemplation, he wrote:

> Contemplation is not vision, because it sees 'without seeing' and knows 'without knowing'. It is a more profound depth of faith, knowledge too deep to be grasped in images, in words or even in clear concepts. It can be suggested by works, by symbols, but in the very moment of trying to indicate what it knows the contemplative mind takes back what it has said and denies what it has affirmed. For in contemplation we know by 'unknowing'. Or, better, we know beyond all knowing or 'unknowing'. (Merton 1962b, 1)

The fact that life as a Trappist was not ultimately satisfying for Merton was not due to the rather harsh conditions in the abbey of Gethsemani but because Gethsemani was a contemplative order without contemplative practice. He criticized that a day in the monastery left almost no space for quiet prayer: 'I thought that contemplative life is more that many hours in church and other places' (Merton 1948, 395). Further, Merton was fascinated by John of the Cross and his mystical theology, but talk about mystical experiences or spiritual 'peak experiences' was not well-received among his fellow monks. His book, *Ascent to Truth,* on the teachings of John of the Cross, which was published in 1951 but initiated as a project in 1947, can certainly be seen as a reaction to the neglect of contemplation and an attempt to make contemplation accessible to his contemporaries.

In 1945, Huxley published his highly influential book *Perennial Philosophy*, which kindled widespread interest in the world's mystical traditions. In its wake, the resultant search for non-dual experience (i.e. mysticism) also connected to a youth movement critical of the establishment and consumerism. The title of Alan Watts's book of 1947, *Behold the Spirit: A Study in the Necessity of Mystical Religion,* is characteristic of the atmosphere of that time. Watts was closely related to Zen Buddhism himself, having married the daughter of Ruth Fuller Sasaki, and was highly influenced by D.T. Suzuki's interpretation of Zen Buddhism as universal and ahistorical but nevertheless Japanese.

Zen Buddhism was an important template of counter culturalism, and people such as John Cage and Jack Kerouac, as well as D.T. Suzuki's lectures at the Columbia University 1952-1957, were formative influences for an entire generation. Merton's first contact with Zen dates back to the late forties or early fifties, when a visitor to the monastery lectured about his time in a Zen monastery in Hawai'i, a fact which is mentioned by Merton in his book, *The Sign of Jonas* (1953).

While Merton was working on his *Wisdom of the Desert Fathers* (1960), he started to correspond with Suzuki, asking him about Zen and sending some quotes of the monks of the fourth century. He also asked Suzuki for an introduction. Suzuki's text was later published in *Zen and the Birds of Appetite* (1968).[5]

It was Merton's old interest in experiences of the absolute, unity and other outstanding words and concepts that was fed in reading books on oriental mysticism under the influence of Huxley. Merton understood Zen to be direct experience of the absolute, as a theist he would say direct experience of God. Such experience, for him, engendered a wholeness which allowed one to see in the most mundane events and objects flashes of the Universal (Thurston 2007, 2). At the same time, he also criticized Christianity for being enslaved by images and ideas of Christ which were human creations and projections that stood in the way of God's freedom. He wrote to Suzuki, 'Christ himself is in us as unknown and unseen. We follow him, we find him, and then he must vanish and we have to go along without him on our side. Why? Because he is even closer than that. He is our self'(Pramuk 2009, 134).

---

5   An overview of the correspondence between Merton and Suzuki can be found at http://merton.org/Research/Correspondence/y1.aspx?id=1947

Paradigmatic changes

Motivations

Both Merton and Lassalle acted under the auspices of globalization. Both were critical of Western superiority and colonialism. Both were aware of the dangers of the Cold War and nuclear proliferation and worked for a peaceful and just future for humankind. Both were critical of consumerism, Merton much more outspokenly than Lassalle. And for both, Hugo Lassalle and Thomas Merton, the Second Vatican Council was the marker of a change in policies of the Roman Catholic church, which released new horizons in many a way. Not only did the documents 'Nostra Aetate' and 'Ad Gentes' open the space for a deep encounter with other religions – for Merton and Lassalle the encounter with Buddhism – but also religious freedom was granted in 'Humani Generis'. According to these documents, Christians could find truth – 'sparks of truth' – in other religions and even in atheism. It was a 180-degree turnaround of the politics of the Roman Catholic Church with respect to other religions.

For Merton it granted sufficient space to follow his leanings to 'be *completely open* to the modern world while retaining the clearly defined, traditionally Catholic position' (Merton 1966, 316). The intellectual encounter with Zen and Buddhism contributed to the fermentation or transformation of Merton as a critical intellectual, who engaged in the anti-racist and anti-war movement. At the same time, he was, as a contemplative, critical of the loss of the contemplative dimension in Christianity, finding new impulses from Buddhist realms (Merton 1951, 491; 1973). Merton's last talk was at the meeting of the Monastic Superiors of the Far East in Bangkok in 1968, later published as 'Marxism and Monasticism' (Merton 1973, 326-343). Lassalle attended the talk, but he was unable to meet Merton in person, since Merton died that evening.

Merton's journey was a typical twentieth century, western, personal story of spiritual quest and transformation, although as a Trappist monk he followed a lifestyle rather untypical for people of his cultural milieu and peer group. Lassalle, however, seventeen years older than Merton, had a slightly different motivation. Having been educated in the framework of nineteenth century German and Jesuit Catholicism, he was nevertheless critical of a Eurocentric Christianity and attempted to identify with Japanese culture. His interest and participation in Zen practice was initially due to his search for an appropriate Japanese style of prayer. Whereas Merton was searching on a very personal and informal level, for Lassalle one strand of motivation for his engagement in Zen practice was to become a legitimate Zen teacher in order to be able to teach Zen in legitimate ways. This both inspired his personal practice as a Jesuit and implemented overall changes in Christian spiritual practice.

A personal journey for paradigmatic change

As a young novice, Lassalle had a deep spiritual experience, which he claimed was deeper than anything he ever experienced in Zen. This is mentioned just once in his diaries (3 March 1973, in Baatz 1998, 42). As a consequence of this experience, his whole life was dedicated to becoming a saint, namely, to surrender to God whatever the cost. His spiritual guide during tertianship, Louis Poullier (1865-1940), had insisted that to be a Christian meant to pursue holiness and the experience of God, including a way of life that accorded to that experience. He introduced Lassalle to the writings of the Spanish mystics, especially to the teachings of John of the Cross. Lassalle realized from the very beginning of his Zen practice that Zen was somehow similar and helpful for this endeavour.

A second motivation concerned his commitment as a priest and a Jesuit 'to care for the people's soul'. As early as 1947, when he was travelling through a Germany devastated by the war, Lassalle had realized that people were no longer interested in rational proofs of God's existence, which was one traditional type of catechesis. Just like Rahner or Merton, he thought that it was important for Christians, and especially priests and nuns, to experience God personally and on a deeper level (thus arguing in accordance with the popular idea of mystical religion).

Zen practice, for Lassalle, was a way for everybody who was willing to become involved. Lassalle referred to Zen practice as '*ungegenständliche Meditation*', a non-representational meditation, in order to stress that it was different from traditional 'meditation', namely rumination. Non-representational stood for a practice without mental objects of concentration, such as images, concepts or biblical references, pointing to '*contemplatio*', a key term in the spirituality of John of the Cross.

In the beginning, Lassalle saw Zen practice as a 'natural practice' (Enomiya-Lassalle 1960), 'natural' referring to a widespread image in nineteenth century Catholic theology, of the two floors, a lower one, the physical and human world, and a higher one, God's grace, which was qualified as 'supernatural'. Since the mental image provided no stairway connecting the two realms, grace could only interrupt into the 'natural', physical, human world (Greshake 1977). Later on, Lassalle ceased to use this dichotomy and instead emphasized Zen as a way to mystical experience, interpreted according to one's respective personal biography and worldview (Lassalle in Baatz 1998, 336). A Christian would experience God, but not necessarily as personal: 'humans alone, not God, draw borders', he wrote in 1977 to Reverend Martin in Karachi (Baatz 1998, 396).

To become a saint, one of the major features of Christian spiritual practice was traditionally mortification of the senses. One crisp winter morning in December 1957, Lassalle found his view of Christian spiritual practice was altered fundamentally. He was riding his motorbike. Suddenly he experienced the cold of the winter as a great pleasure instead of a kind of mortification, which had been his attitude so far. He attributed this sensation to his Zen practice, since nature is better enjoyed with an empty mind, as he noted in his diary.[6]

---

6   'In this frosty, foggy, frost-bound landscape, it was a true pleasure to me. Perhaps the *zazen* has something to do with it. When the mind is empty, one can better enjoy nature. One feels oneself somehow at one with nature. If

A few weeks later, he found in a book by the English devotional writer, Richard Rolle, (*c*.1290-1349) advice which inspired him to shift his focus from renounciation to an 'inner awareness of the perfect' and union with God.[7] The traditional precepts for a Christian spiritual life often involved and involve subduing the senses, since sensual pleasure can be seen as a distraction. Lassalle`s shift in his conception of Christian spirituality was far-reaching: traditional Christian mortification aimed to subdue the senses, whereas Zen practice aimed to transform them. In the Platform Sutra, the Sixth Patriarch, Hui Neng, repeatedly points to the transformation of the physical body and the senses (e.g. Yampolsky 143, 158).

The question of God

During his tertianship, Lassalle received a thorough spiritual training in the Spanish mystics, but his theological training was neo-scholastic and thus focussed more on rational arguments about God rather than apophatic theology. Soon after Lassalle resumed his intensive Zen practice, he realized the inconceivability of God and the inadequateness of neo-scholastic theology in this respect. In these early years of his Zen practice, Merton's *Ascent to Truth* (1951) was crucial for Lassalle, as Merton's account of St. John of the Cross assured him that he was on the right way.

Nowadays accurate information on Buddhism and Zen is widely available, but in Lassalle's times he had to rely on what monks in charge at the monasteries told beginners. While he never considered Buddhism a form of atheism, at first he thought of Buddhism as a kind of monism. While immersing himself more and more into Zen practice, he studied the writings of the Christian mystics available to him through the libraries of Jesuit

---

there were no wickedness in mankind, one might be happy and content with this reality.' Diary entry, 13 December 1957, in Baatz 1998, 264.

7   Following Rolle's example, he was looking for 'inner mindfulness toward perfection, and, if possible, a union with God in the heart.' Diary entry, 27 December 1957, in Baatz 1998, 264.

institutions. He increasingly was able to behold the striking parallels between both traditions, which was especially true for the advice of John of the Cross, 'do not hate anything, do not desire anything, do not worry about anything in your heart, do not mourn about anything', and that of Dogen, 'hope for nothing, fear nothing, persist neither in joy over anything nor in sadness over anything'.[8] However, it took him many more years to find that the kōan '*mu*' referred to Buddha-nature and that 'mu' and God were 'on one line' experientially, as he was able to state in June 1973 (Baatz 1998, 358). Soon after Lassalle's *kensho* (Zen experience of enlightenment) was affirmed by Yamada Roshi and when he had completed his kōan training, Yamada Roshi gave him permission to teach in 1978.

Why can Christians practise Zen?

Lassalle did not adhere to the notion of Huxley's 'perennial wisdom'.[9] Instead, he followed the idea of a 'natural mysticism' that could be found in all religions, including Christian mysticism, which distinguished itself only through the 'supernatural' dimension of Christian faith. The theory of 'natural mysticism' originally emerged through the encounter of Christian theologians and thinkers with non-Christian mysticism through colonialism (Baier 2009, 570-581). It became clear that there was a strong resemblance between the mystical experiences of Christians and non-Christians, which resulted in the theological distinction between 'natural' and 'supernatural' mysticism. Thus, a more ecumenical approach to non-Christian religions gained support among academic theologians, a tradition that would later serve as background for *Nostra Aetate*,[10] which became essential

---

8   'Nichts hoffen, nichts fürchten, in nichts in Freude ausruhen, über nichts traurig sein.' Diary entry, November 10, 1954, in Baatz 1998, 227.

9   The idea of a universal truth as the basis for all religious knowledge. Aldous Huxley, *The Perennial Philosophy* (New York: Harper, 1945).

10   According to this theory, developed from an initial impulse by French scholar Joseph Marordin, S.J.'s (1878-1944) essay of 1908-1909, humans have

to Lassalle's work, since it enabled him to continue with his project even though his Japanese superiors often attempted to block his efforts.

The fact that Yamada, the 'great-grandson' of Harada Daiun Sogaku Roshi (1871-1961) granted Lassalle, a Catholic and a Jesuit priest, permission to teach Zen was a singular and historical event, a complete novelty. Yamada was free to do so, since he was not part of a monastic tradition but head of the lay Zen group, Sanbokyodan, founded by Haku'un Yasutani Roshi (1885-1973), dharma-heir to Harada Sogaku, in 1954 after disrobing as a Soto-monk. Through the lens of traditional monastic Zen, however, this move was certainly illegitimate.

Both of them, Lassalle and Yamada, regarded their faith as absolute, but they were also able to allow within them a place for the core values of other religions. While Lassalle believed that it was possible for everyone to attain mystical experiences and that Zen was a means to this, Yamada Roshi repeatedly affirmed that 'the experience of enlightenment is like a cup of tea, it tastes alike for everybody',[11] an affirmation of the universality of Zen rooted in its nationalistic interpretation. Moreover, both men also had witnessed the terrors of war as soldiers and believed that a practice such as Zen, with its emphasis on selflessness rather than individual interest, would be able to make a lasting contribution to the realization of world peace.

Throughout the 1980s, Yamada also permitted many other Christians to teach Zen. Neither Lassalle nor any of the other

---

an inherent ability to have mystical experiences of God, according to Paul's letter to the Romans (1:20); Christianity, however, also features a 'supernatural' revelation—the eruption into the world of God's revelation through Christ.

11 Yamada Kōun, 'Za-Zen und Christentum', in Baatz 1998, 365. The view that 'Zen is at the heart of all religions' stems from a nationalist interpretation of Zen Buddhism, represented by teachers like D.T. Suzuki as well as the Japanese Kyoto School. Cf. Robert Sharf, 'Whose Zen? Zen Nationalism Revisited', in *Rude Awakenings: Zen, the Kyoto School, and the Question of Nationalism*, eds. James W. Heisig and John Maraldo, Nanzan Studies in Religion and Culture. Honolulu: University of Hawai'i Press, 1995, 40-51.

Christians whom Yamada authorized to teach had to perform *ju-kai* (taking precepts)[12] or accept other Zen Buddhist priestly tasks usually connected with the teaching permission (Baatz 2017a, 341). Yamada, however, maintained the traditional language of Zen for training Western Christians. Lassalle once inquired whether it would be appropriate if he himself or Yamada as well would use Christian terms for teaching Zen to Christians, but Yamada refused to do so. Later, Yamada emphasized that he had transmitted Zen to Christians and that now it was their turn to find the meaning of Zen in Christianity (Baatz 1998, 398). This is a yet unresolved task.

Unresolved tasks – different interpretations

In the first generation of Christian Zen teachers there were different attempts to comply with Yamada's order. Collectively, the following two positions become apparent:

1. The perennialist position (Huxley): Zen is seen as the universal timeless wisdom, which is (a) a gift to Christians who can do with it what they want; or (b) Zen is the universal timeless wisdom, the peak of the development of human consciousness and trans-religious.

Both these views within this first position argue with stereotypes (East = spiritual, West = rational, etc.), which are characteristic of orientalist views, or as Snodgrass argues 'occidentalist' views (Snodgrass 2003, 273), as Japanese Buddhists took up these notions of alterity to revitalize Buddhism in their country. *Shin bukyō* used Western arguments to bolster their position in Japan, for example, claiming that the new Buddhism was a scientific religion (Snodgrass 2003, 211). Perennialists took up not only the nationalistic view of Zen as 'the heart of all religions' but also the idea of Buddhism as scientific. No wonder that some,

---

12 *Jukai* is similar to baptism *and* is compulsory for a monastic Zen career, but *koji* (lay) Buddhists can take jukai also.

Willigis Jäger for example, confounded Zen and a position resembling Haeckel's scientific religion (Monists), constructing Zen as 'trans-religious'. Another feature of a perennialist interpretation of Zen is that the Buddhist tradition is not considered as relevant, because either Zen is seen as 'trans-religious' or as 'a gift' (Baatz 2009, 109-142).

2. Religion is seen as a kind of language (Panikkar). This position regards Zen and Christianity alike as languages in a Wittgensteinian sense, as 'language games' referring to and including forms of life. Therefore, Buddhist traditions are as relevant as Christian traditions. Typically, the representatives of this position are multilingual, and multiculturally socialized, as well as interested in intellectual theological reflections on their position (Baatz 2009, 195-203). Ruben Habito's critical remark vis-à-vis Yamada Koun Roshi, that tea tastes differently to different people according to their habits underscores this position (Habito 1986, 190-191).

Within both of these, a thorough theoretical/theological and comparative reflection would be desirable, but is largely missing.

What do Christians find in Zen? Some sweeping assumptions

For centuries in Europe, religion was part of one's destiny. However, this is no longer so, at least for most European countries, and especially in West and Central Europe. Everybody has to follow the 'heretical imperative' (Berger 1979) and choose the religious perspective. There is no such thing as 'cults' that are controlled by the government, and the guarantees of freedom of religion and freedom of expression enable people to follow their own personal, spiritual quest without forcing them into compulsory religious identities. The end of the established state church is the context in which Zen has become relevant for Christians.

In 1215, the Fourth Lateran Council made compulsory an annual confession during Easter. Confession at that time had already developed from a once-in-a-lifetime event to a regular, individualistic shrift with tariffs. The introduction of compulsory confession was not least due to an attempt to curtail heretical movements within the church and to regain control over spiritual movements. In the long run, the importance of confession steadily increased and Christian spiritual life was transformed. As Karl Baier has demonstrated in his groundbreaking study, *Meditation und Moderne* (2009), one of the consequences of such emphasis on confession was the tendency to also emphasize imaginative and catechetical instruction over contemplation. Moreover, the increasing importance of confession also held political significance, given the intermingled relationship of 'altar and throne', Church and State, which were the two ruling forces supporting each other, as elucidated by the critical thinkers of the Enlightenment.

In contrast to catechetical instruction, contemplation aims at that which is beyond thinking and emotions. Its imperative is 'nada, nada', as John of the Cross advises, a dimension of no object or subject for which the Christian tradition often uses paradox-metaphors such as 'cloud of unknowing' or 'dark light' to express its quality. The appropriate theological mode of reflection would be apophatic or negative theology. Different to Buddhism, contemplation never became a normative experience in Christianity. There was even a growing resistance against it – John of the Cross and Teresa of Avila both ran into problems with the Inquisition. The last blow to contemplation was the quietist controversy at the end of the seventeenth century (1680), which found its end with the condemnation of the priority of contemplation over meditation by Pope Innocent XI in 1687. Thus, the conceptual, imaginative and verbal became predominant, and mysticism remained suspect up until the middle of the twentieth century. To support personal mystical experiences was even a reason for prosecution as 'modernist' (as in the case of the Jesuit George Tyrell). Vatican II initiated a thorough change in this respect, as the 'anti-modernist oath' required from theologians since 1910, was abolished in 1967.

Within this context, Lassalle's contribution cannot be underestimated. His books paved the way for a renaissance of mysticism in Christianity. He and Merton saw the fundamental change taking place in the Roman Catholic Church of today. Thomas Merton wrote: 'At present the Church is outgrowing what one might call the Carolingian suggestion. This is a world view which was rooted in the official acceptance of the Church into the world of imperial Rome, the world of Constantine and of Augustine, of Charlemagne in the west and of Byzantium in the east' (Merton 1966). Lassalle in a very similar way emphasized that the Church had to undergo a thorough change inspired by the mystical experience of Christ (Enomiya-Lassalle 1984, 180).

Today, nearly all Catholic institutional education houses (*Bildungshäuser*) offer courses in mysticism, meditation and sometimes even contemplation. Since the 1960s, more and more of the classical mystical texts have been reprinted and found interested readers. Not all but much of this has happened as a result of Lassalle's lasting influence.

Perhaps most significant for these changes is the meditation bench, which was invented around 1960 by Japanese Zen Masters for lay practitioners and introduced to the West through Lassalle in 1961 (Baatz 1998, 287). It is a significant piece of furniture, since it demonstrates a change in Christian spiritual practices. Today it can be found in many Christian educational institutions as well as in monasteries.

These changes happened despite resistance and attempted suppression from clerical institutions. Maybe this is also the reason why there is almost no proper theological reflection. Lassalle's work was made possible by a narrow window of opportunity, between 1962, when the Second Vatican Council began to liberalize Catholicism's relationship with other faiths, and the late 1970s, with the election of a conservative pope, John Paul II (r. 1978-2005), and the onset of the Islamic Revolution in Iran. Much earlier or much later and Lassalle's achievements would not have been possible.

Bibliography

Ando, Clifford & Jörg Rüpke, eds., 2012. *Religion and Law in Classical and Christian Rome*. Stuttgart: Franz Steiner.

Baatz, Ursula, 1998. *Hugo M. Enomiya-Lassalle: Ein Leben zwischen den Welten*. Zurich: Benziger Verlag.

Baatz, Ursula, 2009. *Erleuchtung trifft Auferstehung. Zen-Buddhismus und Christentum. Eine Orientierung*. Berlin: Theseus. 2009.

Baatz, Ursula, 2017a. 'Hugo M. Enomiya-Lassalle. Zen and Christianity'. In *A Companion to Jesuit Mysticism*, ed. Robert A. Maryks. Leiden: Brill: 335-357.

Baatz, Ursula, 2017b. *Spiritualität, Religion, Weltanschauung. Landkarten für systemisches Arbeiten*. Göttingen: Vandenhoek & Ruprecht.

Baier, Karl, 2009. *Meditation und Moderne: Zur Genese eines Kernbereichs moderner Spiritualität in der Wechselwirkung zwischen Westeuropa, Nordamerika und Asien*, 2 vols. Würzburg: Königshausen & Neumann.

Berger, Peter L., 1979. *The Heretical Imperative, Contemporary Possibilities of Religious Affirmations*. New York: Doubleday.

Bochinger, Christoph, Martin Engelbrecht & Winfried Gebhardt, 2009. *Die unsichtbare Religion in der sichtbaren Religion. Formen spiritueller Orientierung in der religiösen Gegenwartskultur*. Stuttgart: Kohlhammer.

Carr, Anne E., 1988. *A Search for Wisdom and Spirit: Thomas Merton's Theology of the Self*. South Bend: University of Notre Dame Press.

Daggy, Robert E., ed., 1988. *Encounter: Thomas Merton and D.T. Suzuki*. Monterey, KY: Larkspur Press.

DePalma Digeser, Elizabeth, 2006. 'Religion, Law and the Roman Polity: The Era of the Great Persecution'. In *Religion and Law in Classical and Christian Rome*, eds. Clifford Ando & Jörg Rüpke. Stuttgart: Franz Steiner: 68-84.

Dunne, John, 1972. *The Way of All the Earth: Experiments in truth and religion*, New York: Macmillan.

Enomiya-Lassalle, Hugo M., 1960. *Zen-Weg zur Erleuchtung.* Wien: Herder.

Enomiya-Lassalle, Hugo M., 1966. *Zen-Buddhismus.* Köln: Bachem.

Enomiya-Lassalle, Hugo M., 1968. *Zen-Meditation für Christen.* München: O.W. Barth.

Enomiya-Lassalle, Hugo M., 1972. *Meditation als Weg zur Gotteserfahrung.* Köln: Bachem.

Enomiya-Lassalle, Hugo M., 1975. *Zazen und die Exerzitien des heiligen Ignatius. Einübung in das wahre Dasein.* Köln: Bachem.

Enomiya-Lassalle, Hugo M., 1984. *Am Morgen einer besseren Welt.* Freiburg: Herder.

Enomiya-Lassalle, Hugo M., 2015 (1947). *Hiroshima.* Brihuega, Guadalajara: Fundacion Zendo Betania.

Enomiya-Lassalle, Hugo M., 2016 (1974). *Zen unter Christen. Östliche Meditation und christliche Spiritualität.* Graz: Styria.

Finger, Evelyn, 2016. 'Achtung Umarmung!'. In *Die Zeit,* 46/2016, https://www.zeit.de/2016/46/ papst-franziskus-besuch-schweden-deutschland-oekumene (26.11.2018).

Finger, Evelyn, 2017. 'Feuer im Herzen'. In *Die Zeit,* 2017, https://www.zeit.de/2017/07/ kirchenspaltung-protestanten-vatikan-papst-franziskus-treffen (26.11.2018).

Greshake, Gisbert, 1977. *Geschenkte Freiheit. Einführung in die Gnadenlehre.* Freiburg: Herder.

Grosshans, Hans-Peter, Samuel Ngun Ling & Perry Schmidt-Leukel, eds., 2017. *Buddhist and Christian Attitudes to Religious Diversity.* Yangon: Ling's Family Publications.

Habito, Ruben, 1986. 'Total Liberation, Zen Spirituality and the Social Dimension'. In Ruben Habito & Elaine McInnes, *The Zen Experience in a Philippine Context.* Angeles City: Pima Press.

Hadot, Pierre, 1999. *Wege zur Weisheit – oder: Was lehrt uns die antike Philosophie?* Frankfurt am Main: Eichborn.

Hense, Elisabeth, 2011. 'The Quest for interdisciplinary Theories on Spirituality'. In *Towards a Theory of Spirituality,* eds. Elisabeth Hense & Franz Maas. Leiden: Peeters: 5-14.

Huxley, Aldous, 1937. *Ends and Means: An Enquiry into the Nature of Ideals and into the Methods Employed for their Realization*. London: Chatto & Windus.

Huxley, Aldous, 1946. *Perennial Philosophy*. New York: Harper.

Kasimow, Harold, John P. Keenan & Linda Klepinger Keenan, eds., 2003. *Beside Still Waters: Jews, Christians, and the Way of the Buddha*. Somerville, MA: Wisdom Publication.

Kippenberg, Hans G., & Kocku von Stuckrad, 2003. *Einführung in die Religionswissenschaft: Gegenstände und Begriffe*. München: C.H. Beck.

Lactantius, 2011. *Divine Institutes*, transls. and eds., Anthony Bowen & Peter Garnsey. Liverpool: Liverpool University Press.

Lamet, Pedro Miguel, 2016^2. *Arrupe. Testigo del siglo XX, profeta del XXI*. Bilbao: Mensajero.

Livius, Titus, 1957. *Ab urbe condita libri*, Engl: *Livy: with an English translation*, in fourteen volumes. Cambridge, MA: Harvard University Press.

Merton, Thomas, 1948. *The Seven Storey Mountain*. New York: Harcourt & Brace.

Merton, Thomas, 1951. *The Ascent to Truth*. New York: Harcourt & Brace.

Merton, Thomas, 1953. *The Sign of Jonas*. New York: Harcourt & Brace.

Merton, Thomas, 1960. *The Wisdom of the Desert, Sayings from the Desert Fathers from the Fourth Century*. New York: Laughlin.

Merton, Thomas, 1962a. *The New Man*. London: Burns & Oates.

Merton, Thomas, 1962b. *New Seeds of Contemplation*. New York: New Directions.

Merton, Thomas, 1966. 'Is the World a Problem?' *Commonweal-magazine*, New York. bhttps://www.commonwealmagazine.org/world-problem (26.11.2018).

Merton. Thomas. 1968. *Zen and the Birds of Appetite*. New York: New Directions.

Merton, Thomas, 1973. *The Asian Journal*, ed. Naomi Burton, Brother Patrick Hart & James Laughlin. New York: New Directions.

Ōtani, Eiichi, 2014. 'The Movement called "New Buddhism" in Meiji Japan'. In *Modern Buddhism in Japan*, eds. Makoto Hayashi, Eiichi Ōtani & Paul L. Swanson. Nagoya: Nanzan Institute for Religion and Culture: 52-85.

Pramuk, Christopher, 2009. *Sophia: The Hidden Christ of Thomas Merton*. Collegeville, MN: Liturgical Press.

Schmücker, Marcus & Fabian Heubel, eds., 2013. *Dimensionen der Selbstkultivierung, Beiträge des Forums für Asiatische Philosophie*, Freiburg & München: Alber.

Sharf, Robert, 1995. 'Whose Zen? Zen Nationalism Revisited'. In *Rude Awakenings: Zen, the Kyoto School, and the Question of Nationalism*, Nanzan Studies in Religion and Culture, eds. James W. Heisig & John Maraldo. Honolulu: University of Hawai'i Press: 40-51.

Snodgrass Judith, 2003. *Presenting Japanese Buddhism to the West*. Chapel Hill: The University of North Carolina Press.

Suzuki, D.T. 1957. *Mysticism. Christian and Buddhist*. London: Allen & Unwin.

Thelle, Notto R., 1987. *Buddhism and Christianity in Japan: From Conflict to Dialogue (1854-1899)*. Honolulu: University of Hawai'i Press.

Thurston, Bonnie Bowman, ed., 2007. *Merton and Buddhism: Wisdom, Emptiness and Everyday Mind.* Louisville, KY: Fons Vitae.

Watts, Alan, 1947. *Behold the Spirit. A Study in the Necessity of Mystical Religion*. London, Murray.

Woodhead, Linda, 2011. 'Five types of religion'. *International Review of Sociology* 2: 121-143.

Yampolsky, Philip B., 1967. *The Platform Sutra of the Sixth Patriarch, the Text of the Tun Huang Manuscript*. New York: Columbia University Press.

Why Buddhists Taught Zen Meditation to Christians?[1]

Robert Sharf

Abstract

Zen is a large monastic organization in modern Japan, comprising some 60 training monasteries, 21,000 temples, and 24,000 ordained clergy. But only a handful of Zen priests have been actively involved in training Christians, and they have tended to be reformers or lay teachers who left the traditional (Rinzai, Sōtō) monastic organizations altogether. This chapter focusses on who these Zen teachers were, the specific form of Zen practice they were transmitting, and the significance of their teachings on how Zen has come to be understood and practised by Christians.

Keywords: proselytizing, Nishitani Keiji, Thomas Keating, Sasaki Jōshū, Rinzai, *Sanbōkyōdan* (Three Treasures Association), *kōan*, Yamada Kōun, Robert Kennedy, spiritual technology, consciousness, *satipaṭṭhāna*, *vipassanā*, Critical Buddhism

---

1 This chapter was originally written for the conference, 'Meditation in Buddhist-Christian Encounter: A Critical Analysis', sponsored by the European Network of Buddhist Christian Studies and held at Montserrat Monastery on 29 June to 8 August 2017. My thanks to the organisers and participants of that conference for their helpful feedback on my presentation. Thanks also to Joseph O'Leary, Elizabeth Horton Sharf, and Evan Thompson for their astute suggestions on earlier drafts. Note that this short chapter draws on my previously published work, spanning some two decades, on Chan/Zen Buddhism and its transmission to the West (see bibliography).

Introduction

In approaching my assigned topic, 'Why Buddhists Taught Zen Meditation to Christians', I will start with what should be obvious but is sometimes overlooked or misconstrued. Buddhists taught Zen meditation to Christians because Buddhism is a missionary religion that deems itself in possession of a singular, universal and salvific truth. In Mahāyāna Buddhism, which is the tradition found in East Asia, the bodhisattva ideal demands that one places the salvation of others above oneself, and this entails, first and foremost, spreading the Buddha's dharma. But the evangelical orientation of the tradition dates back much earlier than the rise of Mahāyāna; it is evident in our earliest textual sources, in which the Buddha enjoins his monks to adopt an itinerant lifestyle so as to better disseminate his teachings. At the same time, the monks are given dispensation to preach the Buddha's word in the local vernacular, so as to make his teachings accessible to all.[2] Buddhism's early spread was aided and abetted by the patronage of a powerful emperor, Aśoka, who placed religious ideology (dhamma) in service of his political agenda: promoting a pacifist religious message would presumably help to quell unrest in his new empire (Aśoka's role in the early dissemination of Buddhism is, in some respects, comparable to that of Constantine in the spread of Christianity).

Proselytizing in Buddhism

Accordingly, it should not be news that Zen teachers consider proselytizing and conversion (Chinese: *jiaohua* 教化, Japanese: *kyōke*) as part of their vocation; this is, after all, why Bodhidharma came from the West. Yet, this is sometimes missed or unacknowledged in inter-religious encounters. Allow me to draw, in part, on my personal experience, which is admittedly several decades old and thus perhaps a bit out of date. My introduction to formal Zen practice was at Saint Joseph's Abbey, a Trappist mon-

---

2   See, for example, *Araṇavibhanga-sutta*, MN 139.

astery in Spencer, Massachusetts. The abbot of Saint Joseph's, Fr. Thomas Keating (1923-2018), had been inspired by the work of Thomas Merton in the area of inter-religious dialogue, and he invited the Japanese Rinzai teacher, Sasaki Jōshū 佐々木承周 (1907-2014) to lead regular week-long retreats (*sesshin* 接心) at the abbey over a number of years in the 1970s and early 1980s. A handful of Trappists became regular and committed participants in these retreats, taking time off only to celebrate Mass on Sundays. Previously, I had spent a few years in India and Southeast Asia, where I practised Burmese style meditation with teachers in the lineages of U Ba Khin and Mahāsī Sayadaw. The Theravāda retreats attracted a diverse group of students from a variety of cultural and religious backgrounds, but the Western participants tended to be young, spiritual seekers and disaffected hippies who had little experience with the discipline of a cloistered, silent retreat. The Trappists, in contrast, are known for their 'Strict Observance' of the rule of Saint Benedict, and elect to live their lives in silent, meditative seclusion. They are, in some respects, the polar opposite of the agnostic young seekers who congregated at Buddhist meditation centres in the 1970s, and one might have expected the Trappists to have an easier time adjusting to the rigours of a Zen *sesshin*. Yet, the monks at Saint Joseph's struggled with Sasaki's brand of Rinzai training. Sasaki, it should be noted, was a traditionalist, who had little interest in adjusting his teaching to the dispositions of his students, no matter their background. The stumbling block for the Trappists, according to Sasaki, was their theistic faith. Sasaki, who returned to Saint Joseph's annually for several years, became increasingly exasperated with the monks, complaining openly that they would never grasp Zen so long as they clung to their belief in God. Sasaki was, in short, interested in conversion, and the Trappists were proving recalcitrant.

I also recall the celebrated Kyoto School philosopher and Zen enthusiast, Nishitani Keiji, 西谷啓治 (1900-1990) in discussion with visiting Christian theologians at the NCC Center for the Study of Japanese Religions in the mid-1980s (The NCC Center, based in Kyoto, is dedicated to interfaith dialogue between Christianity and the religions of Japan). Nishitani went into a long exposition on the meaning of the Christian trinity; he seemed to have no compunctions about lecturing the theologians on the import of their own Christian faith. Nishitani, like Sasaki, seemed uninterested in the give and take of dialogue. One of the theologians in attendance, John Hick (1922-2012), recounts presenting Nishitani with a copy of his book, *God Has Many Names*, upon which Nishitani murmured, 'The devil also has many names' (Hick 2002, 279).

Finally, I recall the Chinese Chan teacher, Hsuan Hua 宣化 (1918-1995), founder of the Dharma Realm Buddhist Association and the City of Ten Thousand Buddhas, sharing the stage with the eminent Benedictine monk and student of Zen, Brother David Steindl-Rast (b. 1926), at a Buddhist-Christian dialogue conference in Berkeley in 1987. Hsuan Hua, whose monastic name means 'to proselytize', assumed the role of guru, lecturing Steindl-Rast on the truths of Buddhism and showing little interest in an exchange of views. In each case – Sasaki, Nishitani, and Hsuan Hua – little actual dialogue took place. The Christians, inspired by the reforms of Vatican II and the rise of new spiritual practices coming from the East, seemed sincerely intent on exploring areas of common concern, insight and practice. The Buddhist teachers, in contrast, were not there to engage in dialogue but to instruct.

I am not sure if the Christians at these cross-cultural events were aware of the extent of the disconnect, and if so, why they remained politely at the table. I suspect a number of factors were in play beyond simple courtesy. For one, their naïvety about what it is to be an 'enlightened' Buddhist master may have led the Christians to be unduly deferential to their interlocutors. For another, they may have been misled by the popular notion that Buddhism in general, and Zen in particular, is not, properly speaking, a 'religion', and hence Zen masters cannot be said to proselytize. Note that both the Buddhists and the Christians had a stake in perpetuating this fiction: for the Zen teachers, the conceit that Zen is 'not religion' reaffirmed the exceptional status of their tradition. For the Christian clerics, it meant that their interest in Zen need not be construed as compromising their Christian faith.

Thomas Keating served as abbot of Saint Joseph's Abbey from 1961 to 1981. He was an enthusiastic proponent of inter-religious exchange and facilitated the visits of a number of Buddhist and Hindu teachers, including Sasaki Jōshū. Inspired by his exposure to Asian meditation, Keating collaborated with Fr. William Meninger and Fr. M. Basil Pennington (1931-2005) on the development of the 'Centering Prayer', intended as a Catholic counterpart or response to the spiritual exercises being promulgated by the Asian teachers. Keating felt that lay Catholics interested in meditation needed and deserved a properly Catholic option, in part as the Eastern alternatives came with considerable cultural baggage. I wonder if Keating might have taken a different trajectory had his exposure to Zen come through someone other than Sasaki.

As mentioned above, Sasaki was a traditionalist who was unwilling to cut the Trappists any slack, and this set him apart from most other Japanese responsible for spreading Zen to the West. Sasaki's conservatism is nowhere more evident than in his attitude toward sanctioning teachers: despite having taught continuously in America for over fifty years, he died without bestowing dharma transmission (*inka* 印可) on a *single* disciple. Indeed, Sasaki seemed to take a perverse pride in this, as it testified to his high standards and set him apart from most other Zen teachers in the West (Sasaki regarded the other Zen masters [*rōshi* 老師] in America as bush-league wannabes at best, and imposters at worse, and he had no reservations about saying so publicly). But Sasaki's refusal to recognize a successor was not due to pride and obstinacy alone. The traditional Rinzai approach to kōan practice, systematized by Hakuin Ekaku 白隠慧鶴 (1686-1768) and his student Tōrei Enji 東嶺圓慈 (1721–1792) in the Edo period, requires, among other things, a considerable command of Buddhist doctrine and Zen literature. Yet, despite Sasaki's constant prodding, few of his advanced students seemed interested in acquiring such competence.[3] As a result, none of his disciples were capable of filling his shoes: they could not perform, at least to Japanese standards, the two most important tasks required of a Rinzai *rōshi*, namely, *sanzen* 参禅 (formal private interviews in which the master tests a student's understanding of a kōan), and *teishō* 提唱 (ceremonial lectures on Zen literature).

I am guessing that in time Keating came to realize that Sasaki's conservative approach did not offer a way forward for committed Christian monastics or laypersons. Keating's 'Centering Prayer' was devised as an alternative; it did not require that one submit to an Asian master or adapt to a culturally alien form of life.

I mention all of this in order to highlight the difference between more traditional Zen training on the one hand, and the instruction offered by reform-minded teachers associated with the Sanbōkyōdan 三宝教団 (Three Treasures Association) on the other. The latter group was willing and eager to adapt their teaching to Christian clergy. Moreover, they had no qualms about conferring dharma transmission on Christian monks and priests, making them bona fide Zen masters (*rōshi*) after a relatively short course of training. Owing in part to their largesse in sanctioning teachers, the influence of the Sanbōkyōdan on Western Zen has been far out of proportion to its status in Japan. Indeed, insofar as traditional Rinzai and Sōtō monks are aware of the Sanbōkyōdan at all, they view it as a marginal group of amateurs propagating a vulgarized form of kōan practice. Not that I am endorsing this self-interested if not reactionary indictment. It is just that Westerners sometimes fail to appreciate the difference between the education of a monk-in-training (*unsui* 雲水) in a Rinzai or Sōtō monastery (*senmon*

3   Sasaki established the 'Summer Seminar on the Sutras' to fill this lacunae in his disciples' training. These seminars, which began in the 1970s, were first held at Mt. Baldy Zen Center, then at Cornell University, and finally at the Bodhi Manda Zen Center in Jemez Springs, New Mexico; they included leading scholars from around the world and were intended to provide academic training in Buddhism for Sasaki's disciples as well as for interested college students. Yet, his disciples, many of whom had become interested in Zen precisely because it promised experiential truths rather than conceptual understanding, never seemed to take the academic training seriously.

sōdō 專門僧堂) on the one hand, and the training provided at a Sanbōkyōdan *zendō* 禪堂 on the other.

As I have written previously on the history and significance of the Sanbōkyōdan, I will merely summarize my findings here (Sharf 1995b). The organization was founded in 1954 by the Sōtō priest, Yasutani Hakuun 安谷白雲 (1885-1973), as an independent lay society, unaffiliated with any recognized Zen denomination or monastic *honzan* 本山 (head temple). Yasutani's Zen drew on the innovations of his teacher, Harada Sōgaku 原田祖岳 (1871-1961), who, despite Sōtō school proscriptions against the use of kōans, actively incorporated kōans into his teaching.[4] Harada and Yasutani believed that their synthesis of Rinzai and Sōtō practice brought them closer to the original teachings of the founder of the Sōtō school, Dōgen Kigen 道元希玄 (1200-1253). It should be noted, however, that the Sanbōkyōdan use of kōans is much abbreviated compared to what is found in Rinzai. Sanbōkyōdan teachers forgo the use of *jakugo* 著語 ('capping phrases', supplements to particular kōans), as well as the more literary and discursive components of kōan training that come to the fore in later stages of Rinzai practice (Hori 2003; Sharf 2007). As a result, it is possible to complete the Sanbōkyōdan kōan curriculum in a fraction of the time that it takes to complete the kōans in a traditional Rinzai monastery.

Sanbōkyōdan teachers are perhaps most famous (or infamous) for their single-minded emphasis on the attainment of *kenshō* 見性 ('seeing [one's true] nature'); they consider everything else as mere chaff. Yasutani and his heirs believed that their streamlined but intensive approach to kōans and *zazen* made *kenshō* available to the lay public in a relatively short period of time. Indeed, they brazenly declared that it was no longer possible to experience authentic *kenshō* in a traditional Zen *sōdō* 僧堂 (monastic training hall), and that Sanbōkyōdan alone was transmitting the real thing. With their outspoken scorn for orthodox religious institu-

---

4   Kōan practice was proscribed in Sōtō Zen since the reforms of the Edo period; see Foulk 2000 and Bodiford 2006.

tions, their instrumental approach to religious practice, and their promise of rapid and palpable spiritual rewards, the Sanbōkyōdan bears all the signature features of what scholars call a 'new religion' (*shin shūkyō* 新宗教), dozens of which emerged over the period of social upheaval that followed the collapse of the Tokugawa regime (1600-1868) and continued to do so through much of the twentieth century.[5]

Like many of the Japanese new religions, the Sanbōkyōdan sought to reduce the complexity of Buddhist teachings to a simple and accessible technique meant to elicit a tangible or 'empirical' goal. This entailed abbreviating or eliminating many components of traditional monastic practice, including the study of scripture and the mastery of a vast panoply of liturgical practices intended to shape the ritual comportment of a Zen priest. In their place, they taught students to concentrate on kōans in the context of intensive sitting meditation, all of which is directed at realizing *kenshō*. And they claimed a remarkable success rate. Those achieving *kenshō* write up their experiences in personal testimonials, called '*kenshō* records' (*kenshōki* 見性記) or 'records of *kenshō* experience' (*kenshō taiken ki* 見性体験記), that are published in the group's newsletter *Kyōshō* (The use of personal testimonials is another common feature of the Japanese new religions). These testimonials attest to the fact that anyone can realize *kenshō* and even become a *rōshi* in but a few years without giving up their day job.

Yet another element common to both the Sanbōkyōdan and many of the new religions is their universalist orientation. Their leaders welcomed non-Japanese into the group and travelled globally to give talks and offer *sesshin*. Since their Zen was con-

---

5   The Sanbōkyōdan and other new religious movements of the twentieth century have precursors in the 'one-practice' movements of the Kamakura period, namely the Nichiren, Zen, Pure Land (Jōdo-shū), and True Pure Land (Jōdo Shinshū) movements. All tried to make Buddhist practice more broadly available by reducing it to a single, simple exercise: Nichiren practitioners could recite the title of the *Lotus Sutra*, Pure Land practitioners could recite the name of Amida Buddha, and Zen practitioners could engage in simplified forms of *zazen*.

strued as more of a spiritual exercise than a religious rite, non-Buddhists were not required to renounce their prior religious affiliations in order to advance in the organization. This made the Sanbōkyōdan approach to Zen particularly attractive to Christian clergy interested in Eastern meditation, and the Sanbōkyōdan leadership welcomed them in. Yamada Kōun 山田耕雲 (1907-1989), who assumed leadership of the movement after Yasutani's death, took a particular interest in the Catholics, predicting that 'Zen would become an important stream in the Catholic Church one day' (Aitken 1990, 153). In time, well over half of the foreign students who received dharma transmission in the Sanbōkyōdan consisted of Catholic priests and monastics, most of them under Yamada's watch. Indeed, some of the long-time Japanese students complained that their leaders were holding the international students to a lower standard.

The list of Western Zen teachers credentialled in the Sanbōkyōdan line or one of its offshoots includes the Jesuits, Niklaus Brantschen (b. 1937), Hugo Enomiya-Lassalle (1898-1990), Ruben Habito (b. 1947), Robert Kennedy (b. 1933) and Ama Samy, as well as the Benedictine monk, Willigis Jäger (b. 1925).[6] All of them are certified and teach as *rōshi* in either the Sanbōkyōdan or in its offshoot, Maezumi Rōshi's White Plum Asanga, yet they still consider themselves practising Catholics.[7]

---

6   Hugo Enomiya-Lassalle is perhaps the most influential of these figures; see esp. Baatz 2017. Ruben Habito (b. 1947), founder of the Maria Kannon Zen Center in Dallas, has since given up his Jesuit priesthood. Robert Kennedy is member of the White Plum Zen lineage and founder of the Morning Star Zendo in Jersey City; he studied with Yamada Kōun in Kamakura, Maezumi in Los Angeles and with Bernard Glassman (b. 1939), who designated Kennedy a *sensei* in 1991 and a *rōshi* in 1997. According to the Morning Star Zendo website, Kennedy has installed sixteen teachers, including the Trappist monk Kevin Hunt of St. Joseph's Abbey. Many of his teachers have gone on to designate dharma heirs of their own (http://kennedyzen.tripod.com/). Ama Samy is founder of the Bodhi Zendo in Tamil Nadu.

7   The White Plum Asanga was founded by Maezumi Hakuyū 前角博雄 (1931-1995) and his disciple, Bernard Glassman. Maezumi studied and received transmission in a number of lineages, but his teaching style, notably his use of kōans, is taken directly from the Sanbōkyōdan. Far more Catholic

Had Thomas Keating encountered a Sanbōkyōdan teacher instead of a Rinzai traditionalist, he might well have become a *rōshi* himself and not felt the need to develop the Centering Prayer.

Western teachers in the Sanbōkyōdan line are arguably even more profligate in their bestowal of dharma transmission than their Japanese mentors. Robert Kennedy, for example, has recognized some sixteen dharma successors to date. The status of the growing ranks of Western teachers emerged as a matter of controversy among Sanbōkyōdan authorities in Kamakura, and, after Yamada's death in 1989, the Japanese leadership tried to rein in the foreign teachers; they revoked or refused to recognize the status of some, and insisted that the remainder return to Kamakura annually to participate in an 'international Zen teachers' retreat' (*sekai zen shidōsha sesshin* 世界禪指導者接心) under Japanese leadership, if they expected to retain their credentials. Moreover, they declared that foreign *rōshi* are ineligible to confer, independently, transmission of the dharma – they would now have to submit their candidates to Kamakura for final approval. Some Westerners balked at subjecting themselves to Kamakura's authority, and this led them to break their formal ties to the Sanbōkyōdan and establish their own independent organizations.

The tendency for intra-sectarian fragmentation and schism is yet another feature that the Sanbōkyōdan shares with the Japanese new religions. These groups typically experience an initial period of rapid growth based on a promise to democratize charisma, but they quickly find that spreading charisma around – making enlightenment available to all – is corrosive to institutional stability. Nonetheless, one can understand the particular discomfort that the Japanese leadership had with the proliferation of Western and specifically Christian teachers under Yamada. To the Japanese, some of the foreigners must have seemed virtually illiterate when it came to the cultural and conceptual world of Japanese Bud-

---

clergy have been involved with the Sanbōkyōdan style of Zen than I have listed here, including the prolific author, Fr. William Johnston (1925-2010); I have mentioned only those who, to my knowledge, were certified as Zen instructors.

dhism, and they sometimes failed to exhibit the kind of behaviour that the Japanese expected of a Zen *rōshi*.

Not all of the Catholic Zen *rōshi* have come through the Sanbōkyōdan. Another Jesuit *rōshi*, J. Kakichi Kadowaki (b. 1926), founder of the International Zen-Ignatian Training Programme, studied and received transmission from the Rinzai master, Ōmori Sōgen 大森曹玄 (1904-1994). But, like the founders of the Sanbōkyōdan, Ōmori was anything but a traditionalist. He was an innovator, interested in distilling the essence of Zen and combining it with martial arts and calligraphy. And he was similar to the Sanbōkyōdan leaders in another respect as well: he too generated controversy owing to his right-wing nationalist sentiments, a topic to which I will return briefly in my conclusion.

At this point one might ask: so what if the Sanbōkyōdan is a modern, perhaps even radical, reform movement? After all, Zen began as a reform movement – an attempt to recover the Buddha's original insight – and the eighth-century founders of Zen made similarly strident claims that they and they alone preserved the authentic dharma. It is not the scholar's task to issue normative judgments about what is and what is not authentic.

Yet, this critique misses the point I am trying to make, which is not a judgment about the legitimacy of modernist Buddhist movements, but rather about how their claims are understood and contextualized in the West. Here is a parable to make my point.

Imagine, if you will, that a reform-minded Trappist priest from Saint Joseph's, inspired by his experience with Keating's Centring Prayer, leaves the monastery to form a new lay-oriented organization with no formal ties to, or recognition from, the Catholic Church. This organization is devoted solely to spreading the Centring Prayer, and it offers intensive retreats to any and all irrespective of their religious background. As this group deems the Centring Prayer to be the very heart of Catholic spirituality, knowledge of Christian scripture and doctrine, and participation in the Catholic sacraments, is deemed secondary. Indeed, some members of the sect consider scriptural study and ritual practice a hindrance that stands in the way of a direct experience of God.

Imagine, moreover, that the leaders of this movement claim to be able to discern, in formal interviews, the depth of their students' experience of God's presence. They enumerate discrete stages of insight attained through the Centring Prayer, and then publicly recognize students as they pass from stage to stage, presenting them with certificates, bestowing them with religious names and titles, publishing their testimonials in the organization's newsletter, and so on. Those who are judged to have reached the final goal are ordained as 'bishops' and given dispensation to teach and ordain others.

All the while, members of this movement consider themselves Catholics in good standing; this despite the fact that their movement is not recognized by the Church, and that many of their priests, not to mention rank-and-file members, may be largely ignorant of scripture and doctrine, and unversed in the most rudimentary forms of Catholic ritual and worship. Yet, the members are not insecure about their Catholic identity; on the contrary, they consider themselves *more* Catholic than the Church. The Church, in their eyes, is spiritually bankrupt, as it misconstrues Christ's message to be something that could be embodied in scripture, in ritual or in an institution. As such, members of this reform movement are unconcerned that the Vatican does not recognize, much less endorse, their teachings and priestly ordinations.

One can assume that, in America and Europe, few outside the movement would take seriously their claim to embody and preserve the essence of Catholicism. Outsiders are more likely to regard it as an idiosyncratic Christian sect offering seekers a quick spiritual fix. But now imagine that some visiting Japanese Buddhists with no background in, or knowledge of, Christianity join the movement, rise through the ranks, are ordained as priests and bishops, and take the tradition back with them to Japan where they present it, in all sincerity, as authentic Roman Catholicism. Given that most Japanese know next to nothing about Christianity, nobody would be any the wiser.

I offer this parable to illustrate why the Sanbōkyōdan claim to transmit 'real Zen' has gained more traction outside of Japan than within. The parallels with the Sanbōkyōdan are not precise, of course. For one thing, the Catholic Church is more monolithic than either Sōtō or Rinzai, which are subdivided into semi-autonomous monastic orders that oversee the training and installation of their own priests. For another, with the end of clerical celibacy in the Meiji period, the gap between layperson and priest narrowed, and Japanese Buddhist clerics lost much of their standing and authority. All this may make it easier to launch an independent Zen school in Japan than it would be to start an autonomous Catholic movement in the West. But, I do think the parable captures something of the cultural miscues involved in the spread of Zen in the West.

But What about Experience?

One of the signature features of Buddhist modernism is precisely the claim that Buddhism is not a religion but is rather a spiritual technology or 'mind science' intended to foster a non-conceptual (and hence universal) spiritual experience. In Japan this claim predates the Sanbōkyōdan by several decades – we find versions of it in the writings of D.T. Suzuki 鈴木大拙 (1870-1966), Hisamatsu Shin'ichi 久松真一 (1889-1980), and other Buddhist intellectuals who came of age in the Meiji and Taishō periods. The rhetoric of these scholars appealed especially to those within the monastic establishment who were struggling to defend their traditions in the face of secularist critique (The monasteries and temples were struggling economically as well, as the collapse of the parishioner system [*danka seido* 檀家制度] in the Meiji era initiated a period of financial insecurity that continues to the present day). But the attempt to reduce the entirety of the Buddha's teachings to something simple, empirical and accessible has earlier antecedents in East Asia as well; it can be traced back to the very origins of the Chan/Zen tradition in eighth-century China. Once again, as I have written on this topic previously, my comments will be brief and to the point (Sharf 2014b, 2017).

In discussing the emergence of the Chan school, historians sometimes distinguish between 'small-c *chan*' and 'large-C

Chan'. Small-c *chan* refers to the vast panoply of contemplative practices (*dhyāna*) that originated in India and spread to China prior to the rise of the self-styled Chan lineages (*chanzong* 禪宗, i.e., Chan with a 'large-C') in the eighth century. The early practices included: (1) 'contemplations on foulness' (*aśubhabhāvanā, bujing guan* 不淨觀), which comprise meditations on the repulsiveness of the body or of a corpse; (2) repentance rituals (*chanhui* 懺悔), intended to eliminate negative karma and trigger prognostic visions; (3) recollection of the qualities of the buddhas (*buddhānusmṛti, nianfo* 念佛), and so on.[8] These practices are designed to cultivate wholesome (*kuśala*) states and counteract impure states, and they typically involve attending to a specific physical or mental object while recollecting (*smṛti, nian* 念) a particular teaching or virtue. Such exercises were intended for mendicant monks versed in the doctrinal and epistemic underpinnings of the Buddhist path. There were practices available to laypersons, of course, such as making offerings to buddhas and bodhisattvas (*pūjā, gongyang* 供養), and simple forms of *buddhānusmṛti*, but the lay practices were typically directed toward worldly ends such as curing disease, safe childbirth and securing a better rebirth.

Things changed with the rise of what we are calling large-C Chan in the eighth century. This movement emerged, in part, from the efforts of popular and populist *dhyāna* masters in the capital to create a simple practice accessible to laypersons as well as monks. These teachers developed various fast-track practices that promised to engender awakening (*bodhi*) without requiring that one assume an ascetic lifestyle, engage in monastic training, or be familiar with doctrine and liturgy. The largely mythical figure of Huineng 慧能 (638-713) came to epitomize this new 'sudden teaching' (*dunjiao* 頓教). Huineng was an illiterate woodcutter with no prior familiarity with Buddhism, yet he grasped the crux of the teaching immediately upon hearing a single line from the

---

8   On early *dhyāna* practices in China and their relationship with visions and visualization, see esp. Greene 2012.

Diamond Scripture, and he went on to receive dharma transmission and become the Sixth Patriarch of Chan despite his lay status.

There are a number of historical factors that contributed to the rise of this movement. One often overlooked influence may have been the recent arrival of Indian masters of esoteric Buddhism (aka 'Tantra') in the Chinese capital.[9] The teachings of these celebrated Buddhist emissaries emphasized the direct transmission of esoteric knowledge from master to disciple, as well as the conferral of lay precepts in the context of public 'altar rites' (or 'maṇḍala rites', *tanfa* 壇法). But, most important for our present purposes, their newly revealed scriptures and rites taught that mind is intrinsically pure and luminous, and that buddhahood consists precisely in realizing this abiding luminosity. This teaching was transmitted through *maṇḍala* rites that were structured as sacrificial offerings to assemblies of divine beings, yet the point of the rites was to affirm and enact the practitioner's primordial identity with the deity. This notion that the essence of mind is buddha-nature (*foxing* 佛性) was not new in eighth-century China – it is found in a variety of texts including the *Treatise on the Awakening of Faith in the Mahāyāna* (*Dasheng qixin lun* 大乘起信論) – but the stature of the Indian masters and the appeal of their impressive *maṇḍala* technology may have helped to popularize this doctrine among elites at the time (Sharf 2017).

Another factor in the rise of Chan was the growing interest in Buddhism among lay elites in the capital, including officials, aristocrats and even members of the imperial household. Ambitious Buddhist masters responded by vying for their patronage, and some charismatic teachers attracted large lay followings. Perhaps influenced by the Indian esoteric masters, rather than simply offering their lay followers future karmic rewards, the Chan masters promised an immediate taste of awakening itself.

This led to a fertile period of experimentation and innovation. Rival teachers advanced a host of new practices under the ru-

---

9   The most famous were Śubhakarasiṃha (Shanwuwei 善無畏, 637-735), Vajrabodhi (Jin'gangzhi 金剛智, 671-741), and Amoghavajra (Bukong 不空, 705-774).

brics of 'maintaining mind' (*shouxin* 守心), 'maintaining unity' (*shouyi* 守一), 'pacifying the mind' (*anxin* 安心), 'discerning the mind' (*guanxin* 觀心), 'viewing the mind' (*kanxin* 看心), 'focussing the mind' (*shexin* 攝心) and so on. Unfortunately, we know surprisingly little about the specifics of these practices, but the fragmentary evidence, culled largely from Dunhuang manuscripts, suggests that many of them involved focussing attention not on the *content* of conscious experience so much as on the nature or phenomenon of consciousness itself (Sharf 2014b). To use a venerable Buddhist metaphor, consciousness or mind is said to be like a mirror, and the point of meditation is to attend not to the images that appear fleetingly in the mirror, but rather to the intrinsically clear and radiant and still mirror itself.

It is here that we see an interesting parallel with another Buddhist movement that attempted to bring the fruits of monastic practice to the laity, namely, the mindfulness (*satipaṭṭhāna*, *vipassanā*) movement that emerged in Burma (Myanmar) in the first half of the twentieth century. Here too, monastic teachers experimented with novel techniques that were held to lead to advanced stages on the path, including *sotāpatti-magga* (the stage of the stream winner), without the need to abandon one's family and livelihood, or to adopt a renunciate lifestyle, or to study scripture and *abhidhamma*. The new Burmese method, like early Chan, emphasized a technique whereby one attends to the immediacy of conscious sensation; the goal is to detach oneself from the inner narrative, to stop reacting to and judging whatever arises in consciousness, and to focus instead on the selfless and transient nature of mental events. Like the early Chan techniques, the Burmese methods were trying to effect a kind of gestalt or figure/ground shift – shifting attention away from the content of experience to the non-conceptual nature of experience itself (Sharf 2014b, 2015).

I would note one more similarity between the early patriarchs of Chan and their twentieth-century Burmese counterparts: in both cases their teachings provoked suspicion and resistance from conservative voices within the monastic *saṃgha*. We might attribute some of the hostility to the reactionary reflex of entrenched interests, which resisted the 'democratization of charisma', but there were serious doctrinal and ethical issues at stake as well. These mindfulness practices seem to be predicated on the belief that it is both possible and desirable to cultivate a meta-cognitive state that is non-judgmental and non-conceptual. Yet, it is far from clear that the Buddhist scriptural and commentarial traditions allow for or countenance such a state. The existence of non-conceptual (*nirvikalpa, wufenbie* 無分別) cognition has been the subject of ongoing controversy among Buddhist exegetes for over two-thousand years; Sarvāstivāda Ābhidharmikas wrestled with the topic (Sharf 2018), as did the later Mahāyānists. And there were disagreements on the issues even among Madhyamaka commentators (between so-called Svātantrikas and Prāsaṅgikas, for example), and within Yogācāra as well (specifically between Dignāga and Dharmapāla; Sharf 2016). In each case, one side (Sautrāntika, Madhyamaka, Prāsaṅgika, Dharmapāla) accused the other (Vaibhāṣika, Yogācāra, Svātantrika, Dignāga) of unduly reifying consciousness – of rendering it an intrinsically dispassionate yet numinous subject or 'cogito', which was tantamount to the ātman of the heretics.

Indeed, this is the crux of the issue for Buddhist scholiasts: given the Buddhist doctrine of non-self (*anātman*), can any sense be made of cognitive experience (*vijñāna*) in the absence of a modicum of conceptual discrimination (*vikalpa*)? Early Ābhidharmikas interpreted the doctrine of non-self to rule out the notion of an abiding ground or self-intimating (self-reflexive) 'witness' of experience. Since all conscious experience entailed discrimination (*vikalpa*), the suppression of discrimination and conceptualization resulted not in a state of spiritual insight, but rather a condition known as *nirodha*, an exotic yogic state in which consciousness has ceased altogether. To the early Buddhists, *nirodha* constituted a temporary respite from *saṃsāra*, but did not bring about or even contribute to liberation. In fact, they believed this to be a key difference between Buddhist and non-Buddhist practice. The heterodox Brahmanical yogis ignorantly held the ātman to be the unchanging ground of awareness, and thus they aspired to suppress discrimination and conceptualization so as to disclose the natural luminosity of mind itself. To the Buddhists, these benighted yogis mistook *nirodha* for liberation, and it led them to be reborn in the sphere of 'beings without cognition' (*asaṃjñika-sattvāḥ, asāṃjñika-deva*), where they remained, trapped in a zombie-like state, for eons (Sharf 2014a).

These debates might seem unduly scholastic and of little import to meditation practice, but this was not the attitude among leading Chan masters in the Tang and Song periods, who were at the forefront of these debates. And it is easy to understand why: all Chan masters agreed that the goal of the tradition is *prajñā* or wisdom. The pressing question was the relationship between *prajñā*, conceptuality and consciousness, and one's understanding of this relationship would have a profound effect on one's approach to both path and goal. Vehement disagreements over precisely this issue contributed to the splits between the so-called Northern and Southern (or Gradual and Sudden) schools in the Tang period. The same issues emerged at the centre of the Samyé debates (aka 'Council of Lhasa') in Tibet in the 790s, in which the Indian meditation master, Kamalaśīla, took the gradual or conceptualist side, and the Chinese Northern Chan master, Moheyan 摩訶衍, the sudden or non-conceptualist side. And it popped up again in the Song Dynasty controversy over 'silent-illumination *chan*' (*mozhao chan* 默照禪), a debate that would continue to polarize Sōtō and Rinzai Zen in Japan through the centuries. Finally, the same issues animate the more recent Critical Buddhism (*hihan bukkyō* 批判仏教) controversy in Japan; the advocates of Critical Buddhism hold that the buddha-nature idea that came to dominate East Asian Buddhism privileges non-conceptual states and thereby undermines the need for critical discernment and moral judgment. In each case, critics reject the notion that the goal of Buddhist practice can be reduced to a non-conceptual, meta-cognitive, self-reflexive experience – a 'witness consciousness' that can be disaggregated from the rise and fall of the aggregates.

Such a notion, insist the critics, is tantamount to *ātmavāda* – the heterodox theory that posits the existence of an enduring 'self'.

Again, a modern practitioner might claim: so what? Whether or not we deem modern Burmese *satipaṭṭhāna* or Sanbōkyōdan *kenshō* to be orthodox, the reality is that the cultivation of mindfulness – understood generically as a state wherein one is fully present to what is happening in the here and now instead of being lost in thought – did play a role in various Buddhist reform movements since medieval times, and these reforms were intended to make the heart of Buddhism – wisdom and detachment – available to the wider public. In the end, it is irrelevant whether the methods and resulting insight are orthodox or not. In fact, one of the strengths of mindfulness is precisely that it transcends Buddhist or religious orthodoxy; it is a universal human truth. Yet, there is a degree of bad faith in such an argument, since modern practitioners want to believe that these practices, however deracinated, still yield transformative insights and experiences that have a beneficial effect on our spiritual and ethical well-being. Which is to say that they want their cake and they want to eat it too: they want their secularized practices to yield spiritual goals. Consider this: for over one hundred years, European phenomenologists have been interested in the sustained and critical investigation of what is presented to us in the immediacy of consciousness awareness. Husserl called for a return to the 'things themselves' that involves bracketing or setting aside (*epoché*) the 'natural attitude' – the metaphysical assumptions and unexamined concepts and intuitions that condition ordinary waking experience. Most fundamental to the natural attitude is the pre-reflective distinction we make between the perceiving subject (or self or cogito) on the one side, and the objective world on the other (Yogācāra calls this the grasper-grasped [*grāhaka-grāhya*] duality.) While Husserl, Heidegger, Sartre, Merleau-Ponty and their heirs disagree on many things, they all concur that if we set aside our beliefs and simply observe carefully, we find that our life-world is given to us as an integrated or enfolded whole – what Heidegger calls Dasein, and Merleau-Ponty calls the 'fold' in the fabric of the world.

Proponents of modern Buddhist meditation, whether Japanese Zen or Burmese mindfulness, will want to distinguish their techniques from the more analytic and discursive practices of Western philosophy, and indeed from Buddhist philosophy as well. They want their experience of bare presence – of the collapse of subject-object duality – to be non-conceptual on the one hand, but still to bring about positive psychological and moral transformation on the other, which supposedly distinguishes it from mere philosophical inquiry. They want eminently Buddhist virtues such as compassion, empathy, generosity and altruism to arise spontaneously from this non-conceptual state. But there is the rub, since it is not clear how a non-conceptual state that transcends worldly distinctions can yield these vaunted worldly goods. How, in short, can an experience that goes beyond judgment and reasoning give rise to ethical discernment? This is by no means a new problem: it was recognized in Buddhism early on. To pick a single but telling example, the *Scripture on the Perfection of Wisdom in Eight Thousand Lines* (*Aṣṭasāhasrikā prajñāpāramitā-sūtra*), one of the earliest surviving Mahāyāna scriptures dating to the first century BCE, cautions that the wisdom of emptiness must be balanced by the cultivation of compassion and skilful means. Nāgārjuna makes the same point in his *Verses on the Middle Way* (*Mūlamadhyamaka-kārikā*), when he warns that to grasp at absolute truth without understanding conventional truth is akin to grabbing a snake from the wrong end – it is bound to reach around and bite you. In other words, the realization of emptiness does not, and indeed cannot, in and of itself, engender states that we would find morally uplifting. For that you need more than transcendent wisdom (*prajñā*); you need the rest of the Buddhist perfections (*pāramitā*) as well. In short, you need religion.

This is, perhaps, why so many of those associated with modernist Zen movements in Japan – movements dedicated to an experience that transcends Buddhism and religion – took moral and political stances that many today find objectionable. Here I would include Harada Sōgaku, Yasutani Hakuun, Ōmori Sōgen, Nishitani Keiji and others who, like Heidegger, coupled their fascination with the domain of pure presence with an attraction to nationalist and fascist ideologies (Sharf 1995c, 1995d; Victoria 1997, 2003). Is it a coincidence that the teachers most invested in bringing Zen to the West and cultivating Zen practice among Christians were Japanese who believed in the intrinsic superiority of Japanese culture and endorsed Japanese imperialist ambitions in the first half of the twentieth century? So, to return to the question with which I was tasked – why Buddhists taught Zen to Christians – perhaps part of the answer is that in transmitting Zen to Christians, these Japanese teachers sought to accomplish in the cultural and religious domains what eluded them in the political domain.

In conclusion, I submit that the more pressing question for inter-religious dialogue today is not whether we can identify a spiritual method or mystical experience that transcends the particularity of religious teachings – whether Catholic, Zen, or what have you – but precisely why we would want to.

Bibliography

Baatz, Ursula, 2017. 'Hugo M. Enomiya-Lassalle: Zen-Enlightenment and Christianity'. In *A Companion to Jesuit Mysticism* (Brill's Companions to the Christian Tradition, no. 78), ed. Robert Aleksander Maryks. Leiden: Brill: 335-357.

Bodiford, William M., 2006. 'Koan Practice'. In *Sitting with Koans: Essential Writings on Zen Koan Introspection*, ed. John Daido Loori. Somerville MA: Wisdom Publications: 91-115.

Foulk, T. Griffith, 2000. 'The Form and Function of Koan Literature. A Historical Overview'. In *The Kōan: Texts and Contexts in Zen Buddhism*, eds. Steven Heine & Dale S. Wright. Oxford: Oxford University Press: 15-45.

Greene, Eric Matthew, 2012. 'Meditation, Repentance, and Visionary Experience in Early Medieval Chinese Buddhism'. Ph.D dissertation, University of California, Berkeley.

Hick, John, 2002. *John Hick: An Autobiography*. Oxford: One-world Publications.

Hori, Victor Sogen, 2003. *Zen Sand: The Book of Capping Phrases for Kōan Practice*. Honolulu: University of Hawai'i Press.

Sharf, Robert H., 1995a. 'Buddhist Modernism and the Rhetoric of Meditative Experience'. *Numen* 42.3: 228-283.

Sharf, Robert H., 1995b. 'Sanbōkyōdan: Zen and the Way of the New Religions'. *Japanese Journal of Religious Studies* 22.3-4 (*Special Edition: The New Age in Japan*, eds. Haga Manabu & Robert Kisala): 417-458.

Sharf, Robert H., 1995c. 'The Zen of Japanese Nationalism'. In *Curators of the Buddha: The Study of Buddhism under Colonialism*, ed. Donald S. Lopez, Jr. Chicago: University of Chicago Press: 107-160.

Sharf, Robert H., 1995d. 'Whose Zen? Zen Nationalism Revisited'. In *Rude Awakenings: Zen, the Kyoto School, and the Question of Nationalism* (Nanzan Studies in Religion and Culture), eds. James W. Heisig & John Maraldo. Honolulu: University of Hawai'i Press: 40-51.

Sharf, Robert H., 2007. 'How to Think with Chan *Gong'ans*'. In *Thinking with Cases: Specialized Knowledge in Chinese Cultural History*, eds. Charlotte Furth, Judith Zeitlin & Hsiung Ping-chen. Honolulu: University of Hawai'i Press: 205-243.

Sharf, Robert H., 2014a. 'Is Nirvāṇa the Same as Insentience? Chinese Struggles with an Indian Buddhist Ideal'. In *India in the Chinese Imagination: Myth, Religion, and Thought*, eds. John Kieschnick & Meir Shahar. Philadelphia: University of Pennsylvania Press: 141-170.

Sharf, Robert H., 2014b. 'Mindfulness and Mindlessness in Early Chan'. *Philosophy East & West* 64.4: 933-964.

Sharf, Robert H., 2015. 'Is Mindfulness Buddhist? (And Why It Matters)'. *Transcultural Psychiatry* 52.4: 470-484.

Sharf, Robert H., 2016. 'Is Yogācāra Phenomenology? Some Evidence From the *Cheng weishi lun*'. *Journal of Indian Philosophy* 44.4: 777-807.

Sharf, Robert H., 2017. 'Buddhist Veda and the Rise of Chan'. In *Chinese and Tibetan Esoteric Buddhism*, eds. Yael Bentor & Meir Shahar. Leiden: Brill: 85-120.

Sharf, Robert H., 2018. 'Knowing Blue: Early Buddhist Accounts of Non-Conceptual Sense Perception'. *Philosophy East and West* 63.3.

Victoria, Daizen, 1997. *Zen at War*. New York and Tokyo: Weatherhill.

Victoria, Daizen, 2003. *Zen War Stories*. London: RoutledgeCurzon.

Theme 3:
Christian-Buddhist Encounter Through Mindfulness

POPULAR MINDFULNESS: THE WESTERN INTEREST IN MINDFULNESS MEDITATION

Andreas Nehring[1]

Abstract

For at least a couple of decades, we can observe a boom and a wide reception of the Buddhist concept of mindfulness in various functional areas of Western societies. Perceived by its proponents as a non-confessional praxis of self-experience, mindfulness meditation belongs to what social scientists term 'spirituality' rather than a more traditional understanding of 'religion'. Mindfulness, I argue in this chapter, can be analysed as a mirror for the socio-cultural figuration of spirituality in Western societies. Fluctuating between therapy and religious event, object of scientific research and a pedagogical concept, mindfulness allows us to ask how the surplus of an implicit spiritual assuredness that can be trained and transformed during meditation is becoming part of a public discourse in Western societies. The acceptance and effectiveness of mindfulness are intertwined in therapeutic, religious, pedagogical functional areas. I show that the acceptance of mindfulness on the other hand can only be explained by focussing on the cultural preconditions of its reception in the West. Therefore, I argue that an investigation of the mindfulness-concept from a cultural studies perspective should achieve more than just a critique of the dominant empirical research on mindfulness. The question of why mindfulness is so popular in Europe and the North-American con-

---

1   This paper is based on an earlier publication in German by Andreas Nehring and Christoph Ernst, 2013.

text is exactly in its simplicity highly relevant. A cultural studies approach to mindfulness will analyse this concept and practice in the context of the contemporary conditions of its cultural representation. I argue that mindfulness as a praxis is entangled in discourses of its legitimation and interpretation. I do not, therefore, analyse in detail the Buddhist roots of the mindfulness-concept but rather ask why and how this concept has been appropriated and thereby transformed in Western societies.

Keywords: mindfulness, popular spirituality

Hardly ever before has the request that we should all be more mindful been emphasized more strongly in various sections of public discourses than today. And the option to follow this request has multiplied in recent years: mindful cooking, mindful driving, mindful sex and so on, offers we find in books, courses and on the web. The normativity of being mindful throughout the day is probably most visible in a pre-installed health-app on the Apple iPhone in the version of iOS 10 that has been available since 2016. It helps users to stay healthy throughout the day and even the year. The app helps people to observe their sleeping habits, and to digest and control daily food consumption. It monitors sport-activities and finally it helps to improve mindfulness for the user by measuring the time he or she is meditating. These four dimensions: sport, sleep, digestion and mindfulness give this app a holistic flavour. With reference to mindfulness, Apple suggests: 'Quiet your mind. Relax your body. Be in the moment.' Besides the problem that the app does not tell people how to do this, the implicit message is that modern human beings in post-industrial societies lack these promised qualities. What is not mentioned by Apple is that central aspects of what the Company considers to be mindfulness derives from Buddhist conceptualizations of this term.

Plum Village, an organization started by the Vietnamese Zen Master, Thích Nhất Hạnh, offers a series of desktop and mobile-apps, for example a Bell of Mindfulness or a Stillness Buddy that are meant to structure the day of its users:

> Often when we are on our computers or smartphones, we become completely lost in our work and completely disconnected from our body in the here and now. You may like to program a bell of mindfulness on your computer or smartphone and every quarter of an hour (or as often as you like), the bell sounds so you have a chance to stop, breathe and relax. Breathing in and out three times is enough to release the tension in the body and smile, and then continue your work. If we're in the middle of a conversation, hearing the bell of mindfulness can be a helpful reminder to practice mindful, compassionate speech. There are also virtual Sanghas, guided meditations, and other Mindfulness tools available online. You may like to check out Plumline [plumline.org]'. (Plumvillage.org. Be Mindful Online; accessed 19 October 2017)

And the 'Stillness Buddy' promises:

> Stillness Buddy is helping thousands of people around the world to live in the present moment, feel less stressed and happier, alive and more at peace. Using key quotes and inspiring words from leading spiritual teachers, Stillness Buddy is like having a friend that, every now and then, gently reminds you to stop, breathe, center yourself again and then continue. (Plumvillage.org/mindfulness-practice; accessed 19 October 2017)

The Burmese meditation master Mahasi Sayadaw even claims that meditation in due time leads to extraordinary experiences:

> From time immemorial, Buddhas, Arahats and Ariyas have realized Nibbana by this method of Vipassanā. It is the highway leading to Nibbana...Impermanence, suffering and non-self will be realized through direct personal experience, and with the full development of these knowledges, Nibbana will be realized. It will not take long to achieve the objective, possibly one month, or twenty days, or fifteen days, or, on rare occasions, even in seven days for those select few with extraordinary parami. (Mahasi Sayadaw 1995; accessed 19 October 2017)

Slovenian philosopher Slavoj Žižek has this to say:

> The meditative attitude of western Buddhism probably is the
> most effective method to participate completely in the capitalist
> dynamics and at the same time preserve the pretence of mental
> health. (Žižek 2001, 62)

For a couple of decades, but even more so after the turn of the
new millennium, we can observe a boom and a wide reception of
the Buddhist concept of mindfulness in various functional areas
of Western societies. Perceived by its proponents as a non-confessional praxis of self-experience, mindfulness meditation belongs
to the phenomenon that has been labelled by social scientists as
'spirituality' rather than the more traditional understanding of 'religion'. Mindfulness, as Robert Sharf once pointed out, is widely
'interpreted as "bare attention" or "present-centred awareness",
by which is meant a sort of non-judgmental, non-discursive attending to the here-and-now' (Sharf 2015: 472). Seen in this
context, mindfulness can be analysed as a mirror for the socio-
cultural figuration of spirituality in Western societies. Fluctuating
between therapy, anti-stress remedy and religious event, object
of scientific research and pedagogical concept, mindfulness allows us to ask how the surplus of an implicit spiritual assuredness, which can be trained and transformed during meditation, is
becoming part of a public discourse in the West.

The term mindfulness in modern discourse describes a self-
reflexive form of directing one's attention, in which one's own
experiencing of a situation is imagined from the perspective of
second-order observation, and this in the setup of a meditative
praxis. The aim is to achieve a non-judgmental, neutral position
in which thoughts and emotions are observed in their process of
emergence and disappearance. As an attitude of emotional and
rational acceptance of a given situation, mindfulness opens insight into the dynamics of the conscious processes of thinking and
a deepened awareness of the entanglement of thought-processes
with bodily conditions. This is what we can call a psychosomatic
feedback. Through its connectedness with the situated experience
of a meditative praxis, that is, with the help of a highly ritualized

technique, the concept of mindfulness offers the possibility to experience the entanglement of habitualized and automatized patterns of emotion and evaluation with tacit body-knowledge more consciously. And the implicit promise is that this opens new possibilities for their configuration and transformation in daily life. To a great extent derived from the Theravāda Buddhist tradition of *vipassanā* meditation, these features of mindfulness have been appropriated and utilized since the 1970s by Jon Kabat-Zinn, an American molecular biologist, who developed a programme called 'Mindfulness-based stress-reduction' (MBSR) for therapeutic purposes, which has been successfully applied to a great variety of psychosomatic and bodily diseases.

As a philosophical concept and as a meditative practice, mindfulness has been absorbed into the West since the early twentieth century and currently gains in importance far beyond the sphere of religion, namely, in medicine and psychotherapy, in science, in the educational system and in popular culture. It is not an exaggeration to state that mindfulness is presently the most popular keyword when the training of consciousness is concerned. In the economic system, mindfulness meditation is recommended for stressed managers as burn-out prevention. In cognitive neurosciences, we can observe a spike in measuring brain-activity, especially during meditation, in order to prove the constitutional effects of being more mindful. Philosophers like the German professor, Thomas Metzinger, are suggesting mindfulness meditation for the school curriculum, while emphasizing that meditation has nothing at all to do with Buddhism and even less so with religion in general (Metzinger 2009). Schoolchildren should simply be familiarized with the dynamics of their consciousness and its bodily effects. Mindfulness is discussed in pedagogy as a praxis for self-care. In conferences conducted by neuroscientists and Buddhists, like the *Mind & Life* conferences, the impact of meditation on the brain is discussed. And in the field of media, especially where the increased public discussion about psychic processes is translated into questions of the individual's conduct of life, mindfulness is presented as a timely proposition for meaningful living. I would like to call this field a popular mindfulness-discourse.

In order to adequately assess the plurality of references to mindfulness in science and society, it is necessary, in contrast to most of the affirmative research that has been carried out so far, to focus on the interdependency of the various sociocultural lines in the reception and application of mindfulness. It is not only necessary to increase knowledge about the empirical, validatable psychological effectiveness of mindfulness, but to understand better the social and cultural presuppositions surrounding this concept. The acceptance and effectiveness of mindfulness are intertwined in therapeutic, religious and pedagogical functional areas. The question of *why* mindfulness is so popular in Europe and the North-American context is, in its simplicity, highly relevant.

A cultural studies approach to mindfulness should analyse this concept and the practice in the context of the contemporary conditions of its cultural representation. I would argue that mindfulness as a praxis is entangled in discourses of legitimation and interpretation, and therefore has to be analysed as a field of explicit semantics. It is epistemologically trivial but, in opposition to positivistic attempts to empirically confirm the often supposed effectiveness of mindfulness, it has to be pointed out that these semantics are not simply derived interpretations of what has been experienced during meditative praxis, but they themselves structure the experience-dimension of an acted out meditation-praxis in terms of expectations and presuppositions.

What is so challenging about the hype on mindfulness and its multidimensional reception is that the discussion around mindfulness can be seen as a special case of a wider question for social and cultural studies. How, in a given historical situation, is the relationship of an experience that is purely individual and only accessible to personal consciousness, and its representation in forms of communication, shaped? How is a first person perspective transformed through media, such as language and bodily practices, and with the help of images like MRT diagrams, externalized, stabilized and embellished for a reflexive observation in objectively verifiable discourses that we can call third person perspectives. In other words, the question is how a translation takes place between mindfulness as a private sense experience that is open only to one's own consciousness and the public forms of discourses about mindfulness. I would argue that, besides its relevance for understanding the Western interest in mindfulness today, this is one of the key methodological challenges for religious studies in general. This central question of *how* this can be interpreted nevertheless cannot be disconnected from questions about what, when and why.

Therefore, any cultural studies approach to mindfulness, apart from a systematic and analytical approach, has to deal with historical and comparative aspects of the reception of mindfulness in Western as well as Eastern discourses. A recent publication by Jeff Wilson on 'Mindful America' is helpful here (Wilson 2014). One has to bear in mind that the meditation practices, which are appropriated from Buddhist traditions and are applied today, have come to their present shape only through and after the encounter of Buddhism with Western culture and the emergence of the concept of individual experience. The focus on experience, or even pure experience, is not only dominant in the West but, since Friedrich Schleiermacher introduced the idea of a pure religious experience that is considered as foundational for all religion, it has been effectively appropriated in Asian Buddhist circles as well, as Robert Sharf has shown in many of his earlier publications (Sharf 1995, 228-283; Sharf 1998, 94-116; Sharf 2000, 267-287).

The reception of mindfulness in Europe in various ways has been influenced by cultural exchange and transfer-connections. And we have to be aware that the appropriation of mindfulness meditation did not take place in a direct line from Asia to Europe but to a large extent was mediated via North America. Furthermore, this is only one dimension of the mindfulness phenomenon. Not only are the sources of the diverse Buddhist traditions extremely heterogeneous, but also mindfulness as such does not necessarily have to have Buddhist roots. In a similar way, a systematic-analytical perspective cannot reduce mindfulness only to the sphere of the 'religious' and its discourses around the quality of religious experience. Rather, mindfulness as currently promoted seems to be a comprehensive offer for the meaningful conduct of life that can best be described as a form of popular spirituality. As stated, by 'spirituality' I mean a non-organizational, individualistic search for a meaningful life; it can be religious but does not necessarily have to be so. As the German sociologist, Hubert Knoblauch has shown, referring to Thomas Luckmann, the plausibility of the concept of spirituality is that it makes an offer of communication that allows the individual to have specific personal experiences. Such experiences happen within a framework of a popular form of communication, as a highly generalized cultural pattern that is suitable for various connections and interpretations (Knoblauch 2009). Epistemologically, the concept of spirituality can be seen as a dimension of experience that involves an implicit assuredness that serves as the basis for interpretations of life-situations that are experienced and constructed as meaningful. Mindfulness, as an indubitable subjective phenomenon, aims at the deployment of a first-person-perspective; however, this does not have much value in academic argumentation since it is does not yield to observation and inter-subjective replication. This is clearly reflected in an interview between the German neuroscientist, Wolf Singer, and the French Buddhist and biologist, Mattieu Ricard, in a book entitled *Meditation and Brain Research*:

> It does not suffice to ponder how the human psyche works and elaborate complex theories about it, as, for instance, Freud did. Such intellectual constructs cannot replace two millennia of direct investigation of the workings of mind through penetrating introspection conducted with trained minds that have become both stable and clear. Any sophisticated theory that came out of a brilliant mind but does not rest on empirical evidence cannot be compared with the cumulated experience of hundreds of people who have each a good part of their lives fathomed the subtlest aspects of mind through direct experience. (Ricard & Singer 2017, 2)

This statement clearly indicates: we cannot speak of a lack of observability but what we have to take into account is the position and perspective of observation. The phenomenologically interesting potentiality of human awareness consists in the ability to observe itself reflexively. Awareness is always intentional, that is, it is awareness of something, even of oneself. The problem that emerges is the identification of the subject and object of observation. How can human beings perceive the world cognitively? How do we classify and transform information symbolically and at the same time apply these processes, which allow reality to emerge in our minds, to ourselves? A human being creates an image of him or herself as a conscious subject. What is so exciting is that these phenomenologically trivial basic assumptions in various ways are reactivated in contemporary mindfulness-discourses. For example, in the so-called 'philosophy of mind', there is a debate about how a human being transcends the self by centring on himself or herself. Or, in other words, by conceptualizing the mind as in a certain relationship to the brain, this debate also circles around the whole complex of the autonomy of free will (cf. Singer 2002; Ravencroft 2008).

Another aspect is that the form of introspection that mindfulness meditation promises happens on two reciprocal, entangled levels, namely, the psychic and the physical levels. As mentioned before, mindfulness meditation is a body-technique that manipulates the mind via the body, by first of all focussing on the body and its functions. The two most common techniques, developed and popularized by meditation masters in Myanmar during the first half of the twentieth century, are the 'body-scan' and 'breath control', and their somatic effects can be traced by measuring the heart frequency or the oxygen uptake rate. Mindfulness meditation in a way can be seen as a revitalizing of the body-mind relationship, and this revitalizing results in an internal and introspective closure that in popular discourses is often marked with the loaded term 'holistic' or in German 'Ganzheitlichkeit', which enables an interruption of the continuous differentiation of the Self by new experiences.

The central allegation in the popular discourse on modernity now is that, because of the continuous processes of differentiation within society, a new quality of demand emerges for the individual to position himself or herself in his or her own biography. A growing demand in compensating contingency leads to ever more complex processes of decision-making and, for the individual, it is becoming more and more difficult to sustain the postulated unity of the Self or 'Ganzheitlichkeit'. This leads to pathologies like depression or 'burn out', which are interpreted as symptoms of social change, especially within labour conditions. Meditation at this point is seen to be a strategy of problem-solution as well as a means of prevention. And meditation-apps promise to help.

Questionable, nevertheless, is the functionality of mindfulness meditation for daily routine. As a social praxis, mindfulness, in spite of the often postulated distance to all normative claims and religious or otherwise dogmatic positioning, is anything other than a non-normative practice. In every discourse in which mindfulness meditation is received, this meditative practice is ideologically enhanced according to the rules and parameters of the respective discourse. This can include an intentional reference to Buddhism but not necessarily so. Respectively, the ability of mindfulness to be adapted to a variety of life-situations is a sociocultural indicator of its flexibility so that it is perceived as especially attractive for diverse ideological forms of enrichment. The central precondition for this high ability for adaptation in various discourses is, in my opinion, that mindfulness is perceived as a lifestyle that is compatible as a technology of the self. By this I mean that mindfulness is seen as a daily praxis for a reflexive correction of the self. No matter if seen in a medical-therapeutical context or in a philosophy of life perspective, mindfulness, so goes the argument, is helping to increase one's distance from wrong conditions of mind provoked by a disease, by problematic social relationships or by unbearable work-conditions. And popular culture helps to regulate processes of individual self-management by offering life-style possibilities, which are presented in a specific communicative pattern, most of the time in a clear and convincing narrative form. Therefore, in mindfulness-discourse, we often find a semantic of benefit for health, for the psyche and for the individual's sense of meaning.

I have elaborated on this theoretical frame since I believe that if we look at mindfulness as a form of 'spirituality' and, as such, as a popular form of the expression of individual experience, we can analyse the specific aspects of mindfulness in a better way, and we can see how the concept circulates between religion, therapy and technologies of the self. It can also help to identify how references to Buddhist traditions of liberating the self or self-redemption almost impose themselves in this discourse field.

The mindfulness-discourse, therefore, has to be seen in the context of the wider question of what religion is, and, secondly, whether Buddhism is a religion. It is symptomatic that the reception of mindfulness in academic as well as therapeutic contexts in the West is shaped by the positive but very unspecific image of Buddhism, prevalent since the nineteenth century. Buddhism to a large extent has been seen as an analytical and methodological philosophy for the self-inspection of one's own consciousness, and not as a religious movement that is bound to teachings and doctrines. This has led to the notion that there is a high affinity between Buddhism and scientific discourses, and Western concepts of rationality and reason. Further, it is striking that Buddhism is interpreted as a subjectivist approach to problem-solution and this interpretation is even more emphasized in publications that are meant for Western readers. The ultimate justification of the Buddhist religion is grounded in the subject, namely, the starting point of the perception of reality, which is seen as suffering, as well as the potential of redemption.

According to the German monk, Nyanaponika Mahathera, whose publications have been seminal for the reception of mindfulness in America, the subjective perspective of Buddhism culminates in its self-conception as a teaching of the mind. In the opening pages of his widely circulated, *The Heart of Buddhist Meditation*, he states:

> This book is issued in the deep conviction that the systematic
> cultivation of Right Mindfulness, as taught by the Buddha in his
> Discourse on Satipaṭṭhāna, still provides the most simple and di-
> rect, the most thorough and effective, method for training and de-
> veloping the mind for its daily tasks and problems as well as for
> its highest aim: mind's own unshakable deliverance from Greed,
> Hatred and Delusion. (Nyanaponika 1962, 7)

In the German version of this book, he calls this chapter: 'Die
Lehre vom Geist' and his terminology shifts between *spirit*, *mind*
and *consciousness*, by using these terms synonymously. The
praxis of mindfulness helps to recognize, form and liberate the
mind. If the mind is 'the very element in and through which we
live' (Nyanponika 1962, 36), than he argues it is necessary to first
of all attend to 'the basic facts of the mental processes' (Nyanponika 1962, 37). Nyanaponika calls this 'bare attention' and
many scholars, including Robert Sharf (Sharf 2015, 472), have
argued that this term and the concept behind it has its roots in the
Theravāda meditation revival in the early twentieth century. Meditation masters like Ledi Sayadaw (1846-1923) and Mahasi Sayadaw (1904-1982), whom Nyanaponika considered as his teacher,
developed meditation techniques, even for lay-people, that have
become widespread and applied today in various contexts world-
wide. Mindfulness as taught by the Buddha is not only meant for
Buddhists but for the whole of humanity and this is so, according
to Nyanaponika, because, firstly, the mind is the same diachronic-
ally across cultures and, secondly, because the emphasis of the
teaching of the Buddha is on the subjective aspect of perceiving
reality. 'Bare attention' is a possibility for everyone. The personal
and individual aspect of the knowledge acquired in meditation is
the only real help that human beings can look for. Nyanaponika
points out, '[i]n the Buddhist doctrine, mind is the starting point,
the focal point, and also, as the liberated and purified mind of
the Saint, the culminating point' (Nyanaponika 1962, 21). That
this concept of the mind, which Nyanaponika sketches out in his
publications, is already a normative construction, becomes clear
not only when we take into account that he distances himself from

'teachings that claim that a human being can only be saved by the grace of a God' (Nyanaponika 1993, 165), but even more when his concept of the self-liberating mind needs an explicit legitimation. Mindfulness, he claims, is necessary for today because it can serve as a remedy against the 'degenerations of humankind' (Nyanaponika 1993, 21), against the catastrophes of self-destruction, which could be observed in Christian Europe during the twentieth century and, finally, as a remedy against 'mindless dissipations' which are common among Westerners today. Mindfulness, on the other hand, supports the 'evolvement of a high and highest humanity, the true superhuman of whom so many have dreamt and to whom so many misguided efforts have been directed' (Nyanaponika 1993, 21-22).

All the above mentioned aspects of mindfulness we find again in today's therapeutic contexts, in which mindfulness meditation is practised, most famously in the Mindfulness-Based-Stress-Reduction (MBSR) developed by the already-mentioned American molecular-biologist and physician, Jon Kabat-Zinn. Kabat-Zinn has established this kind of meditation as not only an effective therapy for a variety of physical diseases, psychic diseases due to stress, somatoform disorders like fibromyalgia and burnout symptoms, but also for chronic pain provoked by severe diseases. Mindfulness meditation is applied to build up better tolerance of pain and acceptance of the bad situation. An MBSR course is about eight weeks; in it elements of various meditation techniques are combined. Kabat-Zinn has elaborated this programme in his book, *Full Catastrophe Living* (1990), which in its German translation unfortunately received the boring title, *Gesund durch Meditation* (2009). If we follow Kabat-Zinn's argument, then mindfulness is a way of practice that 'can lead to the discovery of deep realms of relaxation, calmness, and insight within yourself' (Kabat-Zinn 1990, 12). And again the focus is on the subject and the inner experience:

> What you will be learning will be coming primarily from inside you, from your own experience as your life unfolds from moment to moment rather than from some external authority or teacher or

belief system. Our philosophy is that you are the world expert on your life, your body, and your mind, or at least you are in the best position to become that expert if you observe carefully. (Kabat-Zinn 1990, 14)

MBSR claims to show the path to a true understanding of the self:

A new territory, previously unknown to you or only vaguely suspected, which contains a veritable wellspring of positive energy for self-understanding and healing shall be explored by the patient. (Kabat-Zinn 1990, 12)

Related to the emphasis on individual experience, Kabat Zinn explicitly argues that mindfulness meditation is a universal concept:

Although at this time Mindfulness meditation is most commonly taught and practiced within the context of Buddhism, its essence is universal. Mindfulness is basically just a particular way of paying attention. It is a way of looking deeply into oneself in the spirit of self-inquiry and self-understanding...In fact one of its major strengths is that it is not dependent on any belief system or ideology, so that its benefits are therefore accessible for anyone to test for himself or herself. Yet it is no accident that Mindfulness comes out of Buddhism, which has as its overriding concerns the relief of suffering and the dispelling of illusions. (Kabat-Zinn 1990, 12-13)

Therefore, Kabat-Zinn consciously refers to the Buddhist tradition of *vipassanā* meditation and his aim is to apply this tradition to the therapeutic system. While in the reception of mindfulness in psychology and philosophy, only the description and exploration of a mindful state of consciousness is in the forefront, Kabat-Zinn aims at something more. Mindfulness for him is a way of life and Buddhist ethics are important. But the universalization and de-contextualization of Buddhist meditation praxis, as can also be observed in the publications of Jack Kornfield, Joseph Goldstein and Sharon Salzberg, have opened meditation to many functional areas of Western societies.

Kabat-Zinn's interpretation of mindfulness meditation is interesting in various ways. First of all, there is the discrepancy between Buddhist-religious and non-Buddhist scientific contextualization of the MBSR Programme. MBSR would be a very good example within which to examine the borderlines between religion and science, not only Buddhism and Science but also how diverse scientific aspects can be mingled together. Mindfulness in Kabat-Zinn's terms is a holistic body-experience that has to be distinguished from 'dis-attention', a term he borrows from the controversial parapsychologist, Gary Schwartz, who describes it as 'not attending to the relevant feedback messages of our body and our mind that are necessary for their harmonious functioning' (Kabat-Zinn 1990, 228). MBSR, therefore, is designed as an attempt to sensitize patients for the reciprocation of body and mind. The central insight that has to be trained is that 'living systems maintain inner balance, harmony, and order through their capacity to self-regulate via feedback loops between particular functions and systems (Kabat-Zinn 1990, 227). Kabat-Zinn develops a conception of health as a dynamic process of interconnectedness. With the help of a biological superstructure, an image of a human being as an entropy producing system is composed and the holistic perspective is produced by connecting the Buddhist concept of dependent origination (*paṭicca-samuppāda*) with the so called Gaia-hypothesis (Kabat-Zinn 1990, 157) derived from systemic ecology, which is based on a systems-theoretical understanding of life.

According to Kabat-Zinn, the body, through feedback-loops which connect all systems, is able to adjust reactively and autopoetically to its environment. With these arguments, he refers to system-theoretical, functionalist and constructivist theories developed in biology, anthropology and neuroscience by Gregory Bateson, Humberto Maturana, Francisco Varela and others. The Dutch scholar of religion, Wouter Hanegraaff aptly has called this field of theory 'New Age Science' (Hanegraaff 1998, 67).

For Kabat-Zinn, the idealistic and natural philosophical speculations about the interconnectedness of body and mind, and the holistic view of the relatedness of all living beings form the specific character of mindfulness meditation that contrasts this praxis to all other forms of stress reduction. Not only is the academic enrichment of the MBSR therapy striking but also that it is connected to a strong concept of individuality. On the one hand, through a stereotypical affirmation of 'Eastern' ideas and practices, a distance to stereotypical 'Western' concepts of individuality is created, and, on the other hand, a welfare promise for the individual is articulated in such a way that each and every individual has to travel his or her own path of mindfulness in order to achieve a holistic state of identity.

To sum up: the dissemination of mindfulness takes place in the framework of a popular form of communication, a cultural pattern that is highly generalized, widely suitable for connection and open to various interpretations. It is comparatively easy to learn, has hardly any preconditions for participation and can be integrated into almost all areas of life. Popular culture is serving in modern societies to regulate processes of individual self-management. And the success of mindfulness is that it provides a framework for a technology of the self that is applicable in daily life. Mindfulness is a body-praxis and a technique of mind that beyond doubt is of therapeutic value but, under ideology-critical aspects, it can be seen as a problematic self-interpretation of modern societies; an analysis of its dissemination and popularity especially reflects on the demands that are arising for the individual today in contemporary society.

Bibliography

Hanegraaff, Wouter J. 1998. *New Age Religion and Western Culture: Esotericism in the Mirror of Secular Thought*. New York: State University of New York.

Kabat-Zinn, Jon, 2009. *Gesund durch Meditation: Das große Buch der Selbstheilung*. Frankfurt a.M.: Fischer.

Kabat-Zinn, Jon, 1990. *Full Catastrophe Living: Using the Wisdom of Your Body and Mind to Face Stress, Pain, and Illness*. New York: Bantam.

Knoblauch, Hubert, 2009. *Populäre Religion. Auf dem Weg in eine spirituelle Gesellschaft*. Frankfurt a.M.: Campus.

Mahasi Sayadaw, 1995. *Satipatthana Vipassana*. http://www.accesstoinsight.org/lib/ authors/mahasi/wheel370.html.

Metzinger, Thomas, 2009. *Der Ego-Tunnel: Eine neue Philosophie des Selbst. Von der Hirnforschung zur Bewusstseinstechnik*. Berlin: Piper.

Nehring, Andreas & Christoph Ernst, 2013. 'Populäre Achtsamkeit – Kulturelle Aspekte einer Meditationspraxis zwischen Präsenzerfahrung und implizitem Wissen'. In *Präsenz und Implizites Wissen*, eds. Christoph Ernst & Paul Heike. Bielefeld: Transcript: 373-401.

Nyanaponika Thera, 1962. *The Heart of Buddhist Meditation: A handbook of mental training based in the Buddha's way of mindfulness*. London: Rider & Co.

Nyanaponika Thera, 1993. *Geistestraining durch Achtsamkeit: Die Buddhistische Satipatthana-Methode*. Stammbach: Beyerlein u. Steinschulte.

Ravencroft, Ian, 2008. *Philosophie des Geistes. Eine Einführung*. Stuttgart: Reclam.

Ricard, Matthieu & Wolf Singer, 2017. *Beyond the Self: Conversations between Buddhism and Neuroscience*. Cambridge, MA: MIT Press.

Sharf, Robert 1995. 'Buddhist Modernism and the Rhetoric of Meditative Experience'. *Numen* 42.3: 228-283.

Sharf, Robert, 1998. 'Experience'. In *Critical Terms for Religious Studies*, ed. Mark C. Taylor. Chicago-London: The University of Chicago Press: 94-116.

Sharf, Robert, 2000. 'The Rhetoric of Experience in the Study of Religion'. *Journal of Consciousness Studies* 7.11-12: 267-287.

Sharf, Robert, 2015. 'Is Mindfulness Buddhist?' *Transcultural Psychiatry* 52.4: 470-484.

Singer, Wolf, 2002. *Der Beobachter im Gehirn: Essays zur Hirnforschung*. Frankfurt a.M.: Suhrkamp.

Wilson, Jeff, 2014. *Mindful America: The Mutual Transformation of Buddhist Meditation and American Culture*. Oxford & New York: Oxford University Press.

Žižek, Slavoj, 2001. *Die gnadenlose Liebe*. Frankfurt a.M.: Suhrkamp.

Thích Nhất Hạnh's Propagation of Mindfulness in the West

Elise Anne DeVido

Abstract

Buddhist monk Thích Nhất Hạnh (b. 1926) is a well-known teacher, poet, peacemaker, prolific author and pioneering proponent of Engaged Buddhism. His teachings on mindfulness have influenced educators, therapists, medical practitioners, politicians, social and political activists, environmentalists and those involved in inter-religious dialogue. In both academic and popular circles, his name is synonymous with the term 'mindfulness' itself. Yet, few works analyze carefully how this came to be. This chapter discusses the evolution of Thích Nhất Hạnh's 'mindfulness' in the context of his life-long mission to actualize a Buddhist practice engaged in all spheres of life. Questions explored include how he fashioned the persona of 'Zen Master' and his place in the history of American Zen; how he developed his ideas and methods on mindfulness as he searched for his niche among other missionizing Asian Buddhists; his ideas and methods regarding mindfulness in light of the recent critiques of the mindfulness movement; and the future of Thích Nhất Hạnh's organization and his legacy for modern Global Buddhism.

Keywords: Thích Nhất Hạnh; Mindfulness; McMindfulness; Engaged Buddhism; Age of Anxiety; American Zen; Global Buddhism

Introduction

Buddhist monk, Thích Nhất Hạnh, secular name Nguyễn Xuân Bảo, was born in 1926 in Huế, French colonial Vietnam.[1] He is a teacher, poet, prolific author and pioneering proponent of 'Engaged Buddhism'. His prodigious list of English and Vietnamese publications for adults and children, many of which have been translated into other foreign languages, include: his teachings and practices (manuals, trainings, exercises) for popular audiences; reports regarding the Vietnam War; history of Buddhism in Vietnam and books on Engaged Buddhism; annotated translations of Buddhist texts; poems, songs, novels, several films, at least one play; and his calligraphic works.[2]

From the late 1970s, Thích Nhất Hạnh spent the following decades developing his craft as a mindfulness and meditation teacher and has met with great acclaim outside his native country and more recently, within Vietnam. His teachings on 'mindfulness' have influenced educators, therapists, medical practitioners, politicians, social and political activists, environmentalists and those involved in inter-religious dialogue.

As yet, there are no in-depth critical studies of his life and work. A biographer would need to be trained in Buddhist studies and the history of global Buddhism, East and Southeast Asian history, and nineteenth and twentieth century intellectual history, as well as know English, Vietnamese, Chinese and French, among other languages, to navigate the vast amount of extant materials, and the various revised and republished editions. It would be best to conduct interviews with him and his disciples, who shape and guard his image, but, for the time being, the possibility for scholars to go beyond the generic and hagiographic accounts of Thích

---

1   I have not yet found details about the first 16 years of his life, for example, details about his family background and early education nor why he became a monk.

2   While I am unaware of a definitive bibliography of his works, readers might refer to Parallax Press for his works in English and other languages, and Lá Bôi for Vietnamese publications in Vietnamese. See also DeVido 2014 for an annotated bibliography of selected works.

Nhất Hạnh and his sangha (both monastic and lay) seems slim due to their rejection of academic scrutiny let alone Thích Nhất Hạnh's poor state of health.[3]

There are however, sympathetic portraits of and paeans to him written by students and devotees, and essays and chapters on his contributions to Engaged Buddhism, to 'Buddhism in the West', and to Christian-Buddhist inter-religious dialogue.[4] He has also become a popular guru and has enjoyed a high degree of visibility in Buddhist publications such as *Lions' Roar* and *Tricycle*, and on television, including the Oprah Winfrey Show. To take but a few examples, he has taught mindfulness trainings at Google Head-quarters to billionaire CEOs and to members of the US Congress, and has promoted mindfulness skills in public schools. Oft-re-peated in reportage and book blurbs is his nomination by Martin Luther King Jr. for the 1967 Nobel Peace Prize and the opinion that '[a]mong Buddhist leaders influential in the West, Thích Nhất Hạnh ranks second only to the Dalai Lama' (Niebuhr 1999).[5]

Though he did not coin the term 'mindfulness' and there have been many other Buddhist teachers of various traditions (includ-ing monks and nuns from Vietnam) who bridge 'East and West', Thích Nhất Hạnh, in both academic and popular circles, is often synonymous with the term 'mindfulness' itself. Yet, few works, academic or not, analyze carefully how this came to be,[6] most likely for the reasons mentioned above about the challenges for

---

3   In late 2014 Thích Nhất Hạnh suffered a major stroke and since then he has been confined to a wheelchair with limited speech. On 13 March 2018, a Thai Plum Village representative emailed me this message: 'Thay has been at Thai Plum Village since 10 Dec 2016. During this period, he went to Vietnam for only 9 days' [autumn 2017]. To me this was surprising due to the unhappy events of late 2009. Note that 'Thầy', with diacritics, means 'master' or 'teacher'.

4   Parachin 2011, for example, considers Thích Nhất Hạnh as a mystic.

5   An interesting connection here: Gustav Niebuhr's grandfather was H. Rich-ard Niebuhr of Yale Divinity School and his grand-uncle Reinhold Niebuhr, who taught from 1928-1960 at Union Theological Seminary in New York City where Thích Nhất Hạnh's studied from 1962-1963.

6   For example, Rosenbaum & Magrid 2016 has no discussion about Thích Nhất Hạnh. A good start in an analytical direction is Wilson 2014.

potential biographers. This paper will discuss the evolution of Thích Nhất Hạnh's 'mindfulness' in the context of his life-long mission (I use the term 'mission' in an evangelical sense) to actualize a Buddhist practice engaged in all spheres of society, solving the problems of modern life. A chapter is not long enough to discuss all aspects of this evolution, so I have chosen to focus on the following topics: in Part One, three key points in the making of Thích Nhất Hạnh's 'mindfulness' before the 1980s, namely, a) Vietnam's Buddhist Revival Movement, b) Princeton Theological Seminary, Columbia University and Union Theological Seminary, c) war. Part Two focusses on 'Mindfulness' and the making of a Vietnamese Zen Master. Part Three engages with mindfulness, while the Conclusion offers an evaluation of his legacy.

I begin with two caveats. First, although this paper focusses on Thích Nhất Hạnh, he has worked over the years with multitudes of friends, colleagues, professionals from many fields and students, as well as with many public and private institutions, and his successes would not be possible without this global community.[7] Second, the terms 'East' and 'West' tend toward essentialism and are better used as discursive tools. Over the past one hundred years, Buddhism has been a globalizing phenomenon, so the categories of 'traditional' and 'modern' or 'Eastern' and 'Western' Buddhism are not easy to delineate and define. 'The West' may include, for example, ethnic Vietnamese of different generations born in or immigrated to the United States from France or other countries, or monastic and lay disciples of Thích Nhất Hạnh, who are not ethnically Vietnamese but have a Vietnamese dharma name and live in Plum Village, France, or other related Communities of Mindful Living worldwide. It is also important to remember the many Vietnamese temples in 'the West' and their sangha communities that preceded or developed in the same time as the Thích Nhất Hạnh phenomenon. As much as possible this paper will refer specifi-

---

7   Thích Nhất Hạnh's closest colleague is Sister Chân Không and they have worked together since the late 1950s to develop Engaged Buddhism in Vietnam and worldwide. This essay cannot do justice to her life and works. For some insights into her life, see Chân Không 1993.

cally to nations such as Vietnam [in some cases, South Vietnam or North Vietnam], the United States, France, Thailand and so on.

Part One: Key Points in the Making of Thích Nhất Hạnh: 'Mindfulness' Before 1980s

Rather than present a biography of Thích Nhất Hạnh, this section will explore three key points that shaped the later development and propagation of his 'mindfulness' platform:[8]

a. Vietnam's Buddhist Revival Movement
b. Princeton Theological Seminary, Columbia University and Union Theological Seminary
c. Vietnam War.

Vietnam's 'Buddhist Revival' Movement

To start with, Vietnam has a rich and diverse religious history. The Vietnamese spiritual landscape has included Śākyamuni and the bodhisattvas together with a wide range of nature deities, tutelary gods and deified historical figures. As for Mahāyāna Buddhism, Linji and Pure Land have predominated since the seventeenth century; the thorny problem of 'Zen' in Vietnam will be discussed later in this paper. Roman Catholicism has over five-hundred years of history in Vietnam. In addition, there are different strains of Theravāda Buddhism and Islam, a number of twentieth century syncretic religions, and various Protestant groups, as well as 'remnants' of Śaiva-Mahāyāna in central Vietnam.[9]

As elsewhere in Asia, some Mahāyāna Buddhist temples and monasteries in Vietnam (from the tenth century on) were closely linked to royal families. In addition, monks and nuns were often

8   For a biography with more details, one can consult Chapman 2007 or DeVido 2014.
9   See Do 2003, Taylor 2007, and Ngo 2015. In this chapter I use the terms Mahāyāna, Theravāda, and other 'religions' as a general guide: I realize the risk of essentialism in the terms. See for example Sharf 2002.

called upon for their expertise in healing, exorcizing divination techniques, and death rituals, and their monasteries functioned as community centres that provided charity and refuge. As is well-known, in the nineteenth and early twentieth centuries, many Asian countries faced crises brought by imperialism and modernity. In this context 'Buddhist revivals' linked with 'nationalist' platforms arose in Sri Lanka, Burma, China, Thailand, Laos, Cambodia, Japan and Tibetan Buddhism.[10]

Likewise, in French colonial Vietnam, from the 1920s, Vietnamese Buddhist monastic and lay reformers sought to reform their religion[11] to lead national rejuvenation, inspired in part by the Chinese monk Taixu's (1890-1947) blueprint to modernize and systematize sangha education and temple administration, and by his idea of 'Buddhism for this world' [renjian fojiao 人間佛教 in Chinese, Nhân Gian Phật Giáo in Vietnamese]. 'Buddhism for this world' emphasized the centrality of education, modern publishing, social work and Buddhist lay groups for Buddhism's future in the modern world. Trí Quang, a major figure in 1960s Buddhist socio-political activism in Vietnam, credited Taixu 'for promoting [Buddhism for this world]…that Buddhists were born to serve human beings, that monastics should not only pray for themselves but to join society; not only think of the dead, but think of the future, to sacrifice for and serve humanity' (Thích Trí Quang 1972: 149-151). To Trí Quang, Taixu was a revolutionary: 'With his call for "a revolution in religious doctrine, a revolution in religious administration, and a revolution in religious property", Master Taixu is the model for the modern sangha in the twentieth century' (Thích Trí Quang 1972: 152).[12]

---

10 See DeVido 2007 for more details about the Buddhist Revival in Vietnam.

11 Here I speak of Mahāyāna Buddhism however there were 'revitalization' movements in Vietnam's Theravāda communities as well as an emergence of a Mahāyāna-Theravāda sect.

12 Trí Quang and other Buddhist reformers went far beyond Taixu and developed a fundamentalist Buddhist nationalism for Vietnam, with its apogee in 1960s South Vietnam. Thích Nhất Hạnh was at once an insider and outsider in that history.

Trí Quang (b. 1924) and Nhất Hạnh are contemporaries and, in addition to their temple trainings from a young age, continued their studies in newly-established Buddhist Institutes.[13] In addition to developing Buddhist education for monastics, Buddhist reformers in China and Vietnam published Buddhist journals with articles by monastics and laypersons. Nhất Hạnh first gained renown in Vietnamese Buddhist circles for his poetry and essays, and his work as editor. Nhất Hạnh speaks about how his ideas for Engaged Buddhism took shape in 1954, just at the time of the Geneva Accords that divided Vietnam into North and South:

> Buddhism is a very ancient tradition in Vietnam, and most of the people have a Buddhist seed in them. Mr. Vu Ngoc Cac, manager of a daily newspaper, asked me to write a series of articles about Buddhism. He wanted me to offer insight as to the spiritual direction we should take in order to deal with the great confusion in the country. So I wrote a series of ten articles with the title, "A Fresh Look at Buddhism." It is in this series of ten articles that I proposed the idea of Engaged Buddhism — Buddhism in the realm of education, economics, politics, and so on. So Engaged Buddhism dates from 1954.
>
> At that time I did not use a typewriter, I just wrote in the old-fashioned way. And they came and they took the article, and the article was always printed on the front page with a big red title. The newspaper sold very, very well because people were very thirsty. They wanted spiritual direction because confusion was so huge.
>
> That series of articles was published as a book later on. Not long after, I visited Hue. Duc Tam, who had been in the same class as me at the Buddhist Institute, was the editor of another Buddhist magazine. In fact, I wrote another series of ten articles with the title 'Buddhism Today,' which was also on the theme of Engaged Buddhism. (Thích Nhất Hạnh 2008)

In 1956 he obtained certificates in Vietnamese literature and the history of philosophy at Saigon University. By the time he went

---

13 Nhất Hạnh studied from 1953-1957 at An Quang Buddhist Institute, Saigon, for a Diploma in Buddhist Studies 1957.

overseas for the first time, he evidenced writing talent in both poetry and prose, possessed wide intellectual interests, and communicated to the public his burgeoning ideas on Engaged Buddhism. However, in his *Journals*, he communicated his disappointment with the Buddhist leaders' (who were in fact the first generation of Buddhist *reformers*) opposition to the efforts by himself and others to create a grassroots Buddhist movement (Thích Nhất Hạnh 1999, 6-7).[14] This is a likely reason that Nhất Hạnh decided to study overseas. And he noted there were more than one hundred libraries in the USA 'with great collections of religious books, including Buddhist texts in Chinese, Sanskrit and Pāli' (Chân Không 1993, 30).

New World Views: Princeton Theological Seminary, Columbia University and Union Theological Seminary

Previous biographical accounts of Thích Nhất Hạnh only mention in passing his USA years, 1961-1963. However, I argue that the inter-cultural and inter-religious encounters of these years were central to his formation as interlocutor among cultures and religions. In 1961 he became a Special Student for one year at Princeton Theological Seminary (PTS), with funding provided by the latter. His advisor at PTS was Professor Edward J. Jurji, a pioneer in comparative religion and the concept of religious pluralism.[15] A number of theological seminaries in the US then and now enjoy close relations and Professor Jurji recommended Thích Nhất Hạnh for graduate study in Religion at Union Theological Seminary (UTC), Columbia University Department of Religion. On 4 June 1963, Thích Nhất Hạnh obtained a joint Master of Arts in Religion with the thesis, 'The problem of knowledge in the phi-

---

14 More details are necessary to understand his conflict with the so-called 'conservative Buddhist establishment' that in fact was not unified in structure or ideas; moreover, so-called conservative Buddhists aided and supported him many times.

15 Princeton Theology Seminary Special Collections for information on PTS and Professor Jurji.

losophy of Vijñānavāda'.[16] This was apt, because twentieth century Buddhist modernists in China and Vietnam paid particular attention to the Yogācāra, 'consciousness-only',[17] as a powerful tool to debate with Western science and philosophy. Whether or not this was true for Thích Nhất Hạnh, Andronic (2011) convincingly argues the importance of 'consciousness-only' to his teachings on 'interbeing' and 'mindfulness' that he developed later in the 1960s-1970s.

Previous studies of Thích Nhất Hạnh did not notice that he studied in the States during a golden age of Protestant theology. According to his student Sr Chân Đức, while at UTS, Thích Nhất Hạnh read *Letters and Papers from Prison* by Dietrich Bonhoeffer, who had taught at UTS in the 1930s: 'The sacrifice, the understanding, and the love of Dietrich Bonhoeffer were very much appreciated by Thay ['teacher', used by Thích Nhất Hạnh's disciples], and helped Thay to make his own breakthrough to feel the true, deep courage needed to be able truly to renew Buddhism' (Than Ngiem 2017).[18] Furthermore, Columbia's graduate programme in religion was founded in 1943 by Columbia's Horace A. Friess with Reinhold Niebuhr and Paul Tillich of UTS, two of the towering public intellectuals of the 'Age of Anxiety', and their 'religious humanism' (in Thích Nhất Hạnh's phrase) was a major intellectual current in seminaries and universities alike in the 1950s and 1960s and influenced Thích Nhất Hạnh as well.

In his letter to Martin Luther King, Jr. of 1 June 1965, entitled 'In Search of the Enemy of Man', Thích Nhất Hạnh sought King's

---

16 Princeton Theological Seminary Special Collections; Registrar Offices of Union Theological Seminary and Columbia University.

17 As Pacey 2014 writes, for Taixu and other Buddhist reformers, Yogācāra 'like science, addressed the nature of the noumenon, discussed epistemology and causality and had a system of logic' (p. 218) and thus could debate and even surpass 'Western' ideas. Andronic 2011 takes another view of Yogācāra thought, its central importance to Thích Nhất Hạnh's 'interbeing' and 'mindfulness'.

18 She did not specify which edition of letter and papers from prison that he read. The original 1951 German text, *Widerstand und Ergebung*, was translated into English in 1953, I am unsure if in whole or part.

support to join the 'world's humanists' and publicly oppose the war in Vietnam. Here I quote from the letter in length to illustrate the force of his argument:

> I am sure that since you have been engaged in one of the hardest struggles for equality and human rights, you are among those who understand fully and who share with all their heart the indescribable suffering of the Vietnamese people. The world's humanists would not remain silent. You yourself cannot remain silent. America is said to have a strong religious foundation and spiritual leaders would not allow the American political and economic doctrines to be deprived of their spiritual element. You cannot be silent since you have already been in action and you are in action because, in you, God is in action too – to use Karl Barth's expression. And Albert Schweitzer, with his stress on the reverence for life. And Paul Tillich with his courage to be, and thus, to love. And Niebuhr. And Mackay. And Fletcher. And Donald Harrington. All these religious humanists, and many more, are not going to favor the existence of a shame such as the one mankind has to endure in Vietnam...In writing to you, as a Buddhist, I profess my faith in Love, in Communion, and in the world's humanists, whose thoughts and attitudes should be the guide for all humankind and find out who is the real enemy of Man. (Thích Nhất Hạnh 1967, 92)[19]

'In Search of the Enemy of Man' certainly fits into what Mark Greif (2015) describes about the mid-century 'age of the crisis of man' discourse: one example among many was Niebuhr's *The Nature and Destiny of Man* (1943). Greif discusses how, in the context of two world wars and the Cold War, thinkers of all political positions pondered how 'to save mankind', or, 'The Family of Man', as in the famous 'humanist photography' exhibit that toured the world from 1955-1963. Thích Nhất Hạnh linked the

---

19 This letter and other writings of Thích Nhất Hạnh did influence King to speak out against the war in April 1967. By enemies of man Thích Nhất Hạnh meant intolerance, fanaticism, dictatorship, cupidity, hatred, discrimination, etc.

fate of Vietnam with the survival of the human race, due to the high-stakes danger of the Cold War.

One response to 'the crisis of man' was the development of the comparative study of world religions.[20] In different ways, Thích Nhất Hạnh's professors played key roles in this development after WWII. Edward J. Jurji of Princeton Theological Seminary was an important figure as mentioned above. At Columbia, the Departments of Religion and studies of East Asia were closely linked. For example, Professors Ryūsaku Tsunoda, Horace A. Friess (Department of Religion chair at Columbia) and William T. de Bary invited D.T. Suzuki to Columbia University, where he taught from 1952-1957. Although Suzuki had left Columbia by the time Thích Nhất Hạnh studied there, Suzuki had already made a deep mark on the American and European intellectual landscape through his lectures and his books.[21] Due to the influence of Suzuki's seminars, Columbia University 'came to be regarded as a significant launching pad for the academic study of Zen' (de Bary 2006, 599-601). At a Japanese Pure Land temple (Thích Nhất Hạnh did not describe what sect) near the Columbia main

---

20 Building upon the spirit of the 1893 Parliament of World Religions illustrated by this quotation by chief organizer John Henry Barrows: 'The solemn charge which the Parliament preaches to all true believers is a return to the primitive unity of the world...The results may be far off, but they are certain'. Later, the founding of Harvard University's Center for World Religions in 1960 is a perfect example of post WWII religious internationalism. As described at its inaugural reception, the Centre was envisioned to be a place for 'East meets West' encounters. The first Director of the Center for World Religions, Robert H.L. Slater, a survivor of the Japanese invasion of Burma, already wrote in 1941 that he dreamed of a super-university 'founded by men [of various faiths] who hold hands...deriving from his own religious conviction a charity which sees beyond nations, beyond continents to a New World' (Slater 1941, 67).

21 I do not know which D.T. Suzuki books Thích Nhất Hạnh read during his studies in the USA, however Suzuki had already published many English works from 1900 on such as *The Awakening of Faith*, *Essays in Zen Buddhism*, *Living by Zen* and *Zen and Japanese Culture*. See http://www.matsugaokabunko.com/en/bibliography/index.html for more titles.

campus, Thích Nhất Hạnh heard a sermon by a Japanese priest and mused:

> The Pure Land sect's efforts to look like Western churches seem to me to reflect their lack of understanding of the true American needs. Americans place a high value on independence. Their children are encouraged to be self-sufficient and self-reliant. A Buddhist approach that emphasizes self-effort and self-realization, like Zen, to build, develop, and awaken the individual, seems to be better suited to the American spirit...[i]n fact, Zen is generating a lot of interest here. Professor D.T. Suzuki's voice has struck a chord across the country. (Thích Nhất Hạnh 1999, 96-97)

Certainly, the success of Suzuki made Thích Nhất Hạnh consider the possibility of propagating a 'Vietnamese Zen tradition' in 'the West'.[22] He continued that '[p]eople who live in a frenetic society, exhausted by interminable plans and thoughts, thirst for the serenity and self-contentment that a path like Zen offers'. An inkling of the 'mindfulness' practices to come?

By 1963, Columbia University had established Chinese, Japanese and Korean studies. Anton Cerbu, a professor of 'Oriental Humanities' with interests in Tibetan and Vietnamese Buddhism, urged Thích Nhất Hạnh to stay there and develop Vietnamese studies. However, Thích Nhất Hạnh decided to return to South Vietnam to participate in the Buddhist nationalist movement made known to the world by a 'lotus in a sea of fire': Thích Quảng Đức's self-immolation on 11 June 1963 (see DeVido 2007).

The Vietnam War

There are many accounts about how Thích Nhất Hạnh's vision of Engaged Buddhism[23] in the 1960s shaped and was shaped by the (South Vietnam) Unified Buddhist Church's (UBC) Buddhist

---

22 The Vietnamese monk Thích Thiên Ân (1926-1980) taught in the USA from 1966-1980 but had modest influence compared to Thích Nhất Hạnh.

23 He exhorted that Buddhists must emerge from the temple and go beyond charity-provision to propose Buddhist solutions, based on compassion and non-violence, to urgent problems of humankind such as poverty, hunger,

nationalism and anti-war movements within and without Vietnam (Thích Nhất Hạnh 1967; King 1996; Chapman 2007; DeVido 2009; DeVido 2014). It is not possible here to relate this complex history, so I will mention two aspects of the war years: the origins of 'interbeing', and his role as interlocutor between Vietnam and 'the West' (and among world faiths). Both of these aspects are inseparable from Thích Nhất Hạnh's mission to propagate 'mindfulness' from the 1980s on.

Interbeing

After he returned to Saigon in 1963, he gathered a group of students to form a new sangha, the Order of Interbeing (Chân Không 1993, 77-79).[24] The name of his new Order was '*Tiếp Hiện*': *Tiếp,* to continue, to be in touch with, and *Hiện,* to actualize in the present moment. Their mission was to carry out Engaged Buddhism. Although I have not found a complete etymology of this term, Thích Nhất Hạnh points to the Chinese term 相即 *xiangji* as one source (Andronic 2011, 22). Huang (2009) discusses the Flower-Adornment Sūtra's 相即相入 *xiangji xiang ru,* which conveys *śūnyatā*, dependent-origination and interpenetration symbolized in 'Indra's Net' (Huang 2009). Yet, in her detailed explanation, Andronic (2011, 22-24) claims that '[h]is interbeing is not the metaphor of Indra's net but rather a description of reality; that is, if we look deeply we see that things are empty, impermanent, and without a separate self, and instead are what they are because of a web of interdependent relationships with other things'. Andronic goes so far to say that '*interbeing* becomes the lens through which Nhất Hạnh re-examines all Buddhist doctrines' (2011, 23).

---

diseases, slavery and war. In sum, he called on Buddhists in Vietnam to lead a non-violent social revolution. See Thích Nhất Hạnh 1965, 14, 21, 26-27.

24 Many Buddhist groups in South Vietnam met in 1964 to form the Unified Buddhist Church to increase Buddhists' socio-political power *vis à vis* the government of South Vietnam and the Roman Catholic Church. Again Thích Nhất Hạnh displayed his complex relationship with the UBC at that time by forming his own sangha (Order of Interbeing) the members of which he ordains himself.

For his sangha, Thích Nhất Hạnh created Fourteen Precepts (later called Fourteen Mindfulness Trainings) based upon the commonly-understood Five Lay precepts and the Eight-Fold Path.[25] Over the years, he and his Plum Village sangha have revised the 'Five Precepts' for lay Buddhists and renamed them as 'The Five Mindfulness trainings'. In one iteration, the Five Mindfulness Trainings include the vocabulary of environmental protection, upholding only committed romantic/sexual relationships, prevention of the sexual abuse of children, and the possible toxic effects of media (Thích Nhất Hạnh 2007). Thích Nhất Hạnh's community modify the Precepts/Mindfulness trainings in accordance with changing contexts.

Interlocutor

In 1966 the Fellowship of Reconciliation and Cornell University's George M. Kahin arranged lectures for Thích Nhất Hạnh in the United States and in Europe, including an audience with Pope Paul VI. He spoke to government officials, helped persuade the United Nations to send a fact-finding mission to Vietnam, gave press conferences, and shared ideas with many religious and peace activists including Martin Luther King Jr., Thomas Merton, the Society of Friends and the Catholic Worker. He communicated to 'The West' the complex war situation in Vietnam, the suffering of the Vietnamese at the grassroots level, and how a 'modern' Vietnamese Buddhist practice might work with other

---

25 Since 1966 Thích Nhất Hạnh has revised the Fourteen Precepts though the kernel remains. One list is: do not be idolatrous to any doctrine or ideology; do not think that knowledge you possess is absolute; do not force others to adopt your views; do not avoid contact with suffering and awaken others to reality of suffering; do not accumulate wealth: live simply and share resources; do not maintain anger and hatred; do not lose yourselves in your surroundings: learn to practice breathing in order to regain composure in body and mind; reconcile conflicts in the community; Right Speech; do not exploit the Buddhist community, stand against oppression and injustice; Right Livelihood; No killing, prevent war; No stealing; Do not mistreat your body; see Chân Không 1993, 77-79.

faiths and other 'humanists' to bring peace and sovereignty for Vietnam. *The New York Review of Books* presented him as 'a Buddhist Poet in Vietnam':

> [Here] are popular poems in free verse and when I write them I feel I am trying to speak very simply for the majority of Vietnamese who are peasants and cannot speak for themselves; they do not know or care much about words like communism or democracy but want above all for the war to end so they may survive and not be maimed or killed. ('A Buddhist Poet in Vietnam', 1966)[26]

Similarly *The Harvard Crimson* reported:

> Thích Nhất Hạnh, director of the School of Social Studies [School of Youth for Social Service] at the Buddhist University of Saigon, called Friday night for a U.S. policy of reconstruction in and withdrawal from South Vietnam. The lecture, 'Self-Determination in Vietnam', was held before a sympathetic audience in Dunster House. Often clasping his hands in a gesture of prayer, the Buddhist priest spoke bluntly, but in a soft and hesitant English. 'I am a messenger from the suffering peasants in South Vietnam', Nhất Hạnh announced, 'and I have come here to tell you that the war must stop.' (Lerner 1966)

Today we question the outdated language, for example, his use of 'peasants' and his claim to speak for an entire group of 'voiceless persons' but Thích Nhất Hạnh's voice-in-person not only linked together disparate religious and secular institutions, and private organizations that may not have met otherwise, but went beyond the earlier 'crisis of man' paradigm towards a new global ethics. Themes from these lecture tours are found in his 1967 book, *Vietnam: Lotus in a Sea of Fire: A Buddhist Proposal for Peace*, which also includes his rendering of Buddhism past and present in Vietnam, and documents such as his peace proposals and his essay 'In Search of the Enemy of Man'. However, *Lotus in a Sea of Fire* does not mention 'mindfulness' even once.

---

26 Thích Nhất Hạnh was actually the author.

We do not know the precise reasons that prevented Thích Nhất Hạnh's return to Vietnam after his lecture tour. What we do know is that the UBC appointed him to lead their overseas office in Paris. The office wrote and printed News Bulletins about the UBC's many war relief and rural reconstruction projects in South Vietnam and fundraised for the same. Peace groups, scholars, overseas Vietnamese and student volunteers made connections through the office. The war in Vietnam finally ended in 1975 but, according to Thích Nhất Hạnh, the Socialist Republic of Vietnam forbade him to return. (The previous paragraph is adapted from DeVido 2014).

Part Two: 'Mindfulness' and the making of a Vietnamese Zen Master

The years from the mid-1970s to the early 1980s were a turning point for Nhất Hạnh and his colleagues: exile from Vietnam; despair over the oppression of Buddhists in Vietnam after 1975; disenchantment with factional politics among international peace activists; and a failed rescue operation to save Vietnamese boat refugees stranded in the Gulf of Siam (Chân Không 1993; Forest 2015). Nhất Hạnh and his colleagues built a retreat called Sweet Potatoes in northeast France and then created Plum Village in southwest France in 1982, home for the Order of Interbeing and retreat centre to growing numbers of students. While at Sweet Potatoes, Nhất Hạnh and his colleagues produced *The Miracle of Being Awake: A Manual on Meditation for the Use of Young Activists* (1974/5) (Forest 2016). This book has been republished with different titles over the years including the imposing *The Miracle of Mindfulness: The Classic Guide by the World's Most Revered Master* (2015). Although Nhất Hạnh has published hundreds of books concerning mindfulness over the years, I find that the *Miracle of Being Awake* contains the core of his teachings; thus, I will summarize its key points.[27] The book is a long letter

---

27 For his interpretation of 'mindfulness' here, he draws upon the *Satipaṭṭhāna Sutta*, *Ānāpānasati Sutta*, the Purification Practices for daily life in the *Avataṃsaka Sūtra*, and 'consciousness-only' of Vijñānavāda.

to his students in Vietnam involved in wartime social service. He defined mindfulness as 'keeping one's consciousness alive to the present reality'. To practice mindfulness was to 'keep one's attention focussed on the work, to be alert and ready to handle any situation which arises'. It was 'the miracle which can call back in a flash our dispersed mind and restore it to wholeness so that we can live each minute of life.' Through practising mindfulness in daily activities and in formal meditation, according to this work, one gains the ability to contemplate interdependence and break through narrow views to realize the Bodhisattva path, and to lessen suffering in ourselves and others near and far: family, classmates, friends, community. Thus, meditation is linked to social action.[28] The book ends with 'Thirty Exercises to Practice Mindfulness' in one's daily life that his subsequent books include in various forms and with good reason: they show his uncanny skill to balance humane warmth and cool clarity to teach the dharma.

Nhất Hạnh's skilful teaching attracted students from France, Thailand, the USA, Holland and elsewhere. In 1983 the Buddhist Peace Fellowship, affiliated with the Fellowship of Reconciliation and with the San Francisco Zen Center (founded by another Japanese Zen pioneer in the USA, Shunryū Suzuki Rōshi) arranged Thích Nhất Hạnh's first retreat in North America, followed by others in 1985, 1987, and 1989. Some retreats addressed general audiences while others were tailored for different professions or different ethnic and religious backgrounds. His students established several monastic centres besides Plum Village as well as 'communities of mindful living' across the globe. Until his stroke in 2014, he regularly toured North America, Europe and several countries in Asia to give retreats, lectures and interviews. (The previous paragraph is adapted from DeVido 2014.)

Nhất Hạnh and his team have strategically applied mindfulness practices to tackle concerns such as healing from trauma, pain and addiction, anger management, 'the search for happiness', work-life balance, communication and reconciliation, American angst

---

28 For a more sophisticated analysis see Andronic 2011, especially page 37.

regarding eating, and healing the wounded inner child. 'The energy of mindfulness is the salve that will recognize and heal the child within' (Nhất Hạnh 2006c, 9). One might say that much in these books is repetitive, yet they are best-sellers and evidently help many people.

The Making of a Zen Master

Just about the same time as *The Miracle of Mindfulness,* Thích Nhất Hạnh published *Zen Keys: A Guide to Zen Practice* (1974), in which he explicates what he believes is a basic understanding of 'Zen' concepts and methods, and gives an overview of *Chinese* (my emphasis) Chan history. His goal is to develop a living Zen tradition in and for 'the West', centred around large and small sanghas. Continuing some 'crisis of man' themes, he calls for a mutually respectful dialogue between 'East' and 'West' and holds that a Zen attitude of compassion towards self and others will rejuvenate humanity and allow us to live in harmony with the natural world. The book includes translations of forty-three *kōans* by the founder of the Trần Dynasty, Trần Thái Tông (1218-1277) as proof of a Vietnamese 'Zen tradition'.

As discussed earlier in this chapter, Thích Nhất Hạnh arrived in the United States at the cusp of a 'Zen boom', from the Beats in the 1950s to D.T. Suzuki.[29] In addition to the layman D.T. Suzuki, there were Sōtō Zen Master, Shunryū Suzuki Rōshi, Seung Sahn, who propagated Korean Seon in the USA, and the Chinese Chan monk, Hsuan Hua, who arrived in the USA in 1959 and founded a number of Chinese Buddhist associations, temples and schools. In this context, Thích Nhất Hạnh uses the recognizable Japanese terms Zen and *kōan* to introduce the 'Thiền tradition' of Vietnam to 'the West'. The 1974 edition of *Zen Keys* included a fulsome introduction by American Zen teacher, Philip Kapleau:

---

29 In 1960, the American philosopher Van Meter Ames discussed the 'Zen boom' in his article 'Current Western Interest in Zen'.

The publication in English of Thích Nhất Hạnh's *Zen Keys* has particular significance for Americans. For not only is his work the first precise statement of Vietnamese Buddhism to come to us – we who have such a deep and tragic karmic connection with Vietnam – but also Thích Nhất Hạnh is not an average Buddhist. He is a Zen monk, trained and developed in a Zen monastery, a man who has realized the wisdom and compassion which are the fruits of Buddhist practice. (Thích Nhất Hạnh 1974, 1)[30]

To understand how Thích Nhất Hạnh constructed this 'Zen monk' identity, helpfully endorsed by Kapleau, it is important to recall the earlier discussion of Vietnam's 'Buddhist Revival'. The reformers needed a model for their Buddhist nationalism; thus, they looked back to a so-called Golden Age of Buddhism in medieval Vietnam during the Lý and Trần dynasties from the eleventh to fifteenth centuries. During this time, the story goes, Vietnamese rulers listened to the counsel of monks, the rulers rid the land of Mongolian invaders, and peace and prosperity reigned. Yet, upon closer look, Buddhist thought of the Lý and Trần dynasties blended with Confucian and Daoist ideas. Furthermore, the Trần Kings' 'Trúc Lâm Buddhism' was probably limited to writings among court elites. Then, from the eighteenth century, a mix of Linji Buddhism (a kind of 'Chan' that still needs research, but see Nguyen Cuong Tu 1997) and Pure Land practices predominated in Vietnam. Furthermore, Thích Nhất Hạnh himself said his monastic upbringing was '*dhāraṇīs* like the Śūraṅgama Dhāraṇī and *Mahā Karuṇā Dhāraṇī*' in the morning and Pure Land liturgy in the evening (Thích Nhất Hạnh 2014). To use the term 'Zen Buddhism' to describe either medieval Vietnamese elite thought or traditional Buddhist monastic training is not apt and even disingenuous.

Instead, the answer lies in the making of an imagined Thiền tradition in the twentieth-century. To appeal variously to 'modern', 'nationalist', 'elite' and 'Western' tastes, Buddhist reformers constructed a discrete Vietnamese Thiền tradition out of medieval

---

30 This book first appeared in Vietnamese (1971) then French (1973).

Buddhist syncretic thought and promoted this imagined Thiền tradition *as* Vietnamese Buddhism, rid of so-called 'superstitions' like Pure Land, and other local ideas and practices (see Nguyen 1997, Nguyen & Barber 1998, and Soucy 2007). But, even if Vietnam did not have Chinese-style 'transmissions of the lamp' or Zen lineages as those associated with Japan, Vietnam does have a rich Thiền literature and over the centuries monastics learned various meditation practices. Thích Nhất Hạnh drew upon these traditions to make his own.

Part Three: A Surfeit of Mindfulness?

Wilson stated, '[S]cores of Thích Nhất Hạnh's books all revolve around the theme of mindfulness, and eventually mindfulness becomes a totalizing hermeneutic for him…'(Wilson 2014, 189). Does the critical term 'McMindfulness' apply to Thích Nhất Hạnh's ideas and methods on mindfulness? (see Purser & Roy 2013). Could Thích Nhất Hạnh's 'mindfulness' be construed as an example of 'spiritual materialism' (Trungpa 1973)?[31] At first glance, it seems so:

> Mindfulness: the art of simply being present. From Oprah to Phil Jackson to Anderson Cooper, it has been embraced by some of the world's most successful people. Featuring testimonies from Deepak Chopra, Thich Nhat Hanh, Sharon Stone, Oliver Stone, and more, this documentary shows you how to embrace mindfulness in your own life. Like mindfulness itself, the film is simple, direct, and effective. (Kasanoff 2015)

Granted, the paragraph just quoted is publicity for a film, not a quotation by Thích Nhất Hạnh himself. But such publicity benefits his enterprise. And for someone who counsels against consumerist desires, his mindfulness merchandise abounds, including calendars, mindfulness bell apps, and a wristwatch of his design with

---

31 'We can deceive ourselves into thinking we are developing spiritually when instead we are strengthening our egocentricity through spiritual teachings' (Trungpa 1973, 1).

every hour marked by the word 'now', not a number. If one only reads these mass market books in a superficial fashion and not his other works that explicate mindfulness as variously presented in the sutras (e.g. Thích Nhất Hạnh 2011), one might have the impression that the goals of mindfulness practices are love, happiness and peace on a personal level. One might miss the key role of compassion, the Bodhisattva path, as Thích Nhất Hạnh himself explicates in *The Miracle of Mindfulness*, or as other Buddhist teachers explain:

> Clearly, the motivation for avowals of mindfulness trainings is compassion. My blessed teacher, H.E. Shyalpa Tenzin Rinpoche ardently reminds us that the most important factor in mindfulness is 'pure intention' – the aspiration to relieve all beings from suffering (bodhicitta). Any other intentionality separates one (to some degree or another) from Right Mindfulness. (Reilly 2016)

An instrumental rendering of mindfulness has its limits:

> The fundamental project of Mindfulness is to benefit oneself, usually in particular ways, and even for particular aims. This is fine, in so far as skills are strengthened (e.g., attentiveness, focus, relatedness) and suffering (e.g., stress, anxiety, depression) is lessened. But how can self-referential Mindfulness liberate one from all (or even most of the ways we experience) suffering? (Reilly 2016)

Richard Reilly further explains:

> As Buddhists well understand, it is (the false attribution of) 'self' ('ego') that is the root of our own suffering and of our causing others to suffer; and that to uproot this source of suffering, as distinct from treating a few symptoms, a more comprehensive remedy – The Noble Eightfold Path – is advised. Herein, moment-to-moment awareness is not awareness of one's thoughts, feelings, emotions, or experiences of phenomena simpliciter; it is awareness of the appearance and of the emptiness (the dependent origination) of thoughts, feelings, emotions, experiences of phenomena.

Those familiar only with Thích Nhất Hạnh's 'mass-market mindfulness' might not recognize his large body of work on the Buddhist textual foundations of mindfulness and Interbeing such as within the *Satipaṭṭhāna Sutta* and the *Mahāsatipaṭṭhāna Sutta* (Discourse on the Four Establishments of Mindfulness and the Great Discourse on the Four Establishments of Mindfulness; *Majjjhima Nikāya* I. 55-63 and *Dīgha Nikāya* II. 290-315); the *Ānāpānasati Sutta* (Discourse on the Full Awareness of Breathing; *Majjjhima Nikāya* III. 78-88)); the *Bhaddekaratta Sutta* (Discourse on knowing the better way to be alone; *Majjjhima Nikāya* III 187-189); the *Prajñāpāramitā Sūtras* (Perfection of Wisdom discourses), including, of course, the Diamond Sutra, the *Avataṃsaka Sūtra* (Flower-Adornment), the *Saddharmapuṇḍarīka Sūtra* (Lotus Sūtra) and others.[32] Andronic (2011) masterfully explicates the key philosophical teachings of Thích Nhất Hạnh, in particular the latter's *Fifty Verses on the Nature of Consciousness*, his interpretation of Yogācāra (consciousness-only). Hiên Thu Lương (2009) explores the contributions of Thích Nhất Hạnh and other 1960s Buddhists to the making of Vietnamese existential philosophy.[33]

The most likely explanation for the plethora of mass market books, their visibility in mass media, the trend of 'corporate mindfulness', and the repackaging and republishing of his 'classics' is the financial imperative: to sustain Thích Nhất Hạnh's global enterprise.[34] One might counter that Thích Nhất Hạnh and any teacher for that matter, religious or not, uses skilful means, *upāya*, as s/he adapts teaching, content and method to suit different audiences. His lectures in Silicon Valley with Google leaders and employees, and other captains of the IT industry might be a case in point:

---

32 For more details see Andronic 2011, Appendix D, 'Lists of Texts in Plum Village Practice Book' and their Pāli and Āgama references.

33 The interaction between various strains of existentialism and Buddhist thought in South Vietnam before 1975 is in need of in-depth study.

34 By no means do I imply that he or his colleagues or students profit individually. I refer to the many institutions that need operating funds and the living expenses for his monastic sangha.

If you know how to practice mindfulness you can generate peace and joy right here, right now. And you'll appreciate that and it will change you. In the beginning, you believe that if you cannot become number one, you cannot be happy, but if you practice mindfulness you will readily release that kind of idea. We need not fear that mindfulness might become only a means and not an end because in mindfulness the means and the end are the same thing. There is no way to happiness; happiness is the way...If you consider mindfulness as a means of having a lot of money, then you have not touched its true purpose...It may look like the practise of mindfulness but inside there's no peace, no joy, no happiness produced. It's just an imitation. If you don't feel the energy of brotherhood, of sisterhood, radiating from your work, that is not mindfulness. (Confino 2014)

The theme of another Google programme was to explore the 'intersection of mindfulness and tech' and the relationship between intention, insight and innovation (Confino 2013), and, most importantly, how not to lose sight of qualities that make us human.

Reasons for his success with 'mindfulness'

Thích Nhất Hạnh was not the first to associate *sati* especially with the English term 'mindfulness.' According to Jeff Wilson, we need to look at the Pāli Text Society, founded in 1881, and writings such as Soma Thera's *The Way of Mindfulness: The Satipatthana Sutta and Commentary* (1941) (Wilson 2014, 26-28 about Pāli Text Society and 33-34 on Soma Thera). But Thích Nhất Hạnh was a key creator of a 'mindfulness culture', along with the modern *vipassanā*/insight meditation movement via Myanmar, and Jon Kabat-Zinn's mindfulness-based stress reduction programmes. In Wilson's view, this mindfulness culture has resonated well with certain strains in the American landscape, such as 'the mind-cure/mental healing' traditions, a therapeutic and counselling culture, 'self-improvement' and 'personal potential' regimes and even American Transcendentalism (Wilson 2014, Chapter One).

There are a number of reasons why Thích Nhất Hạnh has been so successful in the global transmission of mindfulness and 'Buddhism in the West' more generally. First, as mentioned earlier, he has dedicated his life to actualizing Engaged Buddhism and, towards this end, has employed his gifts as translator, interpreter and interlocutor, whether regarding texts, cultures, ideas or emotional states. Future studies about Thích Nhất Hạnh should explore more the fact that, in addition to his monastic training, he spent the first twenty-eight years of his life in colonial Vietnam, and, as discussed earlier in this chapter, the deep influence of French culture in Vietnam (philosophy, literature, education, science, etc.) did not fade after France's defeat in 1954.[35] Thích Nhất Hạnh lived in a multi-cultural environment (Vietnamese; Chinese; French) even before he went to the USA in 1961, and thereafter has written and cross-translated in all three languages.

His undergraduate and graduate degrees obtained in both Vietnam and the US added cachet to his persona as interlocutor or spokesperson, especially to those unfamiliar with Buddhism or sceptical of Buddhist monks. He holds weighty spiritual credentials through his connection with Thomas Merton, Daniel Berrigan, and, especially, Martin Luther King, Jr. Although she did not refer to Thích Nhất Hạnh, Jane Iwamura (2011) suggests that an Orientalist image of 'The Wise Man of the East' attracted some spiritual seekers in the United States. Thích Nhất Hạnh's construction of his persona as a 'Zen Master from Vietnam' embues him with spiritual authority, especially to those unfamiliar with Buddhist history in Vietnam. Most of all, the ethics of his Engaged Buddhism attracted many people who came of age during the Vietnam War, perhaps involved in social movements or in actual war-zones, and these became the first generation of his 'Western' students (including Vietnamese immigrants to France and the USA). One should not underestimate the power of 'Vietnam' as an entire constellation for a generation or more, not the

---

35 See Gadkar-Wilcox 2014 about the deep influence of French philosophy on intellectual culture in South Vietnam.

least for some students and admirers of Thích Nhất Hạnh. In Philip Kapleau's rather ponderous words:

> We in the West must heed this wise and earnest voice speaking out of the heart of Asia if we are to avoid a third world war and the not improbable destruction of most of the human race and our planet earth. Americans especially must listen with an unprejudiced believing heart for not only is our karma with Vietnam and Asia deep…but to a large extent the fate of humanity rests on us. (Thích Nhất Hạnh 1974/1975, 15)

Over the decades, the shadow of 'war-time Vietnam' may have faded for some of his students[36] but Plum Village holds onto the perfume of 'tradition'. It pays respects to 'the ancestors', bestows Vietnamese dharma names on students, celebrates Lunar New Year, including oracle readings based on Vietnam's national epic poem, *The Tale of Kiều*, and has created new traditions for daily life and special occasions.[37] One of his finest creations is *gāthā* (religious verse) for daily life (2006b), inspired by the 'Purification Practices' of the Flower Adornment Sutra to generate, as he says, awareness of being, *samyak-smṛti* (right mindfulness).

Another reason for his success is that since the 1950s he has been savvy about publishing and media access. He was known as a writer and editor in Saigon even before 1961 (first trip to the USA). We need more details about the 1960s lecture tours that he and Cao Ngọc Phượng (the future Sr. Chân Không) took in the USA and Europe: about the important connections with top government officials, and public and private organizations, and how they gained coverage in the media. Such networking talent facilitated Thích Nhất Hạnh's career as 'Zen Master' in the United States from the late 1980s on.

As mentioned earlier, Thích Nhất Hạnh's team are experts in marketing. He has two publishing houses tailored to different cultural audiences: Parallax Press for languages other than Vietnamese and Lá Bối for Vietnamese works. He has the talents to

---

36 I don't presume to generalize for all persons of that period.
37 Plum Village directory of mindfulness practices.

explain complex ideas for a general audience in a clear, concise and lyrical way, often with reference to his own experiences and to vivid imagery from the natural world. He also teaches through calligraphy and song. His creative collaboration with artist-writer Mai Vo Dinh is another story yet to be told.

Thích Nhất Hạnh attracts many with his efforts in inter-religious dialogue and his books, *Living Buddha, Living Christ* (1995) and *The Raft is Not the Shore: Conversations Toward a Buddhist-Christian Awareness* (Hạnh & Berrigan 1975). The Catholic theologian, Paul F. Knitter of Union Theological Seminary, in his book *Without Buddha I Could not be a Christian* (2010), discusses the notion of 'double-belonging' and cites inspiration from Thích Nhất Hạnh.[38] And in 2015, the Roman Catholic Church bestowed the 'Pacem in Terris Peace and Freedom Award' upon Thích Nhất Hạnh, fifty years after Martin Luther King, Jr. won the same award. Finally, whether or not one believes in a karmic connection with a specific master, his personal characteristics attract many: slightly-built and soft-spoken; poetic and artistic; a soothing, patient and non-judging father-figure who indeed calls his students 'children'.

Yet, despite his successes outside Vietnam, with his consistent messages over the years that 'home is where the heart is' and 'I have arrived, I am home/In the here and now…', it seems that his heart could not rest until he fulfilled his mission to reform Buddhist practice in Vietnam. According to one of his senior disciples Sr *Chân Đức,* 'Thay always thought that he would be teaching in Vietnam, renewing Buddhism in Vietnam. But the causes and conditions brought him to the United States, which meant that for more than forty years, since he came in 1962 until today, Thay has been offering a new kind of Buddhism to us in the West' (Than Ngiem 2017).

After many years of difficult negotiations with the Vietnamese government, Thích Nhất Hạnh returned to Vietnam to lead lecture

---

38 Knitter 2009 discusses 'double-belonging' on pages 63-64 and 151-152. He
    refers to Thích Nhất Hạnh on pages 214-215 and 220.

tours in 2005, 2007, and 2008.[39] But in late 2009, Thích Nhất Hạnh's and his monastics were violently expelled from the country. The details are too complex to discuss here. However, I would say Thích Nhất Hạnh's popularity and growing numbers of followers in Vietnam became threatening to the central government and the state-run Buddhist establishment (see DeVido 2014). Also, by calling for freedom of religion, Thích Nhất Hạnh and his community apparently violated his promise to the Vietnamese government not to do so, and his monastics, many of whom were young and unfamiliar with local politics and special interests, were unable to communicate or negotiate skilfully enough.[40] Although Thích Nhất Hạnh was for the second time unable to realize his life-long dream to realize Engaged Buddhism in Vietnam, on my visits to north, central and south Vietnam, I found his photos, books and calligraphy in bookstores and temples, and Buddhist monastics and laypeople practised his 'mindfulness trainings'.

In addition to his successes in 'the West', Thích Nhất Hạnh and his Plum Village sangha have helped transform Buddhism elsewhere in Asia. This is an example of what anthropologist Agehānanda Bhāratī (1970) has called 'the pizza effect'.[41] Such institutions include: the Asian Institute of Applied Buddhism Studies and Practice founded in Hong Kong; the Thai Plum Village in Pakchong, Thailand (where Thích Nhất Hạnh currently resides); and the Nhập Lưu (Stream Entering) Monastery in Victoria, Australia. These centres are for both monastics and lay practitioners. Also, there are lay practice centres in Beijing, Ja-

---

39 See Chapman 2007 for accounts of the 2005 and 2007 tours.

40 Some Buddhist monks in Vietnam whom I consider to have a balanced outlook suggested these two reasons to me.

41 A classic example is the Theosophical Society. See Sharf 1995 and Versluis 1993 for more on the fascinating interactions among 'Western' and 'Eastern' spiritualities, interactions that muddle the categories 'East' and 'West'. In the case of Thích Nhất Hạnh, there are several rounds of pizza: he grew up with Buddhist traditions already being transformed from the 1930s on, then while in Vietnam he sought to reform the reformed version, was unable to do so in Vietnam, then in exile further developed his ideas on mindfulness and Buddhist practice in daily life, then at last exported this to Asia.

pan, India, Indonesia, Korea, Malaysia, Philippines, Singapore and Taiwan. From an instrumental angle, it is smart to expand in Asia with its potential for support by the *nouveaux riches*.

Conclusion: What continues?

Even before his 2014 stroke, Thích Nhất Hạnh and his disciples were preparing for the major transition when he passes away, the typical problem for organizations led by charismatic founders. His senior monks and nuns lead retreats and give dharma talks, manage institutes and retreat centres worldwide,[42] and reach out to younger generations. There is a Thích Nhất Hạnh Foundation for grant-giving and overall support of 'the enterprise'. Parallax Press has published his *Stories and Essential Teachings* 2016, and other writings have been re-issued in 'collectors' format. Noticeably, when I attended his dharma talks over a decade ago in Hồ Chí Minh City, at Bát Nhã Temple in Bảo Lộc, and a retreat in Hong Kong, I noticed how he and his monastic and lay students had created a strong sangha with warm and mutual devotion. In the past, lay 'mindfulness communities' seemed to be at the fore of Plum Village global expansion, but in recent years Thích Nhất Hạnh and his publicity machine have focussed on the monastic sangha that he hopes will continue to promote his mindfulness practices and the overall Plum Village enterprise. Parallax Press has published updated manuals about monastic disciplines, and a liturgy of Buddhist ceremonies and daily practices (2006a). And, the Plum Village sangha is the topic of a 2017 documentary called 'Walk with Me' about Thích Nhất Hạnh's monastic sangha, narrated by Benedict Cumberbatch, a self-described Buddhist.

In a long letter to his students, among other topics, Thích Nhất Hạnh contrasts the physical body with the *dharmakāya* and claims that at the time of the Buddha 'there was not yet the expression

---

42 I do not know the precise number of lay 'communities of mindful living' in the world: the Mindfulness Bell website has a directory; however, such self-governed groups come and go.

Sangha Body. We had to wait twenty more centuries for the expression Sangha Body to arise in Plum Village' (Thích Nhất Hạnh 2014) and that to create a sangha [he implies a sangha trained in his teachings] is the most important responsibility of Dharma Teachers:

> Teachers don't teach the basic practices, but just teach religious doctrines for us to learn by heart and pass on to future generations. This is our very rhetorical way of learning, and we have to change it. Dharma Teachers must teach ways of breathing, walking and sitting, how to handle our mental formations such as anger, sadness, hatred and jealousy; how to handle our pain and suffering, and calm our feelings and strong emotions. Once we know how to do these things, we'll be able to help our brothers and sisters do the same, and we will be able to teach our own students. When we know how to use loving speech and deep listening to bring about reconciliation and re-establish communication, only then can we really build a Sangha Body. (Thích Nhất Hạnh 2014)

Even bolder is this:

> The Buddha, Shakyamuni, our teachers, predicted that the next Buddha would be Maitreya, the Buddha of love…It is possible that the next Buddha will not take the form of an individual. The next Buddha may take the form of a community, a community practicing understanding and loving kindness, a community practicing mindful living. And the practice can be carried out as a group, as a city, as a nation. (Thích Nhất Hạnh 1994, 41)

The next step is nothing less than the transformation of the human species. In September 2017, a senior disciple of Thích Nhất Hạnh accepted on his behalf the Union Medal, awarded by his *alma mater*, the Union Theological Seminary (UTS), and UTS plans a Thích Nhất Hạnh Program for Engaged Buddhism. His disciple, Sister Chân Đức (Annabel Laity), is of British background and is Dean of Practice at the European Institute of Applied Buddhism in Germany, founded by Thích Nhất Hạnh. At UTS she conveyed another of his global and ambitious messages thus:

> [For more than forty years], Thay has been offering a new kind of Buddhism to us in the West. So from that, we can go forward with courage and we can go forward on a path that will help us transform homosapiens into *homoconscious*. A kind of homo that takes care not only of the human species but is able to take care of all species, especially our dear mother earth under our feet, and around us, and above us in the atmosphere...Rather than destroying homosapiens, we can transform *homosapiens* into *homoconscious*, the homo that knows how to live deeply our daily life, with compassion, with loving kindness, with joy, with deep happiness, and deep, deep love. (Than Ngiem 2017)

As Wilson notes, mindfulness is now part of the spiritual vocabulary of North America (Wilson 2014, 48). Years of efforts by Thích Nhất Hạnh and other teachers from various Buddhist traditions have made 'Buddhism' into an American religion as well as a global religion. Beyond this, through his scholarship, his art, his teaching methods and his global efforts for peace and reconciliation, Thích Nhất Hạnh will be remembered not only as one of the world's greatest humanists but one who pointed us towards the hope of *homoconscious*.

Bibliography

Ames, Van Meter, 1960. 'Current Western Interest in Zen'. *Philosophy East and West* 10: 23-33.

Andronic, Mihaela, 2011. 'Key Philosophical Teachings of Thích Nhất Hạnh'. MA in Buddhist Studies, University of Sunderland, England.

Barrows, John Henry, 1893. https://parliamentofreligions.org/parliament/chicago-1893. Accessed 13 September 2018.

Agehānanda Bhāratī, 1970. 'The Hindu Renaissance and its Apologetic Patterns'. *The Journal of Asian Studies* 29.2: 267-287.

Chapman, John, 2007. 'The 2005 Pilgrimage and Return to Vietnam of Exiled Zen Master Thích Nhất Hạnh'. In *Modernity and Re-enchantment: Religion in Post-revolutionary Vietnam,* ed. Philip Taylor. Singapore: Institute of Southeast Asian Studies: 297-341.

Chân Không, 1993. *Learning True Love: Practicing Buddhism in a Time of War*. Berkeley, CA: Parallax Press.

Confino, Jo, 2013. 'Google Seeks Out Wisdom of Zen Master Thich Nhat Hanh'. https://www.theguardian.com/sustainable-business/global-technology-ceos-wisdom-zen-master-thich-nhat-hanh. Accessed 15 December 2017.

Confino, Jo, 2014. 'Thich Nhat Hanh: Is mindfulness being corrupted by business and finance?' https://www.theguardian.com/sustainable-business/thich-nhat-hanh-mindfulness-google-tech. Accessed 15 December 2017.

De Bary, William T., ed., With Jerome Kisslinger & Tom Matthewson, 2006. *Living Legacies at Columbia*. New York: Columbia University Press.

DeVido, Elise Anne, 2007. 'Buddhism for this World: The Buddhist Revival in Vietnam, 1920-51 and its Legacy'. In *Modernity and Re-enchantment in Post-Revolutionary Vietnam*, ed. Philip Taylor. Singapore: Institute of Southeast Asian Studies: 250-296.

DeVido, Elise Anne, 2009. 'The Influence of Chinese Master Taixu on Buddhism in Vietnam'. *Journal of Global Buddhism* 10: 413-457.

DeVido, Elise Anne, 2014. 'Thich Nhat Hanh'. *Oxford Bibliographies Online*. Oxford University Press. http://dx.doi.org/10.1093/OBO/9780195393521-0138. Accessed 14 September 2018.

Do, Thien, 2003. *Vietnamese Supernaturalism: Views from the Southern Region*. London: RoutledgeCurzon.

Forest, Jim, 2015. 'Only the rice loves you: A month with Thich Nhat Hanh in Paris.' http://jimandnancyforest.com/2015/10/only-the-rice/. Accessed 15 Feb. 2018.

Forest, Jim, 2016. 'Getting into the stream: A visit with Thich Nhat Hanh in Fontvannes'. 9 July 1976. http://jimandnancyforest.com/2016/02/getting-into-the-stream/. Accessed 16 March 2018.

Gadkar-Wilcox, Wynn, 2014. 'Existentialism and Intellectual Culture in South Vietnam'. *The Journal of Asian Studies* 73.2: 377-395.

Greif, Mark, 2015. *The Age of the Crisis of Man: Thought and Fiction in America, 1933-1973.* Princeton, NJ: Princeton University Press.

Huang, Chanhua, 2009. *Fojiao gezong dayi – Huayan zong dayi* [The Main Ideas of each Buddhist School – Huayan School]. Jiangsu: Guanling Shushe.

Iwamura, Jane, 2011. *Virtual Orientalism: Asian Religions and American Popular Culture.* New York, NY: Oxford University Press.

Kasanoff, Larry [Director], 2015. 'Mindfulness: Be Happy Now'. http://www.imdb.com/title/tt5192640/. Accessed 3 January 2018.

King, Sallie B., 1996. 'Thich Nhat Hanh and the Unified Buddhist Church of Vietnam: Nondualism in Action'. In *Engaged Buddhism: Buddhist Liberation Movements in Asia*, eds. Christopher S. Queen & Sallie B. King. Albany, NY: State University of New York Press: 321-363.

Knitter, Paul F., 2009. *Without Buddha I Could not be a Christian.* Croydon, UK: Oneworld.

Lerner, Stephen D., 1966. 'Thích Nhất Hạnh on Vietnam'. *The Harvard Crimson*, 31 May, 1966. http://www.thecrimson.com/article/1966/5/31/thich-nhat-hanh-on-vietnam-pthich/. Accessed 1 November 2017.

Lương, Hiên Thu, 2009. 'Vietnamese Existentialism: A Critical Reappraisal'. Ph.D. in Philosophy, Temple University, Philadelphia, PA.

Niebuhr, Gustav, 1999. 'A Monk in Exile Dreams of Return to Vietnam'. *New York Times*, 16 October 1999. http://www.nytimes.com/1999/10/16/us/a-monk-in-exile-dreams-of-return-to-vietnam.html.

Niebuhr, Reinhold, 1941 and 1943. *The Nature and Destiny of Man.* Vol 1: *Human Nature.* Vol. II: *Human Destiny.* New York, NY: Charles Scribners' Sons.

Ngo, Hoang, 2015. 'Building a New House for the Buddha: Buddhist Social Engagement and Revival in Vietnam, 1927-1951'. PhD in History, University of Washington, Seattle, WA.

Nguyen, Cuong Tu, 1997. *Zen in Medieval Vietnam: A Study and Translation of the Thien Uyen Tap Anh*. Honolulu, HI: University of Hawaii Press.

Nguyen, Cuong Tu & A.W. Barber, 1998. 'Vietnamese Buddhism in North America: Tradition and Acculturation'. In *The Faces of Buddhism in America*, eds. Charles S. Prebish & Kenneth Ken'ichi Tanaka. Berkeley, CA: University of California Press: 129-146.

Pacey, Scott, 2014, 'Taixu, Yogācāra, and the Buddhist Approach to Modernity'. In *Transforming Consciousness: The Intellectual Reception of Yogācāra Thought in Modern China*, ed. John Makeham. Oxford: Oxford University Press: 103-122.

Parachin, Victor M., 2011. *Eleven Modern Mystics and the Secrets of a Happy Holy Life*. Pasadena, CA: Hope Publishing House.

Plum Village Directory of Mindfulness Practices, [n.d.]. https://plumvillage.org/mindfulness-practice/gatha-poems/. Accessed 1 March 2018.

Purser, Ron & David Roy, 2013. 'Beyond McMindfulness'. *The Blog: HuffPost*. https://www.huffingtonpost.com/ron-purser/beyond-mcmindfulness_b_3519289.html. Accessed 24 June 2018.

Reilly, Richard, 2016. 'Mindfulness and Right Mindfulness'. *American Buddhist Women: Quarterly Electronic Magazine from Sakyadhita USA*. Issue 10. http://americanbuddhistwomen.com/richard-reilly.html. Accessed 16 March 2018.

Rosenbaum, Robert & Barry Magrid, eds., 2016. *What's Wrong with Mindfulness (And What Isn't): Zen Perspectives*. Somerville, MA: Wisdom Publications.

Sharf, Robert, 1995. 'Whose Zen? Zen Nationalism Revisited'. In *Rude Awakenings: Zen, the Kyoto School, and the Question of Nationalism* (Nanzan Studies in Religion and Culture), eds. James W. Heisig & John Maraldo. Honolulu: University of Hawai'i Press: 40-51.

Sharf, Robert, 2002. 'The Uses and Abuses of Zen in the Twentieth Century'. In *Zen, Reiki, Karate: Japanische Religiosität in Europa*, eds. Inken Prohl & Hartmut Zinser. Bunka: Tübinger interkulturelle und linguistische Japanstudien, band 2. Münster, Hamburg, London: Lɪᴛ Verlag: 143-154.

Slater, Robert H.L., 1941. *Guns through Arcady: Burma and the Burma Road*. Sydney and London: Angus and Robertson Ltd.

Soma Thera, 1941. *The Way of Mindfulness: The Satipatthana Sutta and Its Commentary*. Colombo, Ceylon: Ceylon Daily News Press.

Soucy, Alexander, 2007. 'Nationalism, Globalism and the Reestablishment of the Trúc Lâm Thiền Buddhist Sect in Northern Vietnam'. In *Modernity and Re-enchantment: Religion in Post-revolutionary Vietnam*, ed. Philip Taylor. Singapore: Institute of Southeast Asian Studies: 342-370.

Suzuki, Shunryū, 1970. *Zen Mind, Beginner's Mind: Informal Talks on Zen Meditation and Practice*. New York & Tokyo: Weatherhill.

Taylor, Philip, ed., 2007. *Modernity and Re-enchantment: Religion in Post-revolutionary Vietnam*. Singapore: Institute of Southeast Asian Studies.

Than Ngiem, 2017. '2017 September 6th: Sr. Chân Đức's speech at the Union Medal Award Ceremony, New York City'. Posted on 22 October 2017. https://plumvillage.org/news/2017-union-medal/. Accessed on 2 March 2018.

Thích Nhất Hạnh, 1965. *Engaged Buddhism (with other essays)*. Translated from the Vietnamese by Trinh Van Du. Saigon: Typewritten manuscript.

Thích Nhất Hạnh, 1966. 'A Buddhist Poet in Vietnam'. *The New York Review of Books,* 9 June 1966. https://www.nybooks.com/articles/1966/06/09/a-buddhist-poet-in-vietnam/. Accessed 3 March 2018.

Thích Nhất Hạnh, 1967. *Vietnam: Lotus in a Sea of Fire: A Buddhist Proposal for Peace*. New York: Hill & Wang.

Thích Nhất Hạnh, 1974. *Zen Keys: A Guide to Buddhist Practice*. Garden City, NY: Anchor Press.

Thích Nhất Hạnh, 1974/1975. *The Miracle of Being Awake: A Manual on Meditation for the Use of Young Activists*. Nyack, NY: Fellowship Books.

Thích Nhất Hạnh, 1987. *Interbeing: Commentaries on the Tiep Hien Precepts*. Berkeley, CA: Parallax Press.

Thích Nhất Hạnh, 1994. 'The Next Buddha May Be a Sangha'. *Inquiring Mind: A Semi-Annual Journal of the Vipassana Community* 10.2.

Thích Nhất Hạnh, 1995. *Living Buddha, Living Christ*. New York, NY: Riverhead Books.

Thích Nhất Hạnh, 1999. *Fragrant Palm Leaves: Journals 1962-1966*. New York City, NY: Riverhead Books.

Thích Nhất Hạnh, 2006a. *Chanting from the Heart: Buddhist Ceremonies and Practices*. Berkeley, CA: Parallax Press.

Thích Nhất Hạnh, 2006b. *Present Moment, Wonderful Moment: Mindfulness Verses for Daily Living*. Berkeley, CA: Parallax Press.

Thích Nhất Hạnh, 2006c. *Reconciliation: Healing the Inner Child*. Berkeley, CA: Parallax Press.

Thích Nhất Hạnh, 2007. *For a Future to be Possible: Buddhist Ethics for Everyday Life*. Berkeley, CA: Parallax Press.

Thích Nhất Hạnh, 2008. 'Dharma Talk: History of Engaged Buddhism.' #49 Autumn 2008. http://www.mindfulnessbell.org/archive/2015/02/dharma-talk-history-of-engaged-buddhism-2. Accessed 2 February 2018.

Thích Nhất Hạnh, 2011. *Awakening of the Heart: Essential Buddhist Sutras and Commentaries*. Berkeley, CA: Parallax Press.

Thích Nhất Hạnh, 2014. 'Connecting to our Root Teacher: A Letter from Thay', 27 September 2014. Posted by Plum Village, 26 June 2015. https://plumvillage.org/news/connecting-to-our-root-teacher-a-letter-from-thay-27-sept-2014/. Accessed 2 March 2018.

Thích Nhất Hạnh, 2016. *At Home in the World: Stories and Essential Teachings from a Monk's Life*. Berkeley, CA: Parallax Press.

Thích Nhất Hạnh & Daniel Berrigan, S.J., 1975. *The Raft is not the Shore: Conversations toward a Buddhist-Christian Awareness*. Maryknoll, NY: Orbis.

Thích Thiên Ân, 1975. *Buddhism and Zen in Vietnam*. Rutland, VT & Tokyo, Japan: Charles E. Tuttle Co.

Thích Trí Quang, 1972. *Tăng-già Việt Nam* (The Sangha of Vietnam). Hanoi: Đuốc Tuệ.

Trungpa, Chögyam, 1973. *Cutting Through Spiritual Materialism*. Berkeley, CA: Shambala Publications.

Versluis, Arthur, 1993. *American Transcendentalism and Asian Religions*. London & Oxford: Oxford University Press.

Williams, R. John, 2011. '*Technê*-Zen and the spiritual quality of global capitalism'. https://rjohnwilliams.files.wordpress.com/2010/05/williams-techne-zen-and-capitalism.pdf. Accessed on 8 November 2018.

Wilson, Jeff, 2014. *Mindful America: the Mutual Transformation of Buddhist Meditation and American Culture*. New York, NY: Oxford University Press.

MINDFULNESS (*ACHTSAMKEIT*) AND AWARENESS (*BEWUSSTHEIT/'POSITIVE CONCENTRATION'*) IN THE CONTEXT OF BUDDHIST-CHRISTIAN/ BUDDHIST-WESTERN ENCOUNTER AND ETHICS

Sybille C. Fritsch-Oppermann

Abstract

In this paper I will first deal with mindfulness as a form of atten-tion connected to a special state of perception and consciousness, on one hand, and as a practical (meditation) method to minimize suffering on the other. Although often used synonymously, aware-ness is taken as a more conscious directed form of it, as is 'posi-tive concentration'. I will introduce theoretical and practical sug-gestions from psychoanalysis and psychotherapy (starting with Jon Kabat-Zinn), dealing with awareness, and will concentrate on Fritz Perls's 'Gestalttherapie' as an example.

On the other hand, I will introduce mindfulness (awareness) as a Buddhist concept (wisdom) of meditation and life which is without any goal or focus. Sati *(Pāli; Skt.* smrti*) is an 'attitude' of mindfulness/awareness as explained in the* Ānāpānasati Sutta *(mindfulness of breathing) and the* Satipaṭṭhāna Sutta *(founda-tions and basics of mindfulness). I will then introduce the Japa-nese term 'munen muso' in the sense of non-objective meditation taking Zen, especially Soto-Zen, as an example. Second, I ask how encounter between Buddhist and Christian/Western ways of medi-tation could foster the mutual understanding of the concepts of Ego, Self and God/*Śūnyatā. *Third, I ask how awareness and med-itation could lead to a new ecological understanding of the Bud-dhist term,* pratītyasamutpāda, *on the one hand, and the concept* *of 'deep incarnation' (Gregersen 2015), on the other, and how this could lead to further developments of a Buddhist-Christian ethics. Finally, I will ask whether the newly discussed concept of EQ, emotional intelligence, could function as a hermeneutical bridge builder, not only between science and theology but also between Buddhist and Christian ecological ethics.*

Keywords: awareness, Buddhism, Christianity, ecological ethics, mindfulness, Buddhism

Introduction

In this paper I will first deal with the Buddhist understanding of mindfulness, introduce the use of this term within Western psychoanalysis/psychotherapy and critically comment on it. Although 'mindfulness' and 'awareness' are often used synonymously, 'awareness' is taken in this paper as a more conscious and directed form of mindfulness – as is 'positive concentration'. In a second step I will ask how, given this background, encounter between Buddhist and Christian/Western ways of meditation (and contemplation) could foster the mutual understanding of, for example, concepts of Ego, Self and God/*Śūnyatā* and, therefore, could inspire and enrich anthropology and ethics as well as (creation) theology and soteriology. In a third step I ask how, with the help of the Buddhist term *pratītyasamutpāda* (dependent co-origination) and the (overall) Christian concept of 'deep incarnation' (Gregerson 2015), this could lead to a revision of our understanding of ethics and ecology. I will also ask whether the concept of 'emotional intelligence' could serve as a hermeneutical bridge between Buddhist and Christian ethics.

1. Mindfulness and Awareness/Positive Concentration in Buddhism and Psychotherapy

In the following I differentiate between the Buddhist understanding of 'mindfulness' and the more active concept of 'awareness', the latter often connected with a special state of perception and mind (consciousness), especially when Buddhist meditation practices were introduced to the West without making a clear distinction between the two terms. In doing so, I am aware of the many different language levels that enter any kind of discourse and the questions that arise from this, such as:

- Do I argue from a more confessional level? And if so, does this lead to a scientific intercultural and interdisciplinary discourse? Or, do I rather have to stick to a more or less narrative exchange of personal belief(s)?
- Am I aware of what has been pointed out in the natural sciences for quite a while as the 'observer standpoint' ('Beobachterstandpunkt' in German)?

For many scholars in the natural sciences this has led to hermeneutics being seen as an important 'method' as well (Jaeckelen 2005; Reynhout 2013). Therefore, it is important to add that my perception of Zen is shaped by Japanese Soto-Zen and the philosophy of the Kyoto School, and that the structures of my argumentation are most probably more shaped by a constructivist understanding of Kantian philosophy than, say, by a Hegelian thought tradition. It is with these elements as background that I think and meditate and do research about what I call 'a modern Buddhist understanding of mindfulness in the tradition of Zen'.

The literal meaning of *sati* in the context of Early Buddhism and the Vedic tradition of India, is memory and recollection. In the work of Robert Sharf, it means to maintain awareness of reality, whereby the true nature of phenomena can be seen (Sharf 2014). Thus, I will use the word 'mindfulness' to translate the key Buddhist terms *sati* (Pāli) and *smrti* (Sanskrit). It then describes a meditative state of mind,[1] a wisdom that is gained through or which leads to enlightenment (*bodhi*). In contradistinction to this, I reserve the word 'awareness' for a form of (emotional) knowing (also in the sense of EQ) and a more focussed form of concentration (and meditation). The German translation I prefer for mindfulness is *Achtsamkeit*. *Achtsamkeit* and its synonym, *Aufmerksamkeit*, are sometimes, for example, in the German 'Duden' dictionary, said to have their roots in the Latin *attendere* (ad tendere). But then and differently from the way I will use the word 'mindfulness' and *Achtsamkeit* here, both words are understood more as an active process of conscious discernment within a human or individual conscience. Mindfulness in modern Buddhism indeed has been described as an attitude expressing liberation from suffering and stress. But in most cases it is nevertheless described as a 'method', in which neither goal nor focus plays a role (as a 'state of presence/ of mind').[2] Yet, there is an active, focussing aspect in it, a goal to be reached, even if that goal is stress reduction, though I would prefer to retain this aspect for mindfulness.[3]

The same is to be stated for another 'definition' of an 'ideal state of mindfulness' as '*weitwinkelartige 'Aufmerksamkeits' einstellung*' (wide-angled attitude of 'attention') in the sense of an all-encompassing (embracing), clear and fully awake openness to the total multitude of perception. Chögyam Trungpa, following Tibetan Buddhism, characterizes this state of mind as 'panorama-awareness' (Chögyam Trungpa 1978, 96; Chögyam Trungpa

---

1   Robert Sharf 2014, 'Mindfulness and Mindlessness in Early Chan', *Philosophy East & West*, 64.4: 933-964.

2   Here I am following, in part, the elaborations of Thanissaro Bhikkhu, a Buddhist monk born and living in the US though adhering to the Thai Forest Tradition.

3   Thanissaro Bhikkhu 1999, where *sati* describes the quality of mind to remember something, to keep something in one's mind, and is translated as awareness, whereas *samma sati* (right awareness) remembers certain and special things and keeps them in mind. In this explanation, for mainly Western readers and students of Buddhist meditation, one clearly sees a goal-oriented connotation in the sense of what I call awareness (and in German *Bewusstheit*). To me this is a good example of mixing mindfulness (*Achtsamkeit*) and awareness (*Aufmerksamkeit*)). See also Gethin 1998, 174-194.

1989, 76; Kittel 2010). But again the stress on perception here is slightly misleading in the sense that a subject perceives an object often in observing it and defining it.

1.1 The Term Mindfulness in Buddhism – by way of (Soto) Zen

'Mindfulness' as a Buddhist concept (as Buddhist wisdom) is exercised and experienced in meditation and practised in life. Two discourses of the Buddha in the *Sutta Piṭaka*, the *Ānāpānasati Sutta* (concerning mindfulness of breathing in meditation; *Majjhima Nikāya* III, 78-88) and most of all the *Satipaṭṭhāna Sutta* (concerning the foundations of mindfulness; *Majjhima Nikāya* I. 55-63, which, as far as content is concerned, is identical with the *Mahāsatipaṭṭhāna Sutta*; *Dīgha Nikāya* II. 290-315) describe mindfulness and how to practise it.

Following Thích Nhất Hạnh's interpretation of the *Satipaṭṭhāna Sutta*, there are four 'foundations of mindfulness':

– body mindfulness
– emotions mindfulness (good, bad or neither good nor bad)
– mind mindfulness (actual state or changes in state, for example distracted, concentrated, confused)
– objects of mind mindfulness, i.e. all outer and inner objects/things perceived at this moment (Nhất Hạnh 1990).

Again, this is what I would translate as awareness. This is important, since I will argue that concentrative meditation comes rather close to what I call 'awareness' and to what is partly dealt with in Western therapy under the label of 'mindfulness', in the sense of 'positive concentration', as used in Fritz Pearls's earlier works on Gestalt therapy, meaning to focus (!) one's view on a certain object, for example a line of writing, and apply one's whole attention to this limited realm of perception – not least with the goal of attaining a status of total calmness.

'Mindfulness', as used in this paper, is to a certain extent contrary to this 'attentive concentration'. Mindfulness does not have the latter's directionality. It does not so much focus on whatsoever perception, but opens and widens mind and body and soul. Contrary to 'attentive concentration' (and also to what I call 'awareness'), there is no purposeful constraint.

'Mindfulness' is more in the sense of a direct, whole-body-and-mind 'enlightenment' to the present moment in the tradition of (Soto) Zen (and later on Kyoto School), which was brought to China by the Indian monk Bodhidharma, who later became famous as the first patriarch of Zen (Chan in China).[4] On the way to Buddhahood (Enlightenment) he introduced a strict sitting meditation of thinking nothing or 'thinking the unthinkable'.

Enomiya Lassalle, a Catholic theologian and expert on Japan and Buddhism (especially Soto Zen), translated '*asphanaka samādhi*' (Sanskrit), which in Japanese is '*munen muso*' (no mind no thought), as 'non-representational meditation' (*ungegenständliche meditation*) (Stachel 1986). For him meditation is not to be seen as meditation on objects or a concentration on objects. Again, neither goal nor focus (are allowed to) play a role. At stake is a non-discriminating state of mind in which the separation between subject and object is overcome.

1.2 Mindfulness' in the Theory and Practice of Psychoanalysis and Psychotherapy – taking Gestalt therapy as an example

When the Buddhist practice of mindfulness spread in the West as a set of techniques of 'mindfulness', the work of Daisetz Teitaro Suzuki, Alan Watts and Eugen Herrigel, besides others, played an important role. Since the 1960s, the attention to meditation techniques has been closely related to a growing interest in forms of expansion of consciousness in the fields of psychotherapy, especially psychoanalysis (C.G. Jung, Erich Fromm), and of humanist psychotherapy (Fritz Perls, Carl Roger, Charlotte Selver). There

---

4   Bodhidharma is asked by the Chinese Emperor: what is the highest sense of reality? And his answer is 'open width – nothing holy'. The conversation goes on with the Emperor asking: who are you standing in front of me?' and Bodhidharma answering, 'I do not know'. See Wilhelm Gundert, 1973.

are different aspects of 'mindfulness' (and acceptance) in psycho-analysis, for example, the free associations of the analysand and the evenly suspended attention of the analyst, which Sigmund Freud called 'indiscriminating introspection' (Michal 2004, 365). Also and especially, Gestalt therapy, client-centred psychotherapy and the method of Focussing and body-oriented procedures (for example, Hakomi) draw on mindfulness (Bundschuh-Müller 2004).

It is interesting that the term 'techniques' is already being used at this early stage, especially as the above mentioned 'non-represen-tational meditation', as an appropriate equivalent for mindfulness meditation. This meditation is not – and on purpose is not – a tech-nique in the traditional sense; far more, it is an emptying, step by step, without any focussing on whatsoever the object or aim (goal) is.

Later and in the realm of experimental psychology, the first EEG-studies were done on meditating persons. The first scientific studies on the 'use' of 'mindfulness'-meditation in the realm of psychotherapy took place in the late 1970s. A crucial influence was brought to it by the work of Jon Kabat-Zinn. He had been using 'mindfulness' techniques first of all for mindfulness-based stress reduction (MBSR), in which 'mindfulness' is understood as a form of intentional awareness, referring to the present mo-ment (Kabat-Zinn 1982, 33-47). Since then research interest in the area of 'meditation' has grown steadily and also some other approaches have developed, mostly oriented towards cognitive-behavioural therapy, for example, Acceptance and Commitment Therapy and mindfulness-based Cognitive Therapy (MBCT; see Keng, Smoski & Robins 2011; Redemann 2008; Brown & Ryan 2004; Brown, Ryan & Creswell 2007).[5] Indeed, the efficacy of mindfulness-based Cognitive Therapy (MBCT) for prevention of fallback in the case-history of people with several depressive epi-sodes meanwhile is seen as sufficiently proved.

Kabat-Zinn, in his book *Im Alltag Ruhe finden*, argues that concentration always has to be deepened by mindfulness exer-cises, since lacking the latter's energy, namely, curiosity, the urge

---

5   Within Brown & Ryan 2004, 'mindfulness' is defined formally as receptive 'mindfulness' and awareness of momentary happenings and experiences.

towards knowledge and understanding, openness and engagement with the whole spectrum of human experience is weakened.[6] Therefore, although pointing towards the aspect of unfocussed and open meditation, he stresses energy and urge for knowledge in 'Achtsamkeit'.[7] Kabat-Zinn states:

> Back in 1979, when I started Mindfulness-Based Stress Reduction, I came up with an operational definition of mindfulness that still serves as well as anything else: mindfulness is the awareness that arises from paying attention on purpose in the present moment nonjudgmentally. That doesn't mean you won't have any judgments. In fact, when we start paying attention, we realize that we almost have nothing but judgments going through our heads. Mindfulness is about getting access to our own awareness with equanimity and without falling into a stream of conceptual thinking that goes on and on and on.[8]

---

6   See for example, '...so intensiv und befriedigend es auch sein mag, sich in der Konzentration zu üben, bleibt das Ergebnis doch unvollständig, wenn sie nicht durch die Übung der Achtsamkeit ergänzt und vertieft wird. Für sich allein ähnelt sie (die Konzentration) einem Sich-Zurückziehen aus der Welt. Ihre charakteristische Energie ist eher verschlossen als offen, eher versunken als zugänglich, eher tranceartig als hellwach. Was diesem Zustand fehlt, ist die Energie der Neugier, des Wissensdrangs, der Offenheit, der Aufgeschlossenheit, der Engagements für das gesamte Spektrum menschlicher Erfahrung. Dies ist die Domäne der Achtsamkeitspraxis (Kabat-Zinn 2007, 75)

7   Bishop, Lau, Shapiro et al 2004 suggest an operational definition of 'mindfulness' with two components. First, what is at stake is a self-regulation of 'attention', which remains focussed on immediate experience; a growing realization of mental processes in the present moment becomes possible, as for example, the arising of thoughts, emotions or sense impressions, also a change of attention back to present experience, when a thought, emotion or sense impression has come up in consciousness, a non-elaborative realization, i.e. a hindrance of elaborative, secondary processes concerning arising thoughts, emotions and sense impressions – an identification with the present experience. Second, an orientation towards present experience is marked by curiosity, openness, acceptance. No specific state (for example, relaxation) or changing of upcoming emotions is aimed at. The state and contents of the actual conscience are nothing but realized. This comes rather close to what I use as the concept of Buddhist mindfulness.

8   See https://www.psychotherapynetworker.org/blog/details/511/mindfulness-and-awareness-according-to-jon-kabat-zinn.

A practice of mindfulness and meditation, which 'looks' for such 'open width' (as, for example, with the French biologists Ricard and Singer in dialogue about brain science and meditation; Ricard & Singer 2008), a step by step approach leads towards 'full mindfulness'. In this state mind is 'wide as the firmament', very clear and transparent (Ricard & Singer 2008, 77). This also comes very close to what I explain as the modern Buddhist understanding of mindfulness in the Zen tradition. But it still has a more active, oriented attitude. Those who do mindfulness meditation in this Western therapeutical tradition do not try to overcome the subject-object-dichotomy at the deepest level. And again, following Kabat-Zin in therapeutical practice and in brain science, the stress moves towards a sort of goal-focussed awareness.

To sum up: the Western uses of 'mindfulness' (meditation) introduced so far differ more or less from the Buddhist one I suggest and rely on in this paper. The terms 'mindfulness' and 'awareness', i.e. 'concentration', are sometimes used synonymously. There is, for therapeutic reasons, a certain focus on the active and technical aspects. The greatest difference can be seen when comparing the Soto Zen use; modern Buddhist interpretations (especially to Western readers and followers) being much closer to Western ones in focussing on the active and technical aspects. Moreover, in my view, a technique is always in the end connected with a more discriminating state of mind, which is rather contrary to what I define here as Buddhist mindfulness (meditation) in the Soto Zen tradition.

I note that Andreas Nehring, in his chapter in this volume, points out, that, for a couple of decades, there has been a new 'millennium boom' in various functional areas within Western societies going hand-in-hand with a non-confessional praxis of self-experience ('spirituality' versus 'religion'). Here, the use of and debate about 'mindfulness meditation' can be seen as a mirror for the sociocultural figuration of this spirituality. It fluctuates between therapy and religious event, object of scientific research and a pedagogical concept, its surplus being an implicit spiritual assuredness. Nehring explains 'mindfulness' mainly by focussing on the cultural precondition of its reception and, with this cultural studies approach, the concept and practice of 'mindfulness (meditation)' is entangled in discourses about its legitimation and interpretation, the ideologically critical aspect of it being an even stronger form of activity and technique, that is a self- mastering technique!

2. An Enriching Encounter with Buddhism: Ego and Self, God and Emptiness

Further following Nehring, epistemologically 'mindfulness (meditation)' has to be seen as inward assuredness with questionable scientific value, since no discourse about it is possible, the main problem being that a subject and object of observation emerge. Here I agree and yet disagree. In science there is a growing agreement (and such is the case even in natural science) that truth is not a metaphysical (absolute) constant, but develops and is in process (process philosophy) and is two- or many-fold. Quite a while ago, this was realized through Einstein's theory of relativity and the work of the Copenhagen School. A thesis is true as long as it is not falsified. The traditional concept of 'scientific truth' is varied and the subject-object dichotomy is overcome. Aesthetics is becoming part of scientific thought and of theology (theo-poetics). Although systematic theology and its truth question should not totally merge into poetics, the latter allows us, hermeneutically, to watch out, for example, for analogies in different 'truth systems'. That is especially important in interreligious encounter, when thought and language structures as different as those in Buddhist and Western (Christian) contexts are at stake.

So a critical discussion of the Western adaptation(s) (and misuses) of Buddhist mindfulness meditation, on the other hand, leads to a deeper encounter between Buddhist and Western understanding of the concepts of Ego, Self and God/Emptiness and also concepts of hermeneutics and ethics, namely, truth and reality. I suggest that we agree on the thesis that those forms of Buddhist and Western mindfulness meditation practices introduced in this paper, in spite of their clear differences, in a strong or weak way, aim at overcoming subject-object dualism/dichotomy.[9]

There is neither time nor space here to include aspects of (Christian) mysticism in more detail. But if we would follow this track, it would be worthwhile to discuss the concept of 'unio mystica' (mystical union) as analogous to the state of non-duality in mindfulness meditation and finally enlightenment. Mindfulness meditation and mystical experience in fact might then be understood as more existential and not so much essentialist perceptions of truth, i.e. final reality. There is neither metaphysics nor substance ontology in enlightenment gained through mindfulness meditation and its philosophy.

When Bodhidharma, to the question, 'What could be the highest sense of holy reality?' answered, 'Open width – nothing holy', did he not also point to this state of mindfulness, and, if so, to *śūnyatā* (emptiness), as the final 'law' of human beings (and other beings)? Some of his followers even argued that, because of this final reality of emptiness, all (human) beings already had Buddha-nature deep within their ground, already there, although often unknown. And would this then (necessarily) lead to a form of attentive acting in the world of *pratītyasamutpāda* (dependent co-origination) as well?

2.1 Mindfulness (and Meditation) in Buddhism and Christianity

Again in (Zen) Buddhist mindfulness meditation as well as, in a weaker way, in Western forms of it, we can speak (at least of the goal) of overcoming the separation between subject and object. In Christian mysticism and contemplation, a strict separation between profane and holy, between God and human beings, becomes questionable or obsolete in the mystic's experience of *unio*

---

9 For Western Gestalt therapy, this, for example, means that also the often disturbing dualisms between doctor (subject) and patient (object) are overcome – or, at the least, it means that the latter are highly questionable concepts in constituting a clear hierarchy and dependency between those healing and those to be healed.

mystica with God (often referred to then as *deitas* and no longer as *deus*, namely, not a (personal) counterpart, but a more all-embracing and – in an ontological sense – non-substantial Godhead, 'Godhead'). A separation between subject and object, and also a dualism of being and non-being here seems rather analogous to what is experienced as enlightenment in Buddhist mindfulness meditation. If this is the case, we then could see an analogy between awareness and meditation and one between mindfulness and contemplation. And we could speak of Buddhist mindfulness meditation as analogous to Christian contemplation, to stress the non-directed, 'non active' aspect of it. And since Christian (and monastic) meditation practice in general is nurtured by mysticism or nowadays enriched by the practice of Buddhist meditation (here again especially Zen), this could lead, and has led, to a Christian concept of mindfulness, which implies an inner Christian theological widening of horizon, in anthropology and ethics, but also in the doctrine of God and soteriology. Thích Nhất Hạnh's puts this point in an active and focussed way:

> Mindfulness is the energy of being aware and awake to the present moment. It is the continuous practice of touching life deeply in every moment of daily life. To be mindful is to be truly alive, present and at one with those around you and with what you are doing. (Plum Village website)

2.2 Nirvana soku Samsara – beyond Time and Space: a God Embracing us

Bodhidharma's 'Open width – nothing holy' clarifies that, according to dharma, the final reality to be achieved in enlightenment is emptiness (*śūnyatā* and, following Suzuki 1970, *nirvāṇa* in a more psychological sense), the way to enlightenment being mindfulness (meditation). For some Buddhist philosophers of the Japanese Kyoto School, such as Masao Abe, and especially in the tradition of Dōgen, enlightenment can be gained at once and in this life-time, and in enlightenment we also realize, that, at the ground of our self (ego), our real Self, namely Buddha-nature, already awaits us.[10] Dualisms between God and his creation (still present in theism and theist theologies), between holy and profane, and between human and non-human beings, for instance, cease to exist. And this insight into the dependent co-origination of all that 'is' (*pratītyasamutpāda*) leads to 'attentive acting'. In other words, it is possible and desirable to create a state of non-conceptual cognition (through meditation), within which virtues and insights spontaneously arise.

This 'acting', however, does not take place in obedience towards an almighty God and his divine commandments but in devout listening to what for us is the meaning of Buddha-nature, to what *actio* should follow *contemplatio* and *unio*, to what the Pauline Χριστος εν εμοι, (Christ in me) 'tells' me to do. This is a special interpretation of dependent (co-)origination (*pratītyasamutpāda*), in line with the Japanese Kyoto School, especially Masao Abe, who started as a Zen practitioner and philosopher, and later became deeply interested into Jodoshin-shu. For Abe, in the end, *pratītyasamutpāda* is not ultimately *dukkha* (suffering or anguish). And this is partly so because he sees a *soku*-relation[11] between *saṃsāra* and *nirvana*, between emptiness and the world as it is.

It might be that Abe refers here to Dōgen, who claimed, because of the inseparability between *saṃsāra* and *nirvāṇa*, that beings do not have Buddha-nature, they *are* Buddha-nature.

Even if Abe in his (Buddhist) philosophy of religion is non-mainstream and even if Dōgen's thought was incompatible with most forms of Buddhism, this should not hinder us from taking up their special teachings in order to develop suggestions for our intercultural/comparative philosophy of Emptiness and Fullness.

---

10 In Dōgen, 2007, his most famous work, for the first time the idea of Buddha-nature comes up in the *Tathāgatagarbha Sūtra*. Dōgen's interpretation of it is especially taken up by the philosophy of the Kyoto School in modern Japan. See also Heine 1992.

11 Later and in conversations he could even exclaim: 'I do not die I do not have cravings'. A good introduction to Abe's teaching is LaFleur 1985. See also Fritsch-Oppermann, 2000.

Emptiness is more than (empty) form and enlightenment is more than the awakening experience. And it is deeply connected (in what I want to call here a sort of '*soku*-dialectics') to *saṃsāra*. That we claim Buddha-nature for all sentient and non-sentient, living and non-living beings does not mean that we are on a direct path to quietism or worshipping *saṃsāra*. It means that there is a chance for acting and changing the world for the better, and this because of the Buddha-nature underlying all reality.

The concept of emptiness in some of its aspects seriously questions substance ontology and instead takes a mainly epistemological point of view. This shapes ethical aspects and anthropology in a unique way – and questions about absolute truth are left aside altogether. What matters instead is the search for what one could and should better call '(final) reality'. This of course also leads to a strong criticism of metaphysics and theology in their tendency towards absolutist claims.

Emptiness opens the way to a deeper self-observation in deconstructing the ego and human self in order to – with the help of mindfulness meditation – awaken to the final Self, Buddha-nature, and re-construct the person and worldly self from this viewpoint of enlightenment. Whether also psychology and psychotherapy, especially constructivist psychotherapy and theory of knowledge, and whether meta-theoretical epistemology and neurology can be informed by this comparison, has to be left to their representatives and specialists. I cannot deal with such comparisons within this chapter's compass.

3. Mindfulness – Starting Point and Signpost for a New Understanding of Ecology

Buddhist mindfulness, as used in this paper, can be seen as having a twofold connotation of fullness (enlightenment) and thoughtfulness in a more ethical sense. Furthermore, human beings are different from other beings and non-sentient beings in a special but not superordinate way, since all have Buddha-nature as final reality and exist in dependent co-origination (*pratītyasamutpāda*).

This is good news: we can find liberation from all imprisonment within ego-centrism, greed and 'violent anthropocentrism'. Such an understanding of human beings and their con-vironment, with concomitant ethical effects, could and should have considerable influence on world-wide concepts of ecology and economy.[12]

When human beings, according to Buddhist 'doctrine' and philosophy, awaken, through mindfulness (meditation) to emptiness as final reality and to their Buddha-nature, they know and sense that emptiness is the final reality also of non-human beings, sentient and non-sentient, already in *saṃsāra*. Insight into *pratītyasamutpāda* leads towards attentive acting and, as a thesis for further thought, to detached compassion and an epistemic ecology of 'living systems' reacting auto-poetically to their con-vironment – this being an analogy to *pratītyasamutpāda* in the terminology of sociology and natural (bio)sciences.[13]

From recent dialogues between Christian theology and the philosophy of religion with (natural) science (as noted), there arises a debate about a concept introduced by Niels Gregersen, namely, 'Deep Incarnation'.[14] Gregersen points to the Logos, incarnate in all of creation, as the cosmic Christ. For him and for many others, the usual dichotomy between the particular and the universal is by no means helpful. His concept of deep incarnation is a walk-able bridge towards religions other than Christianity. And, from my perspective, it also suggests 'salvation' for non-human beings and maybe even for non-sentient beings. Perhaps Gregersen's theory grounds certain ecological conclusions that come close to those of Buddhism in that they oppose all anthropocentrism and androcentrism and submit a convincing teaching of the coherence and

---

12 If we argue, that there is no final difference between human beings and other sentient and non-sentient beings it would be worthwhile to no longer speak of environment but rather of con-vironment.

13 Auto-poiesis was introduced into the scientific debate, especially biology, to describe the organizational characteristics found in living systems, by Humberto Maturana.

14 Gregersen 2015, 'The Extended Body of Christ: Three Dimensions of Deep Incarnation', 225-251.

'salvation' of all that is. And it is from this point that an interesting dialogue could also start with science.

Another topic that needs to be addressed in the future derives from this, namely, the need for a closer look at the dialogue between the natural sciences and religion/theology and the newer concept of Emotional Intelligence (EQ),[15] with a view to assessing whether it can become a relevant and a helpful discussion-partner in Buddhist-Christian encounter. As Karl Baier's chapter demonstrates, in meditation and contemplation, images connect thoughts with emotions. The concept of Emotional Intelligence in neurobiology and brain science, on the other hand, leads to a definition of intelligence which is indeed analogous to the Buddhist concept of mindfulness, in taking thinking as one of the senses. This concept of intelligence would enable us to act and to 'understand' each individual and subject as creative components of a greater whole. And so what I have suggested as a modern Buddhist understanding of mindfulness would have, in addition to the main argument of this chapter, an interesting analogy in modern neuroscience – both leading to a more holistic approach when explaining our perceptions and definitions of reality and truth.

Bibliography

Abe, Masao, 1985. *Zen and Western Thought*, ed. William R. LaFleur. Honolulu: University of Hawai'i Press.

Bishop, Scott R., Mark Lau, Shauna Shapiro, Linda Carlson, Nicole D. Anderson, James Carmody, Zindal V. Segal, Susan Abbey, Michael Speca, Drew Velting & Gerald Devins, 2004. 'Mindfulness: A Proposed Operational Definition'. *Clinical Psychology: Science and Practice* 11.3: 230-241.

---

15 Sybille C. Fritsch-Oppermann, 2013. 'The Intelligence of Emotions – Emotional Intelligence' (Review Article), in European Society for the Study of Science and Theology *ESSSAT News & Reviews* 23.3: 8-18.

Brown, Kirk Warren & Richard M. Ryan, 2004. 'The Benefits of Being Present: Mindfulness and Its Role in Psychological Well-Being'. *Journal of Personality and Social Psychology* 84.4: 822-848.

Brown, Kirk Warren, Richard M. Ryan & David Creswell, 2007. 'Mindfulness: Theoretical Foundations and Evidence for its Salutary Effect'. *Psychological Inquiry* 18.4: 211-237.

Bundschuh-Müller, Karin, 2004. '"Es ist was es ist sagt die Liebe..." Achtsamkeit und Akzeptanz in der Personenzentrierten und Experimentellen Psychotherapie'. In *Achtsamkeit und Akzeptanz in der Psychotherapie. Ein Handbuch,* ed. Thomas Heidenreich & Michalak Johannes. Tübingen: DGVt-Verlag.

Chögyam Trungpa, 1978. *Jenseits von Hoffnung und Furcht. Gespräche über Abhidharma.* Wien: Octopus.

Chögyam Trungpa, 1988 (1972). *Aktive Meditation. Tibetische Weisheit,* Olten: Walter.

Chögyam Trungpa, 1989. *Spirituellen Materialismus durchschneiden.* Küsnacht: Theseus.

Chögyam Trungpa, 1989. *Der Mythos Freiheit und der Weg der Meditation.* Küsnacht: Theseus.

Dōgen, 2007. *Shōbōgenzō: The True Dharma-Eye Treasury*, volumes I-IV, BDK English Tripiṭaka series. Berkeley: Numata Center for Buddhist Translation and Research.

Fritsch-Oppermann, Sybille C., 2000. *Christliche Existenz im buddhistischen Kontext. Katsumi Takizawas und Seiichi Yagis Dialog mit dem Buddhismus in Japan.* Berlin-Münster-Wien-Zürich-London: LIT-Verlag.

Fritsch-Oppermann, Sybille C., 2013. 'The Intelligence of Emotions – Emotional Intelligence' (Review Article). *ESSSAT News & Reviews* 23.3: 8-18.

Gethin, Rupert, 1998. *The Foundations of Buddhism.* New York: Oxford University Press.

Gregersen, Niels H., ed., 2015. *Incarnation. On the Scope and Depth of Christology.* Minneapolis: Fortress Press.

Gundert, Wilhelm, ed., 1973[3]. *Bi-Yän-Lu: Meister Yüan-wu's Niederschrift von der Smaragdenen Felswand, verfasst auf dem Djia-schan bei Li in Hunan zwischen 1111 und 1115*. In *Druck erschienen in Sütschuan um 1300*, 3 vols. München & Wien: Hanser.

Heine, Steven, ed., 1992. *A Study of Dogen: His Philosophy and Religion*. Albany, New York: SUNY Press.

Hölzel, Britta K., 2007. *Achtsamkeitsmeditation: Aktivierungsmuster und morphologische Veränderungen im Gehirn von Meditierenden*. PhD thesis, Justus-Liebig-Universität Giessen.

Jaeckelen, Antje, 2005. *Time and Eternity: the Question of Time in Church, Science and Theology*. West Conshohocken: Templeton Foundation Press.

Kabat-Zinn, Jon, 1982. 'An outpatient program in behavioural medicine for chronic pain patients based on the practice of mindfulness meditation: Theoretical considerations and preliminary results'. *General Hospital Psychiatry* 4.1: 33-47.

Kabat-Zinn, Jon, 2007. *Im Alltag Ruhe finden. Das umfassende praktische Meditationsprogramm*. Freiburg: Herder.

Kabat-Zinn, Jon & Rich Simon, 2015. 'Mindfulness and Awareness according to Jon Kabat-Zinn'. Interview. Accessed: https://www.psychotherapynetworker.org/blog/ details/511/mindfulness-and-awareness-according-to-jon-kabat-zinnHomepage.

Keng, Shian-Ling, Moria J. Smoski & Clive J. Robins, 2011. 'Effects of mindfulness on psychological health: A review of empirical studies'. *Clinical Psychology Review* 31.6: 1041-1056.

Kittel, Ingo-Wolf, 2010. '"Panoramabewusstheit" – fact or fiction?'. In *Meditation und Yoga. Achtsamkeit, Heilung, Selbsterkenntnis*, eds. Harald Piron & Renaud van Quekelberghe. Eschborn & Magdeburg: Klotz: 187-194.

LaFleur, William R., ed., 1985. *Zen and Western Thought*. University of Hawai'i: Macmillan.

Michal, Matthias, 2004. 'Achtsamkeit und Akzeptanz in der Psychoanalyse'. In *Achtsamkeit und Akzeptanz in der Psychotherapie. Ein Handbuch*, eds. Thomas Heidenreich & Johannes Michalaik. Tübingen: DGVt-Verlag.

Nhat Hanh, Thich, 1990. *Umarme deine Wut: Sutra der vier Verankerungen der Achtsamkeit*. Küsnacht: Theseus.

Perls, Frederick S. 1978. *Das Ich, der Hunger und die Agression: die Anfänge der Gestalttherapie*. Stuttgart: Klett-Cotta.

Perls, Frederick S., Ralph E. Hefferline & Paul Goodman, 2015. *Gestalttherapie. Grundlagen der Lebensfreude und Persönlichkeitsentfaltung*. Stuttgart: Klett-Cotta.

Reddemann, Luise, 2008. *Imagination als heilsame Kraft: Zur Behandlung von Traumafolgen mit resourcenorientierten Verfahren*. Stuttgart: Klett-Cotta.

Reynhout, Kenneth A., 2013. *Interdisciplinary Interpretation: Paul Ricoeur and the Hermeneutics of Theology and Science*. Plymouth, UK: Lexington Books.

Ricard, Matthieu in dialogue with Wolf Singer, 2008[4]. *Hirnforschung und Meditation*. Frankfurt: Suhrkamp.

Stachel, Günter, ed., 1986. *Munen muso – ungegenständliche Meditation. Festschrift für Pater Hugo M. Enomiya-Lassalle zum 80. Geburtstag*. Mainz: Matthias-Grünewald.

Suzuki, Daisetsu Teitaro, 1970, ed. Christmas Humphreys. *Essays in Zen Buddhism*. London: Rider.

Thanissaro Bhikkhu, 1999. *The Wings to Awakening: An Anthology from the Pali Canon*: Barre: Dhamma Dana Publications.

THEME 4:
THE HESYCHAST TRADITION
AND ITS AFFINITIES TO BUDDHISM

MEDITATION IN THERAVĀDA BUDDHISM AND THE HESYCHAST TRADITION OF CHRISTIANITY

Nicholas Alan Worssam

Abstract

This paper looks at the echoes of Buddhist categories of meditation practice to be found in the Christian tradition of hesychastic prayer. Hesychia *is a Greek term signifying silence or stillness, and is a word used to describe a variety of practices, but is most commonly linked to the use of the Jesus Prayer (Lord Jesus Christ, Son of God, have mercy on me!) to still the mind, and the practice of watchfulness (Greek:* nepsis*) to become more aware of the thoughts which disturb the mind during prayer, both being taught in the collection entitled* The Philokalia*. These will be compared to the practice of* samatha *(calm) and* vipassanā *(insight) meditation in the tradition of Theravāda Buddhism, focussing on the Pāli canon and Buddhaghosa's classic work, the* Visuddhimagga *(The Path of Purification). Particular correspondences explored include the Eight Thoughts (Greek:* logismoi*) and the Five Hindrances (Pāli:* nīvaraṇa*), the causation of thoughts (Greek:* peirasmos */ Pāli:* paṭicca-samuppāda*), and the practice of meditation on love (Greek:* agapē */ Pāli:* mettā*) leading to meditative absorption and the experience of radiant light.*

Keywords: Meditation, Theravāda Buddhism, The Path of Purification, Hesychasm, *The Philokalia*, Mindfulness, Watchfulness, the Five Hindrances, the Eight Thoughts, Causation, Lovingkindness, Absorption, Light

Introduction

Meditation and prayer are core practices of Theravāda Buddhism and Orthodox Christianity. In this chapter I will look first at some verses of the Buddhist *Dhammapada,* and the Christian writer, Evagrius of Pontus, to point out some basic similarities in the structures of the practice of meditation. Then I will examine some foundational Buddhist meditative practices under the titles of Effort, Mindfulness and Concentration, comparing them with the Christian practices of Watchfulness and the Jesus Prayer. Then I will discuss in more detail some particular meditational practices: mindfulness of breathing, mindfulness of death, and contemplation of states of mind and their causality. This leads into a discussion of one of the primary antidotes to unskilful states of mind: the cultivation of compassionate loving-kindness. Finally, I compare the Buddhist and Christian descriptions of absorption in deep meditation, with the accompanying experiences of radiant light.

Although this chapter attempts to hold in creative tension the similarities and differences between Theravāda Buddhist and Orthodox Christian practices of prayer and meditation, this is not necessarily an easy tension to maintain. 'Theravāda' means the Teaching or Way of the Elders, a title that the Orthodox Christian tradition would no doubt welcome also; but to suggest that there may be two valid ways of the elders would leave many proponents of either path rather aghast. The fundamental Buddhist text, the *Mahāsatipaṭṭhāna Sutta* (The Greater Discourse on the Foundations of Mindfulness) begins (in the translation of Maurice Walshe): 'There is, monks, this one way to the purification of beings, for the overcoming of sorrow and distress, for the gaining of the right path...' (*Dīgha Nikāya* ii 290; Walshe 1987, 335). This would seem to exclude other descriptions of the path to liberation. But, although considered by the Pāli commentaries as a possible translation, this '*Ekāyano maggo*' can alternatively be translated as 'the direct path', as for example by Bhikkhu Bodhi in his translation of the *Majjhima Nikāya* version of the text (*Satipaṭṭhāna Sutta, Majjhima Nikāya* I 55-56, Ñāṇamoli & Bodhi 1995, 145), or as Sarah Shaw translates the passage: 'This monks, leads only one way…to the disappearance of suffering and pain, to the attainment of the way, to the realization of *nibbāna*' (Shaw 2006, 80). Perhaps both Buddhists and Christians are walking in the same direction, or at least towards the same end.

Christianity is itself not unfamiliar with talk of a unique way apart from which no-one gains salvation. Timothy Ware, writing in his classic work, *The Orthodox Church*, says that: 'Orthodoxy, believing that the Church on earth has remained and must remain visibly one, naturally also believes itself to be that one visible Church…' (Ware 1963, 250f.).[1] And many members of the Orthodox Church question the appropriateness of non-Orthodox Christians practising hesychastic prayer.[2] But here, too, there are dissenting voices in the tradition. One such comes from the Macarian Homilies, probably composed in Syria in the fourth century:

> After I received the experience of the sign of the cross, grace now acts in this manner. It quiets all my parts and my heart so that the soul with the greatest joy seems to be a guileless child. No longer am I a man that condemns Greek or Jew or sinner or worldling. Truly, the interior person looks on all human beings with pure eyes and finds joy in the whole world. He really wishes to reverence and love all Greeks and Jews. (Maloney 1992, 83)

For Macarius, or the author writing in his name, the experience of the revelation of God leads to a breaking down of barriers, and the

---

1 This concern for unity and exclusivity is found also in the writings of Archimandrite Sophrony, the founder of an Orthodox monastery in England, who says that, 'If a certain similarity either in their practice or their outward manifestations, or even their mystical formulation, can be discerned, that does not at all imply that [Orthodoxy and other traditions] are alike fundamentally. Outwardly similar situations can be vastly different in inner content' (Sophrony 1977, 119).

2 A very interesting exploration of this Orthodox anxiety has been published by Christopher Johnson (2010). Using not just authors such as Ware and Sophrony, but delving into the book reviews populating the Amazon website, Johnson maps the way many Orthodox Christians fear that their tradition of spirituality is being taken out of context, possibly to the spiritual harm of such eclectic seekers at the fringes of church membership.

inclusion of others in one's compassionate and reverent regard. Here, too, there are signs of hope for an attitude to spiritual practice that includes rather than excludes the other.

So I begin my explorations with some short verses by two poets of the spiritual life. These verses are chosen because they allow an introductory look at some of the key terms and issues involved in the comparative study of Buddhist and Christian meditation. First, two sayings of the Buddha as recorded in the *Dhammapada*:

> The monk who dwells in loving kindness,
> Confident in the Buddha's teaching,
> Attains the peaceful state,
> The blissful stilling of conditioned things (verse 368)

> There's no meditation in one without wisdom,
> Or wisdom in one who doesn't meditate.
> The one in whom are both meditation and wisdom
> Is close to *nibbāna*. (verse 372; Roebuck 2010, 72-73)

The first verse I chose because for me the spiritual path has to begin with loving kindness. It has to be intellectually rigorous, while rooted in the heart. In the Mahāyāna tradition, this motivation to practice is known as *bodhicitta* (thought of awakening), which includes the wish for the enlightenment of all beings, and the dedicated commitment to practise to that end. But this motive is at the heart of the Theravāda tradition also. One practises for the sake of 'the good, the benefit, the happiness of humans and gods,'[3] and one does so based on faith, being 'confident in the Buddha's teaching'.[4] Furthermore, this love and this faith lead

---

3   Cf. the words of the Buddha commissioning his followers: 'Monks, I am free of all ties, human and divine, and so are you, monks, free from all ties, human and divine. Monks, take to the road. Travel for the good of the many, for the happiness of the many, out of compassion for the world, travel for the good, the benefit, the happiness of humans and gods. Preach the Doctrine, which is good in the beginning, good in the middle, and good at the end.' *Mahāvagga* (Vinaya 1, 21) quoted in Wijayaratna 1990, 132.

4   '[The monk] acquires perfect confidence in the Buddha thus: "The Blessed One is accomplished, fully enlightened, perfect in true knowledge and conduct, sublime, knower of worlds, incomparable leader of persons to be

to peace and the bliss of stillness or calm, which are the fruits of practice. Then, in the second verse quoted, the importance of both meditation and wisdom is emphasized. Perhaps here there is an intimation of the categories of *samatha* or calm, and *vipassanā* or insight, the two wings of Buddhist meditation (Gethin 1998, 174).

Turning to the Christian tradition, I begin with Evagrius Ponticus, one of the first to systematize the wisdom of the earliest monks and nuns of the Christian tradition in the Egyptian desert of the fourth century. Evagrius says:

> The state of prayer can be aptly described as a
> habitual state of imperturbable calm.
> It snatches to the heights of intelligible reality
> the spirit which loves wisdom
> and which is truly spiritualized
> by the most intense love.
>
> If you are a theologian you truly pray.
> If you truly pray you are a theologian.
>
> (*Chapters on Prayer, 52 and 60*; Bamberger 1981, 63 and 65)

Evagrius first speaks of calm, in Greek *apatheia*: this is an important term meaning not apathy but dispassion, or impassability, or, as the Buddhists might say, equanimity. This dispassion is rooted in the practice of stillness (Greek: *Hesychia*, hence the term 'hesychasm'[5]): both outwardly refraining from speech and inwardly

---

tamed, teacher of gods and humans, enlightened, blessed.".…He considers thus: "I am possessed of perfect confidence in the Buddha," and he gains inspiration in the meaning, gains inspiration in the Dhamma, gains gladness connected with the Dhamma. When he is glad, rapture is born in him; in one who is rapturous, the body becomes tranquil; one whose body is tranquil feels pleasure; in one who feels pleasure, the mind becomes concentrated.' *Vatthūpama Sutta, Majjhima Nikāya* I.37, (Ñāṇamoli 1995, 118-119).

5   Kallistos Ware defines Hesychasm as follows: 'The term "Hesychasm" can be used in a variety of ways. It is derived from the Greek word *hesuchia*, meaning "quiet" or "stillness"… the word 'Hesychast' may be used in an exterior and spatial sense, to denote a hermit or solitary as contrasted with a monk in a cenobitic community. But more commonly it is employed in an

cleansing the mind of all images.[6] Dispassion is itself the necessary preparation for love (Gk. *agape*) as it roots out the obscura-
tions of self-concern. It is dispassionate love which in turn leads
to wisdom or knowledge (Gk. *gnosis*), the direct intuitive awareness of reality, which is the sphere of the liberated mind or *nous*.[7]
Combatting the passions and enabling true love is a large part of
the work of prayer, but more of that later in the chapter.

Then comes a famous couplet by Evagrius, affirming that
prayer and theology are not two different things. True knowledge
of God can only be the result of prayer. For Evagrius, theology
means the direct apprehension of the divine, not intellectual debates about abstract concepts. In Buddhist terms, theology is closer to insight (Pāli: *vipassanā*), or wisdom (*paññā*), rather than the
pejorative term 'views' (*diṭṭhi*). As such, for Evagrius, theology is
inseparable from imageless pure prayer, the latter being perhaps
the Christian equivalent of the calm of *samatha* meditation.

Moving on from these initial verses, I would like to look more
closely into what the two traditions actually teach about meditation and prayer. Here, to define some terms, it is useful to turn to
Buddhaghosa, the great exegete of the Pāli scriptures and author
of the *Visuddhimagga* (The Path of Purification). In the following
texts we see Buddhaghosa explaining three key terms: Energy,
Mindfulness and Concentration. These he later describes in the
context of the Buddha's Noble Eightfold Path, where they form
the section of the Path devoted to meditation (Pāli: *samādhi*) or
practice (Pāli: *bhāvanā*).[8] In the passages quoted below, Buddhag-

---

interior sense, to indicate one who practises inner prayer and seeks silence
of the heart' (Jones et al, 1986, 243).

6   'Stand guard over your spirit, keeping it free of concepts at the time of
prayer so that it may remain in its own deep calm.' Evagrius in *Chapters on
Prayer*, 69, (Bamberger 1981, 66).

7   'Love is the offspring of impassibility, and impassibility is the blossom of
the practical life.' 'The kingdom of heaven is impassibility of the soul accompanied by true knowledge of beings.' *Praktikos* 2 and 81, (Sinkewicz
2003, 97 and 110).

8   The Right Effort of the Path (Pāli: *sammā vāyāma*) is closely related to the
faculty of energy (*viriya*): 'One's energy, which is in conformity and associ-

hosa explains the terms as part of his analysis of the aggregates (*khandha*s), the factors that together comprise what is mistakenly perceived to be the self. Although I take each of the three faculties in turn, it is important to see their interconnections and the fluidity of the definitions. These faculties work together as a connected set of disciplines, and their descriptions overlap.[9]

Buddhaghosa explains the terms one by one, beginning with Right Effort and its closely related term 'energy':

> Energy (*viriya*) is the state of one who is vigorous. Its characteristic is marshalling (driving). Its function is to consolidate conascent states. It is manifested as non-collapse. Because of the words 'Bestirred, he strives wisely' (*Anguttara Nikāya* ii, 115) its proximate cause is a sense of urgency; or its proximate cause is grounds for the initiation of energy. When rightly initiated, it should be regarded as the root of all attainments. (*Visuddhimagga* 464; Ñāṇamoli 1975, 523)

Meditation is hard work; it is not primarily a matter of bliss, though that may come later and almost as a surprise. It is a matter of close observation of the mind and weeding out unskilful patterns of thought, while encouraging and maintaining skilful, wholesome mental states.[10] This urgency and intensity of practice

---

ated with that [right view], cuts off idleness, and that is called right effort. It has the characteristic of exerting...' Buddhaghosa, *Visuddhimagga* 510 (Ñāṇamoli 1975, 583).

9   As Bhikkhu Anālayo points out in his commentary on the *Satipaṭṭhāna Sutta*, these three themes (and wisdom) are frequently repeated in the definition refrain of the sutta, describing the monk as 'diligent, clearly knowing, and mindful, free from desires and discontent in regard to the world', which Anālayo interprets as referring to the faculties of energy, wisdom, mindfulness and concentration (see Anālayo 2003, 34).

10 'And what, bhikkhus, is right effort? Here, bhikkhus, a bhikkhu generates desire for the nonarising of unarisen evil unwholesome states; he makes an effort, arouses energy, applies his mind, and strives. He generates desire for the abandoning of arisen evil unwholesome states...He generates desire for the arising of unarisen wholesome states...He generates desire for the maintenance of arisen wholesome states, for their nondecay, increase, expansion and fulfilment by development; he makes an effort, arouses energy, applies

is echoed in the opening paragraphs of *On Watchfulness and Holiness* by St Hesychios the Priest, writing perhaps from a monastery at the foot of Mount Sinai in the eighth century:

> Watchfulness (Greek: *nepsis*) is a spiritual method which, if sedulously practised over a long period, completely frees us with God's help from impassioned thoughts, impassioned words and evil actions...
> This watchfulness and this Prayer must be intense, concentrated and unremitting. (*On Watchfulness and Holiness*; *The Philokalia* I, 162, 164)

'Watchfulness' is a key term in the hesychastic tradition.[11] In the English version of *The Philokalia*, the editors define it as: 'Literally, the opposite to a state of drunken stupor; hence spiritual sobriety, alertness, vigilance. It signifies an attitude of attentiveness...maintaining guard over the heart and intellect...It is closely linked with purity of heart and stillness' (*The Philokalia* I, 366). Scriptural foundations to the practice are found in passages such as Proverbs 4:23: 'Keep your heart with all vigilance, for from it flow the springs of life' (New Revised Standard Version).[12]

Watchfulness is perhaps most closely matched by the Pāli term *sati*, usually translated as mindfulness, which is defined by Buddhaghosa as follows:

> By its means they remember...thus it is mindfulness (*sati*)...Its function is not to forget. It is manifested as guarding, or it is manifested as the state of confronting an objective field...like a

---

his mind, and strives. This is called right effort.' (*Samyutta Nikāya* V, 45. 8; Bodhi 2000, 1529).

11 The full original title of the work known as *The Philokalia*, the compendium of texts on prayer often quoted in this paper is: 'The Philokalia of the Neptic [watchful] Saints gathered from our holy Theophoric ['God-bearing'] Fathers, through which, by means of the philosophy of ascetic practice and contemplation, the intellect is purified, illumined, and made perfect' (Cook 2011, 6). For an excellent introduction to the writings collected in *The Philokalia* see Bingaman & Nassif 2012.

12 See, for example, John Cassian, *The Monastic Institutes* (Bertram 1999, 101).

door-keeper because it guards the eye-door, and so on. (*Visuddhimagga* 464; Ñāṇamoli 1975, 524)

The references to guarding the mind or the sense-doors are particularly resonant of the hesychast teaching on watchfulness.[13] Hesychios gives his take on watchfulness as guarding the mind as follows:

> Watchfulness is a continual fixing and halting of thought at the entrance to the heart. In this way predatory and murderous thoughts are marked down as they approach and what they say and do is noted; and we can see in what specious and delusive form the demons are trying to deceive the intellect. If we are conscientious in this, we can gain much experience and knowledge of spiritual warfare. (*On Watchfulness and Holiness*; *The Philokalia* I, 162)

Hesychios, and many of the early Christian writers, talk freely of the role of demons in the process of the arising of destructive thoughts. This may sound strange to our ears now, but is not unfamiliar in the Pāli suttas, with their vivid descriptions of the battles of the Buddha with Māra (lit. the killer – the personification of evil) and his cohorts. But, whether we take these descriptions literally or as symbolic of the sometimes overpowering effect of human neuroses, the element of struggle in prayer and meditation is freely admitted and resolutely faced. In Christian terminology, this is spiritual warfare, not a holiday retreat.

Lefebure, in his Christian commentary on the *Dhammapada*, compares the hesychast practice of watchfulness with the Pāli Buddhist term '*appamādo*' or vigilance, as described in chapter two of the *Dhammapada*. Verse 24 of this chapter combines many of the terms I have already been exploring: 'For one who is vigilant and restrained, who is energetic and mindful, who acts care-

---

13 *Sati,* mindfulness, is further elaborated in the Buddhist teaching in the sutta on the 'Four Foundations of Mindfulness', more of which later in this chapter, which contains a number of direct parallels with Christian meditative practice such as mindfulness of breathing (*ānāpānasati*) or the awareness of states of mind (*cittānupassanā*).

fully and purely, who lives the Dharma, fame grows' (Lefebure & Feldmeier 2001, 43). However, Lefebure goes on to say: 'One central difference between the Buddhist and Christian traditions is that Christian vigilance is always awaiting the arrival of the God whose coming cannot be predicted' (Lefebure & Feldmeier 2001, 55).

In response I would say that the actual moment by moment practice of Buddhist and Christian vigilance is remarkably similar, and both are closely focussed on the awareness of the thoughts themselves as they arise and pass away. Of course, it is true that the Christian practice is set against the backdrop of the overall view of salvation history as described in the Bible. A classic text is Mark 13:35-37 where Jesus warns the disciples: 'Therefore, keep awake – for you do not know when the master of the house will come, in the evening, or at midnight, or at cock-crow, or at dawn, or else he may find you asleep when he comes suddenly. And what I say to you I say to all: Keep awake.' These verses bring to a close the 'Little Apocalypse', the teaching of Jesus summarizing what will happen at the great judgement scene of the coming Kingdom of God. Buddhist practice has a different view of the world and time, more cyclical than linear, more psychological than the mythological framework of Christianity. But does this say anything more than that *appamādo* occurs in the Buddhist framework and *nepsis* in the Christian framework? I would argue that, although not interchangeable as terms – their meaning emerges from their different contexts – nonetheless their function within these different contexts is comparable, and the lived practice of each one, when shared, informs and enriches the other. Their function is attentiveness to the vagaries of the mind in the present moment, purifying the mind in preparation for a clearer vision of what is ultimate and unconditioned.[14]

---

14 Maximus the Confessor (580-662) shows the depth of Hesychast theological reflection on the meaning of the coming of God in the *Parousia* saying that at that time the world is 'the image and appearance of the light that never appears, a perfectly exact mirror, completely transparent, untouched, immaculate, catching in itself – if one may dare to say it – the full radiance of

Having said that, there is indeed something important in the phrase used by Lefebure: 'awaiting the arrival of the God whose coming cannot be predicted'. The unpredictability of the coming of God in the Christian tradition points to the irreducible factor of grace in the Christian spiritual path. Whatever practice of prayer or meditation is adopted by the Christian, one can never presume to have attained anything by one's own unaided efforts; the grace of God goes before us, 'prevents' us in the sixteenth century English of the Anglican Book of Common Prayer. At first sight, the Buddhist path seems different: in the *Ariyapariyesanā Sutta*, the Buddha talks of his attainment of enlightenment by his own striving. And yet is there not grace in this account? It is surely found precisely in the next section of the sutta, where the Buddha, at the prompting of the god Brahma, gratuitously decides to teach the dhamma, which few are likely to understand. The Buddha says: 'Then I listened to Brahma's pleading, and out of compassion for beings I surveyed the world with the eye of a Buddha.' And speaking of those 'with little dust in their eyes', the Buddha says: 'Open for them are the doors to the Deathless, let those with ears now show their faith' (*Majjhima Nikāya* I 167-179; Ñāṇamoli & Bodhi 1995, 259-262). The eye of a Buddha is full of compassion, full of grace and truth; the ear of a noble disciple is full of faith in response.

Finally, after discussing Energy and Mindfulness, Buddhaghosa examines *samādhi*, concentration, in the practice of meditation:

> It puts consciousness evenly on the object, or it puts it rightly on it, or it is just the mere collecting of the mind, thus it is concentration (*samādhi*)...It is manifested as peace. Usually its proximate cause is bliss. It should be regarded as steadiness of the mind, like the steadiness of a lamp's flame when there is no draught. (*Visuddhimagga* 464; Ñāṇamoli 1975, 523-524)

---

the primordial beauty, made like God yet no less itself, radiating – insofar as it is capable – the goodness of the silence hidden in the abyss' (*Mystagogia* 23; quoted in von Balthasar 2003, 352). Could that last phrase be a Christian definition of the Buddhist term *Nibbāna*?

Buddhaghosa goes on to describe many forms of concentrative techniques, using objects ranging from handmade disks of different colours (*kasiṇa*) to the 'divine abidings' of loving kindness, compassion, joy and equanimity. In the contemporary Thai forest tradition, one commonly used method of concentration is the repetition of the word 'Buddho', half on the inbreath and half on the outbreath. For example, Ajahn Mahaboowa describes Ajahn Mun meditating this way as he paced back and forth doing walking meditation. The local villagers seeing him walking this way, staring at the ground, wondered what he had lost, to which he replied: 'I've lost my Buddho!' (Tiyavanich 1997, 162). In the Pāli canon, the Buddha recommends that affirmations be associated with the breath, such as: 'I shall breathe in experiencing the mind'…'I shall breathe out gladdening the mind'.[15]

The practice used to enter states of concentration in Christian hesychasm is most often the devotion known as the Jesus Prayer, either in the form of a sentence (Lord Jesus Christ, Son of God, have mercy on me) or simply the ceaseless repetition of the name 'Jesus'.[16] Hesychios speaks of this attentiveness and endless in-

---

15 *Ānāpānasati Sutta, Majjhima Nikaya* 118 (Ñāṇamoli & Bodhi (trans.) 1995, 941-948). Many modern Theravāda teachers use repeated aspirations or affirmations, particularly in the practice of the development of loving kindness (Pāli: *mettā bhāvanā*). See for example Salzberg 1997.

16 There is some debate among scholars as to which is the earliest form of the prayer. Some see the name itself as the basic form of the prayer; see Gillett 1987, 93. Others see the prayer as necessarily involving some kind of invocation of mercy or compassion. As an example of the ambiguity of the texts, see the saying of Diadochos of Photike (c.400-485): 'No one, it is written, can say "Lord Jesus" except in the Holy Spirit (1 Cor. 12:3). Let the intellect continually concentrate on these words within its inner shrine with such intensity that it is not turned aside to any mental images. Those who meditate unceasingly upon this glorious and holy name in the depths of their heart can sometimes see the light of their own intellect' (*The Philokalia* I, 270). This is interpreted by a disciple of Abba Philimon (6/7th c.) as a reference to the longer form of the prayer: 'Keep watch in your heart; and with watchfulness say in your mind with awe and trembling: "Lord Jesus Christ, have mercy upon me." For this is the advice which the blessed Diadochos gave to beginners' (*The Philokalia* II, 347). The reference by Diadochus to the light of the intellect is picked up later in this chapter.

vocation of the name of Jesus as leading to inner stillness (Greek: *hesychia*):

> Attentiveness (*prosoche*) is the heart's stillness, unbroken by any thought. In this stillness the heart breathes and invokes, endlessly and without ceasing, only Jesus Christ who is the Son of God and himself God. (*The Philokalia* I, 163)

This stillness or silence (*hesychia*) into which the name of Jesus is continuously spoken, or silently breathed, would seem to be, after watchfulness, the second main aspect of the hesychastic teaching on prayer. Although watchfulness is sometimes given a broad definition,[17] covering all the faculties separately defined in Pāli as *viriya*, *sati* and *samādhi* (energy, mindfulness and concentration), more often Hesychios follows a binary pattern:

> Watchfulness and the Jesus Prayer, as I have said, mutually reinforce one another; for close attentiveness goes with constant prayer, while prayer goes with close watchfulness and attentiveness of intellect... The Jesus Prayer requires watchfulness as a lantern requires a candle. (*The Philokalia* I, 178 and 180)

Thus watchfulness could be compared to the Pāli terms *viriya* and *sati*, energetic mindfulness, with the Jesus Prayer forming the element of concentration, *samādhi*. In the same way, referring back to my opening quotations from the *Dhammapada*, watchfulness could be seen as *vipassanā*, literally clear seeing; while the Jesus Prayer is part of the discipline of *samatha*, the closely focussed and attentive mind.

So, with sufficient guidance to hand referring to the common factors of energy, mindfulness and concentration in Buddhist and

---

17 For example, at one point he describes four different types of Watchfulness: 'One type of watchfulness consists in closely scrutinizing every mental image or provocation;...A second type of watchfulness consists in freeing the heart from all thought, keeping it profoundly silent and still, and in praying. A third type consists in continually and humbly calling upon the Lord Jesus Christ for help. A fourth type is always to have the thought of death in one's mind' (*The Philokalia* I, 164, 165).

Christian meditation, I can turn to the practical foundations of mindfulness, quintessentially found in meditation on the breath:

> And how, bhikkhus, does a bhikkhu abide contemplating the body as a body? Here a bhikkhu, gone to the forest or to the root of a tree or to an empty hut, sits down; having folded his legs crosswise, set his body erect, and established mindfulness in front of him, ever mindful he breathes in, mindful he breathes out. Breathing in long, he understands: 'I breathe in long'; or breathing out long, he understands: 'I breathe out long'...
> (*Satipaṭṭhāna Sutta, Majjhima Nikāya* I 56; Ñāṇamoli & Bodhi 1995, 145-146)

Contrast this elegantly simple practice with the rather more laboured method of St Symeon the New Theologian (949-1022), or his disciple, in *The Three Methods of Prayer*:

> Then sit down in a quiet cell, in a corner by yourself, and do what I tell you. Close the door, and withdraw your intellect from everything worthless and transient. Rest your beard on your chest, and focus your physical gaze, together with the whole of your intellect, upon the centre of your belly or your navel. Restrain the drawing-in of breath through your nostrils, so as not to breathe easily, and search inside yourself with your intellect so as to find the place of the heart, where all the powers of the soul reside. To start with you will find there darkness and an impenetrable density. Later, when you persist and practise this task day and night, you will find, as though miraculously, an unceasing joy.
> (*The Philokalia* IV, 72, 73)

There are some quite significant parallels with Buddhist practice here. First, the meditator begins with a call to solitude and silence (perhaps the Buddha would have recommended the base of a tree rather than a quiet cell), and the renunciation of all that is transient (Pāli: *anicca*). Then, there is the focussing of the attention on the breath, using what the Indian tradition would refer to as the 'chakras' or energy centres of the heart or navel. Next, there is the full experience of 'darkness and impenetrable density', which could be related to the direct experience of suffering (*dukkha*) in

Buddhism. Finally, there is the miraculous breakthrough into joy, reflecting the Buddha's teaching on joy or rapture (*pīti*) as one of the first factors of absorption in meditation (*jhāna*).

As a guide to the physical exercise of meditation, however, this text is perhaps not to be recommended. The downward bent neck and the restraining of the breath are not often found in Buddhist teaching. The crossed legs and straight back typical of representations of the Buddha are surely a better way to attain meditative equipoise. St Gregory of Sinai (c.1265-1346) goes even further. He says:

> Sitting from dawn on a seat about nine inches high, compel your intellect to descend from your head into your heart, and retain it there. Keeping your head forcibly bent downwards, and suffering acute pain in your chest, shoulders and neck, persevere in repeating noetically or in your soul 'Lord Jesus Christ, have mercy'.
> (*On Stillness*; The *Philokalia* IV, 264)

The Buddha practised austerities like this for six years before his enlightenment, but made a definite break with such an approach, teaching instead the Middle Path between the extremes of sensual pleasure and self-mortification.[18] Also, although the meditator is encouraged to know the breath as long or short, there is no indication in the Pāli suttas that he or she is to forcibly make the breath long or short, restricting the breath as recommended (under due guidance) in the hesychast tradition.

Nonetheless, it is important to note that, although using the breath in meditation is an ancient practice in the Christian tradition, it is by no means necessary or even widely encouraged by hesychast teachers. One of the earliest references to the use of the breath would seem to be by John Climacus (c.579-649): 'Let the remembrance of Jesus be present with your every breath. Then indeed you will appreciate the value of stillness' (Luibheid 1982, 270).[19] But later teachers counsel moderation in this prac-

---

18 E.g. *Saṃyutta Nikāya* IV. 354 (Bodhi 2000, 1350).

19 Although medieval hesychasts such as St Gregory of Sinai (*The Philokalia* IV, 265) read this saying in quite a literal way, more recent scholars have

tice; for example, Bishop Ignatii Brianchaninov (1807-1867) says:

> This teaching of the Fathers [on the use of breathing techniques] has created and continues to create many perplexities for its readers, although in fact there is really nothing difficult about it. We advise our beloved brethren not to try to practise this mechanical technique unless it establishes itself in them of its own accord... The mechanical method described in these writings if fully replaced by an unhurried repetition of the prayer, a brief pause after each prayer, quiet and steady breathing, and enclosing the mind in the words of the prayer. With the aid of such means we can easily achieve a certain degree of attention...The essential, indispensable element in prayer is attention. Without attention there is no prayer'. (Kadloubovsky 1966, 104)

In Buddhist terms, this is a *samatha* technique, a way of calming the mind, or, as the hesychast would say, taking the mind into the heart. But again, the question needs to be asked: Are these merely similarities of outward form or parallels of inner content? Attention is clearly a common factor, but the direction of the attentive mind is not necessarily the same. Buddhists primarily seek direct insight into the three marks of impermanence, suffering and nonself; Christians direct the attentive mind to devotion to God in and through the Lord Jesus Christ. In their introduction to '*The Three Methods of Prayer*', attributed to St Symeon the New Theologian, the translators of the English version of *The Philokalia* offer dire warnings against making superficial comparisons between Christian and other religious practices. They say:

> Modern Western writers have compared this psychosomatic technique [of meditating with the breath] with certain methods used in Yoga and Sufism, but the parallels should not be exaggerated. The author of *The Three Methods* places the technique in a specifically Christological context: its purpose is to prepare us for

---

sometimes interpreted this as simply a reference to unceasing prayer in general, rather than a conscious use of the breath in meditation; see Chryssavgis 2004, 231.

'the invocation of Jesus Christ'. Any such technique is certainly to be employed with prudence, and its misuse can inflict grave damage on a person's physical and mental health. Significantly *The Three Methods* emphasizes the importance of obedience to a spiritual father who can act, in this and all matters, as our unerring guide. (*The Philokalia* IV, 65)

The first point, that hesychasm is Christocentric, is of course true; but if that means that all discussion and comparison ends at this point then there can be no benefit in comparative studies. But, as we noted earlier, meditation in the Theravāda is itself undertaken upon the foundation of faith or confidence (Pāli: *saddhā*). Theravāda Buddhism retains such a warmth of devotion, particularly in its Asian context, that Kate Crosby can give a chapter of her book on Theravāda Buddhism the title: 'Buddha Worship' (Crosby 2014). Devoted recollection of the excellent qualities of the Buddha is a legitimate practice in Theravāda Buddhism, as is awareness of transience and suffering in hesychasm.[20]

As for the second point, about the need for a spiritual guide, this would be warmly endorsed by the Theravāda tradition. One clear example of this is the Buddha's teaching on the Good Friend (Pāli: *kalyānamitta*). In response to Ananda's claim that good friendship is surely half the holy life, the Buddha gives him a friendly rebuke:

> This is the entire holy life, Ānanda, that is good friendship, good companionship, good comradeship. When a bhikkhu has a good friend, a good companion, a good comrade, it is to be expected that he will develop and cultivate the noble Eightfold Path... By relying upon me as a good friend, Ānanda, beings...are freed from sorrow, lamentation, pain, displeasure, and despair. (*Saṃyutta Nikāya* 1.88; Bodhi 2000, 180)

Buddhaghosa in the *Visuddhimagga* has a long section on how the Good Friend should be relied on to give good advice as to the adoption of a meditation object. He also provides the best envi-

---

20 See the discussions on Buddhist faith and Christian watchfulness above.

ronment for the disciple, depending on the disciple's particular personality type:

> What suits one of what kind of temperament? A suitable lodging for one of greedy temperament has an unwashed sill and stands level with the ground...it ought to be spattered with dirt, full of bats, dilapidated, too high or too low, in bleak surroundings, threatened [by lions, tigers etc.] with a muddy, uneven path, where even the bed and chair are full of bugs...A suitable place for one of hating temperament is not too high or too low, provided with shade and water, with well-proportioned walls, posts and steps...with bed and chair covered with well-spread clean pretty covers, smelling sweetly of flowers, and perfumes and scents set about for homely comfort, which makes one happy and glad at the mere sight of it...The right lodging for one of deluded temperament has a view and is not shut in, where the four quarters are visible to him as he sits there...for his mind becomes more confused in a confined space... (*Visuddhimagga* 107-110, Ñāṇamoli 1975, 109-111)

Perhaps for some monks or nuns the moral of the story would be to convince your Good Friend that you have a hating temperament, or at least a deluded one...

Another possible similarity between Buddhist and Christian meditation is in the practice of the Mindfulness of Death. As part of the Four Foundations of Mindfulness, the Buddha teaches:

> Again, bhikkhus, as though he were to see a corpse thrown aside in a charnel ground, one, two, or three days dead,...a bhikkhu compares this same body with it thus: 'This body too is of the same nature, it will be like that, it is not exempt from that fate.' (*Satipaṭṭhāna Sutta, Majjhima Nikāya* I 58; Ñāṇamoli & Bodhi 1995, 148)

In the Buddha's teaching, contemplating a dead body is an '*asubha*' practice: a reflection on the non-beautiful or loathsome nature of the physical body, chiefly as an aid to counteracting sensual desire. But there is another kind of Mindfulness of Death where the emphasis is more on the sense of urgency instilled by recollection of the precariousness of life:

> If, upon review, the bhikkhu knows: 'I have bad unwholesome qualities that have not been abandoned, which might become an obstacle for me if I were to die tonight,' then he should put forth extraordinary desire, effort, zeal, enthusiasm, indefatigability, mindfulness, and clear comprehension to abandon those bad unwholesome qualities…But if, upon review, the bhikkhu knows thus: 'I do not have any bad unwholesome qualities that have not been abandoned, which might become an obstacle for me if I were to die tonight,' then he should dwell in that same rapture and joy, training day and night in wholesome qualities. (*Aṅguttara Nikāya* III, 307; Bodhi 2012, 879)

Here, this recollection is a basis for entering states of blissful meditation, up to the level of 'access concentration' according to Buddhaghosa (*Visuddhimagga* 248; Ñāṇamoli 1975, 258). Compare this with a passage by St Philotheos of Sinai in *The Philokalia,* perhaps from the tenth century:

> Having once experienced the beauty of this mindfulness of death, I was so wounded and delighted by it – in spirit, not through the eye – that I wanted to make it my life's companion; for I was enraptured by its loveliness and majesty, its humility and contrite joy, by how full of reflection it is, how apprehensive of the judgment to come, and how aware of life's anxieties. (*Forty Texts on Watchfulness 6; The Philokalia* III, 18)

Philotheos finds it a beautiful practice and a delight, not at all 'morbid' in the pejorative sense. It is possible that he sees it in these terms because he is thinking ahead to the joys of heaven – which would be a rather lowly motivation in the Buddhist scheme of things. More likely, though, we just need to assume that what he has found through meditating on death is indeed the joy of renunciation, the relief of letting go of clinging to a body destined to decay.

Another point of contact would seem to be the third foundation of mindfulness: contemplation of states of mind. In the Buddha's words:

> And how, bhikkhus, does a bhikkhu abide contemplating mind as mind? Here a bhikkhu understands mind affected by lust as mind affected by lust, and mind unaffected by lust as mind unaffected by lust. He understands mind affected by hate as mind affected by hate, and mind unaffected by hate as mind unaffected by hate. He understands mind affected by delusion...unaffected by delusion...He understands liberated mind as liberated mind, and unliberated mind as unliberated mind. (*Satipaṭṭhāna Sutta, Majjhima Nikāya* I 59; Ñāṇamoli & Bodhi 1995, 150)

This intimate knowledge of the states of mind as they arise and pass away would seem to be closely paralleled in the Christian practice of keeping watch over the thoughts. For example, Evagrius teaches that:

> If there is any monk who wishes to take the measure of some of the more fierce demons so as to gain experience in his monastic art, then let him keep careful watch over his thoughts. Let him observe their intensity, their periods of decline and follow them as they rise and fall. Let him note well the complexity of his thoughts, their periodicity, the demons which cause them, with the order of their succession and the nature of their associations. (*Praktikos* 50; Bamberger 1981, 29-30)

Evagrius teaches that there are eight principle thoughts (Greek: *logismoi*) that plague the mind of one intent on prayer:

> First is that of gluttony, then impurity, avarice, sadness, anger, *acedia* [boredom, listlessness], vainglory, and last of all, pride. It is not in our power to determine whether we are disturbed by these thoughts, but it is up to us to decide if they are to linger within us or not and whether or not they are to stir up our passions. (*Praktikos* 6; Bamberger 1981, 16)

It is important for the person praying to clearly name each thought, and the demon which instigates them, because then it is possible to come back with a scriptural retort. One of the books of Evagrius entitled '*Antirrhetikos*' or 'Talking Back' is a long list of appropriate sayings, many from the Psalms, in order to name the demons and stop them in their tracks. It is a practice not dissimilar to that of the Burmese monk, Mahasi Sayadaw, who recommends labelling thoughts as they appear in the mind (e.g. Mahasi Sayadaw 1990, 27ff). The list of the five hindrances (Pāli: *nīvaraṇa*), one of the contemplations of the Fourth Foundation of Mindfulness (Pāli: *dhammānupassanā*), could be compared to the Eight Thoughts of Evagrius: sensual desire could be related gluttony and impurity; aversion to anger and sadness; sloth-and-torpor to *acedia*; restlessness and worry to avarice; doubt to vainglory and pride. Of course, these are not equivalent terms, especially the last pairing, but they represent similar kinds of hindrances to meditation, a full list of which would include rather more than just five or eight items.

For Evagrius, these eight thoughts can be summarized as irascibility and desire, which represent the distortions of the two powers of the soul: the incensive aspect (Greek: *to thumikon*) and the appetitive aspect (*to ephithymitikon*). Evagrius says:

> One cannot divest oneself of impassioned memories without taking care for one's irascibility and desire, by consuming the former with fasting and vigils and sleeping on the ground and calming down the latter by being long-suffering, free from grudges and charitable with alms. From these two passions arise nearly all the demonic thoughts who bring the mind 'to ruin and destruction' [1 Tim. 6:9]. (*On Thoughts* 3; Casiday 2006, 92)

Evagrius also privileges the attainment of knowledge (Greek: *gnosis*),[21] as it pertains to the third faculty of human nature, the intelligent aspect (*to logisitikon*), such that his teaching parallels the Buddha's teaching that desire and aversion, together with ignorance, are the principle causes of suffering in the world.

Evagrius also sees that in the causes of suffering are to be found the path of escape. These three aspects of human nature can be turned around to act as they were supposed to do in God's good plan: 'The rational soul operates according to nature when the fol-

---

21 *On Prayer* 86: 'Knowledge! The great possession of humanity. It is a fellow-worker with prayer, acting to awaken the power of thought to contemplate the divine knowledge' (Bamberger 1981, 69).

lowing conditions are realized: the concupiscible part desires virtue; the irascible part fights to obtain it; the rational part, finally, applies itself to the contemplation of created things' (*Praktikos* 86; Bamberger 1981, 37). Salvation is not about the suppression of the soul's natural powers, rather it is their liberation to act according to their original nature; virtue is more fundamental in human nature than vice, and the tripartite structure of the soul manifests most naturally as goodness, energy and understanding.

This search for the causation of suffering is intricately explained in the Buddhist doctrine of dependent origination. For the purposes of meditation practice, the central links in the chain are: 'with the six sense bases as condition, contact; with contact as condition, feeling; with feeling as condition, craving; with craving as condition, clinging; with clinging as condition, existence...' (*Samyutta Nikaya* II.1; Bodhi 2000, 533). The key link in the chain is that between feeling and craving: if sensory experience does not lead to craving or thirst (Pāli: *taṇhā*), then there is the possibility of release from conditioned existence.

The Christian hesychastic teachers also explore the nature of causation as it applies to thought processes. Evagrius recognizes the key role of feeling or sensation: 'Now desire precedes every pleasure, and it is feeling which gives birth to desire. For that which is not subject to feeling is also free of passion' (*Praktikos* 4, Bamberger 1981, 16). Various extended patterns of the causation of thoughts are presented in *The Philokalia*, beginning with Mark the Ascetic in the early fifth century. He emphasizes the necessity of understanding the mind by direct experience of the process of causation of thoughts, beginning with 'provocation':

> In our ascetic warfare we can neither rid ourselves of evil thoughts apart from their causes, nor of their causes without ridding ourselves of the thoughts...The devil initiates the whole process by testing a person with a provocation which they are not compelled to accept; but the person, urged on by self-indulgence and self-esteem, begins to entertain this provocation with enjoyment. Even if their discrimination tells them to reject it, yet in practice they take pleasure in it and accept it. If someone has not per-

ceived this general process of sinning, when will they pray about it and be cleansed from it? And if they have not been cleansed, how will they find purity of nature?...and how will they behold the inner dwelling-place of Christ? (*On those who think they are made righteous by works,* 170, 224; *The Philokalia* I, 140, 145)

Mark the Ascetic lists the stages of temptation (Greek: *peirasmos*) as provocation, enjoyment, acceptance, prepossession and passion.[22] For the hesychasts, provocation and momentary disturbance of the mind are unavoidable; it is when the meditator entertains the thoughts and assents to them that the entrainment of passion begins.[23] In this way they are mapping the same territory as that explored by the Buddha in his doctrine of dependent origination (*paṭiccasamuppāda*), particularly in the steps leading from contact through feeling, clinging, and craving to becoming. In both traditions, it is 'self-indulgence and self-esteem', wrong views about the self, which are the cause of suffering.

One antidote to the passion of anger, common to both Buddhist and Christian traditions, is meditation on loving-kindness. As the Buddha explains:

[The bhikkhu] abides pervading one quarter with a mind imbued with loving-kindness (*mettā*), likewise the second, likewise the third, likewise the fourth; so above, below, around, and everywhere, and to all as to himself, he abides pervading the all-encompassing world with a mind imbued with loving-kindness, abundant, exalted, immeasurable, without hostility and without ill will... (*Vatthūpama Sutta. Majjhima Nikāya* I 38; Ñāṇamoli & Bodhi 1995, 120)

---

22 *On the Spiritual Law,* 138-170; and *No Righteousness by Works,* 224 - *The Philokalia* I, 119-121 and 145). See also Cook 2011, 73-92 for a full survey of the process of Temptation (Greek: *peirasmos*).

23 Hesychios gives the following sequence: 'The provocation comes first, then our coupling with it, or the mingling of our thoughts with those of the wicked demons. Third comes our assent to the provocation, with both sets of intermingling thoughts contriving how to commit the sin in practice. Fourth comes the concrete action – that is, the sin itself' (*On Watchfulness and Holiness,* 46; *The Philokalia* I, 170).

Such a practice, although not systematically taught, is clearly evidenced in the homilies of St Isaac of Syria:

> An elder was asked: 'And what is a merciful heart?' 'It is the heart's burning for the sake of the entire creation, for people, for birds, for animals, for demons, and for every created thing; and at the recollection and sight of them, the eyes of the merciful pour forth abundant tears. From the strong and vehement mercy that grips their heart and from their great compassion, their heart is humbled and they cannot bear to hear or to see any injury or slight sorrow in creation. For this reason they offer up prayers with tears continually even for irrational beasts, for the enemies of the truth, and for those who harm them, that they be protected and receive mercy...because of the great compassion that burns without measure in their heart in the likeness of God.' (Isaac of Syria 2011, 491)

As Hilarion Alfeyev points out, 'In Isaac's understanding, God is above all immeasurable and boundless love. The conviction that God is love dominates Isaac's thought: it is the source of his theological opinions, ascetical recommendations, and mystical insights' (Alfeyev 2000, 35f). For Isaac, love and justice do not form the two sides of God's nature: God is wholly love. Being lost in the love of God the person of prayer experiences a kind of 'sober inebriation', and a sweetness and delight that floods the whole body (Alfeyev 2000, 252).

Some Christian writers, however, while admitting to points of contact between the two traditions, particularly on the theme of loving-kindness, conclude that there are nonetheless irreconcilable differences. For example, in his comparison of Buddhaghosa and John of the Cross, Feldmeier concludes his chapter on the path to holiness:

> While both paths describe similarities in the aspirant's growth in joy and freedom, there is a central quality in the experience of the path that radically differentiates them. This is the experience of love...John's is a mysticism of love, while Buddhaghosa's is one of deep, penetrating, impersonal insight. In this regard, they cannot be further apart. (Feldmeier 2006, 72-73).

While not denying the development of compassion in Theravāda Buddhism, Feldmeier sees the basic direction of the two traditions as ultimately different. Two responses at least could be made here. The first is to question whether Buddhaghosa and John of the Cross truly are representatives of Buddhism and Christianity respectively. Although undoubtedly widely revered by their co-religionists, they each take their scriptural traditions to a logical conclusion that would sound strange to the ears of many who had not made an extensive study of their writings. They represent polarities of their respective traditions rather than a middle ground that may be a firmer base for dialogue. Secondly, and rather more importantly, in both Buddhism and Christianity, there is a wide spectrum of practice considered to be directly on the path to holiness, including both love and knowledge. There are debates within the two traditions themselves over the relative weight to be given to each of these fundamental aspects of the path. For example, from the Eastern Christian tradition, Evagrius would place a higher value on knowledge (*gnosis*), while the Macarian homilies stress rather the experience of love (*agape*), the two streams being united in writers such as Diadochos of Photike. In Western Christianity there is a similar debate, this time exemplified in the fraternal rivalry of the Dominicans and Franciscans:

> The various schools of Christian spirituality have attempted to explicate the proper relationship between love and knowledge… In the West, Dominicans have stressed the primacy of the intellect and identified the vision of God as the goal of the spiritual journey, with love as the fruit of knowledge. Holding to the primacy of the will, Franciscans have tended to see knowledge as necessary but insufficient, so that knowledge is but an intimation of the ecstasy of love in which God is more 'tasted' than 'seen'. (Arthur Holder in Sheldrake 2005, 396)

This is an intra-religious debate within traditions (and individuals), not just an inter-religious debate between traditions. It is all too easy to pick as one's representative a teacher or a school of thought that represents one side, or leans to one side, of the multi-faceted reality that each religious tradition has become.

Another challenge to the linking of Buddhist and Christian teachings on love is that it could be said that the Buddhist teaching on loving kindness and compassion carries with it the fundamentally different background of the teaching of non-self (Pāli: *anattā*), so that ultimately there is no one to love or be loved. The meditative development of compassion (*mettā-bhāvanā* and *karunā bhāvanā*) thus culminates in the experiences of infinite space, infinite consciousness and nothingness.[24] In reply, the Christian could point to the doctrine that God is Being Itself, that the nature of reality is not irreducibly dualistic, and that the goal of the spiritual path is the divinization of humanity, that people 'may become participants of the divine nature' (2 Peter 1:4). This doctrine is represented visually in the nimbus or halo depicted around the head of Christ in Orthodox icons, in which is often inscribed the Greek words: 'ὁ ὤν' ('*ho ōn*'), 'the One Who Is', thus affirming that created being has only a contingent existence. When this is deeply experienced in prayer, the meditator 'becomes completely light, completely mind, completely transparent…The mind is taken up into divine vision; and mixing takes place. Man is transformed and becomes one with God, such that he doesn't recognize himself, just as iron becomes one with fire.'[25]

Taking this argument one step further, following the lead of the sixth century Syrian monk writing in his *Mystical Theology* under the name of Dionysius the Areopagite, and the slightly later Maximus the Confessor, it could be said that God is better described by negation than by affirmation:

> He who is and who will be all things to all – and who exercises this role precisely through the things that are and that will come to be – is in himself no part of the realm of things that are and come to be, in any way, at any time, nor shall he become so, because he can never be categorized as part of any natural order of beings. As a consequence of his existence beyond being, he is more properly spoken of in terms of not-being. (from *Mystagogia,* Maximus the Confessor (580-662); quoted in von Balthasar 2003, 89)

---

24 See Anālayo 2015, 70.
25 See Elder Joseph the Hesychast (20th c.), in Middleton 2003, 120.

Could there be a link here with the Buddhist teaching of *nibbāna* as being the only unconditioned element, not so much a noun as a verb, the blowing out of the flame of desire? Are Christian practitioners attaining such a realization aided by the experience of Nothingness in the deep absorption of meditative experience?

The outcome of concentrated meditation techniques, whether using the breath, a repeated phrase, or a 'divine abiding' such as loving-kindness or equanimity, can be an absorption in meditation known in the Pāli tradition as '*jhāna*'. These states begin in great rapture and happiness, and become progressively more refined the deeper the absorption becomes. Buddhaghosa describes how meditation on an object such as the breath can lead to the arising of a sign (Pāli: *nimitta*), which allows the mind to focus more strongly. This 'counterpart sign' is 'like a mother-of-pearl dish well washed, like the moon's disk coming out from behind a cloud' (*Visuddhimagga* 126, Ñāṇamoli 1975, 130). Other experiences of light occur in the fourth *jhāna*. Here, the bhikkhu 'sits suffusing his body with a pure bright mind, so that there is no part of his entire body not suffused by a pure bright mind... When his mind is thus concentrated, pure and bright...he directs and inclines it to knowledge and vision' (*Samaññaphala Sutta, Dīgha Nikāya* 1, 75-76; Bodhi 1989, 43-44).

Such experiences of light are found in a number of places in the hesychast tradition, going right back to the early centuries of the Common Era. Evagrius says in his work *Reflections*:

> If someone should want to behold the state of his mind, let him deprive himself of all mental representations, and then he shall behold himself resembling sapphire or the colour of heaven. It is impossible to accomplish this without impassibility, for he will need God to collaborate with him and breathe into him the connatural light. (*Reflections* 2; Sinkewicz 2003, 211)[26]

This is a light that is natural to every soul, simply obscured by the passions. When dispassion or equanimity (*apatheia*) is attained,

---

26 Sinkewicz points out that this may be a reference to the throne of God as described in Exodus 24:10 (Sinkewicz 2003, 284 note 1).

such an absorption in the experience of light becomes possible, just as when the five hindrances are attenuated in the Buddhist schema, the *nimitta* appears and the absorption of *jhāna* becomes possible. So these experiences of light in the Christian tradition can be directly related to *samatha*-type meditation in both traditions, and are full of love, joy and understanding, as described by Theoliptos, Metropolitan of Philadelphia (c.1250-1322), in *On Inner Work in Christ*:

> For when the mind unceasingly repeats the name of the Lord and the intellect gives its full attention to the invocation of the divine name, the light of the knowledge of God overshadows the entire soul like a luminous cloud. Concentrated mindfulness of God is followed by love and joy...' (*The Philokalia* IV, 181)

An example from the seventh century writings of Maximos the Confessor (580-662), brings out the clear elements of absorption in meditation and inner illumination in his work *Four Hundred Texts on Love*:

> When in the intensity of its love for God the intellect goes out of itself, then it has no sense of itself or of any created thing. For when it is illumined by the infinite light of God, it becomes insensible to everything made by Him, just as the eye becomes insensible to the stars when the sun rises. (*The Philokalia* II, 54)

This text would seem to imply that Maximos and those like him have reached at least the first if not the fourth *jhāna* in their meditation practice.[27] This would also be implied by the presence of the psychic powers (Pāli: *iddhi*) such as hearing and see-

---

27 There is some debate among contemporary scholars about how absorbed the first *jhāna* really is: for the Burmese monk Pa Auk Sayadaw the schema of Buddhaghosa is strictly followed, with deep concentration required before it can be said that the first *jhāna* has been attained; others, such as Leigh Brasington, a disciple of the late German nun Ayya Khema, interpret the suttas as requiring a lesser degree of concentration. See Brasington 2015.

ing things at a great distance, reported by St Gregory Palamas,[28] but restricted in the Buddhist scheme to those who have mastered the fourth *jhāna*.[29]

Conclusion

So, at the end of all this can we say that the masters of the Christian Hesychast tradition have 'done what had to be done' and have lived 'the holy life' with 'nothing further beyond'? Or that the Buddhist masters have been divinized by the Holy Spirit in the all-encompassing love of God who both is and, perhaps more accurately, is not? It is difficult to say. Christian writers rarely use the language of the realization of non-self, and Buddhist writers certainly do not speak of God in any ultimate sense. At the end of the path the final metaphors seem to divide. The followers of the Buddha reach the end of their long journey and are released into *nibbāna*, while the followers of Christ go right back to the beginning, are restored to their original state, and re-enter paradise. How can the two possibly be reconciled? And yet I do believe that there is a significant degree of contact between the two traditions in the experience of prayer and meditation, as recorded by two sets of people who most likely had absolutely no direct contact with each other. There is much further to go in such comparisons. If I were to take this study further, I would go into the question of deification – the summit of the Orthodox hesychastic path – and see how it might relate to the experience of *nibbāna*. But that is a topic for another paper. For now it can simply be affirmed that there are numerous areas for fruitful dialogue, in particular the comparison of mindfulness and watchfulness, concentration and

---

28 St Gregory Palamas (1296-1359), *To the most reverend nun Xenia*, 62; *Philokalia* IV 318-319.

29 One celebrated example of such an experience of light is found in the life of the Russian mystic, St Seraphim of Sarov (1759-1833). He ascribes these matters to the grace of the Holy Spirit, as exemplified in the Transfiguration of Christ as recorded in the Gospels, and revealed in a dialogue between Seraphim and his friend Motovilov. See Zander 1975, 90.

the Jesus Prayer, the focus on the breath and on developing loving-kindness, the analysis of mind-states and patterns of thought, and the experience of light and states of meditative absorption. Here, there is at least the beginning of a fruitful conversation.

Bibliography

Alfeyev, Hilarion, 2000. *The Spiritual World of Isaac the Syrian*. Kalamazoo: Cistercian Publications.

Anālayo Bhikkhu, 2003. *Satipaṭṭhāna: The Direct Path to Realization*. London: Windhorse.

Anālayo Bhikkhu, 2015. *Compassion and Emptiness in Early Buddhist Meditation*. London: Windhorse.

von Balthasar, Hans Urs, transl. Brian Daley SJ., 2003. *Cosmic Liturgy: The Universe According to Maximus the Confessor*. San Francisco: Ignatius Press.

Bamberger OSCO, J.E., transl., 1981. *Evagrius Ponticus: The Praktikos & Chapters on Prayer*. Kalamazoo: Cistercian Publications.

Bertram, Jerome, transl., 1999. *John Cassian: The Monastic Institutes*. London: Saint Austin Press.

Bingaman, Brock & Bradley Nassif (eds.), 2012. *The Philokalia: A Classic Text of Orthodox Spirituality*. Oxford: Oxford University Press.

Bodhi, Bhikkhu, transl., 1989. *Discourse on the Fruits of Recluseship: The Samaññaphala Sutta*. Kandy: Buddhist Publication Society.

Bodhi, Bhikkhu, transl., 2000. *The Connected Discourses of the Buddha: A Translation of the Saṃyutta Nikāya*. Boston: Wisdom.

Bodhi, Bhikkhu, transl., 2012. *The Numerical Discourses of the Buddha: A Complete Translation of the Aṅguttara Nikāya*. Boston: Wisdom.

Brasington, Leigh, 2015. *Right Concentration: A Practical Guide to the Jhānas*. Boulder: Shambhala.

Casiday, A.M., 2006. *Evagrius Ponticus.* London: Routledge (The Early Church Fathers).

Chryssavgis, John, 2004. *John Climacus: From the Egyptian Desert to the Sinaite Mountain.* London: Ashgate.

Cook, Christopher C.H., 2011. *The Philokalia and the Inner Life.* London: James Clarke & Co.

Crosby, Kate, 2014. *Theravada Buddhism: Continuity, Diversity and Identity.* London: Wiley Blackwell.

Feldmeier, Peter, 2006. *Christianity Looks East: Comparing the Spiritualities of John of the Cross and Buddhaghosa.* New York: Paulist Press.

Gethin, Rupert, 1998. *The Foundations of Buddhism.* Oxford: Oxford University Press.

Gillett, Lev ('A monk of the Eastern Church'), 1987. *The Jesus Prayer.* New York: St. Vladimir's Seminary Press.

Isaac of Syria, 2011. *Ascetical Homilies of Saint Isaac the Syrian: Translated from the Greek and Syriac by the Holy Transfiguration Monastery*, revised 2nd Edition. Boston: Holy Transfiguration Monastery.

Johnson, Christopher, 2010. *The Globalization of Hesychasm and the Jesus Prayer: Contesting Contemplation.* London: Continuum.

Jones, Cheslyn, Geoffrey Wainwright & Edward Yarnold SJ, eds., 1986. *The Study of Spirituality.* London: SPCK.

Kadloubovsky, E. & E.M. Palmer, eds. and transls., 1966. *The Art of Prayer: an Orthodox anthology, compiled by Igumen Chariton of Valamo.* London: Faber & Faber.

Lefebure, Leo D. & Peter Feldmeier, 2011. *The Path of Wisdom: A Christian Commentary on the Dhammapada.* Leuven: Peeters.

Luibheid, Colm, transl., 1982. *John Climacus: The Ladder of Divine Ascent* (Classics of Western Spirituality). New York: Paulist Press.

Mahasi Sayadaw, 1990. *Satipaṭṭhāna Vipassanā: Insight through Mindfulness.* Kandy: Buddhist Publication Society, Wheel 370/371.

Maloney, George A., transl., 1992. *Pseudo-Macarius: the Fifty Spiritual Homilies & the Great Letter* (Classics of Western Spirituality). New York: Paulist Press.

Middleton, Herman A., 2003. *Precious Vessels of the Holy Spirit: The Lives and Counsels of Contemporary Elders of Greece: Volume 1*. Thessalonica: Protecting Veil Press.

Ñāṇamoli Bhikkhu, transl., 1975. *The Path of Purification (Visuddhimagga)*, by Bhadantacariya Buddhaghosa. Kandy: Buddhist Publication Society.

Ñāṇamoli, Bhikkhu & Bhikkhu Bodhi, transls., 2001 (1995). *The Middle Length Discourses of the Buddha: A Translation of the Majjhima Nikāya*. Boston: Wisdom.

Palmer, G.E.H., Philip Sherrard & Kallistos Ware, eds. and transls. Four volumes: 1983, 1990, 1995, 1998. *The Philokalia: The Complete Text, Compiled by St. Nikodimos of the Holy Mountian and St. Makarios of Corinth.* London: Faber and Faber. (Referenced in the text as '*The Philokalia*' with volume number).

Roebuck, Valerie J., transl., 2010. *The Dhammapada.* London: Penguin.

Salzberg, Sharon, 1997. *Loving-Kindness: The Revolutionary Art of Happiness*. Boulder: Shambhala.

Shaw, Sarah, ed. and trans., 2006. *Buddhist Meditation: An anthology of texts from the Pali canon.* London & New York: Routledge.

Sheldrake, Philip, ed., 2005. *New SCM Dictionary of Christian Spirituality*. London: SCM Press.

Sinkewicz, Robert E., trans., 2003. *Evagrius of Pontus: The Greek Ascetic Corpus.* Oxford: Oxford University Press.

Sophrony, Archimandrite, 1977. *His Life is Mine.* London: Mowbrays.

Tiyavanich, Kamala, 1997. *Forest Recollections: Wandering Monks in Twentieth-Century Thailand.* Honolulu: University of Hawai'i Press.

Walshe, Maurice, transl., 1987. *Thus Have I Heard: The Long Discourses of the Buddha*. Boston: Wisdom.

Ware, Timothy, 1963. *The Orthodox Church.* London: Penguin.

Wijayaratna, Mohan, 1990. *Buddhist Monastic Life: according to the texts of the Theravada tradition,* transls. Claude Grangier and Steven Collins. Cambridge: Cambridge University Press.

Zander, Valentine, 1975. *St. Seraphim of Sarov.* London: SPCK.

HESYCHASM AND TIBETAN BUDDHISM: ANTHROPOLOGICAL PATTERNS AND EXPERIENTIAL PARALLELS

Elizabete Taivāne

Abstract

Although not connected culturally or historically to each other, Hesychasm and the Buddhism of Tibet share several basic features in common. Utilizing the phenomenological method of research, it is possible to identify a correspondence between the anthropological ideas of Hesychasm, the Abhidharma tradition and Tantric Buddhism. On the experiential level, there are clear parallels between the introversive processes taking place in consciousness during Hesychast prayer and Buddhist meditation. They both culminate in a vision of darkness and light. Convergences in the two traditions are interpreted in this chapter as being rooted in common structures of human experience whereas the divergences are explained by the prevalence of gnostic religious instinct in tantric Buddhism and the agapeic one in Hesychasm.

Keywords: Tibetan Buddhism, Hesychasm, Comparative Mysticism, Light, Darkness

'Yes' or 'No' to Cross-Cultural Analysis of Mystical Experience?

This paper concerns the comparative analysis of two completely different and mystically[1] oriented religious traditions, namely Hesychasm and Tibetan Buddhism, which are not linked to each other historically or culturally. It is worth noting that comparative mysticism and mysticism as a whole are controversial fields of exploration today, and there are several reasons for this.[2] Hence, at the beginning, it would be helpful to underscore what the capacities and limitations of comparative mysticism are.

Scholars in the field such as Steven Katz claim that it is not possible to distinguish mystical experience from its interpretation. This means that the former is a derivative of the latter. To put it differently, a mystical experience is always constructed or determined by the context. If not contextually connected, this argument proceeds, two or more experiences cannot be compared (King 2005, 316). Katz's constructivism has attracted a number of critical responses concerning his claim that an un-mediated mystical experience is not possible (King 2005, 317). For instance, to Robert Forman, the essence of mystical experience is the so called

---

1   The adequacy of the term 'mysticism' in the context of non-Christian religions has been discussed by many experts in the field. For instance, Geoffrey Parrinder underscores the correlation between the words 'mysticism', *yoga* and *tawḥīd* (Parrinder 1995 (1976), 15), whereas Ninian Smart asserts that mystical experience and the numinous one are two different experiences (Smart 1999, 167-168). Similarly, Robert A.F. Thurman in his *Essential Tibetan Buddhism* claims that 'Buddha Shakyamuni's enlightenment is not mystical, in the sense of 'contrary to reason'' (Thurman 1995, 11). A profound search for manifold meanings of the term 'mysticism' and their equivalents in Sanskrit is offered by Audrius Beinorius (Beinorius 2005, 221-222).

2   One of the most important problems of mystical experience (and of religious experience as a whole) is its intangibility and, hence, a lack of verification means for its exploration. Besides, according to cognitivists, religious experience is not a phenomenon *per se*, because there does not exist any scientific criteria for distinguishing the religious experience from the non-religious one. The suggestion of Ann Taves is to use the term 'experiences deemed religious' instead of 'religious experience' (Taves 2011, xiii-xiv).

'pure consciousness event', that is an encounter with awareness *per se* or awareness itself, namely, an un-mediated awareness without a particular object. Citing different sacred texts, spiritual teachers and modern seekers, Forman tries to prove the reality of un-mediated experience or a pure consciousness event, contrasting his position with that of Steven Katz (Grabowitz 2014, 14-15).

The Lithuanian expert in the field of indology and philosophy, Audrius Beinorius comes to similar conclusions about the possibility of 'unmediated awareness of reality' (*aparokṣa jnāna*), 'pure consciousness' (*puruṣa*) and 'a state of unconstructed and concentrated awareness' (*nirvikalpa samādhi*), analysing the texts of Hindu and Buddhist scholars (Beinorius 2006, 113-114). With reference to the search for the concept of consciousness as the common denominator of mystical experiences, K.G. Jung and E. Husserl should also be mentioned. The Jungian 'collective unconscious' together with its archetypes, as well as Husserlian intentionality deal with the same notion of consciousness. Nevertheless, these concepts from Jung and Husserl concern the content of consciousness, whereas Robert Forman develops the idea of awareness *per se*. At the same time, they all indicate that there could be some common features, belonging to all human beings, which allow contextually disconnected mystical traditions to be compared.

The total dependence on the context of research in the field of comparative mysticism is contested also by Jonathan R. Herman. He asserts that it is important 'to work within the prevailing... concern for context, but to do so with a renewed methodological self-consciousness and a receptivity to the types of resonances that may indicate connections buried beneath the surface' (Herman 2000, 98). He implicitly recommends a change or a widening of the meaning of the word 'context' (Herman 2000, 97-98).

To summarize, we have three options to explore contextually disconnected mystical traditions. The first one is to emphasize the cultural context and investigate the mystical traditions as isolated and unique entities without an endeavour to compare them. The second option is to compare them utilizing the concept of the awareness *per se* as some sort of common denominator and to ignore the cultural context. The third path is to create a common basis or context for the culturally disconnected traditions, namely, to make use of Herman's suggestion, and to compare the mystical traditions in this new context. To choose the third option, it is important to define this new common context.

The concept of a pure consciousness event seems to be helpful in trying to substantiate the convergences in the culminating stages of culturally disconnected mystical experiences such as the vision of darkness and light. The notion, however, cannot be utilized in comparisons of divergent – culturally and conceptually coloured – experiences, for instance, visions of Christ in Christianity and those of peaceful and wrathful deities in Tibetan Buddhism. Hence, it is necessary to be aware of the different states or levels of consciousness of a mystic during meditation/prayer: those which are and those which are not determined or mediated by cultural, historical and doctrinal context, and to identify a general term for both of them. My suggestion is to make use of the notion of 'universal patterns of human experience' or 'common structures of human experience' in order to include the convergent states of consciousness and the divergent but similarly structured ones. In short, I will use the notion of universal patterns or structures of human experience as the common basis or context for the present cross-cultural comparison.

A Method for Cross-Cultural Analysis of Mystical Experience

The present research is situated in the field of the phenomenology of religion,[3] which charts a middle path between essentialism

3   James V. Spickard in his article on the methodological principles of phenomenology of religion asserts that what is commonly considered phenomenology of religion is not 'phenomenology' in a rigorous sense of the term. Phenomenology can only concern the empirical research of 'subjective experiences of religious subjects' (Spickard 2014, 336). It is necessary to

and constructivism (Allen 2005b, 206). Douglas Allen suggests a method of 'phenomenological induction'. He explains that, according to this method,

> essential structures and meanings are based on, but not found fully in, the empirical historical data. The phenomenologist of religion is engaged in a process of imaginative construction and idealization. By reflecting on particular, contingent, contextualized, religious data, the phenomenologist constructs the ideal religious structure, "the pure case", the exemplary universal meaning. (Allen 2005a, 18)

Allen suggests that 'a structural "web" of religious symbols and their intended meanings' can be identified (Allen 2005a, 18). His 'universal meanings founded on and not fully in the particular data' allow the discovery of some sort of entity of 'pure cases' or ideal structures that are only partially incarnated in the particular context.

The nature or the source of 'pure cases' is not clearly defined by Allen. On the one hand, he asserts that 'pure cases' are constructed by the phenomenologist. On the other hand, he refers to philosophical phenomenology and uses the notion of the 'radical intentionality of human consciousness'. I am not going to restrict myself either to Husserlian intentionality of consciousness or to any other notion and approach suggested by philosophical phenomenology or neo-perennialism. Utilizing Allen's method of phenomenological induction, I will refer to the above-mentioned 'common structures of human experience'. By doing this it is possible to assert that the latter, mediated or unmediated, manifest in various cultural and historical contexts. The common structures are just fiction if not incarnated in the particular data. They derive from the particular data. Therefore, my task is to examine convergent structures of human experience, on the one hand, and, on the

indicate, however, that the phenomenology of religion does not just analyse religious experience, rather it is interested in various observable phenomena such as ritual acts and objects. Besides, as Douglas Allen contends, it is possible to differentiate four groups of scholars who use the term 'phenomenology of religion' in different ways (see more in Allen 2005b, 185).

other, to explain the divergences in experiences determined by the cultural, historical and doctrinal contexts.

To make the method technically clear, it is enough to mention two basic principles of research in the postmodern phenomenology of religion. In order to 'intuit, interpret and describe the phenomenological essence of religious phenomena' (Allen 2005a, 17), the researcher uses the method of *epoché* or the suspension of all personal preconceptions, as well as the principles of empathy and sympathetic understanding. For phenomenologists, the latter means 'to place themselves within the religious "life-world" of others and to grasp the religious meaning of the experienced phenomena' (Allen 2005b, 198). Ninian Smart explained the method of empathy as the 'informed empathy: that is gathering the data and mustering the imagination so that we may know what it is like to be the other' (Smart 1991, 30).

Searching for a Clue to Divergences

In order to explain differences between Hesychast and Buddhist experiences and notions determining the experiences, I will take a lead from Aloysius Pieris, S.J. Trying to classify and characterize Christianity and Buddhism in order to compare them, Pieris contends that the criteria of the classification should not concern the geographical location of religion. The main criterion should concern mystical mood or religious instinct. He posits two: the gnostic and the agapeic. Buddhism represents the gnostic, whereas Christianity represents the agapeic. Pieris writes:

> in the case of religious and spiritual phenomena, 'east' and 'west' should be made to connote, respectively, the *gnostic* and *agapeic* instincts of the human person regardless of his or her geographical provenance...*Gnosis* is salvific knowledge and *agape* is redemptive love...They are two mystical moods that can alternate according to the spiritual fluctuations of individuals, groups, and even of entire cultures...Any valid spirituality, Christian or otherwise, *must* and, as history shows, *does* retain both poles of religious experience. (Pieris 1990, 9-10)

In another place in his book he adds that 'we are actually dealing with the *poles of tension not so much geographical as psychological*' (Pieris 1990, 27). Hence, on the one hand, Pieris tries to escape the geographical context of religion, context in the usual sense of the word. On the other hand, he suggests an original constructivist approach that is oriented psychologically to a larger map than the geographical. Pieris does not ignore the cultural environment that may be subject to spiritual fluctuations. Hence, his approach leaves a free space for the reconstitution of religious experience, as well as for an open-ended interpretation of religious phenomena.

It is significant that the same two mystical moods defined by Pieris are identified by the prominent researcher in the field of Christian mysticism, Evelyn Underhill, as 'the two eternal passions of the self, the desire of love and the desire of knowledge: severally representing the hunger of heart and intellect for ultimate truth' (Underhill 1955, 72). Indeed, there exists some sort of correspondence between the *gnostic/agapeic* classification of religion and the *monistic/theistic* one. The Buddhism of Tibet, to a large extent based upon the ideas of *ālaya vijñāna* ('storehouse' consciousness) and *tathāgatagarbha* (embryonic Buddha/Buddha nature), presupposes the oneness of all things. Humans are Buddha in their innermost being. If so, humans are able to communicate the Ultimate only in the process of introspection, culminating in introversion of consciousness.[4] Such a transformation is fully a result of human effort. Any kind of divine support is completely excluded. This sort of experience is qualified as knowledge because humans acquire some sort of *gnosis* of themselves and reality. Giuseppe Tucci, discussing religious charac-

---

4   I have borrowed the terms of introspection and introversion of consciousness from the work of Russian buddhologist, V.G. Lisenko, devoted to early Buddhist philosophy (В.Г. Лысенко, 1994. Ранняя буддийская философия // В.Г. Лысенко, А.А. Терентьев, В.К. Шохин, Ранняя буддийская философия. Философия джайнизма (Москва: Восточная литература РАН: cc. 186-188). The introversion of consciousness is a going inwards without any effort, a natural state of seeing things as they are.

teristics of Tantrism, whether Hindu or Buddhist, attributes the tantric tradition to the gnostic religious model. This process of transformation, including different rituals which are intended to destroy emotional impulses, is fully a result of human effort. Any kind of divine support is completely excluded in Tantrism (Tucci 1976/1995, 75).

Hesychasm, in its turn, has a theistic world-view, dealing with the Ultimate Other situated beyond the human horizon of being. Theoretically, the Ultimate cannot be experienced in the process of introspection and introversion of consciousness; rather, a supernatural or divine 'intervention' from without is anticipated. At the same time, union with God is not possible without some sort of 'ecstasy', namely, a complete transcending of the human entity. The main agent in the experiencing of God and salvation is divine Grace. The path of Grace, when humanity and God cooperate (Gr. συνεργεία), is based on *agapē*. God loves humanity and initiates the salvific process, through which humanity accepts (or refuses) the divine Grace. The quintessence of this scheme is perfectly expressed in the words of Archimandrite Sophrony Sakharov in his prominent book dedicated to Staretz Silouan (1866-1938):

> Christian life is the cooperation (согласие) of two wills: Divine will and the created human one. God is able to visit man on all his paths, in any moment of time and in any spiritual and physical place, but being beyond any compulsion He never forces His image's freedom, and if a created free will is selfishly turned to itself or claims to be the uncreated divine source, it is closed to the activity of Divine Grace notwithstanding any high levels of contemplation. (Сахаров 1991, 147)

S.S. Horuzhy explains that, according to this paradigm, the nature of Grace excludes any forced attainment of it by humans, whether by capture, conquest, buying, merit or hard work. In order to receive Grace, humans are not required to perform any actions, rather they cultivate a state when their being becomes completely transparent for Grace (Хоружий 1998, 128-131).

My classification is not so strict when incarnated in the living body of religious experience. The lived experience of Hesychasm does not avoid introversion of consciousness and effort on the path to God, whereas the Buddhism of Tibet has accepted the idea of compassionate buddhas and bodhisattvas. The proportions of the agapeic and gnostic elements in the two traditions, however, differ with a predominance of *gnosis* in Tantric Buddhism and *agapē* in Hesychasm.

Concerning the Object of Comparison

The central object of the present comparison is mystical experience. The experiential stratum of religious life and its doctrinal interpretation intensively interpenetrate each other, determine each other, and, hence, cannot be compartmentalized. The Orthodox theologian, V.N. Lossky, in the context of the Orthodox Christian tradition, underscores that an individual experience can never be distinguished from the whole corpus of religious doctrine. The former is an individual manifestation of the common faith; the latter is a common expression of what can be experienced individually (Лосский 1991, 8-11). Hence, research dedicated to comparative mysticism cannot escape the analysis of religious ideas supporting a certain episode or type of mystical experience.

However, it is rather difficult to compare such metaphysical concepts as God the Creator in Christianity and Buddhahood or Buddha nature in Buddhism. The Buddhist and Christian concepts concerning Ultimate Reality have different notional foundations. As is underscored by Agehānanda Bharati, the Graeco-Roman-Judaeo-Christian terminology, which is usually employed by Western scholars in order to interpret notions of Buddhist and Hindu philosophy, is never free from its Aristotelian and Thomistic flavour, and, thus, is not acceptable in Asian studies (Bharati 1976, 42-43).

My suggestion here is to turn attention to anthropological ideas rather than to the metaphysical ones. Although not completely separated from the latter, anthropology (its parallel in Buddhism is psychology)[5] is close to the experiential stratum of religion, which is able to propose practical rather than abstract explanations of experience. The anthropological/psychological ideas in Christianity and Buddhism are easily comparable and helpful in an endeavour to analyse Christian and Buddhist experiences systematically.

The second object, linked to the theme of experience, is the means of its attainment. I will start with consideration of Christopher Emory-Moore's assertion that 'the clearest parallel between the two methodologies of inner light accomplishment [in Hesychasm and Gelug-pa Buddhism] is the shared practice of linking mantra recitation to the breath in order to draw consciousness into the heart' (Emory-Moore 2016, 126). He adds that the Jesus prayer is analogous to mantra for it embodies 'the essential qualities of the Christian deity...in the words: 'Lord Jesus Christ, Son of God''' (Emory-Moore 2016, 126).

My first critical note concerns the understanding of what the Jesus prayer is. It is sufficient to note that there is a great difference between the idea of mantra and the Jesus prayer. Mantra's central function - to incarnate a deity in the subtlest vibrations,

---

5   The notion of *anthropology*, namely teaching about the human situation, is normative for Christian theology, the European mentality on the whole being a derivative of Western *anthropocentrism* and this is the sense in which I am using the term 'anthropology'. Hesychasm has developed the idea of humanity's exalted status among other creatures. Gregory Palamas proposed a long list of arguments in favour of anthropocentrism (see Керн 1996, 361-364). Humanity's exalted status as permanent being is linked to the idea of the only and unique body. For these reasons there exists anthropology, i.e. a discipline dedicated to the exploration of humanity.
The position of humanity in Buddhism differs due to the absence of anthropocentrism. Human beings represent one of six ontologically equal categories of living beings. The absence of the once given unique human body in Buddhism co-operates with the basic ideas of impermanence and reincarnation. The equal ontological status of all sentient beings means the paramount role of the consciousness principle in the discourse and the inferior role of the forms of its rebirth. Not man but the consciousness principle is central. The discipline exploring it can be denoted as 'psychology' and not as 'anthropology' (Розенберг 1991, 106-108).

having semantic roots in the Hindu idea of Śabda-brahman – is completely different from the Christian understanding of prayer as invocation. The Jesus prayer is a meaningful text 'sum[ming] up in the brevity of its words the plenitude and depth of all Ortho-dox prayers' (Corneanu 1995, 16) and, therefore, has nothing in common with the idea of phonic evolution.[6]

My second critical note concerns the divergence between the common principles of Hesychast and Tantric psycho-techniques. It would be difficult to ignore that such tantric means of libera-tion as visualization and sexual practices are completely absent in Hesychasm. Any endeavour to use imagination during prayer is considered an erroneous path in the Eastern Christian tradition. In addition, the principles of Orthodox asceticism are incompat-ible with the tantric method of transforming the passions. The divergences are rooted in two different paradigms of the salvific body. Tibetan Buddhism accepts the tantric doctrine of the dia-mond body (*vajra śarīra*) that allegedly is 'the medium in and through which truth can be realised…it is the epitome of the uni-verse or, in other words, it is the microcosm, and as such embod-ies the truth of the whole universe' (Dasgupta 1974, 146). The diamond body is a perfect means of liberation. Representing the gnostic religious model, Buddhism in general is not familiar with any kind of agnosticism concerning the samsaric horizon of be-ing as a whole (Рудой, Островская 2000, 56) and the reality of *vajra śarīra* in particular. Tantric Buddhism elaborates a sophisti-cated theory of the diamond body as well as a complex of psycho-techniques (including visualizations, recitation of mantra, sexual

---

6 Phonic evolution is the process of emanation in the form of sound. Accord-ing to postulations of tantric Hinduism, the world evolves from Brahman in the form of sound (Śabda-brahman). Mantra's effect is opposite: it initiates the process of involution, i.e. of returning to Brahman using the path of the same sound. During the evolution, the subtle creative sound becomes grosser and grosser constituting psychic and physical phenomena. During the recitation of mantra, the gross reality in the form of sound grows subtler and subtler taking the meditator back to Brahman that is the source of being. The idea of phonic evolution and mantra as a means of the returning to the source is quite similar in tantric Buddhism.

practices). Therefore, the paradigm of the salvific body in Tibetan Buddhism is represented by *vajra śarīra*.[7]

It would be difficult to underestimate the role of psycho-techniques in Hesychasm. They are termed by Orthodox theologian, John Meyendorff, as 'psycho-physical methods of prayer' (Мейендорф 1997, 204) and include asceticism, breath control and typical postures that help to collect all the limbs around the heart (a contemplator is kneeling; his head is bent forward and his attention is directed to his chest). The mentioned methods are combined with the recitation of the Jesus prayer which, joining breath and mind, is supposed to leave the brain and reach the heart.

Although there are some important similarities between tantric and hesychast practices, the psycho-physical techniques in Hesychasm are supposed to be a practical means for beginners, tending to calm and gather the wandering mind; these methods are helpful, but are not compulsory. This was also stressed by Emory-Moore. He underscores that 'for Palamas the Hesychast's method of the Jesus prayer is neither contract nor cause. It is a mere preparative condition for the divine encounter' (Emory-Moore 2016, 127).

John Meyendorff, analysing the legacy of Gregory Palamas, underscores that the task of all the practices is the introversion of mind, namely a deepening into the depth of consciousness, by the means of attention (προσοχή), whereas the next step – the vision of God – cannot be achieved mechanically (Мейендорф 1997, 204-205). According to Palamas, 'the body which is united to us has been attached to us as a fellow-worker' (Palamas 1983, *The Triads* (2,2,5), 48). Meyendorff notes that Palamas never tried to transform any physiological problem into a dogma. Revelation deals with eternal matters and not too much with physiology. The Spirit has not revealed the questions of physiology clearly, thus, each of us is authorized to explain the topic as he desires (Мейендорф 1997, 208). Hence, what is quite natural and acces-

---

7   A profound analysis of anatomy and physiology of the diamond body is present in Namkhai Norbu, 2000, 121-125; Hopkins 1979, 13-20; Kelsang Gyatso 1982, 17-32; Powers 2007, 336-339.

sible for human cognition in Buddhism, lies within the mysterious sphere of Grace in Christianity.

Because of the paramount meaning attributed to divine intervention, the salvific body in Hesychasm is the body of Christ. Citing the *Triads* of Palamas (I,3,38), Meyendorff turns our attention to the notion of incarnation that is a central point within Orthodox Christology. Christ has accepted the human hypostasis and gives himself to his devotees through the communion of his holy body; he becomes co-corporeal to Christians (σύσσωμος ἡμῖν γίνεται). Meyendorff comments that the notion of σύσσωμος (co-corporeal) originated in Ephesians 3:6 and has always been interpreted by the Fathers as union with Christ in the Eucharist. The christocentric and sacramental mysticism of Palamas is the main justification of hesychast asceticism (Мейендорф 1997, 211). The differences concerning the idea of the salvific body are the source of the divergences in practice. Being rather complicated and sophisticated, Tantric psycho-techniques are unique and do not have parallels in hesychast practice. For this reason practice in its comparative mode is not discussed here.

About the Sources

To analyse hesychast experience, I have chosen the texts listed by S. Horuzhy (Хоружий 1998, 160). As Horuzhy stresses, sources discussing contemplative methodology are innumerable, whereas those that focus on the experiential are few, namely the works compiled by Macarius the Egyptian, Symeon the New Theologian, Gregory Palamas and Archimnadrite Sophrony. The latter represents Russian Hesychasm in the second part of the twentieth century and is attributed to the Athonian period. I will not analyse the mentioned texts *per se*, but mainly deal with the interpretation of Orthodox scholars of the twentieth century, including those by V. Lossky, S. Horuzhy, John Meyendorff, S.M. Zarin, P. Minin and V. Korzhevsky.

My criterion in the selection of Buddhist sources is rather similar. The primary sources chosen for the comparison are mainly

322   *Elizabete Taivāne*

Tibetan texts concerning death and liberation through death. The reason for this is that all Tibetan *yoga*s are based on simulating death. The imitation of death during meditation is termed by Jung Young Lee as *thanatomimesis* (Jung Young Lee 1974, 56). I have selected texts from various traditions of Tibet, among them *Bar do thos grol* (Thurman 1994), tantras on death and liberation representing the *rDzogs chen* tradition (Orofino 1990) and the texts of a later period (the eighteenth century) by *dbYangs can dga'ba'i blo gros* on death, the intermediate state and rebirth, belonging to the *dGe lugs pa* tradition (Lati Rinbochay 1979).

Important *rDzogs chen* texts discussing lumenophany are translated and annotated by John Myrdhin Reynolds, Samten Gyaltsen Karmay and others. I also engage with the reflection of tantric teachers such as Namkhai Norbu Rinpoche and Lama Lodo, no less than Western scholars such as Giuseppe Tucci, Agehānanda Bharati, Jung Young Lee and Jeffrey Hopkins.

Comparative Analysis of Hesychast and Abhidharmic Anthropological Ideas

Tibetan Buddhism, when discussing the stages of introversion of consciousness during meditation/death, refers not only to the concepts of tantric anatomy but also to the Abhidharmic concept of the human. For this reason it is helpful to compare the hesychast constitution of the human with that of Abhidharmic tradition.

In Hesychasm, humans are soteriologically oriented as integral psycho-physical organisms. There is no space for a dualism wherein only the spiritual constituent of the human is saved and the body is annihilated. How the body collaborates with the soul in repentance and divine glory is discussed by Gregory Palamas in his *Triads* I, 3, 31-33.[8] The anthropological model suggested by Palamas is in conflict with the dualistic approach of Barlaam

---

8   Св. Григорий Палама, 1995, Триады в защиту священно-безмолвствую-щих (I, 3, 31-33), пер. В. Вениаминов, 93-96. *The Triads* are translated into Russian from two editions, which are almost identical: J. Meyendorff, ed. *Défense des Saints Hésychastes*. Louvain, 1973; Γρηγορίου τοῦ

(Хоружий 1991, 22-23). A similar holism within the human being is present in abhidharmic Buddhism, where all *saṃskṛita*
*dharma*s (conditioned elements) constituting both the spiritual
and sensual parts of the sentient being, including those of *rūpa*
(the physical part of the human) are supposed to attain tranquillity, namely *nirvāṇa* (О.О. Розенберг 1991, 134, 225).

Due to the idea of *anātman* (non-self) in Buddhism, personality is postulated to be deprived of any substantial or unchanging
core, consisting of a huge number of *dharma*s. There are various
ways to group them. According to the most popular classification,
humans consist of five aggregates called *skandha*s.[9]

According to Orthodox anthropology, there are the two-fold,
the three-fold and the four-fold classifications of the constituents of
the human. The latter is rooted in the Aristotelian anthropological
model and is employed, for instance, by Macarius the Egyptian. It
can be compared with the five *skandha*s within Buddhism.[10] According to the fourfold classification in Christianity, a human consists of two major parts, the body and the soul. The body is represented by the five senses and is a parallel to the *rūpa-skandha*
of Buddhist doctrine. The soul, in its turn, consists of three parts
or 'activities'. The first one is the 'sensual'. It is responsible for
pleasant, un-pleasant and neutral feelings in the same way as the
vedanā skandha in Buddhism. The 'cognitive' activity of the soul
deals with intellectual processes bearing resemblance to *saṃjñā*
skandha. Finally, the 'passionate' activity of the soul, called 'will'
in Christianity, is a source of desire and certain deeds. This last
constituent is an equivalent of *saṃskāra skandha* in Buddhism.
The only *skandha* which does not have its equivalent in Christian
classification is *vijñāna skandha*. This aggregate is interpreted as
the awareness of psychic processes or consciousness. According

---

Παλαμᾶ Συγγράμματα. Ἐκδίδονται ἐπιμελείᾳ παναγιώτου Κ. Χρήστου. Τ.
Ά. Θεσσαλονίκη 1962, σελ. 367 sq.

9   For a detailed analysis of Abhidharmic classifications of *dharma*s see: О.О.
    Розенберг 1991, 121-135.

10 For a detailed analysis of the fourfold anthropology in Orthodox tradition,
    see Коржевский 2004, 43-226.

to the Christian scheme, the same awareness (together with the self-awareness) is not mentioned among the constituents of the soul, but rather among the 'features' of the soul.

Finally, there is another expanded hesychast anthropological model skilfully analysed by S.S. Horuzhy. The human consists of a huge number of energies[11] which, in their turn, can be arranged into three configurations. The notion of energies and their configurations resembles the abhidharmic idea of *dharma*s and their various compositions. But, unlike Buddhists, Hesychasts were not too interested in compiling lists of energies; the only energies, systematized by ascetics, were passions. The three compositions of energies mentioned by Horuzhy are the *supernatural* (all energies in the human are subordinate to the divine Grace), the *natural* (a chaotic passionate configuration) and the *unnatural* (a passionate configuration wherein a certain passion subjects the other passionate energies and organizes them around itself) (Хоружий 1991, 76).

It is discernible that the notion of 'supernatural' is extraneous for Buddhism. The term is a derivative of the *agapeic* and *theistic* religious model, which insists upon the existence of two different natures: the super-nature of God and the created nature of man. In Buddhism there is no place for any 'nature' beside the 'dependent origination of things'.

The transition from one configuration of energies to another is performed in Christianity by 'synergy' (συνέργεια). S. Horuzhy defines synergy as one of the energies possessed by humans, namely, the energy of the fundamental aspiration. Synergy is indestructible; it is given to humans initially and can never be destroyed completely. Even when the energies of humans are unnaturally organized, the seeds or sparks of synergy are present in humans. They ensure the possibility for humans to escape from the passionate order of existence (Хоружий 1991, 78).

---

11 Orthodox theology accepts the Aristotelian interpretation of the term *energy* (ἐνεργεια) as the actualization of potencies. To be precise, energy is the process of actualization or motion.

To anticipate the comparative analysis of Tantric and Hesychast anthropological ideas, the indestructible seeds of synergy
bear resemblance to the indestructible drop of tantric physiology. Affinities of this kind allow me to draw a conclusion that
in Hesychasm and in Tantric Buddhism the human is potentially
saved/liberated. The mentioned structure can be called the 'gene
of spiritual growth'.

Constitution of the Human in Tantric Buddhism and Hesychasm

Tantrism elaborates the concept of the diamond body (*rdo rje'i
lus* (/ *sku*) in order to create the base for *sādhana* or religious
practice. According to Chögyal Namkhai Norbu, the main components of the diamond body are winds (*rlung, prāna*), channels
(*rtsa, nāḍī*) and drops (*thig le, bindu*) (Namkhai Norbu 2000, 121-
122). The winds are united inseparably with the correspondent
levels of consciousness (*sems*) called 'consciousnesses'. As John
Powers contends, 'in tantric physiology, consciousnesses are said
to travel throughout the body "mounted" on the winds, which
serve as their support. Consciousnesses cannot function without
the support of the winds, but the winds lack direction without
consciousnesses' (Powers 2007, 284).

'The basic idea of Tantrism is that both the mind and the body
are different forms or modes of manifestation of one and the same
Reality' (Pandit 1991, 170). All the winds and drops have their
starting point in the heart channel wheel; they are supposed to
return to the heart during death and meditation. *Rlung* is endowed
with the gross, subtle and very subtle level. The gross level is
represented by the five root winds (*rtsa ba'i rlung lnga*) serving as the support for particular elements (*'byung ba*). The most
important root wind is the life-bearing wind situated in the heart.
The branch winds take their origin from it. They each flow to a
particular sense organ. The life-bearing wind has three levels: a
gross (*rlung rags pa*), subtle and very subtle. The subtle level
manifests only during death, meditation and the dreaming state.
The subtle level of the wind (*phra ba'i rlung*) is of three types: the

wind mounted by the mind of white appearance (*snang ba dkar lam pa'i sems*); the wind mounted by the mind of red increase (*mched pa dmar lam pa'i sems*); the wind mounted by the mind of black near-attainment (*nyer thob nag lam pa'i sems*). The very subtle wind (*shin tu phra pa'i rlung*) and the very subtle mind or consciousness (*shin tu phra pa'i sems*), mounted on the life-bearing wind, are indestructible and travel from life to life.

So the human can be imagined as a *yantra* or a *mandala* with its principal centre and periphery. Similarly, in Hesychasm any mental or spiritual energy originating in the heart, fulfils its aspiration completely only when it returns to the heart. For both traditions the heart is the *axis mundi*. In Tantric Buddhism, the diamond body is the epitome of the universe with the heart as its centre. In Hesychasm, the heart is considered to be the *axis* piercing through and keeping together both the spiritual and the bodily life of humans (Юркевич 1990, 73).

Insisting upon the idea of the heart as the unique and all-embracing basis, P.D. Yurkevich assumes that the heart can never be treated as mere 'flesh', rather it is 'becoming flesh' (or 'embodiment') (Юркевич 1990, 73). It is typical for Orthodox authors to link the theme of the heart to the concept of Incarnation. This takes us back to the question of the salvific body in Christianity. Christ the incarnated gives salvation to humans united with him in the depth of his being, namely, in the heart.

The heart is the focus of the indestructible union of the soul and the body (Голынский-Михайловский 2000, 176). Being an embodiment or a point of encounter between the Divine reality and the created one, the heart is termed the field where the salvation of the cosmos takes place. Staretz Silouan underscores this cosmic meaning of the heart: 'When unceasing prayer becomes established in the depths of the heart all the world is transformed into a temple of God' (Sophrony 2001, 75).

In Tantric Buddhism as well as in Hesychasm, the heart is the place where the individual mode of being is destroyed. Evelyn Underhill writes that the heart is the entity 'seeking to transcend the limitations of the individual standpoint and to surrender itself to ultimate Reality' (Underhill 1955, 71-72). In Tantric Buddhism, the heart is a seat of non-individualistic, very subtle consciousness. The destruction of the individual has been called by Jung Young Lee 'regression' that is the opposite of 'individuation' (or 'embodiment') (Lee 1974, 49).

Divergences in the understanding of the heart reality in the two traditions are as follows. Hesychasm formulates the heart reality in an abstract and emotional manner, whereas Tantrism prefers the exact and even dry physiological interpretation. The crux of the matter lies in the fact that, in Hesychasm, the term 'heart' has two meanings: (1) the heart as a metaphysical unit, and (2) the heart as a concrete place or abode of this metaphysical unit. Tantrism, in its turn, accepts the latter meaning of the heart, but ignores the former one. Although the idea of metaphysical reality embodied in the heart is perfectly elaborated in tantric Buddhism, this very reality is almost never termed as the 'heart'.[12] Tantrism distinguishes (1) the heart of the subtle body as the abode or reservoir of the metaphysical reality (Wangyal 2000, 158), and (2) the metaphysical reality as such, called 'mind'. In Hesychasm these two entities are often fused under the concept of 'heart' as is noticed by S.M. Zarin (Зарин 1996, 375). The dispassionate character of the heart in Tantrism differs from the Hesychast idea of the heart as a source of love and any other emotion. Obviously, this divergence is a derivative of gnostic and agapeic types of religiosity.

The Hesychast parallel of the Tantric very subtle mind (*shin tu phra pa'i sems*), in its turn, is the mind (νοῦς) called also spirit (πνεῦμα). Mind is the highest faculty of the soul in Orthodoxy; as the active core of the soul it is inclined to the Absolute (Коржевский 2004, 45) and constitutes personality.[13] The mind is

---

12 Exceptions, however, are present in the Tantric literature. For instance, Francesca Fremantle calls the indestructible *bindu* the 'awakened heart-mind', underscoring the metaphysical meaning of the term 'heart' in a way similar to the Hesychast traditional manner. Here the awakened consciousness (or awareness) is identified with the heart (Fremantle 2001, 193).

13 'Personality' is an Orthodox term designating a deified man deprived of any individual tendencies (Хоружий 1991, 15-17).

able to manifest only after 'the cessation of all intellectual activity' (Palamas, *The Triads* (I, III, 17), 35). During contemplation 'the mind becomes supercelestial, [...], and contemplates supernatural and ineffable visions, being filled with all the immaterial knowledge of a higher light' (Palamas, *The Triads* (I, III, 50), 33). Hence the glorified mind is an obvious equivalent of the very subtle mind (manifesting as the Clear Light of bliss) in Tantrism. According to Palamas the mind, purified of any psychic activity and contemplating God, is situated in the heart[14] in the same way as the very subtle mind manifests as Light in the heart in Tantrism.

Like tantric practitioners, Hesychasts have noticed the 'scattered' nature of an ordinary human mind. Gregory Palamas taught that 'nothing in the world is in fact more difficult to contemplate and more mobile and shifting than the mind' (Palamas, *The Triads* (I, II, 7), 45). This can be compared with *The Tibetan Book of the Dead*'s discussion of the extremely mobile character of the mind in the between: 'Driven by the swift wind of evolution, your mind is helpless and unstable, riding the horse of breath like a feather blown on the wind, spinning and fluttering' (Thurman 1994, 84).

Although irrelevant in Hesychasm, the idea of *rlung* is represented in *The Triads* by implication. Palamas mentions the essence of the mind (which can be compared with the Tibetan *sems*) and its energy (the equivalent of *rlung*): 'The essence of the *mind* is one thing, its energy another' (Palamas, *The Triads*, (I, II, 5), 44). He discusses the idea of Dionysius about the straight and circular movements of the mind (Palamas, *The Triads*, (I, II, 5), 44). The straight movement is an ordinary cognitive possibility directed to external objects. This kind of mind activity can be compared with the tantric idea of the circulation of consciousnesses and correspondent winds in the body. Dionysius's circular movement of the mind, then, is similar to the Tantric idea of consciousnesses and their winds moving to the heart by the force of meditation.

---

14 Св. Григорий Палама, Триады в защиту священнобезмолвствующих (I, 3, 41), 104.

Introversion (In-Going) of Consciousness in Tibetan Buddhism and Hesychasm

The core of the mystical experience in Hesychasm as well as of Tantric Buddhism is the salvific/liberative vision of light. In order to achieve this state, some sort of in-going or introversion of consciousness has to take place. According to Tantrism, the winds of an ordinary person flow through most of the channels excluding the central one. By the force of meditation, the winds together with their consciousnesses can be gathered and dissolved in the heart channel wheel of the central channel (Kelsang Gyatso 1982, 24). Tantric Buddhism has elaborated a sophisticated and exact scheme of the subsequent dissolution of winds and their consciousnesses. The main basic stages are the destruction of (1) the gross winds and consciousnesses; (2) the subtle ones.

Hence, the process starts with the entering and dissolution of gross winds in the heart channel-wheel. Here the four basic (or root) winds (*rtsa ba'i rlung lnga*) are implied, namely, the earth element wind, the water element wind, the fire element wind and the wind element wind. The aggregates are not forgotten in the tantric scheme of dissolution of the winds. It includes the *skandhas*, as well as the *indriyas* and *viṣayas* of the Abhidharmic tradition. Each mentioned wind is related to one of *skandhas*, to one or two *indriyas* or sense faculties and to one or two *viṣayas* or objects perceived by the sense faculties.[15] The only *skandha* which remains after the four winds are dissolved is the *vijñāna-skandha* or the aggregate of consciousness. It has gross and subtle levels. The last gross mind associated with *vijñāna-skandha* to dissolve is that of the eighty indicative conceptions. The abolition of the eighty conceptions is the fifth cycle of dissolution (Kelsang Gyatso 1982, 81-82).

The Hesychast introversion of the mind is defined as a turning-about in consciousness or the turning of consciousness 'from without to within' (отвне внутрь) (Хоружий 1998, 107). The process, when the scattered mind is unified and taken to its centre, is desig-

---

15 The process of dissolution is described in detail by Kelsang Gyatso 1982, 68-90 and Hopkins 1979, 15-18.

nated as 'taking the mind down to the heart' (κατάβασις τοῦ νοός εἰς καρδίαν) (Хоружий 1998, 105). Hesychasm and the Orthodox tradition as a whole has not elaborated any conventional scheme of pacification of bodily and psychic activities. Such schemes are rarely present in the works of Orthodox masters of contemplation. Usually the defined stages of introversion of consciousness are just two or three and, hence, cannot be exhaustive.[16] There are also chaotic and fragmentary mentions of pacification of the body, thoughts and passions in other treatises of Hesychasts. However, it is possible to notice one common feature of the descriptions: the pacification starts with the grossest sensual activities and ends with the subtlest ones, as is also the case in Tantric dissolution. The same stages are summed up by P. Minin as (1) the release of the spirit from its attachment to matter and from matter as such; and (2) liberation from the empirically rational content of consciousness (П. Минин 1991, 358). The subversion of the senses can be compared to the first four cycles of the Tantric dissolution, namely, to that of gross consciousnesses together with their winds, senses and sensuous objects. Pacification of the discursive mind and abolition of conceptions, produced by the mind, has much in common with the fifth cycle of the Tantric dissolution, the destruction of eighty conceptions.

Although Hesychasts have not elaborated on the scheme for the pacification of psychic activities, they have a clear scheme connected with the development of passions. Its parallel in Buddhism is the scheme of the development of karma (represented I would argue by the Buddhist concept of the *skandha*s). Besides, the latter scheme coincides with the sequence of the dissolution of gross winds during Tantric meditation. It means that if we find correspondence between the Christian scheme of the development of passions and that of the development of karma in Buddhism and that of Tantric dissolution of winds, then utilizing the principle of analogy, it will be possible to make a conjecture that

---

16 See, for example, Gregory of Nyssa, *The Life of Moses* (156-159) or *The Mystical Theology* (1, 3) by Pseudo-Dionysius.

the sequence of pacification of psychic activities in Christianity is identical with the mentioned three schemes.

The process of the development of karma has been described by Lama Anagarika Govinda as follows. Impressions from the outer world are transmitted through sense organs (*rūpa skandha*) to the emotional (*vedanā skandha*) and intellectual (*saṃjñā skandha*) cognition. The reactions produced become an object for volitions and intentions (*saṃskāra skandha*). It is only the latter which become effective as deed (karma) and which produce the visible and tangible fruit or effect (*vipāka*) (Govinda 1975, 68-69).

According to Gregory Palamas, the starting point of cognition and the development of the passions is the material world, perceived by senses. The perception is accompanied by pleasure or pain. Pleasure usually yields attachment at the level of thoughts (Palamas, *The Triads* (II, II, 9), 50-51). The scheme suggested by Palamas is rather similar to that described by Anagarika Govinda.

The equivalents in Hesychasm of *saṃjñā* and *saṃskāra skandha* are 'thoughts' and 'passions'. There are two types of thoughts: cognitive or non-passionate thoughts and the passionate or sinful ones. The cognitive thoughts (literally, non-passionate thoughts, ἀπαθεστερος λογισμος, бесстрастный помысел) and images (the link between the sensual experience and thoughts) are the equivalent of *saṃjñā skandha*. The cognitive thoughts are the source of the passionate ones (διαλογισμός, помысел). The latter, in turn, are the source of the passions (Зарин 1996, 428-434). Strictly speaking, the passionate or sinful thoughts are situated at the border of *saṃjñā* and *saṃskāra skandha*, whereas the equivalent of passions is *saṃskāra skandha*. To be precise, the last stage of the development of the passions is the act of will accepting the passionate thought and, consequently, giving birth to passion. Passion (πάθος) is defined by S.M. Zarin as the decease of will (Зарин 1996, 236-240). Symeon the New Theologian wrote, 'Consider, brother, that what is called perfect retirement from the world is the complete mortification of self-will' (Symeon the New Theologian 1980, 126). The designation 'demons' or 'spirits of the certain sins' is the equivalent of the passions and is

conventional among Eastern ascetics (Керн 1996, c. 408). Therefore, *saṃskāra skandha* defined as volitions and intentions can be
easily compared with Christian passions.

It is interesting that Hesychasts designate the state of sacred
silence or inner peace after the thoughts are abolished as ἡσυχια,
which conveys tranquillity, peace and silence. Horuzhy underscores that this state beyond words differs from the state beyond
passions; ἡσυχια is not yet ἀπαθεια. Passions are not yet mortified
and are able to attack the ascetic again (Хоружий 1998, 92).

To resume, the process of the development of the passions in
Christianity coincides with that of the originating of karma and
that of the dissolution of winds in Buddhism. The principle of
analogy allows us to make a conjecture that if there exist parallels
between the Buddhist scheme of the dissolution of the winds and
that of the development of karma, the process of the pacification
of natural capacities during prayer and that of the development
of the passions in Hesychasm may also be identical. If so it is
possible to restore the Hesychast sequence of the pacification of
the natural abilities of the human that looks as follows: in the
beginning senses are pacified; after that sensual emotions, images
and cognitive thoughts, passionate thoughts and finely passions
become inactive. The restored scheme, however, does not pretend
to be absolutely correct. More important for me was to find Christian equivalents for the Buddhist gross phenomena subject to dissolution and to show that, independently of cultural environment,
Buddhists and Christians deal with the same psychic phenomena
during the introversion of consciousness.

Entering Mysterious Darkness

According to the foundations of Tantric physiology, human consciousness may be compared to a luminous core covered by the
layers of different psychic activities. When the layers represented
by gross consciousnesses and winds dissolve, those presented by
subtle consciousnesses and winds arise. The first subtle consciousness to manifest is the 'mind of white appearance' (*snang ba dkar*

lam pa'i sems). When it arises, the meditator perceives the vision of whiteness. The subtle level of consciousness is represented by two drops (*bindu, thig le*). This means that the manifestation of the mind of white appearance is none other than the releasing of the white drop obtained from the father and its descent from the upper *cakra* to that of the heart (Kelsang Gyatso 1982, 72, 85-86). When the subtle wind mounted by the mind of white appearance dissolves, the mind of red increase arises. The sign is the vision of an empty sky pervaded by sunlight. The red drop that is obtained from the mother and is situated in the navel channel-wheel ascends to the heart channel wheel (Kelsang Gyatso 1982, 72-73, 86). The mentioned signs of the dissolution of the winds, the vision of whiteness and that of an empty sky pervaded by sunlight are not mentioned in the treatises of Hesychasts. The white and red drops meet in the heart and envelop the very subtle mind and its wind (the same indestructible drop) like a box. It is experienced as a vision of thick darkness (Kelsang Gyatso 1982, 86). The process is known as the manifestation of the mind of 'black near-attainment' or 'the great-empty'. The vision of darkness transforms into the state of 'swoon' or near-unconsciousness.[17] The 'near-attainment' means the condition near the clear light.[18]

According to the foundations of Orthodox theology, the notion of darkness has several meanings. As V. Lossky admits, it can be interpreted in the ethical sense of the word (σκότος τὸ ἐξώτερον). Darkness as γνόφος means the incomprehensibility of God in the context of apophatic theology (Лосский 2000 (b), 68-69). The third meaning of darkness is the experience of total pacification of psychic activities during prayer. This Hesychast parallel of Buddhist darkness is designated by Staretz Silouan as the 'darkness of divestiture' (тьма совлечения), namely the state

---

17 Yang-jen-ga-way-lo-dro, Lamp Thoroughly Illuminating the Presentation of the Three Basic Bodies – Death, Intermediate State and Rebirth. In Lati Rinbochay & Hopkins 1979, 43-44.

18 Yang-jen-ga-way-lo-dro, Lamp Thoroughly Illuminating the Presentation of the Three Basic Bodies – Death, Intermediate State and Rebirth. In Lati Rinbochay & Hopkins 1979, 44.

when 'the ascetic strips himself of all presentment and imaginings, all intellectual concepts, arresting mind and imagination and withdrawing himself from thought of this world'. Like Tibetan masters of meditation, Staretz Silouan taught that darkness lay on the bournes of uncreated light (Sophrony 2001, 111).

Archimandrite Sophrony discovers a link between the experience of the darkness of divestiture and the heart. In the heart, darkness and light are experienced. When the mind enters the heart, it simultaneously destroys any image and notion, and the entrances of the heart close. Thereby the human experiences a darkness that is a precondition of meeting with God (Сахаров 1991, 128). The heart of Sophrony can be compared to the above mentioned Tibetan image of the closed box (Kelsang Gyatso 1982, 86). It has also something in common with the 'castle' of Dharmakaya mentioned by Tenzin Wangyal. Referring to *Zhang Zhung Nyan Gyud*, Wangyal admits that 'in the heart there is pure emptiness, which is the Dharmakaya; this generates light which is the Sambhogakaya' (Wangyal 2000, 158).

The state of darkness is mentioned also by St. Symeon the New Theologian. Quoting from Psalm 18:11, 'He made darkness his covering' (ἔθετο καὶ γὰρ ἀποκρυβὴν τὸ σκότος), Symeon underscores that God, being the only light, has covered His luminosity by darkness.[19] Discussing the condition of the contemplating mind, Symeon describes the experience of darkness and light together: during prayer the mind becomes motionless 'being covered completely by the Divine darkness (γνόφου) and light'.[20] That γνόφος is used instead of σκότος means that we are dealing with a sophisticated transition from the darkness of divestiture to the experience of Divine darkness. Commenting on the passage, Archbishop Basil

---

19 Συμεων ο Νεος Θεολογος, Υμνοι (ΚΑ=21) // Φιλοκαλια των Νηπτικων και Ασκητικων 19 Ε: Συμεων ο Νεος Θεολογος, Υμνοι (Α-ΚΖ), ἐπόπτης ἐκδόσεως Παναγιωτης Κ. Χρηστου, ἐπιμελητὴς ἐκδόσεως Ελευθεπιος Γ. Μερετακης, μεταφραση ἀπὸ τὸν Ιγνατιο Σακαλη, Θεσσαλονικη: Το Βυζαντιον; Γρηγοριος ο Παλαμας, 1990, σ. 282.

20 *Cap.* (=*Chapitres Theologiques, gnostiques et pratiques*) (2), 17-18, ed. Darrouzes, *Sources Chretiennes* 51, 1957. (Cited by Кривошеин 1996, 249.)

Krivoshein assumes that St. Symeon meant an ecstatic psychic state accompanied by an almost unconscious state (Кривошеин 1996, 249). It is not easy to find descriptions of this state in the treatises of Hesychasts. Therefore, the interpretation of Krivoshein is a helpful link to this Tantric state, transforming gradually into light vision.

Experience of Light in Hesychasm and Tibetan Buddhism

The culmination of the introversion in both traditions is the apparition of light. It is called the 'uncreated light' in Hesychasm and the 'clear light of bliss' in Tibetan Buddhism. According to the Tibetan doctrine of the human, the clear light, embodied in the indestructible very subtle mind and its wind, is innate to the human from the beginning.[21] The experience of clear light is denoted also as 'all empty because it is empty of all gross and subtle winds' (Kelsang Gyatso 1982, 75).

The description of the disclosed very subtle mind as being 'naked' is usual for Tibetan sources. For instance, in *Bar do thos grol*, it is called the 'immaculate naked awareness' (Thurman 1994, 122); in the *rDzogs chen* text called *sGron ma drug gi gdams pa* (Doctrine of the Six Lights) 'one sees the state of pure Awareness in its complete nakedness' (Orofino 1990, 72). The term 'naked awareness' (*rig pa rjen pa*) is usual for the participants of rDzogs chen (Garab Dorje 1996, 98).

In Buddhism the light arises from within whereas in Hesychasm it is 'implanted' (the term of Winkler 1986, 23), received or kindled by God. Gregory Palamas underscores that light illumines (Palamas, *The Triads* (I, III, 18), 62). According to Symeon the New Theologian, light comes from above (ἄνωθεν), namely, it descends from Heaven into the heart of Symeon (ἐξ οὐρανῶν μέχρις ἐμῆς καρδίας).[22]

---

21 Yang-jen-ga-way-lo-dro, 'Lamp Thoroughly Illuminating the Presentation of the Three Basic Bodies – Death, Intermediate State and Rebirth.. In Lati Rinbochay & Hopkins 1979, 45.

22 Συμεων ο Νεος Θεολογος, Υμνοι (ΚΕ=25) // Φιλοκαλια των Νηπτικων και Ασκητικων 19 Ε: Συμεων ο Νεος Θεολογος, Υμνοι (Α-ΚΖ), σ. 372.

One of the most popular images of the mind in Tibetan Buddhism is the sky. In the *Lamp Thoroughly Illuminating*, the very subtle mind and its wind are associated with the 'vacuous sky'.[23] Due to the 'Doctrine of the Six Lights', 'the Basis of All is like the *sky*, without any limitations. Innate wisdom, like the *sun*, shines equally in all directions' (Orofino 1990, 62-63). The symbolism of the sky has its semantic roots in the image of *gNam* (the god of blue sky), associated with permanence in ancient Bon (Pao 2002, 128). The images of the sky and the sun are present in Christian literature as well. For instance, according to Evagrius, the mind is experienced as the 'sapphire' and the 'sky' that is the same naked mind (νοῦς γυμνός).[24] St. Symeon the New Theologian, in turn, writes: 'Having thus brought me to this state Thou didst clear the heaven of every mist. By "the heaven" I mean the soul Thou hast cleansed in which Thou comest invisibly [...]' (Simeon the New Theologian, 1980, 365).[25]

One more feature of light in the two traditions is its apophatic and transcending character. Gregory Palamas describes the light as being 'supernatural and supercelestial, different from all things' (Palamas, *The Triads* (I, III, 22), 38-39). To Symeon, God shows His face as the sun without image (ἥλιον ἄμορφον),[26] tracing (σχῆμα), look (εἶδος) and imprint (ἐκτύπωμα).[27] The prefix 'super' is vital in the context of agapeic categories of 'natural' and 'supernatural'. The negative or incomprehensible character of light is mentioned also in *Bar do thos grol,*

23 Yang-jen-ga-way-lo-dro, *Lamp Thoroughly*, in Lati Rinbochay 1979, 45.

24 Евагрий Понтийский, *Kephalaia gnostica* III, 6. (In Лосский 2000 (a), 210.)

25 The translator doesn't give precise information about the source. Nevertheless, the cited Discourse is called by the translator 'The Mystical Experience of Grace in the Form of a Thanksgiving'; it is a translation of *Euch.* (=*Eucharistie Hymns*) 1 in Syméon le Nouveau Théologien, 1965, ed. Basile Krivocheine, III vol., *Sources Chrétiennes* (113), Paris: Éditions du Cerf.

26 *Euch.* (=*Eucharistie Hymns*) (2), 175-180. (In Кривошеин 1996, 245.)

27 *Eth.* (=*Traité éthique*) (1.3), 99-103. (In Кривошеин 1996, 246.)

> Just as your breath stops, the objective clear light of the first be-
> tween will dawn as previously described to you by your teacher.
> Your outer breath and you experience reality stark and void like
> space, your immaculate naked awareness dawning clear and void
> without horizon and center. (Thurman 1994, 122)

Similarly, in the *mKhas pa sri rgyal po'i khyad chos* (The Special
Teaching of the Wise and Glorious King), the state of immediate
intrinsic awareness is represented as being startled, directly penetrating and indescribable (Garab Dorje 1996, 44). One's own primordial state or the clear light is characterized by Tibetan masters
of meditation as the 'inherent *translucent* radiance (*rang gdangs*)'
(Garab Dorje 1996, 158).[28]

Typical, too, of the light experience in both Tibetan Buddhism
and Hesychasm is the graduality of its appearance. Geshe Kelsang Gyatso explains that 'in the same way that slowly removing
the lid of a box exposes more and more light inside, the separation
of the two enclosing drops results in the experience of the clear
light' (Kelsang Gyatso 1982, 86). The gradual appearance of light
during visions is described in an emotional manner by Symeon
the New Theologian in his *Hymns*.[29] Archimandrite Sophrony,
in his turn, explains the phenomenon of gradual appearance like
this: 'Divine Light is constant in itself but man's receptivity varies' (Sophrony 2001, 109). Certain experiences of the Divine
Light during this life are essential in order to see it in the future
age (Кривошеин 1996, 263). This idea is clearly expressed in the
numerous treatises of Tibetan masters. In order to be recognized
during death, light should be experienced in one's lifetime.

Also necessary during meditation or prayer is the condition of
deep peace. Sogyal Rinpoche mentions 'a deep state of stillness'
and calls it a 'pervasive peaceful state': it is 'the Rigpa itself'
(Sogyal Rinpoche 1994, 164-165). Similarly, the sensation of
peace during light vision is mentioned by the masters of Christian

---

28 'Interlinear Commentary to "The Last Testament of Garab Dorje" by the
   Translator' in Garab Dorje 1996.
29 Συμεων ο Νεος Θεολογος, Υμνοι (ΚΒ=22) // Φιλοκαλια των Νηπτικων και
   Ασκητικων 19 Ε: Συμεων ο Νεος Θεολογος, Υμνοι (Α-ΚΖ), σ. 298.

prayer, Gregory Palamas (Palamas, *The Triads* (I, III, 22), 39) and Staretz Silouan (Sophrony 2001, 110). Bliss, too, is another effect of light experience. According to Yang-jen-ga-way-lo-dro, this state is qualified as 'manifesting a subtle bliss consciousness'.[30] During meditation, a person feels a special satisfaction (*bde ba*). Hesychasts also mention emotional satisfaction during the light vision. Symeon mentions spiritual joy, high emotion and incomparable sweetness.[31] Palamas speaks about the 'impassible joy' (Palamas, *The Triads* (I, III, 22), 39) whereas Sophrony experiences 'sweetness of the love of God' (Sophrony 2001, 110).

Finally, accompanying the light vision, is the emotion of love. In Buddhism the clear light of bliss innate to humanity cannot love or be loved. Nevertheless, as a result of enlightenment, being filled with compassion, often allied to love, for sentient beings is experienced.[32] In Hesychast writings, love of God, received during the light vision, is partially expressed as 'compassion and love for those human beings who were severe to the contemplator' as well as 'the painless compassion for the creatures in common' (Сахаров 1985, 175).

The phenomenon of the appearance of two lights in Tibetan tradition is also worth mentioning. Tibetan texts on death usually mention the meeting of the so-called 'son clear light' and 'mother clear light' as the soteriological goal to be achieved. In accord with John Myrdhin Reynolds in his translation and commentary on Garab Dorje, 'This individual Clear Light to which the master introduces us and which we experience again and again in our meditation experience throughout our lifetime, is known as the Clear Light of the Path (*lam gyi 'od gsal*) rather than the Clear Light of the base (*gzhi' 'od gsal*). This luminosity met with on the path is

---

30 Yang-jen-ga-way-lo-dro, Lamp Thoroughly Illuminating the Presentation of the Three Basic Bodies – Death, Intermediate State and Rebirth. In Lati Rinbochay & Hopkins 1979, 27.

31 *Cat.* (=*Catecheses*) (16), 78-107. (In Кривошеин 1996, 241.)

32 Yang-jen-ga-way-lo-dro, Lamp Thoroughly Illuminating the Presentation of the Three Basic Bodies – Death, Intermediate State and Rebirth. In Lati Rinbochay & Hopkins 1979, 27.

also known as the Son Clear Light (*bu'i 'od gsal*), in contrast to the Mother Clear Light (*ma'i 'od gsal*)' (Garab Dorje 1996, 96). Although similar reflections about two lights cannot be found in the works of Hesychasts, Symeon, in the *Catechetical Discourses*, describes his experience of two lights using the third person:

> He was wholly in the presence of an immaterial light and seemed to himself to have turned into light. Oblivious of the world he was filled with tears and with ineffable joy and gladness. His mind then ascended to heaven and beheld yet another light, which was clearer than that which was close at hand. (Symeon the New Theologian 1980, 245-246)

Obviously, Symeon's first light may be compared to the path of luminosity of Tibetan Buddhism and the second one to the base luminosity. Although experiences of light in Tibetan Buddhism and Hesychasm express more convergences than divergences, it is worth noting that unlike the Buddhist paradigm, the Christian union of God and humanity preserves the personal relation between the two. In his *Thanksgivings*, Symeon, utilizing the language of paradox, witnesses:

> As we ascend to that which is more perfect, He who is without form or shape comes no longer without form or without shape. Nor does He cause His light to come to us and be present with us in silence. But how? He comes in a definite form indeed, though it is a divine one. Yet God does not show Himself in a particular pattern or likeness, but in simplicity, and takes the form of an incomprehensible, inaccessible, and formless light. We cannot possibly say or express more than this; still He appears clearly and is consciously known and clearly seen, though He is invisible. He sees and hears invisibly and, just as friend speaks to friend face to face (cf. Ex. 33:11), so He who by nature is God speaks to those whom by grace He has begotten as gods. He loves like a father, and in turn He is fervently loved by His sons. (Symeon the New Theologian 1980, 365)

Commenting on the passage, S. Horuzhy admits that, although the mysticism of light is qualified as impersonal and is opposite to personal mysticism, Hesychasm combines them together. Light in Hesychasm is not the source of annihilation of personality, rather of its growth. Contemplation within Hesychasm is a special type of *trancensus*, uniting the impersonal blending with the Divine of Neoplatonism and the personal communication with God of the Old Testament (Хоружий 1998, 171-172). The Hesychast model differs from the attainment of the rDzogs chen ideal of the rainbow body (*'ja' lus*), that is, the reversal of the emanation of all existing from the Primordial Basis (*gzhi*) (see Karmay 1988, 203-205). The difference is obviously rooted in the agapeic/theistic and gnostic/monistic models of religiosity.

In sum, we have examined the main anthropological and experiential parallels between Hesychasm and Tibetan Buddhism, based on the concept of the common structures of human experience. Parallels, associations and comparisons have been noted. However, it is clear that there are divergences and these are fully rooted in the two types of religiosity, the agapeic and the gnostic, that attention has been drawn to, for they are forms which are determined culturally as well as psychologically.

Bibliography

Sources in English

Allen, Douglas, 2005a. 'Major Contributions of Philosophical Phenomenology and Hermeneutics to the Study of Religion'. In *How to do Comparative Religion: Three Ways, Many Goals*, ed. René Gothóni. Berlin & New York: Walter de Gruyter: 5-28.

Allen, Douglas, 2005b. 'Phenomenology of Religion'. In *The Routledge Companion to the Study of Religion*, ed. John R. Hinnells. London & New York: Routledge: 182-207.

Beinorius, Audrius, 2005. 'Experience and Context: Cross-Cultural Approach to the Epistemology of Mysticism'. In *Contemporary Philosophical Discourse in Lithuania*, ed. Jurate

Baranova, gen. ed. George F. McLean. Washington: The Council for Research in Values and Philosophy: 219-248.

Beinorius, Audrius, 2006. *Imagining Otherness: Postcolonial Perspective to Indian Religious Culture*. Vilnius: Kronta.

Bharati, Agehananda, 1976. *The Tantric Tradition*. Bombay, Calcutta, Madras, Delhi: B. I. Publications.

Corneanu, Metropolitan Nicolae, 1995. 'The Jesus Prayer and Deification'. *St. Vladimir's Theological Quarterly* 39.1: 3-24.

Dasgupta, Shashi Bhushan, 1974. *An Introduction to Tantric Buddhism*. Berkeley & London: Shambala.

Dionysius the Areopagite [Pseudo-Dionysius], 1920: *On the Divine Names and the Mystical Theology*, ed. C.E. Rolt. Grand Rapids, MI, & London: Christian Classics Ethereal Library & SPCK.

Emory-Moore, Christopher, 2016. 'Clear and Uncreated: The Experience of Inner Light in Gelug-pa Tantrism and Byzantine Hesychasm'. *Buddhist-Christian Studies*, 36: 117-130.

Fremantle, Francesca, 2001. *Luminous Emptiness: Understanding the Tibetan Book of the Dead*. Boston & London: Shambhala.

Gregory of Nyssa, 1978. *The Life of Moses*. Mahwah, NJ: Paulist Press.

Herman, Jonathan R., 2000. 'The Contextual Illusion: Comparative Mysticism and Postmodernism'. In *A Magic Still Dwells: Comparative Religion in the Postmodern Age*, eds. Kimberley C. Patton & Benjamin C. Ray. Berkeley, Los Angeles & London: University of California Press: 92-100.

Hopkins, Jeffrey, 1979. 'Preface'. In Lati Rinbochay & Jeffrey Hopkins, *Death, Intermediate State and Rebirth in Tibetan Buddhism*. London: Rider and Company.

Garab Dorje [Tshig gsum gnad brdeg. English], trans. John Myrdhin Reynolds, 1996. *The Golden Letters: The Three Statements of Garab Dorje, the First Teacher of Dzogchen, together with a Commentary by Dza Patrul Rinpoche entitled 'The Special Teaching of the Wise and Glorious King'*. Ithaca, New York: Snow Lion Publications.

Govinda, Lama Anagarika, 1975. *Foundations of Tibetan Mysticism According to the Esoteric Teachings of the Great Mantra OM MANI PADME HŪM.* New York: Samuel Weiser.

Grabowitz, Robert, 2014. *Integrating the Anomalous: Towards a Typology of Religious Transformation* (an abstract of a thesis submitted to the Faculty of Emory College of Arts and Sciences of Emory University in partial fulfilment of the requirements of the degree of Bachelor of Arts with Honors). Emory: Electronic Theses and Dissertation, https://legacy-etd.library. emory.edu/view/record/pid/emory:g0k62, accessed 26 September 2017.

Lee, Jung Young, 1974. *Death and Beyond in the Eastern Perspective: A Study Based on the Bardo Thödol and the I Ching.* New York: Gordon and Breach.

Karmay, Samten Gyaltsen, 1988. *The Great Perfection (rDzogs chen): A Philosophical and Meditative Teaching in Tibetan Buddhism.* Leiden, New York, Kobenhavn, Köln: E.J. Brill.

Kelsang Gyatso, Geshe, transl. Tenzin Norbu, eds. Jonathan Landaw & Chris Colb, 1982. *Clear Light of Bliss: Mahamudra in Vajrayana Buddhism.* London: Wisdom Publications.

King, Richard, 2005. 'Mysticism and Spirituality'. In *The Routledge Companion to the Study of Religion,* ed. John R. Hinnells. London & New York: Routledge: 306-322.

Lati Rinbochay & Jeffrey Hopkins (transls. and annotators), 1979. *Death, Intermediate State, and Rebirth in Tibetan Buddhism.* London: Rider and Company (a translated, annotated version of Yang-jen-ga-way-lo-dro's *Lamp Thoroughly Illuminating the Presentation of the Three Basic Bodies – Death, Intermediate State and Rebirth*).

Namkhai Norbu, Chögyal, 2000. *The Crystal and the Way of Light: Sutra, Tantra and Dzogchen.* Ithaca, New York: Snow Lion Publications.

Orofino, Giacomella, ed. John Shane, 1990. *Sacred Tibetan Teachings on Death and Liberation: Texts from the Most Ancient Traditions of Tibet.* Great Britain: Prism Unity.

Palamas, Gregory, trans. Nicholas Gendle, 1983. *The Triads*. New Jersey: Paulist Press. (*The Triads* are translated into English from Meyendorff's critical edition: Grégoire Palamas, *Défense des saints hésychastes*, 2nd ed. Spicilegium Sacrum Lovaniense, études et documents, fascicules 30 and 31, Louvain, 1973).

Pandit, Moti Lal, 1991. *Towards Transcendence: A Historico-Analytical Study of Yoga as a Method of Liberation*. New Delhi: Intercultural Publications.

Parrinder, Geoffrey, 1995 (1976). *Mysticism in the World's Religions*. Oxford: Oneworld, 1995.

Pieris, Aloysius, S.J., 1990. *Love Meets Wisdom: A Christian Experience of Buddhism*. Maryknoll, New York: Orbis Books.

Powers, John, 2007². *Introduction to Tibetan Buddhism*. Ithaca, New York: Snow Lion Publications.

Smart, Ninian, 1999. *Dimensions of the Sacred: An Anatomy of the World's Beliefs*. Berkeley & Los Angeles: University of California Press.

Smart, Ninian & Steven Konstantine, 1991. *Christian Systematic Theology in a World Context*. Minneapolis: Fortress Press.

Sogyal Rinpoche, eds. Patrick Gaffney & Andrew Harvey,1994. *The Tibetan Book of Living and Dying*. New York: HarperSanFrancisco.

Sophrony, Archimandrite, trans. Rosemary Edmonds, 2001. *The Monk of Mount Athos Staretz Silouan 1866-1938*. Chestwood, New York: St Vladimir's Seminary Press.

Spickard, James V., 2014. 'Phenomenology'. In *The Routledge Handbook of Research Methods in the Study of Religion*, eds. Michael Strausberg & Steven Engler. London & New York: Routledge: 333-345.

Symeon the New Theologian, trans. C.J. de Catanzaro, 1980. *The Discourses* (VI, 8). New Jersey: Paulist Press. (The translation was from *Syméon le Nouveau Théologien, 1963-1965*, ed. Basile Krivocheine, 3 vol., Sources Chrétiennes. Paris: Éditions du Cerf).

Taves, Ann, 2011. *Religious Experience Reconsidered: A Building-Block Approach to the Study of Religion and Other Special Things*. Princeton and Oxford: Princeton University Press.

Thurman, Robert A.F., transl., 1994. *The Tibetan Book of the Dead as popularly known in the West, Known in Tibet as The Great Book of Natural Liberation Through Understanding in the Between*. New York, Toronto, London, Sydney & Auckland: Bantam Books.

Thurman, Robert A.F, 1995. *Essential Tibetan Buddhism*. New Jersey: Castle Books.

Tucci, Giuseppe, 1995 [1976]. *Le religioni del Tibet*. Ristampa, Roma: Edizioni Mediterranee.

Underhill, Evelyn, 1955. *Mysticism: A Study in the Nature and Development of Man's Spiritual Consciousness*. New York: Meridian Books.

Wangyal Rinpoche, Tenzin, 2000. *Wonders of the Natural Mind: The Essence of Dzogchen in Native Bon Tradition of Tibet*. Ithaca, NY: Snow Lion Publications.

Winkler, Gabriele, 1986. *The Jesus Prayer in Eastern Spirituality*. Minneapolis: Light and Life Publishing Company.

Sources in Russian

Голынский-Михайловский, Архиепископ Антоний, 2000. О молитве Иисусовой и божественной благодати. Красногорск. (Golinskiy-Mihaylovskiy, Arhiyepiskop Antoniy, 2000. *O molitve Iisusovoy i bozhestvennoy blagodati. Krasnogorsk*).

Зарин, С.М., 1996. Аскетизм по Православно-христианскому учению. Москва: Паломник. (Zarin, S.M., 1996. *Asketizm po Pravoslavno-hristianskomu ucheniyu. Moskva: Palomnik*).

Керн, Архимандрит Киприан, 1996. Антропология Св. Григория Паламы. Москва: Паломник. (Kern, Arhimandrit Kiprian, 1996. *Antropologiya Sv. Grigoriya Palami. Moskva: Palomnik*).

Кривошеин, Архиепископ Василий, 1996. Преподобный Симеон Новый Богослов (949-1022). Нижний Новгород: Издательство братства во имя святого князя Александра Невского. (Krivoshein, Arhiyepiskop Vasiliy, 1996. *Prepodobniy Simeon Noviy Bogoslov (949-1022)*. Nizhniy Novgorod: Izdatel'stvo bratstva vo imya svyatogo knyazya Aleksandra Nevskogo).

Коржевский, Иерей Вадим, 2004. Пропедевтика аскетики: компендиум по православной святоотеческой психологии. Москва: Центр Информационных Технологий Информатики и Информации. (Korzhevskiy, Iyerey Vadim, 2004. *Propedevtika asketiki: kompendium po pravoslavnoy svyatootecheskoy psihologii*. Moskva: Centr Informacionnih Tehnologiy Informatiki i Informacii).

Лосский, Владимир, 2000 (а). 'Боговидение', пер. В. Рещиковой, А. Бездидько, Ю. Малкова // Владимир Лосский, Богословие и боговидение, ред. Владимир Писляков. Москва: Издательство Свято-Владимирского Братства 112-272. (Losskiy, Vladimir, 2000 (a). 'Bogovideniye', per. V. Reshchikovoy, A. Bezdid'ko, Yu. Malkova // Vladimir Losskiy, *Bogosloviye i bogovideniye*, red. Vladimir Pislyakov. Moskva: Izdatel'stvo Svyato-Vladimirskogo Bratstva: 112-272).

Лосский, Владимир, 2000 (b). 'Мрак и свет в познании Бога', пер. В. Рещиковой // Владимир Лосский, Богословие и боговидение, ред. Владимир Писляков. Москва: Издательство Свято-Владимирского Братства: 67-81. (Losskiy, Vladimir, 2000 (b). 'Mrak i svet v poznanii Boga', per. V. Reshchikovoy // Vladimir Losskiy, *Bogosloviye i bogovideniye*, red. Vladimir Pislyakov. Moskva: Izdatel'stvo Svyato-Vladimirskogo Bratstva: 67-81).

Лосский, В. Н., 1991. Очерк мистического богословия Восточной Церкви. Догматическое богословие. Москва: СЭИ. (Losskiy, V. N., 1991. *Ocherk misticheskogo bogosloviya Vostochnoy Cerkvi. Dogmaticheskoye bogosloviye*. Moskva: SEI).

Мейендорф, Протопресвитер Иоанн, 1997. Жизнь и труды Святителя Григория Паламы: введение в изучение. Пер. Г.В.

Начинкин. Ред. И.П. Медведев, В.М. Лурье. Санкт-Петербург: Византинороссика. (Meiendorf, Protopresviter Ioann, 1997. *Zhizn' i trudi Svyatitelya Grigoriya Palami: vvedeniye i izucheniye*. Per. G.V. Nachinkin. Red. B.G. Medvedev, V.M. Lurye. Sankt-Peterburg: Vizantinarossika).

Минин, П., 1991. Главные направления древне-церковной мистики // Мистическое богословие. Киев: Путь к истине. (Minin, P., 1991. *Glavniye napravleniya drevne-cerkovnoy mistiki // Misticheskoye bogosloviye*. Kiyev: Put'k istine).

Палама, Св. Григорий, 1995. Триады в защиту священно-безмолвствующих. Пер. В. Вениаминов. Москва: Канон. (Palama, Sv. Grigoriy, 1995. *Triadi v zashchitu svyashchenno-bezmolvstvuyushchih*. Per. V.Veniaminov. Moskva: Kanon).

Рао, Рамачандра, 2002. Тантрические традиции Тибета // Рамачандра Рао. Тантра, мантра, янтра. Тантрические традиции Тибета. Москва: Беловодье. (Rao, Ramachandra, 2002. Tantricheskiye tradicii Tibeta // Ramachandra Rao. Tantra, mantra, yantra. Tantricheskiye tradicii Tibeta. Moskva: Belovodye).

Розенберг, О.О, 1991. Труды по буддизму. Москва: Наука. (Rozenberg, O.O., 1991. *Trudi po buddizmu*. Moskva: Nauka).

Рудой, В.И., Островская, Е.П., 2000. 'Буддийская картина мира в традиции постканонической Абхидхармы'. // Категории буддийской Абхидхармы, ред.-сост. Е.П. Островская. Санкт-Петербург: Петербургское Востоковедение: 24-109. (Rudoy, V.I., Ostrovskaya, Ye. P., 2000. 'Buddiyskaya kartina mira v tradicii postkanonicheskoy Abhidharmi'. // *Kategorii buddiyskoy Abhidharmi*, red.-sost. Ye. P. Ostrovkaya. Sankt-Peterburg: Peterburgskoye Vostokovedeniye: 24-109).

Сахаров, Архимандрит Софроний, 1985. Видеть Бога как Он есть. Essex: Stavropegic Monastery of St. John the Baptist. (Saharov, Arhimandrit Sofroiy, 1985. *Videt' Boga kak On yest'*. Essex: Stavropegic Monastery of St. John the Baptist).

Сахаров, Архимандрит Софроний, 1991. Старец Силуан: Жизнь и поучения. Москва: Ново-казачье: Минск: Воскресение. (Saharov, Arhimandrit Sofroniy, 1991. *Starec*

Siluan: Zhizn' i poucheniya. Moskva: Novo-kazachye: Minsk: Voskreseniye).

Хоружий, С.С, 1991. Диптих безмолвия: Аскетическое учение о человеке в богословском и философском освещении. Москва: Центр психологии и психиатрии. (Horuzhiy, S.S., 1991. *Diptih bezmolviya:Asketicheskoye ucheniye o cheloveke v bogoslovskom i filosofskom osveshchenii.* Moskva: Centr psihologii i psihiatrii).

Хоружий, С.С., 1998. Аналитический словарь исихастской антропологии // К феноменологии аскезы. Москва: Издательство гуманитарной литературы: 22-182. (Horuzhiy, S.S., 1998. *Analiticheskiy slovar' isihastskoy antropologii // K fenomenologii askezi.* Moskva: Izdatel'stvo gumanitarnoy literaturi: 22-188).

Юркевич, П.Д., 1990. Философские произведения. Москва: Правда. (Yurkevich, P.D., 1990. *Filosofskiye proizvedeniya.* Moskva: Pravda).

Συμεων ο Νεος Θεολογος. 1990, Υμνοι // Φιλοκαλια των Νηπτικων και Ασκητικων 19 E: Συμεων ο Νεος Θεολογος. Υμνοι (A-KZ). Ἐπόπτης ἐκδόσεως Παναγιωτης Κ. Χρηστου, ἐπιμελητὴς ἐκδόσεως Ελευθεπιος Γ. Μερετακης, μεταφραση ἀπὸ τὸν Ιγνατιο Σακαλη. Θεσσαλονικη: Το Βυζαντιον; Γρηγοριος ο Παλαμας (Symeon o Neos Theologos, 1990, Gmnoi // Philokalia ton Neptikon kai Asketikon 19 E: Symeon o Neos Theologos Gmnoi (A-KZ). Epoptes ekdoseos Panagiotes K. Hrestu, epimeletes ekdoseos Eleuthepios G. Meretakes, metaphrase apo ton Ignatio Sakale. Thessalonike: To Byzantion; Grigorios o Palamas).

APATHEIA AND *ĀŚRAYAPARĀVṚTTI*: MEDITATION AND EPISTEMIC PURIFICATION IN THE *PHILOKALIA* AND YOGĀCĀRA BUDDHISM

Thomas Cattoi

Abstract

*The tradition of the Desert Fathers developed a sophisticated approach to meditation (*theōria*), according to which all actions leave an imprint in the* nous *that is destined to ripen and give fruit, influencing the moral conduct of the individual. The school of Evagrios Pontikos (345-395 ca.) viewed the different stages of contemplation as erasing the traces of past choices from the intellect, ensuring that at the highest stage of* theōria, *the practitioner is utterly detached from the consequences of her choices and is able to achieve a condition of complete dispassion (*apatheia*). The Yogācāra school associated with Asaṅga, for its part, affirmed the existence of two distinct consciousnesses,* klistamanas *and* ālayavijñāna: *the former was associated with deluded awareness, whereas the latter was understood as all-encompassing foundation consciousness. In the* Mahāyānasaṃgraha, *Asaṅga discusses the role of the* ālayavijñāna *as a storehouse in which all impressions (*vasanas*) from past actions are stored as the seeds (*bija*) of future experiences. Through the pursuit of wisdom and compassion, the practitioner can achieve the so-called 'overturning of the basis' (*āśrayaparavrtti*), where the storehouse consciousness is purified of all defilements. The goal of this paper is to explore how these two distinct traditions understand the relationship between meditative practice and cognitive purification, underscoring the points of contact, as well as the irreducible differences*

*between the two approaches. Particular emphasis will be given to
the different ways in which the Philokalic tradition of the Desert
Fathers and Yogācāra Buddhism conceptualize subjectivity, transcendence, and the relationship between the individual practitioner and God or pure consciousness/Buddha nature.*

Keywords: *ālaya-vijñāna, apatheia, Asaṅga āśrayaparāvṛtti,*
discernment of spirits, Evagrios Pontikos, *Kephalaia Gnostika, Mahāyānasaṃgraha, nous,* Origen, *Philokalia, samsara,
Saptadaśabhūmika,* Yogācāra, *Yogācārabhūmi*

Introduction

The purpose of this paper is to bring into conversation the notions
of *ālaya-vijñāna* and *āśrayaparāvṛtti* in a number of Yogācāra
texts, and the notions of *nous* and *apatheia* in the writings of
Evagrios Pontikos (345-390 CE).[1] The main body of the paper
will explore how these two traditions view spiritual progress as a
transformative trajectory leading to a condition of utter tranquil-

---

1   For Yogācāra and its relationship with Madhyamaka, see L.S. Kawamura
    and G.M. Nagao, *Madhyamika and Yogacara: A Study of Mahayana Phi-
    losophies* (SUNY Series in Buddhist Studies. Albany NY: SUNY University
    Press, 1991); Jay Garfield and Jan Westerhoff, *Madhyamaka and Yogacara:
    Allies or Rivals?* (Oxford: Oxford University Press, 2015). The literature
    on Evagrios Pontikos is immense. For a first introduction, see Augustine
    Casiday, *Evagrios Pontikos* (London & New York: Routledge, 2006); Ju-
    lia Konstantinovsky, *Evagrius: The Making of a Gnostic* (London & New
    York: Routledge, 2008); Robert Sinkewicz, *Evagrius of Pontos: the Greek
    Ascetic Corpus* (Oxford: Oxford University Press, 2006). The works refer-
    enced in this essay can be found in G.E.H. Palmer, P. Sherrard and K. Ware
    (transl.), *The Philokalia*, Vol. 1 (London, Farrar Strauss and Giroux, 1983),
    which contains other works from the Evagrian school, and Antoine Guil-
    laumont, *Les Kephalaia Gnostica D'Evagre Le Pontique, et L'Histoire De
    L'Origenisme Chez Les Grecs et Chez Les Syriens* (Paris: Seuil, 1962). A
    new English translation of the *Kephalaia Gnostika* is now available in Ilaria
    L.E. Ramelli (ed.), *Evagrius's Kephalaia Gnostika: a New Translation of the
    Unreformed Text from the Syriac* (SBL Press, 2015).

lity (*apatheia*) and simultaneous engagement with the world of phenomena; in so doing, it will highlight a number of intriguing points of contact between the two traditions, both of which view the highest component of the intellect as the repository of imprints from past actions, as well as the ultimate locus of practice and awakening. The last part of the discussion will then uncover a number of differences in the two traditions, reflecting their distinctive assumptions concerning anthropology, cosmology and the purpose of spiritual practice. It is not the intention of this paper to argue for a historical connection between the Yogācāra tradition and the worldview of the Desert Fathers; rather, its goal is to explore a set of functionally analogous concepts that serve as lynchpins for similar, yet distinctive transformative processes. A careful parallel reading of these texts, attending to their historical and philosophical context, will then illumine the specificities of the two religious traditions, while also uncovering the presence of what may be called 'irreducible differences' between their particular worldviews.

Yogācāra consciousness

The notion of *ālaya-vijñāna* can be traced to the lengthy treatise known as *Yogācārabhūmi* attributed to Asaṅga (ca. 300-370 CE), who, together with his brother, Vasubandhu, is considered to be one of the leading figures of the Yogācāra movement. The *Saptadaśabhūmika* – the so-called 'Basic Section' of the *Yogācārabhūmi* – describes the *ālaya-vijñāna* as a kind of basic consciousness that flows unceasingly within the material sense faculties (Waldron 2003, 92). This basic consciousness contains, in the form of seeds, the causal conditions for different instances of cognitive awareness and behaviour that emerge in connection with their appropriate objects. These arising cognitive and behavioural episodes are known as *pravṛtti-vijñāna*, which is characterized as intermittent, whereas *ālaya-vijñāna* is uninterrupted. In fact, the latter is said to persist even during meditative processes, when the absorption of any input from the material world ceases (*nirodhasamāpatti*). In this text, ālaya-vijñāna is still connected to a bodily experience, largely reflecting the Abhidharmic tradition where, as long as someone is in the flesh, the *vijñāna* (consciousness) continues to 'absorb' the material world within itself (Schmithausen 1987, 12, 18-33).

A slightly later text known as the *Saṃdhinirmocana Sūtra* (The Sutra of the Explanation of the Profound Secrets) develops the notion of *ālaya-vijñāna* further, exploring the relationship between the *ālaya-vijñāna* and the other modes of consciousness that are discussed in the Abhidharma literature; while the earlier tradition viewed the *ālaya-vijñāna* as primarily a receptacle of seeds that come to fruition as long as one remains in the circle of *saṃsāra*, this later rendition of the same notion integrates the earlier reflection on consciousness with the Mahāyāna notion of awakening as an engaged reality (*apratiṣṭhita nirvāṇa*). In the *Saṃdhinirmocana Sūtra*, the *ālaya-vijñāna* undergirds and provides ontological support to the six types of cognitive awareness (the five senses together with our ability to process their input). Since the *ālaya-vijñāna* is always present, all the different forms of cognition happen simultaneously (Waldron 2003, 94-96). The fifth chapter of the *Saṃdhinirmocana Sūtra* actually discusses the role played by the *ālaya-vijñāna* in the cycle of *saṃsāra*: the *ālaya-vijñāna* is said to descend into 'the womb of beings' –which could be the actual mother's womb, or the womb of *saṃsāra*, or perhaps, deliberately, both – takes over the material faculties 'along with their support' (*sādhiṣṭāna-rūpīndriya*), and also appropriates their predisposition towards the creation – in the conventional realm – of images, names, and concepts (*nimitta-nāma-vikalpa*). In this way, the *ālaya-vijñāna*, by way of this two-fold appropriation (*upādāna*), appears to be the engine behind *saṃsāra*. This is different from the *Saptadaśabhūmika*, which only discussed *ālaya-vijñāna* during the periods of *nirodhasamāpatti*; as a dependently arisen form of consciousness, it serves as the *trait d'union* between different lives as it latches onto the karmic deposit that shapes the reincarnation mechanism, and it also underscores the fundamental interrelationship between the body and mind. Of course, the *Saṃdhinirmocana Sūtra* reminds us that this appropriation appears to be twofold (the material faculties on one hand, the ability to attach conceptual labels on the other) only in the conventional realm, or the realm of form – within the formless realm, this distinction ceases to exist (Lamotte 1935, 7-29).[2]

This approach appears to emphasize the agency, or active role, of the *ālaya-vijñāna*, but this is only part of the story, and the later Yogācāra tradition would emphasize the extent to which the *ālaya-vijñāna* itself is modified by this process. The *ālaya-vijñāna* emerges out of the physiological and psychological structures that have accumulated over a whole series of lifetimes; then, in the course of the present life, the *ālaya-vijñāna* receives imprints from the cognitive and behavioural objects that it experiences, in a never-ending spiral. In addition, the *Saṃdhinirmocana Sūtra* (VIII, 37, 1) already views the *ālaya-vijñāna* as itself a cognitive form of awareness: in other words, it is an implicit, yet constantly operative perception of the material world, which constantly impinges on our own sense faculties, and which occurs at the same time as the other six modes of cognition. The text (V, 4-5) compares each of these modes of cognition to waves in a river, which arise if the necessary conditions are present, and which are supported by the stream and simultaneously have an impact on it – a stream – the *ālaya-vijñāna* – which nonetheless never ceases to flow.

The notion of *ālaya-vijñāna* as a mental stream reminds us of the fact that our minds and bodies are manifestations of embedded karma, carrying within themselves the memory of all past actions. At the same time, the notion of a stream should remind us of the fact that the *ālaya-vijñāna* is not a discrete entity but rather a flux that can be conceptualized apart from the cognitive and behavioural manifestations that it supports. In the *Yogācārabhūmi*, the author introduces the notion of so-called 'mental afflictions' – both cognitive and emotional – that operate within the *ālaya-vijñāna* itself, and that bring about further karmic activity in con-

---

2   The quotations from the *Saṃdhinirmocana sūtra* are taken from Lamotte 1935, cited by chapter and section.

junction with the material objects encountered by the sense faculties of the individual sentient being (Waldron 2003, 102). On
the basis of this notion, the so-called *Pravṛtti* (Continued arising)
portion of the *Yogācārabhūmi*'s 'Ālaya' treatise argues that if the
co-dependent arising process, whereby the different cognitive and
behavioural episodes supported by the *ālaya-vijñāna* cease, the
samsaric existence of the individual sentient being will come to
an end. Within the *ālaya-vijñāna*'s stream, there are two distinct
streams: the cognitive and emotional afflictions derived from past
karmic deposit – something that unfolds in a subliminal epistemic
mode known as *manas* – and the manifest awareness of and reaction to external objects (Waldron 2003, 107). Having said that,
these Yogācāra texts are well aware of the fact that some 'unenlightened' readers will misunderstand the nature of the *manas*
process, coming to believe that the *ālaya-vijñāna*, with its store of
afflictions carried over from one life to the next, is actually a permanent self. The author of the *Saṃdhinirmocana Sūtra* must have
foreseen this problem as he claims that the Buddha was initially
reluctant to teach about the *ālaya-vijñāna*, since some less than
perceptive hearers might have regarded it as a permanent self (V).

This interpretation of the *ālaya-vijñāna* as a discrete centre of
subjectivity – or in other words, holding on to certain aspects of
saṃsāra as impermeable to change – echoes the observation in
the *Abhidharmakośa* that sentient beings in the grip of delusion
view *citta* (thought) as identical with the self (Pruden 1988, 196).
Given that the *manas* looks at the *ālaya-vijñāna* as a repository
of memories from the past, it is quite clear why unenlightened
beings may conflate these memories as resting in an unchanging self. Paradoxically, however, it is only thanks to the *ālaya-
vijñāna* that one can engage in karmically skilful actions that are
conducive to enlightenment. The challenge is to be able to make
use of the resource that this karmic repository offers without falling into the trap of thinking that there is a subject enabling us to
engage in these operations. The *Yogācārabhūmi* notes – and this
will be useful for our comparative conversation later – that as
long as the *manas* accompanies the *ālaya-vijñāna*, it is always

going to be accompanied by four 'afflictions', such as a mistaken belief in one's independent existence (*satkāya-dṛṣṭi*) (*Pravṛtti* Portion 4b.B.4), the delusion that one exists at all (*asmimāna*), self-love (*ātmasneha*) and delusion (*avidyā*). The fundamental problem is that as long as all cognitive and behavioural processes are controlled by the *manas*, it is impossible to get rid of the distinction between self and other, or, in other words, to achieve *nirvāṇa* (Waldron 2003, 117-123). It may be worth noting that the Yogācāra distinction between conscious and unconscious operations of the *ālaya-vijñāna* indicates that members of this Buddhist school had conceptualized the notion of the unconscious long before its emergence in Western philosophical thought.

The question at this point is how to eliminate all karmic defilements at the root; in other words, how to bring about the complete cessation of the *ālaya-vijñāna*, since its disappearance will sever the dependently-originated emergence of the sense faculties, and bring about the extinction of *saṃsāra*. The *Yogācārabhūmi* argues that once the two-fold appropriation process mentioned above ceases, the body will only be a floating phantom, since the mechanism that brings about rebirth will have been abandoned (*Pravṛtti* Portion 5b.C.3). The same text, however, notes that the *ālaya-vijñāna* contains the resources both for persisting – indeed, going ever deeper – into delusion, and for moving towards *nirvāṇa*. The *ālaya-vijñāna* contains skilful and unskilful 'seeds'; what practice teaches you is to discern between one and the other set. The *Pravṛtti* (Portion 5b.C.1) notes that the practitioner who is able to 'hoard', so to speak, all the positive seeds, can 'turn the *ālaya-vijñāna* upside down' (*āśrayaṃ parivartate*) through the cultivation of wisdom. Once this overturning (*āśrayaparāvṛtti*) has taken place, the *ālaya-vijñāna* no longer engages in the two appropriations; rather, it enables us to let go of all the defilements. As a result, our life is no longer controlled by conscious and unconscious reactivity, but it is transfigured by the wisdom and compassion sustained by the *ālaya-vijñāna* itself.

What does the *Mahāyānasaṃgraha* tell us about epistemic purification? Asaṅga sets out to develop a model of the mind that has multiple levels, seeking to integrate elements from the earlier Abhidharmic literature and from the texts we have discussed so far. The purpose of this approach is to emphasize that the notion of *ālaya-vijñāna* alone can explain the continuity of co-dependently originated samsaric life and its cessation. The *Mahāyānasaṃgraha* admits that it is not necessary to know about the *ālaya-vijñāna* to achieve awakening: earlier practitioners did not use this term and did not seem to have a clear concept of this mental repository, and they were able to achieve *nirvāṇa* nonetheless.[3] The two aspects of *ālaya-vijñāna* – the transmission of karmic deposits from one life to the next, and the dialectical relationship between the trace of past actions and the imprint of sense objects – are presented as functionally equivalent: while one unfolds over time, the other accompanies any cognitive or behavioural episode (Waldron 2003, 133). The *Yogācārabhūmi* had used the simile of the interdependent arising of the flame and the wick, on one hand, and the bundle of sticks that are 'tied to each other and thus do not fall', on the other (*Pravṛtti* Portion 1b.A.3). The *Mahāyānasaṃgraha* says that the *ālaya-vijñāna* is the result of past karma, and is also the cause of all future epistemic awareness, as it contains all the seeds (*sarvabījaka*) that will cause more defiled *dharma*s. Ultimately, there is a need for a kind of ontological basis for the karmic process to work; without an uninterrupted ground the karmic deposits could not be transmitted from one life to the next, and within this life the imprints of current actions and thoughts could not be carried into the future. For example, according to the *Mahāyānasaṃgraha*, whenever sentient beings experience lust, their stream of mind is not separate from the experience of lust, as the former provides a basis for the latter, and the latter is also coloured by the former, in the same way as a seed can 'perfume' (playing on the meaning of the term *vāsānas*) a flower, but without the flower the seed would not come into being (I.15). In the same way, if you practise the virtues that in the Mahāyāna

---

3   The quotations from the *Mahāyānasaṃgraha* are taken from the 1989 translation by Griffiths, Hakayama, Keenan & Swanson, cited by chapter and section.

path precede meditative concentration, the *ālaya-vijñāna* is necessary in order to retain and transmit in time the resulting mental states that will lead to ultimate awakening.

The paradox of this situation is that, on one hand, individuals pursue higher and higher levels of meditative concentrations, while at the same time they are still also receiving the karmic impact of the experiences they are going through. To understand this aspect of Yogācāra teaching, we must recall how the teaching of Asaṅga builds on the Madhyamaka distinction between conventional and ultimate reality, but the conventional reality splits further between the ordinary realm of our embodied lives and the glorified level of higher 'pure' realms that are more conducive to liberation.[4] The *Mahāyānasaṃgraha* insists that thoughts belonging to one realm are distinct from thoughts that belong to another realm: yet, the process of purification that happens at the level of our embodied lives is spurred by a thought (*citta*) that is influenced by 'seeds' from a higher realm, and thoughts in the higher realm cannot arise without the karmic deposits of thoughts from lives in this ordinary world. As expected, the *ālaya-vijñāna* is established as the bridge that joins the two realms. In addition, however, the *Mahāyānasaṃgraha* also talks of the pure seeds of the formless realm that the *ālaya-vijñāna* contains within itself. This may seem to beg the question: if all seeds and all thoughts only arise because of previous experiences and thoughts, and the sentient being who is undergoing purification is not yet enlightened, where have these seeds come from? The *Mahāyānasaṃgraha* easily solves this conundrum by saying that 'the supra-mundane *citta* emerges from the seeds of the impression of the dharma that was heard in the past, and that emerges out of the perfectly pure *dharmadhatu*' (I, 45). This kind of 'higher' anthropology – or soteriology – typical of Mahāyāna upends the paradox by dissolving the chronological succession between *saṃsāra* and *nirvāṇa*. Simply put, if all sentient beings are already enlightened, they will

---

4   For an introduction to this teaching, and the way it subverts the distinction
     between ontology and epistemology, see Paul Williams, 2008. *Mahāyāna
     Buddhism: The Doctrinal Foundations,* New York: Routledge, 88-92.

carry within themselves traces of this enlightened state, which will blossom when the process of mundane purification is complete and the sentient being can move beyond the world of form. The operative cosmology in these texts actually nuances the Madhyamaka distinction between conventional and ultimate reality, postulating different 'worlds of form' – from our ordinary universe to the most lavishly described 'pure lands' – through which sentient beings move on their way towards *nirvāna*.

It is interesting to note that what really makes it possible to be awakened is the fact that the Buddha – not necessarily the historical Buddha, but a Buddha from ages past – taught the dharma, so that these pure seeds entered the stream of the *ālaya-vijñāna*. The latter then can be the cause of intensifying attachments, but also the cause of liberation; the two elements are mixed with each other, 'like milk and water' says the text, using a classical Sanskrit metaphor that goes back all the way to the *Yajur Veda* (19.73). Yet, with practice, a process begins that gradually transforms all seeds into seeds of liberation: and eventually, as the impressions from hearing the dharma intensify, the consciousness resulting from past seeds fades away, and 'the basis is resolved (*āśrayaparāvṛtti*)' (I.48). It does seem that this approach does retain an emphasis on a process of cause and effect: the *ālaya-vijñāna* with all its seeds is the vehicle of liberation, but the 'resolved' or 'overturned' *ālaya-vijñāna* is the mark of awakening.

Later vernacular manuals in the Yogācāra tradition would systematize the teaching of Asaṅga and of the earlier literature into a system that actually distinguished eight consciousnesses: the five senses, the mind (or *manovijñana*) that apprehends sense perceptions and synthesizes their content, the *manas* discussed earlier (also known as *kliṣṭamanas*, or 'defiled mind') and the *ālaya-vijñāna*. The Indian missionary, Paramārtha (499-569 CE), who moved to China and was renowned for his translations of Yogācāra texts into Chinese, actually argued that whenever the *ālaya-vijñāna* ceases, what emerges is an utterly pure 'ninth consciousness', or *amala-vijñāna* (Paul 1982, 37-69). In China, there were actual controversies as to the status of this purified consciousness. Some emphasized that it was inherently empty, as it had shed all its seeds, and others asserted an ontologically stronger reading, where the *ālaya-vijñāna* is akin to what later would become the *tathāgatagarbha*, or Buddha nature.[5] The *Mahāyānasaṃgraha*'s textual ambiguities make different interpretations possible, but any reading of the *ālaya-vijñāna* as an ontologically discrete and enduring entity would be incompatible with the overall Yogācāra vision.

Earlier scholarship on Yogācāra appeared to suggest that its radical emphasis on the mind really entailed a denial of the existence of the external world. A.K. Chatterje, for instance, claimed that the *Lankavatara Sūtra* contained fully 'idealistic teachings', upholding the sole reality of consciousness and denying the existence of the external world (Chatterje 1962, 37). David Kalupahana echoed this claim and found the same kind of radical idealism in the writings of Asaṅga (Kalupahana 1976, 24-36). Murti's *The Central Philosophy of Buddhism* claims that the fundamental difference between Madhyamaka and Yogācāra is that the former explained everything away as illusory – especially in its *prasaṅgika* form – whereas the latter affirmed the continued existence of the intellectual basis that made these illusions possible (Murti 1980, 54-70). The epistemological vision of the *Mahāyānasaṃgraha*, however, appears to undergird a different ontology: spiritual practice enables the overturning of our cognitive basis and the emergence of a supermundane, non-conceptualizing wisdom, but this does not eliminate the distinction between internal seeds and external stimuli. In other words, awakening marks the cessation of mistaken beliefs about the material world, but it does not entail a denial of its existence.

---

5   See again Williams, *Mahāyāna Buddhism*, 109-119. In Tibet, the debate between the *rang stong* and the *gzhan stong* school hinged on the ontological status of the *tathāgatagarbha*: the former school affirmed the radical emptiness of the Buddha nature, whereas the latter veered in the direction of an ontologically stronger reading, where critics found theistic overtones.

A Christian Approach

The worldview of the Desert Fathers of Egypt, who lived and wrote between the fourth and the sixth century of the Common Era, is of course very different from the speculative vision of these Yogācāra authors. Once the Roman persecutions ceased, fervent Christians who could no longer aspire to martyrdom chose to leave the cities behind, move to the deserts of Egypt and Palestine, and embrace the so-called 'white martyrdom' of asceticism – as opposed to the 'red martyrdom' of blood. Some recent authors such as the Romanian scholar, Dumitru Stăniloae, present the spirituality of the Desert Fathers as part of a linear trajectory of development, which culminates in the classic theology of deification articulated by authors such as Maximos the Confessor (580-662 CE) or later Gregory Palamas (1296-1359 CE) (Stăniloae 2003, 36). This approach to spiritual theology envisages the transformation of the individual as following, albeit in an imperfect manner, the pattern of the hypostatic union – the mystery of the incarnation of the Son of God: while the second person of the Trinity assumed the human nature we all share and invested it with the properties of his divinity, our humanity can, through the practice of contemplation and the virtues, acquire some of the properties of the divine nature.

This manualist approach, however, glosses over a significant plurality of schools of thought, some of which would be absorbed by the mainstream, while others would be condemned as heretical. As the Russian émigré scholar, John Meyendorff outlined in his work *Christ in Eastern Christian Thought*, early Christian spirituality was a far more polyphonic reality – indeed, one whose harmonies could be quite dissonant, as different groups articulated their distinctive understandings of the goal and purpose of Christian practice in radically divergent ways, reflecting their specific cosmology, anthropology and soteriology (Meyendorff 1975, 47-69; 113-131). If the incarnational theology inaugurated by Cyril of Alexandria (376-444 CE), who elaborated a conceptual formulation of the relationship between Christ's divinity and humanity, would become normative in the centuries to come, there was a wholly distinct theological strand in the early church that was deeply influenced by the gnostic currents within Neo-Platonism, and developed a very idiosyncratic soteriology (McGuckin 2004, 3-32). It is in the writings of the Origenist authors, collected in the first volume of the *Philokalia*, an anthology of monastic writers that was edited by Nikodemos the Hagiorite and Makarios of Corinth in the late eighteenth century, that contemporary readers can find an entrée into this alternative spiritual vision.

The extant writings of Evagrios Pontikos, which open up the *Philokalia*'s first volume, are not systematic treatises in the style of Origen's *De Principiis*; rather, they are written as collections – or 'centuries' – of short sayings that can be read day after day as a guide to individual monastic practice. While Evagrios had personally known Gregory of Nazianzos in Constantinople and had likely attended the council of 381 that had affirmed the classical doctrine of the Trinity, little of the mainstream Christological and Trinitarian theology that was being developed in the empire's great urban centres is actually present in treatises such as the *153 texts on Prayers*, or the *Teaching on Asceticism and Stillness* (Palmer, Sherrard & Ware 1983, 31-37; 55-71). The main intellectual source for these works was the lived practice of the Desert Fathers of Egypt, where Evagrios spend the last, but also the most intellectually fruitful, decade of his life, as well as the teaching of Origen of Alexandria (ca. 185-256 CE), who had lived over a century earlier, but whose legacy, while contested, continued to inform monastic spirituality. It should be remembered that Origen had actually not written his works for a monastic readership; rather, he had run a theological academy much in the style of the classical philosophical schools, and his work had been largely exegetical and speculative. After the emergence of monasticism as an important ecclesial and indeed socio-cultural phenomenon, Origenism enjoyed a revival in ascetic circles, leading to the appropriation and the creative reinterpretation of Origen's reading in a way that suited a monastic audience (Daniélou 2016, 296-309).

Origen's cosmology wove together different strands that find a coherent and comprehensive expression in his treatise, *De Principiis*. In line with a broad Neoplatonic sensitivity, but also echoing the teaching of most gnostic schools no less than the Manichean distinction between a material and a spiritual creation, Origen's vision distances itself from the letter of Genesis to postulate an initial noetic creation where no ontological distinction is drawn between the Godhead – an all-encompassing noetic insight – and a plethora of rational beings or *logikoi*. Such undifferentiated noetic reality would then undergo fragmentation, or a 'mystical moulting' – the reason for such an event always remaining clothed in mystery – and this fragmentation would then lead to the emergence of the created order as we know it, with a spiritual as well as a material component. Origen's hierarchy of rational beings ranges from the angels at the top all the way to the demons at the bottom, going through the spirits that move constellations and human beings that inhabit the earth. The boundaries between these categories are fluid and it is quite clear that an individual *logikos* may move from one to another; what characterizes them is their degree of 'thickness' (*pachytēs*), which grows the further they move away from the deity. Origen's ambiguity on the question of metempsychosis is probably deliberate, but, in the broader Origenist tradition, the possibility of reincarnation, and indeed, of a human's possible reincarnation as an angel, or vice-versa, was openly affirmed by many, in defiance of what appears to be the literal meaning of the Jewish and Christian scriptures (Daniélou 2016, 209-220).

The anthropological vision sketched above has distinctive epistemological implications, as well as implications for spiritual practice, both of which are explored at some length in Evagrios's writings. Evagrios views every individual as a *nous* that has fallen into a bodily prison, and is struggling to return to its original condition in the embrace of the divine intellect. Spiritual practice is a preparation for the eventual restoration of eternal unity, and the attainment of *apatheia* is an instance of realized eschatology: the reconfiguration of one's inner life enables one to foretaste in this life what we are destined to experience at the end of time (Ramelli 2015, xlviii-lix). The *exitus-reditus* narrative that under-girds Evagrios's vision views the *nous* as 'growing' a passionate appendix (*pathētikon*) to bridge the gap between itself and the body; the *nous* and the *pathētikon* together constitute the soul, which guides the body in the course of this earthly life. At the end of time, this process is gradually reversed: while, after being sep-arated in death the body and the soul are reunited in a first resur-rection, Evagrios appears to hint that, at the end of time, there will be a final annihilation of the world of corporeality and multiplic-ity, and the *nous* will shed the passions and emerge from the body like a chrysalis, to finally drown in the primordial henad (Ramelli 2015, lxxvii-lxxxi). In other words, the *nous* is the engine of the creative process, but, like the *ālaya-vijñāna*, it is also its rem-edy. The lower and higher passions should not seek to climb the mountain of the *nous*: hence the injunction in Exodus 19, 12-13 to stone to death all cattle (the higher, socially oriented passions) and wild animals (their lower, self-oriented counterpart) that had touched Mount Sinai.

The purpose of Evagrios's writings in the *Philokalia*, as well as the more esoteric treatise *Kephalaia Gnostika*, which survives only in two Syriac translations, is to offer a map for the spiritual journey of the practitioner who seeks to gradually emerge from the clutches of the passions and restore the original purity of the *nous* (Ramelli 2015, xlviii-lix) The practice of the virtues pro-vides the first stage in the restructuring of the inner life, which is the first step for more advanced inner work. This is the mo-ment when the practitioner has to engage in discernment of spirits (*diakrisis pneumatōn*), exploring whether a suggestion or thought is of demonic or angelic origin. The Evagrian tradition would de-velop a sophisticated armoury to help practitioners discern the or-igin of their thoughts, emphasizing that while all knowledge starts in sensory perception – in line with the Aristotelian tradition – hu-man beings relate to the natural order in a manner that is coloured by our memories of past action: indeed, all past actions leave an imprint in the intellect that is destined to come to fruition at some point in the future. If one is subject to temptation (*prosbolē*), and one begins to entertain (*syndesmos*) this thought in one's mind, one puts oneself in danger of falling into serious sin, but what marks the threshold between guiltless intellectual suggestion and actual sinfulness is 'assent' (*synkatathesis*), when the practitioner chooses to heed the demonic suggestion, fully knowing its evil origin, and makes oneself guilty in the eyes of God. The danger is, of course, that this will lead to the development of a habit of sin, which starts with prepossession (*prolēpsis*) – the presence of past sins in the mind – and ends with what is a full-fledged passion (*pathos*) (Palmer, Sherrard & Ware 1983, 31-37).

As one progresses along the spiritual path, outer sensations and ordinary thoughts will calm down, while all other impulses and passions that one has developed over one's whole lifetime will gradually come to the surface. The hesychastic tradition will talk about 'phantasies' (*phantasiai*), which again can be of demonic origin and must be distinguished carefully from the work of the imagination. By way of contemplation (*theōria*) and the practice of the virtues (*praxis*), the *nous* is able to tame the passible part of the soul and induce a condition of inner detachment that is conducive to higher contemplation, where the fruits of the seeds of the passion no longer obstruct the intellect. The condition is known as *apatheia*, which does not indicate 'apathy', as an overly literal English translation may suggest, but the emergence of a *nous* that is free of passionate attachments (Ramelli 2015, lxxvii-lxxxi).

The achievement of *apatheia* does not entail a spiritualizing flight from the senses: indeed, the practitioner who has reached this stage is able to contemplate the natural order in a way that mimics the divine perspective; in other words, as a constellation of signs pointing towards the cosmos's final consummation in God. While Evagrios and his immediate followers tend to emphasize the imperturbable character of *apatheia*, later authors like Maximos the Confessor or Gregory Palamas would integrate the notion of *apatheia* in a broader understanding of practice, where the practice of the virtues is not merely preparatory to a condition of inner tranquillity, but is actually a sign that one has conquered one's passions and dwells in utter tranquillity. Since the practitioner who is *apathos* is ever ready to succour his brethren in need, one could even talk of an 'active *apatheia*' (Stăniloae 2003, 23-36).

For Evagrios, however, even the contemplation of the created order still falls short of the highest stage of contemplation, when one plunges into the mystery of the divine and shortly experiences in one's inner life that communion with God's noetic reality that will be the destiny of all rational beings at the end of time. In the *153 Texts on Prayer*, Evagrios warns us of using images in the highest levels of mental prayer, noting that if we come to see a form or shape in our mind and convince ourselves that that is the deity, we can be certain that this thought is of demonic origin, because the deity has no quantity or form (Palmer, Sherrard & Ware 1983, 55-71). Clearly, the theology of the sacred image that would become such an important marker of Eastern Christian spirituality was yet to come; and certainly there is no room here for an Ignatian theology of the imagination – even if, parenthetically, Ignatius's reflection on the discernment of spirits in the appendix to the spiritual exercises is clearly indebted to Evagrian thought through its appropriation by John Cassian and the Benedictine tradition (Wieck 2009). Some argue that this may have been due to fears of lingering pagan tendencies among the monks of the Egyptian deserts – after all, the theriomorphic character of Egyptian religion had encouraged the production of images of the deities in all shapes and sizes – but while there may be an element of truth in this supposition, this radically aniconic construal of the highest stage of practice dovetails with Origen's overall cosmology, where the very existence of plurality and embodiment is a flaw that has to be overcome (Clark 2014, 43-85).

The role of Christ in this particular spiritual approach is certainly not that of the Son of God offering himself in an expiatory sacrifice to the Father; and in fact, even the classical *Christus victor* Christology, focussing on Christ's defeat of death and the devil in the resurrection, is not yet present in Evagrian thought.

At the same time, the teaching of Christ provides the basis for the practice of spiritual discernment. According to Evagrios, Christ is the one who achieves a radical reordering of his passions and fully subjects them to the power of the intellect. It is thus his teaching, rather than the manner of his death and return to life, that carries the most important soteriological meaning. According to Evagrios's *Kephalaia Gnostika*, which contains his most audacious theoretical speculations, every *logikos* is ultimately identical in dignity with Christ, even if our attachments have obscured this awareness in us. Once we achieve *apatheia* and turn towards the Godhead, we can recover an original insight into our true nature, which eventually will be uncovered when we leave behind the shackles of the flesh (Ramelli 2015, lxxvii-lxxxi). Meyendorff uses the term isochristism to indicate this teaching – one which was, of course, incompatible with the understanding of the incarnation elaborated some fifty years after Evagrios's demise, and which eventually, by the mid-sixth century, contributed to the condemnation of his spiritual vision (Meyendorff 1987, 47-69).

Dialogue

This conversation between two distinct religious traditions uncovers intriguing points of contact between the traditions of Yogācāra and the tradition of the Desert Fathers, despite their distinct underlying assumptions about anthropology, cosmology and the nature of ultimate reality. Evagrios's speculative system finds itself halfway between the cosmology and anthropology of the *Mahāyānasaṃgraha* and the full-fledged incarnational paradigm of Chalcedon. One may, of course, wonder how the tradition of Christian metaphysics would have evolved if this school of thought had become normative; the resulting Christology would have led to a significantly different understanding of the incarnation and of the salvific work of Christ. This, however, would be a different conversation. For the purposes of our discussion, we can conclude that both the Evagrian *nous* and Asaṅga's *ālaya-*

vijñāna serve as springboard for the emergence of the cosmic order, as receptacles and ontological support for human agency, and as engines behind a process that one might call transformative or redemptive. *Apatheia* and *āśrayaparāvṛtti* encapsulate a soteriological vision, where inner tranquillity is the starting point for engaged action on behalf of all *logikoi* or sentient beings. Yet, for Evagrios this epistemic trajectory also entails a real ontological transformation of the subject's inner life, whereas in Asaṅga it uncovers a pre-existent ground of purity, which later authors like Paramārtha, or many representatives of the Tibetan tradition, unlike the earlier Yogācārins, would identify with the *tathāgatagarbha*. Similarly, the monastic tradition of the Desert Fathers presupposes a universe whose temporal arc stretches from an intentional creative act to a final eschatological transformation, whereas the world of the *Mahāyānasaṃgraha* rests in the endless flux of co-dependent origination. Finally, independently of one's take on the ontological status of the *ālaya-vijñāna*, the latter transcends and dissolves the conventional notion of individual subjectivity in a way that the Evagrian *nous* can only do as the universe moves towards an eschatological horizon.

Bibliography

Bhattacharya, ed., 1957. *Yogācārabhūmi of Asaṅga*. Calcutta: University of Calcutta Press.

Chatterjee, Aśok Kumar, 1962. *Yogācāra Idealism*. Varanasi: Banaras Hindu University.

Clark, Elizabeth A., 2014. *The Origenist Controversy: The Cultural Construction of an Early Christian Debate*. Princeton: Princeton University Press.

Daniélou, Jean, transl. Walter Mitchell, 2016. *Origen*. Eugene, OR: Wipf and Stock.

Evagrios Pontikos, 1983. *153 Texts on Prayer*. In *The Philokalia* Vol. 1, transls. G.E.H. Palmer, Philip Sherrard and Kallistos Ware. London: Farrar, Strauss and Giroux: 55-71.

Evagrios Pontikos, 1983. 'Outline Teachings on Asceticism and Stillness'. In *The Philokalia* Vol. 1, transls. G.E.H. Palmer, Philip Sherrard and Kallistos Ware. London: Farrar, Strauss and Giroux: 31-37.

Griffiths, Paul J., Noriaki Hakayama, John Keenan & Paul Swanson, 1989. *The Realm of Awakening: A Translation and Study of the Tenth Chapter of Asaṅga's Mahāyānasaṃgraha*. New York: Oxford University Press.

Guillaumont, Antoine, 1962. *Les* Kephalaia Gnostica *d'Evagre le Pontique, et l'Histoire de l'Origenisme chez les Grecs et chez les Syriens*. Paris: Seuil.

Kalupahana, David J., 1982 (1976). *Buddhist Philosophy: A Historical Analysis*. Honolulu: Hawai'i University Press.

Lamotte, E., 1935. 'L'Ālaya-vijñāna' (Réceptacle) dans la Mahāyānasaṃgraha (Chapter II)'. *Mélanges Chinois et Bouddhiques* 3: 169-225.

Lamotte, E., ed. and transl., 1935. *Saṃdhinirmocana Sūtra. L'Explication des mystères*. Louvain: Louvain University Press.

McGuckin, John, 2004. *Saint Cyril of Alexandria and the Christological Controversy*. Crestwood, NY: St. Vladimir's Seminary Press.

Meyendorff, John, 1987. *Christ in Eastern Christian Thought*. Crestwood, NY: St. Vladimir's Seminary Press.

Murti, T.R.V., 1980 (1955). *The Central Philosophy of Buddhism*. London: George Allen and Unwin.

Paul, Diana, 1982, 'The Life and Time of Paramārtha (499-569)'. *Journal of the International Association of Buddhist Studies* 5.1: 37-69.

Pruden, Leo M., transl., 1988. *Abhidharmakośabhāṣyam*. Berkeley: Asian University Press.

Ramelli, Ilaria L.E., ed., 2015. *Evagrius's* Kephalaia Gnostika: *A New Translation of the Unreformed Text from the Syriac*. Atlanta, GA: SBL Press.

Schmithausen, Lambert, 1987. *Ālaya-vijñāna: On the Origin and Early Development of a Central Concept*. Tokyo: International Institute for Buddhist Studies.

Stăniloae, Dumitru, 2003. *Orthodox Spirituality: A Practical Guide for the Faithful and a Definitive Manual for the Scholar*. Waymart, PA: St Tikhon's Seminary Press.

Waldron, William S., 1994. 'How innovative is the Ālayavijñāna?' *Journal of Indian Philosophy* 22: 199-258 (part 1); also (1995) 23: 9-51 (part 2).

Waldron, William S., 2003. *The Buddhist Unconscious: The ālaya-vijñāna in the Context of Indian Buddhist Thought*. London & New York: Routledge Curzon.

Wieck, Anthony, 2009. 'Discernment of spirits in Evagrios of Pontus and Ignatius of Loyola: a comparative study', unpublished STL dissertation, Jesuit School of Theology at Berkeley CA.

Williams, Paul, 2008². *Mahāyāna Buddhism: The Doctrinal Foundations*. New York: Routledge.

THEME 5:

MEDITATION AND ACTION
IN BUDDHISM AND CHRISTIANITY

Contemplative Practice, Social Analysis and Compassionate Action: Toward Integrating Aspects of Buddhist and Christian Epistemology

John Makransky

Abstract

This essay argues that effective compassionate action must address two kinds of human cause of suffering. The first kind, pointed to by Buddhist epistemology, are universal tendencies of misperception and mis-reaction, tendencies of delusion, greed and ill-will. The second kind of cause of suffering, pointed to by Christian liberation theologies, are socio-economic systems that incorporate individuals into structures of inequity that organize resources and ways of knowing in oppressive ways. Effective contemplative practice is essential to address the first cause of suffering: deluded misperception and reaction, since social analysis alone does not remove the pervasive and unconscious misperception that some persons matter more than others, a misperception that distorts anyone's attempt to build better social systems. Contemplative practices that deconstruct that delusive tendency can also empower human capacities of discernment, love, compassion, inner peace and responsiveness essential for effective work for social change. On the other hand, social analysis is essential to address the second cause of suffering, oppressive social structures, which promulgate systemic patterns of harm while socially conditioning individuals into the first cause of suffering, delusion, greed and ill-will. Contemplative practice that lacks social analysis may also prop up oppressive structures, by improving people's ability to tolerate, but not to challenge, those structures. The conclusion is that neither Buddhist epistemology nor Christian liberation epistemology alone, and neither contemplative practice nor social analysis alone, effectively addresses enough human made causes of suffering. Each must inform and empower the other to provide what is necessary for effective compassionate action.

Keywords: Buddhist epistemology, Christian epistemology, liberation theology, social ethics, social justice, contemplative practice, Buddhist-Christian dialogue, comparative theology

Introduction

I will define compassion here as an empathetic, caring concern for suffering beings that motivates action to free them from the causes of the suffering. My focus here is on human-made causes of suffering. What are those causes? Classical Buddhist traditions and modern Christian liberation theologies focus on different root causes of suffering as the basis for a compassionate response.

Buddhism has traditionally focussed on psychological causes of suffering in individuals: deluded perception, greed, ill will and their karmic effects. Buddhist compassionate action, then, seeks to free people from those mental causes of suffering, by imparting practices that undercut them. Christian liberation theology, drawing on the prophetic traditions of Judaism and Christianity, focusses on oppressive social systems as primary causes of suffering (social sin), and on methods of social-historical analysis to empower people to liberate themselves from those systems.

Each tradition says we remain largely unconscious of the primary cause of suffering that it identifies unless we adopt the epistemology that it offers—Buddhist methods to become aware of oppressive patterns of mind that contrast with enlightened mind, or Christian methods to become newly aware of sinful social structures that contrast with God's kingdom. This essay will argue that neither Buddhist epistemology nor Christian liberation epistemology alone are sufficient to identify enough man-made causes of suffering, and that neither contemplative practice nor social analysis and activism alone are enough to address those causes. Each of these traditions, and each of these modes of practice, must inform the other to provide what is needed for effective compassionate action.

(1) Definition of the person

For what follows, I need first to define what is meant here by 'person'. To do so, I will draw on some threads of Indian Mahāyāna and Tibetan Buddhism. I define the person here as awareness embodied, embodied subjectivity. A person's basic awareness is the pre-conceptual basis in consciousness for all of her thoughts, perceptions, emotions, feelings, intentions and attitudes. One's basic awareness thus encompasses the person as a whole, not just one aspect or part. This awareness, as the basis of all contents of experience, is, in itself, primordial, unconstructed, unconfined, open to an unlimited horizon, insubstantial (empty) and cognizant. Harmful patterns of thought and reaction in persons arise out of this basic awareness, from one's conditioning or cultivation. But this basic awareness also possesses a great underlying capacity for positive powers of mind and heart (sometimes referred to as Buddha nature) — such as love, empathy, compassion, inner peace and freedom, deep discernment, joy, gratitude, energy and creative responsiveness, which can be cultivated to ever-increasing power, inclusiveness and unconditionality. The tremendous positive potential of each person's awareness gives each individual great dignity and worth.

This understanding of persons as embodied awareness or subjectivity is a Buddhist way of establishing what Christians call a theological anthropology—the understanding that all human beings possess a great dignity, worth and potential given in the ground of their being, although it is obscured by self-centred patterns of thought and reaction that are individually and socially conditioned. In the Buddhist traditions I draw from, this basis of unconditional worth and potential in persons is called primordial awareness (Tibetan *rigpa*, Sanskrit *vidyā*), Buddha nature (T. de bzhin gshegs pa'i snying po; S. *tathāgata-garbha*), the deep nature mind (T. *sems nyid*, S. *cittatvam*) or obscured suchness (T. dri bcas de bzhin nyid; S. *samala tathatā*) (Makransky 2007, 34-35; Tsoknyi Rinpoche 1998, 37-38, 43, 226; Longchen Rabjam 1998, 37; Ray 2001, 267-268; Ray 2000, 421-422, 434-435; Wellwood 2002, 157, 165, 238). In Christian theology, various interpretations of the image of God in human beings (*imago dei*) support diverse theological anthropologies, some of which can be seen as analogous to the Buddhist anthropology I am using here. The theological anthropology of Karl Rahner is resonant with my Buddhist understanding of the person, in Rahner's assertion that there is a pre-thematic, unobjectified level of awareness in human beings that is the primordial basis of all their conscious activities, and which opens to an infinite horizon, manifest in the unlimited human urge toward greater knowledge, love and freedom (Rahner 1974, 154-156; Carr 1995, 21-22; Johnson 2007, 33-37, 41-42).

The implication of this kind of Buddhist or Rahnerian anthropology is that persons have an unconditional worth and potential given in the ground of their being, which transcends any reductive labels or concepts that we may have of them. This anthropology also lends itself to the existential terminology that the philosopher Martin Buber employed. We tend, from our conditioning, to relate to others within a framework that Buber called 'I-It', reacting to others as objects of our own need or use, as tools to an end. If we become attuned to the fuller reality of persons as embodied awareness endowed with great dignity and potential, we would relate to them as what Buber called 'I-Thou', as subjects rather than reductive objects, as ends in themselves, beings who transcend all of our self-centred measures of their worth (Buber 1970, 53-68).

(2) A core human problem: the pervasive habit of misperception that contributes to all human-made suffering

In this section, I will continue to draw mainly on Buddhism, especially areas of Buddhist epistemology. What I said above implies that the fundamental identity of persons, their personhood, should not be identified either with our limited thoughts of them nor with their limited thoughts of themselves. The basic identity of persons is their fundamental embodied awareness, possessed of great dignity, worth and capacity, from which all thoughts, emotions and reactions arise according to conditioning or cultivation. Yet we do not routinely perceive or sense everyone around us in their basic identity as beings of great dignity, worth and potential. If we did, we would naturally respond to them all with reverence, care and compassion.

Instead, from their conditioning, our minds tend to label everyone in reductive ways, then to mistake our own reductive thoughts of the persons for the persons, thereby impeding our underlying capacity for more stable and inclusive attitudes of care and compassion toward them all. At the root of this deluded tendency is the mind's unease with the insubstantial nature of its being, which is impermanent, empty of substance, inter-dependent with all, and thus unlimited, unbounded. The mind's fear of its insubstantial and unbounded nature generates a compulsive urge to think up a self that would feel bounded, substantial, and thereby secure; the thought of self as a seeming refuge from the frighteningly insubstantial and unlimited nature of reality as it is. But this thought of a substantial self, per se, is just an ephemeral thought. So the mind, in its attempt to make passing thoughts of self seem substantial, strings the thoughts together into a chain, thereby sustaining the impression of a narrowly delimited, unchanging self. The mind thus *reifies* its limited thoughts of self, mistaking them for one's full personhood. Correlated with this reified construction of self, the mind also reifies its thoughts of everyone else, mistaking its thoughts of them *for them*. In this way, the mind continually categorizes everyone into in-groups that support its current construct of self and out-groups that do not, routinely re-acting to persons as reductive objects of possessiveness, apathy or ill-will, as what Buber called 'I-It' (Gethin 1998, 147; Gross in Gross & Reuther 2001, 110-111; Makransky 2007, 103-107).

There is nothing wrong with thoughts of self and others, *if* they are recognized *as* limited thoughts that do not capture anyone's full being or personhood. Such thoughts help organize the ele-ments of our experience so we can carry out our functions in so-ciety. But when the mind *reifies* its reductive thoughts of self and others, it does not recognize them *as* thoughts. Instead, the mind takes a few qualities that it has attributed to a person, totalizes them as the entire person under a conceptual label, and thereby reduces the person to one reductive label of her. We thus routinely mistake our own limited labels of others, in the moment, for their *whole personhood*: 'just a janitor', 'just an old guy', 'just a girl', 'just one of those people (in some out-group)'. We then react to our reductive representation of the person as if it *were* the person, which hides their fuller being, life experience, dignity and mys-tery from us (Dalai Lama 1999, 36, 41, 94, 108-110). In authentic moments of loving connection, we momentarily commune with others in their fuller personhood, sensing them in their dignity and worth as I-Thou. Yet, much more than we are conscious, we almost continually relate to others as I-It, mistaking our reductive labels for the persons, thereby impeding our underlying capac-ity to commune with their fuller personhood from our own fuller personhood.

Again, this pervasive tendency of deluded perception is based in the mind's continual attempt to establish a substantial self out of insubstantial thoughts of self. Life conditioned by this habit is a struggle, because each situation feels like it must be interpreted to establish the concreteness of a self that is actually just a se-ries of ephemeral thoughts. Buddhist psychology calls this con-tinual, unconscious, self-centred struggle the 'suffering of condi-tioned reaction' (*samskāra-dukhatā*). And this supports a second level of suffering called the 'suffering of transience' (*pariṇāma dukhatā*). The suffering of transience is felt in the mind's attempt to find firm ground by grasping at transient phenomena—material goods, pleasant experiences, pleasant people, and so forth—as if such things could provide lasting safety and well-being for the concrete self, which they can never provide, since they do not last, and since there is no such concrete self (Makransky 1997, 161-162).

The social psychologist, Ernest Becker identified this urge to flee from our mortality as a central motivation for the tendency of societies to inflict suffering on masses of vulnerable people. Roberto Goizueta, a Catholic liberation theologian, has elaborated on Becker's point:

> [The] need to deny our mortality…is what drives us to construct personal identities, social institutions, ideologies and belief systems that can make us feel invulnerable and ultimately invincible… [This] process ultimately deals death, to…others against whom the individual must assert his or her singular invulnerability…we run from weak, powerless, vulnerable, [and] wounded persons in particular, for they especially threaten our sense of invulnerability. They are the mirrors of our own souls, whose very existence threatens our sense of invulnerability, security, and control. (Goizueta 2009, 15-17)

Traditional Buddhism explains the mind's reified misperceptions of persons, including its attempt to create an invulnerable self, as a root cause of suffering for that individual. But the same habit of deluded perception can also be viewed, from perspectives of social psychology and liberation theology, as a fundamental cause of social suffering, contributing to systemic structures of inequity and injustice, by directing resources and opportunities to oneself and one's in-groups, misperceived as the only ones truly worthy of care. From our social conditioning, we misperceive each other according to social location as I-It more than we notice, generating causes of suffering not only in individual relationships but also in our ways of organizing wealth and power. When each of us is unable routinely to sense all persons in their unconditional worth as I-Thou, how could we possibly create societies in which we actually treat all others as if they had great dignity and worth?

How could such an ideal be realized when, in our daily lives, we so little feel it?

(3) Why effective contemplative practice is needed to address this pervasive problem of misperception

Social analysis and activism alone do not address the pervasive habit of misperception described above. A contemplative discipline is needed to expose how much our reductive thoughts have hidden the fuller identity of persons from us, as beings of great dignity, worth and potential; as Thou. When working for social justice, we may think we avoid reductive ways of perceiving others by standing in solidarity with the oppressed. Yet, the same delusive tendency of perception is generally still operative, restricting the scope of our care, so we view the oppressed as the ones worthy of care and their oppressors as lesser beings, unworthy of care. To view one group as more fully human than the other in this way, and to 'choose sides', is to replicate the epistemology of oppression in the name of opposing it, by maintaining the perspective that some persons matter and others do not.[1]

The problem is not just that we lose the fuller personhood of 'oppressors' when we mistake our reductive label of them for the persons, nor that each of us is also an oppressor in ways that are not fully conscious to us. The larger problem is that when we perceive and feel one group as worthy of care and another group as not, we reinforce our underlying tendency to mistake *everyone* for our own reductive labels of them. If we stay committed to a relationship of I-It with regard to some people, the 'oppressors', the basic framework of I-It remains in place, unrecognized and unchallenged, narrowing our perception of everyone else and affecting our actions toward them.

---

1   For further Buddhist arguments against the tendency among Christian liberation and other social activists to frame their work for justice as 'choosing sides', see Nhat Hanh 1987, 70; Nhat Hanh 1995, 79-81; Knitter 2009, 173-174, 205-207; Makransky 2014, 641-644.

This deluded habit of misperception is not solved by social analysis or activism alone, because the mind that engages in social analysis is the same mind that unconsciously mistakes everyone included in its analysis for its reductive thoughts of them, perpetuating habits of misperception that exclude many from genuine care and compassion, even when we think we are working for social justice. When those of us seeking to dismantle oppressive social systems remain unconsciously identified with our own patterns of deluded perception, those patterns become woven into whatever new social system we may create (Knitter 2009, 200). In recent history, this has been evident, for example, in the actions of communist regimes of Russia, China, Cambodia and Eastern Europe, which came into power under high ideals of social equity, then instituted death-dealing policies against masses of people whose lives held little value within the new regime.

Another sign that this basic habit of misperception is operative when we work for social change is how often dysfunctional rage and anger are experienced by social justice activists, anger that lacks awareness of its own tendencies of misperception. Many social justice activists report that, over time, they become caught in recurrent feelings of painful rage and anger, making it difficult to work effectively or to attract support, often contributing to burnout (Gross in Gross & Reuther 2001, 181; Knitter 2009, 175; Makransky 2016, 89-90). Such dysfunctional anger is supported by the habit of reification and misperception described above, which triggers endless reactions to our own fragmented images of ourselves and others. Such reactive habits of anger, in themselves, lack any means to stay in touch with the fuller humanity and potential of everyone involved, especially those who oppose our positions. Such habits prevent us from accessing our fuller capacities for discernment, more inclusive care, inner replenishment, inspiration and energy (Dass & Gorman 1985, 159-160).

By pointing out this tendency to mistake our reductive thoughts of persons for the persons, I am not arguing against the need to confront oppressive social systems and behaviours. Rather, to confront such things effectively we need a kind of knowing that can maintain awareness of the fuller personhood of everyone involved, including those we may confront, and for this a contemplative practice is essential. The Buddhist epistemology I draw on here assumes that there is much to be confronted in persons—all their ways of thinking and acting that are harmful to themselves and others. But in the moment that we confront others out of anger, even supposedly righteous anger, we tend not to sense their deep dignity and human potential beyond the single, reified image that our anger has made of them. And to declare our anger 'righteous' does nothing to correct that error.

For this reason, the power to confront harmful persons in many traditional Buddhist stories is understood as a fierce form of compassion rather than any ordinary form of anger. This is exemplified in stories of bodhisattva figures that fiercely confront an individual or group, out of compassion for all involved, and is also imaged in wrathful tantric Buddhist images of enlightenment. Fierce compassion is a power forcefully to confront someone who thinks and acts harmfully, *both* on behalf of those he harms *and* on behalf of his own underlying potential, his fuller personhood or Buddha nature.[2]

For effective work for social change that is motivated by fierce compassion rather than dysfunctional forms of anger, we need a practice that helps us distinguish *the person* as embodied awareness, endowed with unconditional worth and capacity, from that person's *habits of thought and action*, many of which may be destructive. Such a practice must also distinguish the person from our own reductive thoughts of him or her, revealing the contrast between I-It and I-Thou, not only as a matter of belief at a superficial level of consciousness but as a way of knowing from a deeper

---

2   On fierce compassion as a Buddhist principle of confrontation, see Chogyam Trungpa Rinpoche 1975, 21; Tsang Nyon Heruka 1995, xix-l; Makransky 2007, 179-185; Makransky 2016, 89-95. This principle is depicted in many stories where a Buddhist teacher fiercely challenges his disciples or the larger community, as in several of the Zen stories in Rep 1957 and in stories from Tibet in Surya Das 1992. Fierce compassion as confrontation also takes form as social criticism in Buddhist cultures, e.g. Paltrul Rinpoche 1994, 204-209, 354.

level of consciousness.[3] What I am calling 'fierce compassion' is also exemplified in how Christian figures like Martin Luther King, Archbishops Desmond Tutu and Oscar Romero, Dorothy Day and Thomas Merton upheld unconditional love as a fierce power of resistance to oppressive structures and regimes. Such a fierce, confronting care for everyone involved, a care that includes both 'oppressed' and 'oppressors', is only possible if it expresses a de-reifying wisdom rather than a reifying anger. And to realize such a de-reifying awareness requires an effective contemplative practice.

An effective contemplative practice is a practice that makes our almost continual deluded misperception of persons newly conscious, by introducing a perspective that transcends the misperception, so it can be newly recognized *as deluded* by contrast with a way of knowing that is not. Such a transcendental perspective, in Buddhist terms, is called de-reifying wisdom (*nirvikalpa-jñāna*), a kind of knowing that releases us from identification with our reductive, reified thoughts of persons to sense them in their fuller personhood and mystery, in their Buddha nature. A central purpose of Buddhist practice, then is to empower this kind of transcendental, de-reifying awareness in order to be liberated from our identification with reductive, deluded perceptions of self and others that have led to countless harmful actions and sufferings, in order to sense everyone more fully in their primal dignity and potential, their fuller personhood. And I would argue that some means of cultivating de-reifying awareness must inform any attempt to work against social injustice, if we are to avoid the habits of misperception that contribute to the dynamics of injustice itself.

In Buddhist terminology, the heart of contemplative awakening occurs in the moment when the cognizant aspect of our awareness glimpses the *emptiness* of all its reified perceptions. In that moment, awareness now recognizes its deluded habit of misperception as delusion, by seeing how it mistook its labels of beings for the beings, and by sensing that there is a fuller depth and mystery

---

3   This is exemplified in Roshi Glassman's response to Paul Knitter in Knitter 2009, 173: 'You won't be able to stop the death squads [in El Salvador] until you realize your oneness with them.'

to them all that transcends the delusion. To realize emptiness thus provides a space of freedom for the mind's cognizance to express more all-inclusively and unconditionally its underlying capacities for love, compassion, discernment and creative responsiveness, which can be cultivated to increasing strength and stability.[4]

Buddhist practitioners engage in many kinds of mutually supportive practice to help liberate their awareness from its habit of identifying with its reified misperceptions, in order to sense and respond to persons in their fuller personhood (their Buddha nature), as beings unconditionally worthy of care and compassion. Practitioners study and reflect on the epistemological causes of suffering, the possibility of transcending them, and various ways of doing so, such as through meditations of calm abiding (*samatha*) and penetrating insight (*vipaśyanā*). Such meditations help practitioners access meditative absorptions of de-reifying insight into the emptiness of all reified perceptions. Devotional practices of reverence, offering, repentance and purification position practitioners before a communal field of buddhas, bodhisattvas or other enlightened figures. This field of enlightened beings blesses and empowers the practitioner to learn to join them in their enlightened activity to liberate beings, and ultimately to merge with them in the empty awareness of enlightenment (*dharmakāya*) that is primordially undivided from the practitioner and from all other beings in their Buddha nature. Ethical guidelines and practices discourage harmful attitudes and actions that flow from reductive misperceptions of beings, while encouraging attitudes and actions of generosity and compassion that help a practitioner's awareness become less identified with those misperceptions, instead to recognize and compassionately respond to beings in their fuller personhood, their Buddha nature.[5]

---

4   In Mahāyāna Buddhist terms, this synergistic cultivation of insight into emptiness together with cultivations of all-inclusive love, compassion and associated capacities comprises the path of enlightenment.

5   For informative summaries of these diverse kinds of Buddhist practice, and ways that they inform each other, see e.g. Harvey 2013, 237-375; McMahan 2002, 143-174; Gregory 1986.

Such contemplative and ritual practices are prominent in Buddhist traditions, but Christian (and other theistic traditions) also provide practices that, from the Buddhist perspective above, can be seen also to help liberate the mind from its habitual identification with reductive misperceptions of beings by empowering responsiveness to their fuller personhood, as beings of great dignity, worth and potential.

As an example of de-reifying aspects of Christian practice, for brevity, I give one quote from a co-authored work by two contemporary theologians, Michael and Kenneth Himes, who relate theological understandings of poverty, creation and sacramental vision to Christian practice as a whole. The Himes's write,

> The only reason for anything to exist is the free agape of God... Utterly poor in itself, creation is divinely gifted. Thus, to see creation as a whole, or any particular creature, as what it is...is to see revealed the grace which is its foundation in being. [Thus,] everything is a sacrament of the goodness and creative power of God...The more richly developed our sacramental vision, the more sacraments crowd in upon us...The recognition of the other as...that which exists because it is loved by God, cannot occur where that other is regarded as 'it.' By its nature, a sacrament requires that it be appreciated for what it is, and not as a tool to an end, in Buber's terms, a sacrament is always a 'Thou.'... The whole of Catholic praxis is training in sacramental vision. Liturgy and social action, marriage and parenthood, prayer and politics, music...and the visual arts, all educate us to appreciate the other as sacramental, worthy companions of our poverty and our engracedness. [All such practices] teach us to see things as they are. (Himes & Himes 1993, 111-113)

According to the Himes's, a fundamental purpose of all Christian practice is to confront our idolatrous habit of falsely identifying beings with our limited impressions of them as I-It, so we can respond to them as I-Thou, as beings of great dignity and worth who transcend our reified, reductive perceptions of them.

In making this comparison, I am not arguing that Christian sacramental vision is the very same thing as the de-reifying wisdom cultivated by Buddhists. I am only pointing out that aspects of Christian practice also implicitly promote de-reifying ways of knowing in their own ways, at least to some degree. Other examples include the practices of liturgical communion and prayer that help incorporate worshippers into God's transcendental perspective and all-inclusive love, helping them recognize and respond to the dignity in all persons that transcends all reified, self-interested perceptions of them. Many other examples can be drawn from teachings attributed to Jesus, for example, 'You have heard it said, "You shall love your neighbour and hate your enemy." But I say to you, Love your enemies and pray for those who persecute you, so you may be children of your Father in heaven, who makes [the] sun rise on [both] the evil and the good…'. Jesus's words invite us to join him in a perspective that transcends our familiar reductive labels of 'neighbour' and 'enemy', the reified labels we have mistaken for the persons, by praying for the persons beyond the labels, possessed of great dignity and potential. Jesus thereby invites us into a kind of de-reifying awareness. (Matthew 5:45). Explicit forms of de-reifying analysis can also be found in various Christian contemplative writers, such as Thomas Merton, Meister Eckhardt, Nicholas of Cusa, the author of the *Cloud of Unknowing* and Jan Van Ruusbroec.

(4) What contemplative practice lacks if not informed by social analysis

I argued above that effective contemplative practice is necessary to confront the cause of suffering emphasized by Buddhist epistemology: the mind's deluded attempt to ground itself by reifying its reductive thoughts of persons, then mistaking its reified thoughts of persons for the persons, thereby routinely and unconsciously reacting to them as objects of greed, apathy and ill-will; as I-It instead of I-Thou. If this deluded perception is not newly revealed and addressed by an effective contemplative practice, any attempt to remake unjust social systems tends to replicate the delusion at the core of injustice—the mistaken view that some persons matter and others do not.

But the greed, apathy and ill-will that proceed from deluded perception take shape not only in individual minds but also in economic and political structures that unequally distribute resources and power, causing suffering to the poor and marginalized through policies that favour the few (Loy 2003, 164-167; Knitter 2009, 200). When we participate in inequitable systems without challenging their inequities, we contribute to the harm they cause, even when we do not consciously intend harm. Contemplation that makes us conscious only of our own habits of misperception, if not informed by the experience of people in other social locations, remains too little aware of the suffering effects of social systems upon many others.

Classical Buddhist karma theory focusses on actions with a conscious intention to harm others as the cause of harmful karmic effects. But, as Rita Gross argues, that traditional understanding can prevent Buddhists from questioning their participation in destructive social systems if they do not personally intend to do harm. For example, regarding patriarchal gender norms, Rita Gross has written: '…usually it is not an individual man who wants to cause me suffering by…limiting my options as a woman, but the male dominated system in which he participates, often without [conscious] intention to do harm' (Gross in Gross & Ruether 2001, 177). Or, regarding oppressive economic conditions, Paul Knitter has noted that a person might have a transformative meditation of love and compassion, then put on sneakers made by children in a foreign sweatshop and go for a run while remaining unaware of those children's sufferings.[6] In other words, through contemplative practice we may realize our relation to other individuals as I-Thou, yet participate in, and thereby support, social and economic arrangements that treat masses of individuals as I-It.

Christian liberation theology highlights this second order cause of suffering: oppressive social systems. I refer not just to liberation theologies that emerged in Latin America, but also to those that have taken shape in Asian, African, feminist and wom-

---

6   Personal communication.

anist theologies. Liberation theologians argue that the prophetic tradition of Judaism and Christianity discloses God's special attention to those who are oppressed, and God's fierce challenge to those who exploit them. This prophetic focus culminates in the Christian assertion that God chose, by incarnating in Jesus, to live among the marginalized and to undergo the ignominious death of the cross in oneness with society's non-persons. Jesus's life, death and resurrection reveal both the social sinfulness of the world, and the power of divine love and justice to help liberate the world from it.

It can be argued that, through its understanding of social sin, the prophetic tradition was the first so fully to reveal to human consciousness the destructive nature of oppressive social systems. In this way, the prophetic tradition can be viewed as foundational for all modern disciplines of critical social analysis. It could also be argued that the prophetic tradition, in part through Christian and Jewish social ethics and liberation theologies, has contributed to the very possibility of a modern, socially engaged Buddhism that critically addresses social problems.

Christian liberation theology contrasts with classical Buddhism in its ability to point rigorously and specifically to the suffering brought about by oppressive social systems.[7] This ability derives from a key part of its method, the 'hermeneutic privileging of the oppressed'. Although Buddhist texts describe rebirths of bodhisattvas in all realms of suffering from their compassion for beings, Buddhism has lacked liberation theology's 'preferential option for the poor', which foregrounds the experience of the oppressed and disinherited as the hermeneutic key to the social sinfulness of societies. For liberation theologians, it is the perspectives of the poor and marginalized that shine most light on

---

7   Early liberation theologies of Latin America have been criticized for their association with Marxist ideas and movements. I firmly reject authoritarian Communism as a social solution to problems of inequality, for reasons noted in section (3). But I argue here that liberation theology's laser-like focus on the experience of the marginalized and oppressed is crucially important to inform social ethical understanding and action.

the painful effects of oppressive systems, effects that go largely unnoticed by privileged groups. As Paul Knitter has noted, 'We tend to ignore those who suffer differently from us in order to avoid critically inquiring into the social systems that bring us so much benefit'.[8]

(5) Epistemology and action are mutually informing

Thus far I have argued that the epistemologies of both Buddhism and Christian liberation theology are necessary for effective action in the world. Conversely, action in the world is necessary to inform those epistemologies in ways that personal experience alone, or social analysis at a distance from others, cannot do. Taking action, in this context, means coming to know others in their human dignity and potential, learning from and empathizing with them in the specifics of their experience, and working with them for needed change. Action to address suffering also concretizes the doctrinal teachings of Buddhism and Christianity, and informs their contemplative and ritual practices in fundamental ways.

Within the Buddhist eight-fold path of enlightenment, for example, the three components of embodied action—right action, speech and livelihood—are understood to inform and be informed by every other component of the path, including right intention, view, mindfulness, effort and meditation (Gethin 1998, 81). Similarly, all six perfections of the Mahāyāna bodhisattva path arc understood to be included in each other, which means that embodied action in service to others, which involves the perfections of giving, altruism, patience and perseverance, is essential to inform the perfections of meditation and wisdom, and vice versa (Yangsi Rinpoche 2003, 360).

One thus learns through synergistic practice of contemplation and action to stay in touch with the emptiness of one's reified projections and with the Buddha nature of persons (I-Thou), even under trying conditions of service and action that would ordinar-

---

8   Personal note.

ily trigger reified I-It ways of reacting. Work with and for others is essential to inform empathy and compassion for them, to expose unconscious, self-protective, I-it habits of reaction that hide the fuller realities of self and others, to cut through those habits with de-reifying forms of practice, and to bring out capacities for enlightened action, including de-reifying wisdom, love, compassion, equanimity and creative responsiveness, in increasingly strong, inclusive and sustainable forms (Chodron 2001, 32, 48, 57-59, 102-103, 132-133). Yet the perspectives of the poor and marginalized are not foregrounded in classical Buddhist epistemology or action.

As noted, Christian liberation theology focusses more than classical Buddhism on systemic structures of oppression as the main cause of man-made suffering, which God, through the prophets, has called on humanity to take action to overturn. Therefore, social action is essential to reveal the meanings of God's love and justice for humanity in light of sinful social structures. Gustavo Gutierrez wrote:

> Participation [by action] in the process of liberation is an obligatory and privileged locus for Christian life and reflection. In this participation will be heard nuances of the Word of God which are imperceptible in other existential situations and without which there can be no authentic and fruitful faithfulness to the Lord. (Gutierrez 1988, 32)

Gutierrez also wrote:

> The annunciation of the Gospel…is made real and meaningful only by living and announcing the Gospel from within a commitment to liberation, only in concrete, effective solidarity with people and exploited social classes. Only by participating in their struggles can we understand the implications of the gospel message and make it have an impact on history. (Gutierrez 1988, 153)

Social action is thus essential for receiving God's ongoing revelation. To work in concrete ways for social justice as a Christian is to be tutored by God, through the Spirit of Christ in oneself and in the oppressed, in how to co-create God's Kingdom:

> Our conversion to the Lord implies [our] conversion to the neigh-
> bour...Conversion means a radical transformation of our selves;
> it means thinking, feeling and living as Christ—[who is also]
> present in exploited and alienated persons...To be converted is to
> know and experience the fact that, contrary to the laws of phys-
> ics, we can stand straight, according to the Gospel, only when our
> center of gravity is outside ourselves. (Gutierrez 1988, 118)

And as Lee Cormie wrote:

> An understanding of faith informed by the notion of praxis, such
> as that articulated by liberation theologians, insists that the activ-
> ity of God in shaping the content of faith includes the activity of
> believers, so that this action feeds back into their perception of
> the word of God. (Cormie 1978, 179)

Yet, specific attention to the habit, pointed out by Buddhism, of mistaking our own reductive impressions of everyone for the persons, virtually every moment, remains largely unnoticed in the writings of liberation theologians.

Action that entails coming to know and empathizing with others in the specifics of their experience reveals many aspects of the human condition and possibilities for positive change, which personal contemplation or social analysis alone do not reveal. To learn from and work with others in action is necessary for one's compassion to become knowledgeable in its care and empathy, more conscious of the personal and systemic causes of suffering, and more aware of creative possibilities for addressing those causes. Action is also necessary to deepen one's understanding, and embodiment, of the very meanings of Buddhahood or God's Spirit. Thus, both Buddhist and Christian traditions understand that their respective epistemologies and contemplative practices must be informed by action in the world. Yet what is missing in each tradition's epistemology in light of the other tradition is not fully corrected by action alone. Specific learning from the other tradition is also needed.[9]

---

9   My thanks to Robert Sharf and Paul Knitter, whose early feedback suggested
    I add a section on epistemology and action, which has become section (5).

(6) Conclusion: Buddhist and Christian liberation epistemologies need to be informed by each other for effective compassionate action

Buddhism points out unconscious, conditioned habits of misperception in individual minds, to be addressed by effective contemplative practice. Liberation theology points out unconscious habits of misperception conditioned by our locations in social systems, to be addressed by social analysis that privileges perspectives of the oppressed. Effective contemplative practice newly reveals the habit of reductive reification that is operative in our minds, which de-centres the reified self with its deadening framework of I-It, to open a space to recognize and creatively respond to persons as I-Thou. Social analysis that privileges the experience of the oppressed newly reveals the social inequities of history, thereby de-centring the dominant perspectives of powerful groups to open a space for creatively imagining more caring, compassionate institutions and policies (Cormie 1978, 168, 175).

If the tendencies of delusion, greed and ill-will in individuals, which are highlighted by Buddhism, are not confronted by effective contemplative practice, they keep taking expression in oppressive social systems that institutionalize apathy, greed and violence (even in the name of social revolution). If oppressive social structures, which are highlighted by Christian liberation theology, are not confronted with effective social analysis, they keep instilling tendencies of delusion, greed and ill-will into individuals by social conditioning, which inhibits everyone's ability to realize their fuller capacities of love, compassion and wisdom.[10]

Phrased another way: social analysis and activism that lack effective contemplative practice do not sufficiently uproot the delusive tendencies of individuals, tendencies that will continue

---

10 As Rosemary Radford Ruether has written: 'Structures of privilege and oppression, and our socialization into them, dim our awareness of our larger potential [for discernment, empathy, and social challenge]'. In Gross & Ruether 2001, 136.

to manifest in systemic forms. And contemplative practice and action that lack social analysis do not sufficiently uproot the systemic conditioning that reinforces those delusive tendencies in each individual. Indeed, it has been observed that contemplative practices like mindfulness, lacking social analysis, are being employed now in neo-liberal capitalist institutions, in part, to avoid addressing systemic problems in those institutions and in society, by enhancing the ability of workers to tolerate oppressive systems without providing the critical awareness and tools to challenge those systems (Purser 2015, 40-41).

In sum, individual forms of delusion, greed and ill-will have been the focus of Buddhism as the main cause of suffering, while systemic forms of delusion, greed and ill-will have been the focus of Christian liberation theology as the main cause of suffering. Yet both of these causes of suffering, individual and systemic, are mutually conditioning and mutually reinforcing. Neither can be adequately addressed unless the other is also addressed. This means that neither contemplative practice and action alone, nor social analysis and activism alone, are sufficient to address the world's man-made suffering. Each such practice must inform and empower the other. Another conclusion is that neither classical Buddhist epistemology nor Christian liberation epistemology alone are enough to inform effective compassionate action in the world. Both are needed to effectively address man-made suffering, and to illumine critical elements of the process toward individual and social awakening and liberation.

Bibliography

Buber, Martin, transl. Walter Kaufmann, 1970. *I and Thou.* New York: Charles Scribner's Sons.

Carr, Anne E., 1995. 'Starting with the Human'. In *A World of Grace: An Introduction to the Themes and Foundations of Karl Rahner's Theology*, ed. Leo J. O'Donovan. Washington, DC: Georgetown University: 17-30.

Chodron, Pema 2001. *Start Where You Are: A Guide to Compassionate Living*. Boston: Shambhala

Cormie, Lee, 1978. 'The Hermeneutic Privilege of the Oppressed'. *Catholic Theological Society of America Proceedings* 33: 155-181.

Dalai Lama, 1999. *Ethics for the New Millennium*. New York: Riverhead.

Dass, Ram & Paul Gorman, 1985. *How Can I Help?* New York: Alfred A. Knopf.

Gethin, Rupert, 1998. *The Foundations of Buddhism*. New York: Oxford University.

Gregory, Peter, 1986. *Traditions of Meditation in Chinese Buddhism*. Honolulu: University of Hawaii.

Gross, Rita & Rosemary Radford Reuther, 2001. *Religious Feminism and the Future of the Planet: A Buddhist-Christian Conversation*. New York: Continuum.

Guizueta, Roberto, 2009. *Christ Our Companion: Toward a Theological Aesthetics of Liberation*. Maryknoll, New York: Orbis.

Gutierrez, Gustavo, transls. & eds. Caridad Inda & John Eagleson, 1988. *A Theology of Liberation: History, Politics, and Salvation*. Maryknoll, NY: Orbis Books.

Harvey, Peter, 2013. *An Introduction to Buddhism: Teachings, History and Practices*. New York: Cambridge University.

Himes, Michael J. & Kenneth R. Himes, 1993. *Fullness of Faith: The Public Significance of Theology*. New York: Paulist.

Johnson, Elizabeth A., 2007. *Quest for the Living God: Mapping Frontiers in the Theology of God*. New York: Continuum.

Knitter, Paul F., 2009. *Without Buddha I Could Not Be A Christian*. Oxford: Oneworld.

Longchen Rabjam, 1998. *The Precious Treasury of the Way of Abiding*. Junction City, CA: Padma.

Makransky, John, 2007. *Awakening Through Love: Unveiling Your Deepest Goodness*. Boston: Wisdom.

Makransky, John, 2014. 'A Buddhist Critique of, and Learning from, Christian Liberation Theology'. *Theological Studies* 75.3: 635-657.

Makransky, John, 2016. 'Confronting the "Sin" out of Love for the "Sinner": Fierce Compassion as a Force for Social Change'. *Buddhist-Christian Studies* 36: 87-96.

McMahan, David L., 2002. *Empty Vision: Metaphor and Visionary Imagery in Mahāyāna Buddhism*. London: RoutledgeCurzon.

Nhat Hanh, Thich, 1987. *Being Peace*. Berkeley, CA: Parallax.

Nhat Hanh, Thich, 1995. *Living Buddha, Living Christ*. New York: Riverhead.

Patrul Rinpoche, 1994. *The Words of My Perfect Teacher*. San Francisco: HarperCollins.

Rahner, Karl, transl. David Bourke, 1974. 'The Experience of God Today'. In *Theological Investigations, Volume XI*. London: Darton, Longman and Todd: 149-165.

Ray, Reginald, 2001. *Secret of the Vajra World: The Tantric Buddhism of Tibet*. Boston: Shambhala.

Ray, Reginald, 2000. *Indestructible Truth: The Living Spirituality of Tibetan Buddhism*. Boston: Shambhala.

Reps, Paul, 1961. *Zen Flesh Zen Bones*. New York: Doubleday Anchor.

Surya Das, 1992. *The Snow Lion's Turquoise Mane: Wisdom Tales from Tibet*. San Francisco: Harper.

Trungpa Rinpoche, Chogyam, 1975. *Visual Dharma: The Buddhist Art of Tibet*. Berkeley, CA: Shambhala.

Tsang Nyon Heruka, transls. Nalanda Translation Committee, 1995. *The Life of Marpa the Translator*. Boston: Shambhala.

Tsoknyi Rinpoche, 1998. *Carefree Dignity: Discourses on Training in the Nature of Mind*. Boudhanath, Nepal: Rangjung Yeshe.

Wellwood, John, 2002. *Toward a Psychology of Awakening: Buddhism, Psychotherapy, and the Path of Personal and Spiritual Transformation*. Boston: Shambhala.

Yangsi Rinpoche, 2003. *Practicing the Path: A Commentary on the Lamrim Chenmo*. Boston: Wisdom.

MEDITATION AND ACTION
IN BUDDHIST-CHRISTIAN RELATIONS

Leo D. Lefebure

Abstract

The Christian spiritual tradition has long related the practice of prayer and work. Traditional Catholic meditation practice often involved careful listening to sacred texts and openness to transformation, and contemplation practice invited practitioners to rest quietly in God's presence without words. Benedictines, Franciscans, Dominicans, Carmelites and Jesuits related meditative practice to transformative action for others, include welcoming strangers, caring for the poor and sick, and protesting injustice in society. These traditions find many points of contact with Buddhist values and practices. Many Christians today include Buddhists texts and practices in their meditation and cooperate with Buddhists in acting for shared values in society. In his encyclical on ecology and care for the earth, Pope Francis draws upon the Catholic spiritual tradition of prayer and work, and appeals for interreligious dialogue and cooperation in responding to the ecological crisis.

Keywords: Meditation, contemplation, Benedictines, Franciscans, Dominicans, Carmelites, Jesuits, Pope Francis, hospitality, social justice, ecology

The Path of the Benedictines

I came to the venerable Abbey of Santa Maria de Montserrat, the location of the conference that inspired this publication, as a pilgrim accompanied by Buddhist and Christian companions. As I approached the threshold of the community of the sons of Benedict, I found a welcome inscribed in the *Rule of Benedict*, Chapter 53: 'All guests who present themselves are to be received as Christ, for He will say: *I was a stranger and you took me in* (Matthew 25:35)' (Benedict 1997, 121). Benedict explains and applies this rule in a way that reverses the priorities of our usual class consciousness, expressing a preferential welcome for the poor: 'In the reception of the poor and of pilgrims the greatest care and solicitude should be shown, because in them Christ is more especially received: For the very awe we have of the rich insures that they receive honor' (Benedict 1997, 123).

Many years ago as a college student in Europe, I unwittingly put this rule to the test by showing up unexpected on the threshold of the Abbaye Saint-Pierre de Solesmes, near Tours, France, on the afternoon of Holy Saturday, the most solemn time of the Catholic liturgical year. The guest master of the monastery told me honestly that if he had known I was coming, he would have told me not to come: every room was full and he could not house me. He went on to note that they had this provision in the rule to receive every guest as Christ, and so he found a small hut for me on the other side of the monastery grounds. Even though the hut had no heating, he gave me extra blankets and I was fine. I heard the marvellous singing of Gregorian Chant throughout the lengthy services for Holy Saturday and Easter Sunday. 'Receive every guest as Christ' – for Christ was a stranger who sought shelter; a rule for seeing can transform our manner of acting, and a rule for acting can transform our manner of seeing.

My life has long been shaped by the wisdom of the sons and daughters of Benedict. The motto of my high school preparatory seminary on the south side of Chicago was the age-old Benedictine motto: *ora et labora* (pray and work), which provides the framework for the distinctively Benedictine approach to the topic of meditation and action. The key to this programme is the dynamism of the Latin word *et* (and), through which multiple energies pass: prayer transforms work, and work transforms prayer. On both levels, the Catholic practice of prayer and work can open out to Buddhist practices, welcoming them, listening to them and being transformed by them. At Montserrat we have learnt from our Benedictine hosts that the favoured Benedictine form of *meditatio* for centuries has been a moment within *lectio divina.* This practice begins with *lectio,* a slow, meditative reading of the text, allowing the sacred text, whether from the Bible or a great spiritual writer, to enter our awareness and play with us. From *lectio* we move to *meditatio,* meditation. This form of meditation is above all a form of listening; the Rule of Benedict begins with a call to listen. In this practice we do not try to master the text through our philological, historical, philosophical or archaeological competencies; the process of *meditatio* calls us to let go of the desire to control the text, to become vulnerable, to allow our deeper conscious and unconscious self to enter into the text, to identify with particular figures and listen to what happens to us in a dynamic process of transformation. The rumination of *meditatio* calls us to allow the text to speak to us without preconditions, without knowing where it will lead us, to hear the call to *metanoia,* to conversion of mind, emotions, morals and religious path. Meditation is opening ourselves to a path of transformation that we cannot predict or control. One example of this comes in what I have already noted in chapter 53 of Benedict's Rule: 'All guests who present themselves are to be received as Christ, for He will say: *I was a stranger and you took me in* (Matthew 25:35).' Meditation on the sayings of Jesus in the gospel can lead to new ways of seeing and acting in relation to those in need.

In the traditional Roman Catholic vocabulary, *meditatio* can lead to *contemplatio,* a quiet resting in God's presence beyond words. Guigo II, a twelfth-century Carthusian reformer of Benedictine practice, proposed a four-fold path from reading to meditation to prayer to contemplation (MacCulloch 2013, 100-101).

What can be confusing is that in English translations, what is meant by 'meditation' in Buddhist practice is often more similar to what Catholics have traditionally called contemplation. This form of prayer has roots in the Bible and the early church. The Apostle Paul tells us that 'the Spirit helps us in our weakness; for we do not know how to pray as we ought, but that very same Spirit intercedes with sighs too deep for words' (Romans 8:26). Paul's admonition inspired an ancient Christian tradition of prayer without words, including Evagrius Ponticus, who recommended prayer that is too deep for words: 'Strive to render your mind deaf and dumb at the time of prayer and then you will be able to pray' (Evagrius 1981, 57). Prayer without words is one traditional form of Christian prayer, which continues to be a point of contact with the Buddhist practice of meditation.

The Benedictine practice of *ora et labora* sets a framework for meditation and action. Benedict trusted that we need a healthy rhythm of alternating between work and prayer. If we enter deeply into prayer, we can bring this awareness into our work, allowing prayer and meditation to transform all our activities. In the Benedictine communities of the Middle Ages, there were lay brothers who did manual labour in the fields; for them work was physical, demanding, transformative of the earth and productive of nourishment for the community. For the choir monks, most of whom were ordained priests, work often meant the life of study, of copying manuscripts from the ancient world. Benedict acknowledged the dignity of all forms of labour. The age-old Benedictine form of action has often involved education.

At a time when Western European culture and society went into a state of near collapse, Benedictine monks continued the rhythm of prayer and work, chanting the Psalms, farming the fields, copying the manuscripts, and writing monastic theology in ways that preserved cultural heritage and reinvigorated society. However, the path of the Benedictines is not simply a response to societal collapse (Dreher 2017; Demacopoulos 2017).[11] It is

---

11 George Demacopoulos offers a helpful response and correction to Dreher's interpretation of Benedict, warning that 'it is particularly unfortunate that

a long-term path for all ages, whether outward conditions are propitious or not. Whether things in the world are going well or not, whether everything around the monastery is falling apart or not, whether society is flourishing or collapsing, when society is stable or when all things are shifting on a scale one cannot imagine, the Benedictine programme is to continue the rhythm of *ora et labora*. However, the relation between meditation and action can lead to many different outcomes, not all of them pleasant. At one point in his career, Benedict was reportedly trying to impose discipline on his monastic community, but the monks found him too strict and so they allegedly tried to assassinate him (Dysinger 1997, xix).

In North America, the most moving encounters of Buddhists and members of the Benedictine family have been the Gethsemani Encounters organized by Monastic Interreligious Dialogue at the Trappist Abbey of Our Lady of Gethsemani near Louisville, Kentucky, where Thomas Merton had lived. The first dialogue was held in the summer of 1996 to explore aspects of Buddhist and Catholic monastic life, including meditation. I participated as an advisor to the board of Monastic Interreligious Dialogue. In accordance with the Rule, the Catholic monastics received their Buddhist guests as Christ, welcoming them into the chapter room of the monastery which lies at its heart; the Buddhist monastics quickly felt welcomed in an atmosphere that values silence, meditation and hospitality. While our preparations had envisioned discussions of the forms and practices of monastic life, the presence of His Holiness the XIVth Dalai Lama, the Patriarch (Sangharaja) of Cambodian Buddhism, Maha Ghosananda, and Trappist Fr. Armand Veuilleux, who had recently retrieved the remains of the Trappist monks who were killed in Algeria, brought our awareness to the problems of violence and how to respond. So our conversations repeatedly turned to the question of right action in a world of violence.

---

the presentation of the actual, historical St. Benedict in *The Benedict Option* is misleading.'

Catholic monastics constantly referred to the Rule of Benedict in a variety of ways, and a number of the Buddhists present were so moved and intrigued by these repeated references, that they decided to study the Rule and offer a Buddhist response, *Benedict's Dharma: Buddhists Reflect on the Rule of Saint Benedict* (Fischer et al. 2001). Judith Simmer-Brown, a distinguished representative of Tibetan Buddhism, responded movingly to Benedict's rule regarding guests, the sick and the elderly:

> Especially significant in Benedict's comments about the treatment of the sick, elderly, young, and visitors is the injunction to see them as Christ himself...How can this be understood in Buddhist terms?...When we look into the face of a sick person, we are taken out of ourselves and our self-confirming habits. We are aroused to compassion and service. Similarly, when we encounter the guest, one we would normally consider an outsider, stranger, even a foreigner, we are exposed to the world beyond our making. (Fischer et al. 2001, 82-83)

These Buddhist teachers noted that the Buddha and Benedict both reversed the social judgments of their respective societies, commenting that 'the Buddha was a social revolutionary. The monastic community did away with caste, putting all renunciants in the same arena. Similarly, Benedict upended Roman convention, which despised manual labour, by saying that free-born persons should work with their hands' (Fischer et al. 2001, 83-84). The distinguished Zen leader, Norman Zoketsu Fischer stressed the shared Buddhist and Benedictine emphasis on the dignity and value of work and the importance of education (Fischer et al. 2001, 84). Fischer warned of the danger of spiritual consumerism and urged: 'Real and effective contemplation must be based on a firm commitment to and practice of ethical conduct, ordinary common sense, kindness, and care with one's behavior' (Fischer et al. 2001, 91).

The second Gethsemani Encounter in 2002 addressed directly different forms of suffering and Catholic and Buddhist modes of response (Mitchell and Wiseman 2003). The third Encounter addressed the issues of ecological suffering and proposed *Green Monasticism* (Mitchell & Skudlarek 2010). One of the most important developments of recent decades is that Christians are increasingly including Buddhists texts in the process of *lectio divina*. Catherine Cornille is editing a series of books, *Christian Commentaries on Non-Christian Sacred Texts*, in which Christians meditate upon scriptures or classical spiritual writings from other religious traditions, including Buddhism. What many of us have found is that while Buddhist and Catholic cosmologies differ profoundly and deeply, the practical values for living often converge.

The Path of the Franciscans

In later centuries, one wave of religious renewal and reform after another came through Spain, giving new meaning to the programme of *ora et labora*. Beginning in the early thirteenth century, new approaches to meditation and action came from the friars mendicant, including Franciscans, Dominicans and Carmelites. The young Francis of Assisi heard a call from God to 'repair my house which, as you see is falling completely into ruin,' (Bonaventure 1978, 191) and he responded not only by physically repairing a chapel that was in disrepair but also by reaching out and touching lepers from whom he had previously pulled back. Where Benedict had directed monks to receive poor guests at the monastery as Christ, Francis went out in the streets of the world looking for lepers and the poor and welcoming them. By acting in a new way, Francis came to see in a new way. St. Bonaventure tells us:

> From that time on [Francis] clothed himself with a spirit of poverty, a sense of humility and a feeling of intimate devotion. Formerly he used to be horrified not only by close dealing with lepers but by their very sight, even from a distance; but now he rendered humble service to the lepers with human concern and devoted kindness in order that he might completely despise himself, because of Christ crucified, who according to the text of

the prophet was despised *as a leper* (Isaiah 53:3). (Bonaventure 1978, 189-90)

Because Francis saw Christ in the lepers, contact with them, which had earlier seemed deplorable to him, now seemed enjoyable. Bonaventure tells us that 'with great compassion [Francis] kissed their hands and their mouths' (Bonaventure 1978, 190). His actions transformed his way of seeing and praying. As Benedictines welcomed strangers, the poor, the elderly and the sick in the monastery as Christ, Franciscans went through the streets of the towns and villages of Italy seeking them out. Francis broadened the practice of Christian meditation by pondering Psalm 19:

> The heavens are telling the glory of God;
> And the firmament proclaims his handiwork.
> Day to day pours forth speech,
> And night to night declares knowledge. (Psalm 19:1-2)

Inspired by this perspective, Francis of Assisi composed the Canticle of the Sun, calling for God to be praised '*per*' the sun, the moon, even death. Francis of Assisi prayed:

> Praised be You, my Lord, with all creatures, especially Sir Brother Sun, Who is the day and through whom You give us light... Praised be you, my Lord, through Sister Moon and the stars, in heaven You formed them clear and precious and beautiful... Praised be You, my Lord, through our Sister Mother Earth, who sustains and governs us, and who produces varied fruits with colored flowers and herbs. (Francis & Clare 1982, 38-39)

The Umbrian/Italian word '*per*,' which St. Francis of Assisi used in his hymn, had multiple meanings: it can mean God is to be praised for the Sun, the Moon, the Air, the Waters and Fire. It can also mean that God is praised by them. This interpretation echoes the Psalm: 'The heavens proclaim the glory of God.' 'Per' can also mean 'through', which suggests both the role of creatures in praising God and also a sense of God's mystical presence in all of creation. Francis of Assisi refers to the beauty of the Sun and the Moon, both as a reflection of God's presence and also as active agents praising God. Franciscan meditation includes all creation, including realities that Christians have traditionally viewed as non-animate, in praise of God, leading to service of neighbour. St. Bonaventure reflected on the prayer of St. Francis, noting that Francis saw all creatures as a reflection of the divine beauty, through which we can glimpse the presence of the goodness of God in creation (Bonaventure 1978, 262-63).

Franciscan meditation frequently involves visualization. One Christmas Eve, Francis as a deacon reportedly wanted to visualize the scene of the birth of the Christ child in the manger at Bethlehem, and thus was born the tradition of the *crèche*, the *presepio*. Francis meditated on the crucifixion of Jesus to the point that he received the stigmata, the wounds of Christ (Bonaventure 1978, 303-14); later Franciscans meditated on the life of Francis as a lens for reading the life of Jesus. Bonaventure's *Itinerarium Mentis in Deum* (The Soul's Journey into God) is a profoundly moving meditation on the presence of God in all creation, in human awareness, and the significance of the cross for entering the divine presence. The visual images of the life of Francis of Assisi offered concrete meditations on the life of Christ and what it meant to be a disciple. Francis prayed, and found a call to serve God by ministering to lepers. In the action of caring for people whom he had earlier been afraid of, his awareness and his prayer life were changed. In recent decades, Leonardo Boff has reflected on the implications of Franciscan meditation for liberation theology (Boff 1988) and Pope Francis has proposed the implications for ecological awareness.

The Path of the Dominicans

During this period, Saint Dominic, an older contemporary of Saint Francis who was born in Castile, founded the Order of Preachers to respond to the challenge to preach the gospel with credibility and power. Dominicans developed the programme of *ora et labora* in reference to the patterns of the active and contemplative life. St. Thomas Aquinas judged the active life of the Christian to be good, but, like most medieval Catholics, he praised the contemplative life as a higher good. However, he proposed that the best Christian practice was *contemplata aliis tradere:* to hand on to others what one has contemplated. Later generations of Dominicans accepted this programme and sought to hand on to others what they had contemplated.

One of the greatest Dominican contributions to meditation and action came in the Caribbean in the early years of the Spanish conquest of the Americas, regarding the commandment of the Torah invoked by Jesus to love one's neighbour as oneself (Leviticus 19:18; Mark 12:33; Matthew 5:43 and 22:39; Luke 10:27-28). According to the gospel of Luke, a lawyer famously challenged Jesus regarding this commandment, 'And who is my neighbour?' (Luke 10: 29). Dominicans took up this challenge in relation to the Spanish *encomienda* system, which was causing untold horrors to the indigenous peoples. The Dominican friars on the island of Hispaniola, present-day Haiti and the Dominican Republic, decided to protest, and so on the Fourth Sunday of Advent, 1511, Dominican friar Antonio Montesino, with the full support of his superior, Pedro de Cordoba, unleashed a ferocious attack on Spanish atrocities against the Amerindians. The only record of it comes to us from Bartolomé de Las Casas, who quotes Montesino preaching to the *encomenderos*:

> Tell me, with what right, with what justice, do you hold these Indians in such cruel and horrible servitude?...How is it that you hold them so crushed and exhausted, giving them nothing to eat, nor any treatment for their diseases, which you cause them to be infected with through the surfeit of their toils?...Are they not human beings? Have they no rational souls? Are you not obligated to love them as you love yourselves? Do you not understand this? Do you not grasp this? How is it that you sleep so soundly, so lethargically? Know that for a certainty that in the state in which you are you can no more be saved than Moors or Turks who have not, nor wish to have, the faith of Jesus Christ. (Gutiérrrez 1993, 29)

Contemporary Dominican friar and liberation theologian, Gustavo Gutiérrez comments that Montesino connects greed and death, drawing upon both the Law of Nations and the Gospel of Jesus

Christ. Above all, Gutiérrez emphasizes Montesino's view of the American Indians as neighbours whom Christians are called to love as themselves: 'The various questions of Montesino's homily are interconnected, of course. But the one that recalls the Indian's quality as 'neighbor' to the Spaniards, which the missioners see as entailing a duty to love, is the furthest-reaching question, and the one that gives meaning to the others' (Gutiérrrez 1993, 31). The meditation of Montesino on the call of Jesus Christ led to a demand for action; Las Casas, who would later courageously continue the protest of Montesino, tells us that while many were astonished at Montesino's message, 'no one, so far as I have heard, converted' (Gutiérrrez 1993, 31).

To carry out the programme of *contemplata aliis tradere*, the Dominicans engaged in a far-reaching social interpretation of the gospel and a vigorous defence of the human rights of American Indians. The example of the early Dominicans in the Americas lives on as another witness to the link between meditation and action. Gustavo Gutiérrez continues this tradition today, insisting on the power of the poor in history and calling us to sing and set free, namely to sing the praise of God together with all creation and to work for liberation (Gutiérrez 1987, 93-103).

The Path of the Carmelites

Another powerful tradition of meditation developed in Spain during the sixteenth century through the ministry of the Carmelite Saints and mystics, Teresa of Avila and John of the Cross. Inspired by the example of the prophet Elijah, who encountered God in what has been paradoxically called 'a sound of sheer silence' at Mt. Horeb (1 Kings 19:12; New Oxford Annotated Bible 2007), the Carmelite tradition of Catholic spirituality has long valued silent meditation and the letting go of all thoughts and ideas about God. John of the Cross described the process of purification of disordered appetites, intellect, memory and will through repeated negations in what he called the dark night of the senses and the dark night of the soul (John of the Cross 1991). The practitioner goes through a painful process of purgation to reach the flame of living love. Often during the journey the practitioner becomes more passive, resting in God's presence and surrendering everything to God's grace.

A number of scholar-practitioners have compared John of the Cross to Buddhist practice (Feldmeier 2006). Carmelite leaders Kevin G. Culligan, Mary Jo Meadow and Daniel Chowning have integrated insight and loving-kindness meditation into a spiritual practice inspired by St. John of the Cross (Meadow et al. 2007). These leaders compare and combine the teachings and practices of John of the Cross with those of Shakyamuni Buddha for training the mind (Culligan et al. 1994, 13). The Carmelites begin with Jesus's beatitude: 'Blessed are the pure in heart, for they shall see God' (Matthew 5:8). They comment: 'Jesus teaches that we must purify our entire interior life if we want the happiness of seeing God' (Culligan et al. 1994, 23). They then cite the words of Shakyamuni Buddha in *Dhammapada* verse 236: 'When you are cleansed of all impurity and the stain of all sinful passions is gone, you can enter the blessed abode of the saints' (Culligan et al. 1994, 29). They note that the Buddha taught meditation as 'the practice that cleanses the heart. It purifies the heart of disordered desires, hateful thoughts, harmful memories, fear and other negative emotions, and, in their place, engenders sharp mental awareness, clear understanding, strength of will and attentiveness to each passing moment' (Culligan et al. 1994, 29). They observe that John of the Cross describes the painful but healing process of purification of desires, thoughts, emotions and memories. Thus the Carmelites 'bring these two venerable traditions—Buddhist meditation and the Christian spirituality of St. John of the Cross—together into an ascetical practice we call Christian insight meditation' (Culligan et al. 1994, 30). In a companion volume, Mary Jo Meadow describes the complementary practice of loving-kindness meditation, which extends loving-kindness, compassion, appreciative joy and equanimity to oneself, to one's neighbours and friends, to one's enemies and to all sentient beings (Meadow 1994). The ancient Buddhist practices find an important place in contemporary Christian spirituality.

From a slightly different perspective, the late Irish Jesuit, William Johnston compared the dark nights of the senses and of the soul as described by John of the Cross with aspects of Japanese Zen Buddhist practice; and he found here an opening to Buddhism and to reconciliation:

> To describe this night, St. John of the Cross speaks of 'nothing'—*nada, nada, nada*—and of emptiness. His *todo y nada* (all and nothing) is so similar to the *mu* (nothing) and *ku* (emptiness) of Asia that he has been called a Buddhist in Christian disguise. To this I would say, however, that the Buddhist *mu* and *ku* may well be an experience of the same unknowability of God. Perhaps mystics of all religions are called to unite in atoning for the ugliness of the world and facing the unknowable mystery that cannot be put into words. (Johnston 2006, 88)

Johnston came to see the Jesuit *Spiritual Exercises* as horizontal prayer, while the contemplative prayer of John of the Cross, similar to the practice of Buddhist meditation, involved what Johnston called vertical prayer, which 'draws one down into the deeper, unconscious levels of the personality. It leads one into the cloud of unknowing where one is frequently silent, in love with God' (Johnston 2006, 87). While Johnston sat for a time under the guidance of Yamada Roshi, he did not claim to practise or teach Zen; nonetheless, he found much support in Zen for his practice of Christian contemplative prayer. Informed by Japanese Buddhist commitment to non-violence, Johnston came to a new perspective on the conflicts in his native Northern Ireland, rejecting the violence of the Irish Republican Army, which his family had supported.

The Path of the Jesuits: Contemplation in Action

Perhaps the most famous pilgrim to come to the Abbey of Santa Maria de Montserrat was Inigo López de Loyola, a nobleman who had earlier sought military renown and popularity with women, but who came to Montserrat when he was going through a conversion and was searching for a new path. He would later adopt the name Ignacio or Ignatius and is generally known by this name today. The transformation of Ignatius's life began on 17 May 1521, when he was in battle, fighting with the Spanish army against the French at Pamplona, and a cannon ball shattered his right leg and wounded his other leg (Ignatius 1991). The doctors had trouble treating his legs, and they performed various operations, but he had a limp for the rest of his life. During the long convalescence, there was nothing available to read except a Life of Christ by Ludolph of Saxony and a collection of the lives of the saints, *The Golden Legend of Jacopo da Voragine*. He was bored and so he read them. He was a natural psychologist, and he spontaneously engaged in a form of *lectio divina*, allowing the text to transform his life. He noticed that when his mind followed the lives of the saints he came to greater comfort, peace and tranquillity than when his mind followed his usual dreams of military glory and success with women. With the latter pattern he felt a dryness and agitation in his mind. With the way of the saints, he found serenity. So he decided to embark on what was for him a totally new way of life. Knocked out of military action by a cannon ball, he probed meditation and came to a new style of Christian action, which he would eventually call being a contemplative in action.

At the Benedictine monastery in Montserrat, Ignatius spent a night in prayer before the Black Madonna. He gave her his sword and renounced the life of a nobleman and military leader; he began to wear the garments of a pilgrim. The monastery had a practice of preparing novices over a period of ten or more days to make a lifetime confession, reviewing everything they had done and asking God's mercy. In this type of examination of conscience, the dangers that Buddhists name as the three poisons are very much in evidence. Ignatius did a shorter form of this examination of conscience in three days and wrote down his sins as his way of renouncing his past ambitions. He wanted to go to Jerusalem as a pilgrim. But first he went to Manresa, a little town in the vicinity, planning to reflect on what had happened for a few days and then move on. However, there was a plague, and so he stayed there about a year. While in Manresa, he discovered *The Imitation of Christ* by Thomas a Kempis, and this moved him. He adopted an extreme ascetic regimen and went through acute periods of doubt over whether his confession was valid, felt tempted to commit suicide, and felt a dryness of soul. Eventually, he relaxed the extreme asceticism and learnt to find guidance by listening within, and he came back to a state of serenity with God. He had religious visions and a powerful mystical experience. This was the basis for the *Spiritual Exercises,* which present a path for discernment and experiencing the love of God. This is a development of the Benedictine practice of *lectio divina,* which was influenced by the Franciscan practice of visualizing events from the life of Jesus Christ.

The prayer of Ignatius expresses his paradigm for turning away from sin and turning one's life over to the grace and care of God:

> Take, Lord, and receive all my liberty, my memory, my understanding, and all my will—all that I have and possess. You, Lord, have given all that to me. I now give it back to you, O Lord. All of it is yours. Dispose of it according to your will. Give me your love and your grace, for that is enough for me. (Ignatius 1991, 177)

The goal of Ignatius and his first companions was to help people find God in all things (O'Malley 1993, 18). This included not only spiritual guidance but also feeding the hungry, nursing the sick and educating children.

The *Spiritual Exercises* develop the Christian practice of meditation by visualizing the details of a biblical story, placing oneself within the setting, and then at the end of the narrative imagining oneself alone with Jesus and listening for his call. By the end of the retreat, the person is encouraged to be a contemplative in action. In Japan, a number of Jesuits, including J.K. Kadowaki, Hugo Enomiya Lassalle, Robert Kennedy, Thomas Hand and Ruben Habito, practised the path of Zen, and sought to live Zen-inspired lives as contemplatives in action. The late Thomas Hand commented to me once that the practice of Zen helped him to realize the Jesuit ideal of being a contemplative in action better than anything in the *Spiritual Exercises* of Ignatius. Ruben Habito has related Christian Zen practice to ecology and to action for liberation, and he has reflected on Zen and the Spiritual Exercises. The late American Jesuit, Daniel Berrigan became acquainted with the *Thien* (Vietnamese Zen) Buddhist path of Thích Nhất Hạnh during the time of protesting against the United States' involvement in the war in Vietnam. In their discussions in their book, *The Raft Is Not the Shore,* they explored how in both the Christian and *Thien* traditions meditation and social non-violent action for justice go hand in hand (Nhat Hanh & Berrigan 2001).

Aloysius Pieris, a Jesuit in Sri Lanka, has developed *An Asian Theology of Liberation*, drawing upon the wisdom of the Pāli canon and Catholic principles of social justice (Pieris 1988a).[12] Pieris honours the tree of wisdom of Shakyamuni Buddha and the tree of the cross of Jesus Christ as respective symbols of their paths of transformation, and he chides Buddhists and Christians alike for not acknowledging the reciprocity between their traditions (Pieris 1988b, 113).[13]

The Path of Pope Francis: *Laudato Si'*

Pope Francis draws from all these Catholic traditions in presenting his call for both meditation and action in caring for the earth

12 In his practice Pieris seeks to draw upon both the Buddhist quest for transformative, liberating wisdom, which he calls by the Greek word *gnosis,* and the Christian quest for redemptive love, which he calls by the Greek word *agape*. Pieris believes that the Buddhist tradition has a deep element of *agape*, and the Christian tradition has a deep element of *gnosis*, and they can learn from each other to develop what has been traditionally undeveloped (Pieris 1988b, 111).

13 '[T]here is a *Christian gnosis* that is necessarily agapeic; and there is also a *Buddhist agape* that remains Gnostic. In other words, deep within each one of us there is a Buddhist and a Christian engaged in a profound encounter that each tradition—Buddhist and Christian—has registered in the doctrinal articulation of each religion's core experience. What seems impossible—the interpenetration of the two irreducibly distinct idioms—has already taken place both within Christianity and within Buddhism' (Pieris 1988b, 113).

in his encyclical, *Laudato Si'* (Francis 2015). This encyclical is a powerful appeal for interreligious cooperation in addressing the current global crisis of technocratic reason, abuse of the earth, mistreatment of migrants and oppression of the poor. Pope Francis begins *Laudato Si'* by quoting the hymn of Francis of Assisi: 'Praise be to you, my Lord, through our Sister, Mother Earth, who sustains and governs us, and who produces various fruit with coloured flowers and herbs' (#1). Then he immediately issues a dire warning that we are harming our sister the earth because 'We have come to see ourselves as her lords and masters, entitled to plunder her at will. The violence present in our hearts, wounded by sin, is also reflected in the symptoms of sickness evident in the soil, in the water, in the air and in all forms of life' (#2). This sets the stage for the central tension that runs throughout the encyclical. Pope Francis cites the words of Saint Paul that the earth 'groans in travail' (Romans 8:22) and he chides us for forgetting that 'we ourselves are the dust of the earth (cf. Genesis 2:7); our very bodies are made up of her elements, we breathe her air and we receive life and refreshment from her waters' (#2).

According to Francis, the current problems 'cannot be dealt with from a single perspective or from a single set of interests' (#110). Thus, science and technology must be studied in dialogue with philosophy and social ethics. In the absence of this dialogue, there are no 'genuine ethical horizons to which one can appeal. Life gradually becomes a surrender to situations conditioned by technology, itself viewed as the principal key to the meaning of existence' (#110). Francis calls for interreligious dialogue and co-operation in shaping an integral ecological culture.

Buddhists have frequently critiqued anthropocentrism as a source of unnecessary suffering; Pope Francis laments that in the modern period a radical anthropocentrism placed humans at the centre of the cosmos and measured everything according to human criteria that were all too narrow. Warning that this was only an apparent gain, Francis insists again and again that all things are connected: neglect of nature leads to neglect of the value of human life (#117). Repeatedly, Francis calls for an integral vision, which resonates deeply with many themes from the Buddhist tradition: 'There can be no renewal of our relationship with nature without a renewal of humanity itself. There can be no ecology without an adequate anthropology' (#118). He emphasizes further: 'If the present ecological crisis is one small sign of the ethical, cultural and spiritual crisis of modernity, we cannot presume to heal our relationship with nature and the environment without healing all fundamental human relationships' (#119). In this context, Francis insists: 'A misguided anthropocentrism leads to a misguided lifestyle' (#122).

In this context, Pope Francis links the practice of meditation and the value of human labour, and recalls that St. Benedict taught the monastic value of prayer and work, 'combining prayer and spiritual reading with manual labour (*ora et labora*). Seeing manual labour as spiritually meaningful proved revolutionary' (#126). He draws out the implications of this for the environment: 'This way of experiencing work makes us more protective and respectful of the environment' (#126). Francis decries the loss of contemplative practice: '[O]nce our human capacity for contemplation and reverence is impaired, it becomes easy for the meaning of work to be misunderstood' (#127). Instead of valuing work as a vocation, today humans too often view work as merely instrumental and devoid of dignity.

Pope Francis calls for a worldwide dialogue from a global perspective, believing that such a revolution must be informed by religious and ethical principles that go beyond the domain of empirical science. He acknowledges that believers have not always been 'faithful to the treasures of wisdom which we have been called to protect and preserve', but nonetheless calls for a return to the sources of religious traditions in order to respond to current needs (#200). In this context, he calls for renewed interreligious dialogue on these issues.

Francis concludes with a call for the ecological conversion of both individuals and communities: 'The ecological conversion needed to bring about lasting change is also a community conversion' (#219). He returns to the statement of Jesus that not one of the birds of the air is forgotten by God (Luke 12:6) and asks, rhetorically, 'How then can we possibly mistreat them or cause them harm? I ask all Christians to recognize and to live fully this dimension of their conversion' (#221).

Francis recalls the principles of Christian spirituality that encourage simplicity and contemplation. After many pessimistic predictions and ominous warnings, Francis closes his encyclical on a note of hope with a mystical meditation on the value of rest:

> The universe unfolds in God, who fills it completely. Hence, there is a mystical meaning to be found in a leaf, in a mountain trail, in a dewdrop, in a poor person's face. The ideal is not only to pass from the exterior to the interior to discover the action of God in the soul, but also to discover God in all things. (#233)

The last phrase comes directly from Pope Francis's mentor in Jesuit religious life, St. Ignatius Loyola, who taught his followers to find God in all things. This vision also is grounded in Francis of Assisi and Bonaventure's *The Soul's Journey into God.* Pope Francis moves on to the Carmelite tradition, citing another mystic, St. John of the Cross, on the experience of God in all things so that, properly understood, 'all things are God.' Francis explains: 'Standing awestruck before a mountain, he or she cannot separate this experience from God, and perceives that the interior awe being lived has to be entrusted to the Lord' (#234).

Buddhist-Catholic Dialogue in Castel Gandalfo and Rome in June 2015

During the week after this encyclical was issued in June 2015, I attended a dialogue in Castel Gandolfo and Rome with a group of about forty-five Buddhists and Catholics from the United States. Jean-Louis Cardinal Tauran, the President of the Pontifical Council for Interreligious Dialogue, invited us to ponder how we can understand the forms of suffering in the United States today, and respond together as Buddhists and Christians to relieve suffering:

'In a world where diversity is seen as a threat, our coming together today in friendship and peace is a sign of our openness towards one another and our commitment to human fraternity.' Cardinal Tauran elaborated: 'We are all pilgrims and I see this Buddhist-Catholic dialogue as part of our ongoing quest to grasp the mystery of our lives and the ultimate Truth.' He noted three stages that are important for the journey of dialogue. First is carrying less baggage, in other words: 'Overcoming prejudices, wounds, fears in order to listen to one's heart and to that of one's religious neighbour.' The second stage is crossing borders, journeying to know the other side while remaining firmly rooted in our beliefs. This process 'can thus turn ignorance into understanding, a stranger into a friend, hostility to hospitality and divergence into convergence.' The final stage is returning home 'transformed by what we experienced.'

On Wednesday, June 24, the group travelled to the Vatican for a personal audience with Pope Francis, who welcomed us, saying, 'It is a visit of fraternity, of dialogue, and of friendship. And this is good. This is healthy. And in these moments, which are wounded by war and hatred, these small gestures are seeds of peace and fraternity. I thank you for this and may God bless you' (Francis 2015b). Throughout the week's discussions, many Buddhists responded enthusiastically to Pope Francis's appeal in *Laudato Si'*. At the conclusion of the dialogue, the participants issued a Joint Statement that briefly described the week's activities and outcomes. The statement commented: 'The dialogue strengthened mutual understanding concerning human suffering and means of liberation, as well as deepened relationships as a basis for interreligious cooperation based on shared values.' It noted that participants would return to their respective regions with a commitment to explore joint action in several areas:

- addressing global climate change on the local level
- creating outreach programmes for youth in the cities
- collaborating in prison/gaol ministries and restorative justice matters

- developing resources for the homeless, such as affordable housing
- educating and providing resources to address the issue of immigration
- collaborating to create projects with local Catholic parishes and Buddhist communities to address neighbourhood social issues
- developing social outreach programmes for value education to families
- witnessing our shared commitment as brothers and sisters, our religious values and spiritual practices, and our social collaboration with our religious communities and others in our cities.

Participants agreed to meet in their respective regions to discuss the concrete next steps to be taken. After the dialogue concluded, participants repeatedly expressed their profound gratitude to the organizers and the other participants for this moving experience. From the ancient Benedictine practice of welcoming guests as Christ to Pope Francis's appeal for cooperation in caring for the earth, Christian and Buddhist practices involving meditation and action converge in many aspects.

Bibliography

Benedict, transl. Luke Dysinger, 1997. *The Rule of Saint Benedict Latin & English.* Trabuco Canyon, CA: Source Books.

Boff, Leonardo, transl. John W. Diercksmeier, 1988. *Saint Francis: A Model for Human Liberation.* New York: Crossroad.

Bonaventure, transl. with an introduction by Ewert Cousins, 1978. *The Soul's Journey into God; The Tree of Life; The Life of St. Francis.* New York: Paulist Press.

Culligan, Kevin G., Mary Jo Meadow & Daniel Chowning, 1994. *Purifying the Heart: Buddhist Insight Meditation for Christians.* New York: Crossroad.

Demacopoulos, George, 2017. 'The Benedict of History Versus the Benedict Option'. *Public Orthodoxy* June 28, 2017; https://publicorthodoxy.org/2017/06/28/benedict-vs-the-benedict-option/, viewed 27 July 2017.

Dreher, Rod, 2017. *The Benedict Option: A Strategy for Christians in a Post-Christian Nation.* New York: Penguin Random House.

Dysinger, Luke, 1997. 'Introduction.' In Benedict, *The Rule of Saint Benedict Latin & English,* transl. Luke Dysinger. Trabuco Canyon, CA: Source Books: v-xxvi.

Evagrius Ponticus, translated, with an introduction and notes by John Eudes Bamberger, 1981. *The Praktikos; Chapters on Prayer.* Kalamazoo, MI: Cistercian Publications.

Fischer, Norman, Joseph Goldstein, Judith-Simmer-Brown, Yifa, ed. Patrick Henry with an afterword by David Steindl-Rast, 2001. *Benedict's Dharma: Buddhists Reflect on the Rule of Saint Benedict.* New York: Riverhead Books.

Francis of Assisi & Clare of Assisi, transls. Regis J. Armstrong and Ignatius C. Brady, 1982. *Francis and Clare: The Complete Works.* New York: Paulist Press.

Francis, Pope, 2015a. *Laudato Si' Praise Be to You: On Care for Our Common Home.* Vatican City: Libreria Editrice Vaticana/ San Francisco: Ignatius Press.

Francis, Pope, 2015b. 'Pope Francis Meets with Buddhist Leaders.' *Rome Reports,* https://www.youtube.com/watch?v=w6X1YKtETqg, viewed 27 July 2017.

Gutiérrez, Gustavo, transl. Matthew J. O'Connell,1987. *On Job: God-Talk and the Suffering of the Innocent.* Maryknoll, NY: Orbis Books.

Gutiérrez, Gustavo, transl. Robert R. Barr, 1993. *Las Casas: In Search of the Poor of Jesus Christ.* Maryknoll, NY: Orbis Books.

Ignatius Loyola, eds. George E. Ganss with the collaboration of Parmananda R. Divarkar, Edward J. Malatesta & Marin E. Palmer, 1991. *The Spiritual Exercises and Selected Works.* New York: Paulist Press.

Johnston, William, 2006. *Mystical Journey: An Autobiography.* Maryknoll, NY: Orbis Books.

MacCulloch, Diarmuid, 2013. *Silence: A Christian History.* New York: Viking.

Meadow, Mary Jo, 1994. *Gentling the Heart: Buddhist Loving-Kindness Practice for Christians.* New York: Crossroad.

Meadow, Mary Jo, Kevin Culligan & Daniel Chowning, 2007. *Christian Insight Meditation: Following in the Footsteps of John of the Cross.* Somerville, MA: Wisdom Publications.

Mitchell, Donald W. & William Skudlarek, eds., 2010. *Green Monasticism: A Buddhist-Catholic Response to an Environmental Calamity.* New York: Lantern Books.

Mitchell, Donald W. & James Wiseman, eds., 2003. *Transforming Suffering: Reflections on Finding Peace in Troubled Times by His Holiness the Dalai Lama, His Holiness Pope John Paul II, Thomas Keating, Thubten Chodron, Joseph Goldstein, and Others.* New York: Doubleday.

New Oxford Annotated Bible with the Apocryphal/Deuterocanonical Books, 2007. Michael D. Coogan, New Revised Standard Version. Augmented 3rd edition. Oxford: Oxford University Press.

Nhat Hanh, Thich, & Daniel Berrigan, 2001. *The Raft Is Not the Shore: Conversations toward a Buddhist-Christian Awareness.* Maryknoll, NY: Orbis Books.

O'Malley, John W., 1993. *The First Jesuits.* Cambridge, MA: Harvard University Press.

Pieris, Aloysius, 1988a: *An Asian Theology of Liberation.* Maryknoll, NY: Orbis Books.

Pieris, Aloysius, 1988b: *Love Meets Wisdom: A Christian Experience of Buddhism.* Maryknoll, NY: Orbis Books.

Daily Examination of Consciousness: Ignatian and Vietnamese Truc Lam Zen Approaches to Transformation

Thao Nguyen, SJ

Abstract

After King Tran Thai Tong, a Vietnamese emperor in the thirteenth century, renounced his royal throne to become a Buddhist monk, a new school of Buddhism known as Zen Buddhist Truc Lam was established. Tran Thai Tong's major contribution to Vietnamese Zen Buddhist spirituality was his invention of the daily repentant rituals that examine the six human senses: seeing, hearing, thinking, touching, feeling and encountering. The repentant rituals in the Truc Lam school have significantly shaped the way in which Vietnamese Zen Buddhist monks, nuns and lay people practice Buddhist teachings. In the West, St Ignatius of Loyola, a sixteenth century Spanish knight, also renounced his worldly ambition to pursue a contemplative life and found a religious Order known as the Society of Jesus, or Jesuits. Saint Ignatius's major contribution to Christian spirituality was the Spiritual Exercises featuring the daily examination of consciousness through five steps: awareness, gratitude, affection, repentance and hope for the future, which has transformed millions of Christians. This chapter first introduces the historical development of the meditation methods that employ the human senses in the Truc Lam school and in Ignatian spirituality. Second, it notes significant parallels between these two methods of prayer as well as their significant impacts on the spiritual lives of Buddhists and Christians respectively. Third, the chapter suggests that, given their significant similari-

ties, Buddhist and Christians might want to broaden their inter-religious conversations using a spiritual and practical approach rather than focussing on theological or doctrinal differences.

Keywords: Truc Lam Zen, Ignatian Spirituality, comparative spirituality, rituals of repentance, examination of consciousness

After the Vietnamese Emperor Tran Thai Tong renounced his royal throne in the thirteenth century to become a Zen Buddhist monk, he constructed a formula of daily repentance rituals known as *Six-Period Rituals of Repentance*, by which one examines the six human senses: seeing, hearing, smelling, tasting, touching and thinking (Thich, T.T. 2015).[1] In the sixteenth-century West, Spanish knight, Ignatius of Loyola, likewise renounced his military career to become a Catholic priest and founded a religious Order known as the Society of Jesus or Jesuits. Ignatius's major contribution to Christian spirituality was the Spiritual Exercises, by whose five steps one examined one's consciousness daily. Those five steps are: gratitude, petition for light, examination of conscience, repentance and resolution (Gallagher, 2006, 163). This article first discusses the historical development, structures and content of the *Six-Period Rituals of Repentance* in Vietnamese Zen Buddhism or the Truc Lam Zen school[2] and the daily Examination of Conscience of the Ignatian tradition. Second, it notes

---

1   Although Tran Nhan Tong, grandson of Tran Thai Tong, was officially considered to be the founder of the Vietnamese Truc Lam Zen school, Tran Thai Tong was a pioneer in synthesizing the existing Zen schools and his works significantly influenced his grandson, King Tran Nhan Tong, and shaped the Truc Lam Zen school. In the twentieth century, Master Thich Thanh Từ, one of the most respected reformers of the Truc Lam school, has also applied Tran Thai Tong's Repentance Rituals in all of the Truc Lam monasteries.

2   The birth of the Truc Lam Zen school marked a great shift in Vietnamese Buddhism in various ways. First, while other Zen traditions in Vietnam prior to the Tran dynasty were of Chinese origins and their founders were Chinese or Indians, the Truc Lam Zen tradition was founded by a Vietnamese and it was modified and developed for the Vietnamese. Tran combined three existing Zen traditions introduced to Vietnam from China: Tì Ni Va Lưu Chi

significant parallels between these two methods of prayer as well as their significant impacts on the spiritual lives of Buddhists and Christians respectively. For example, the fruits of these practices can be seen through a process of transformation that encompasses self-awareness, sensitivity, freedom, joy, detachment, a balanced life, conversion and transformation. Third and finally, the article suggests that, given their significant similarities, Buddhist and Christians might want to broaden their inter-religious conversations using a spiritual and practical approach rather than focussing on theological or doctrinal differences.

Radical Life Paths: Tran Thai Tong and Ignatius of Loyola

I begin with an overview of Tran Thai Tong and Ignatius of Loyola, without which their methods of reflection lack context. King Tran Thai Tong was enthroned in 1226 and he became the first emperor of the Tran Dynasty (Dao 2010, 213-220).[3] He resigned from his post in 1258 and became a Zen monk at the age of forty-one (Thich, T.T. 2016, 266). Long before this, Tran was already devoted to Buddhist meditation, so much so that, growing up, he had wanted to dedicate his life to studying and practising Buddhism (Thich, T.A. 1975, 120-30). His dream could not be realized for, as a member of the royal family, he was supposed to participate in and assume leadership of national affairs. However, his political life did not bring him fulfilment. Politics within the royal family and personal struggles motivated Tran to abdicate his throne and dedicate the rest of his life to Buddhist ideals as a monk (Thich, T.A. 1975, 120-121).[4] Tran's decision to renounce

---

(Vinitaruci), Vô Ngôn Thông (Wu-Yen Tung), and (Thảo Đường) Zen Pure Land (Thich, T.A. 1975, 120-30).

3   Prior to the Tran dynasty, Vietnam was governed by the Ly dynasty (Dao 2010, 213-20).

4   Although some Vietnamese emperors in the Ly dynasty were fond of Buddhism, Tran Thai Tong took Buddhism more seriously by pursuing Buddhist ideals as a Zen monk (Thich, T.A. 120-121). Political conflicts within the royal family during Tran's reign also created inner turmoil that Tran had to deal with (Nguyễn. H.H, 1996, 7-10).

his throne was particularly difficult because he was keenly aware that his kingship was endowed from above. Influenced by the Confucian tradition, the Vietnamese emperor regarded himself as 'Thiên Tử' or Son of the Heavenly Lord or Ông Trời (Dao 2005, 524). As such, the task of the emperor was to discern the Mandate of Heaven in order to govern the nation effectively. Quitting such a pre-ordained vocation was therefore no easy decision, and it is understandable why, prior to his formal abdication, he had left his palace twice. One night, he secretly went to Mount Yen Tu, a high mountain in *Quang Ninh* city in North Vietnam. A few days later, state and royal family members found him in a temple and begged him to return and take care of the country (Nguyen, T.T. 2008, 131-34). He agreed and returned. In the following years, after sufficiently instructing his son, Tran Thanh Tong, on national affairs, he left the palace a second time and spent the rest of his life practising Zen at Mt. Yen Tu until he passed away in 1277.

Tran composed Buddhist poems and wrote important works that shaped Vietnamese Buddhism in the following centuries. His most important works include: *Thiền Tông Chỉ Nam, Kim Cương Tam Muội Kinh Chú Giả, Lục Thời Sám Hối Khoa Nghi, Bình đẳng Lễ Sám Văn, Khóa Hư Lục,* and *Thi Tập* (Thich, T.A. 1975, 125). Among these works, the *Lục Thời Sám Hối Khoa Nghi* (Six- Period Rituals of Repentance) has played an important role in guiding Buddhist followers to prepare themselves for Zen meditation. One of those followers was his own grandson, King Tran Nhan Tong, who later followed his grandfather's path and also became a monk-emperor in 1294. King Tran Nhan Tong later founded the Truc Lam Zen school and he became the first patriarch of Vietnamese Zen tradition (Thich, Q.H., 2015). In the twentieth century, Master Thich Thanh Từ, a southern Buddhist monk, successfully reformed the Truc Lam Zen tradition and this school has not only thrived in Vietnam but has also spread to other countries such as Canada, Australia and the United States (Thich, Q.H. 2015).

Ignatius of Loyola lived a couple of centuries later, having been born in 1491 to a noble family in the Basque region of

Spain. In his youth, he very much enjoyed life in aristocratic circles, including the royal family. He developed a taste for music and literature, and romantic tales of chivalry among Spanish nobles (Modras 2004). He joined the army when he was eighteen years old and enjoyed a military career for twelve years. In 1521, while engaged in the Battle of Pamplona, he was hit by a cannonball that broke his right leg. He was brought back to his hometown of Loyola to recover. It was during his months of recovery that Ignatius experienced an overwhelming spiritual conversion. It took nine months for Ignatius to recover fully. When he was finally able to walk again, he desired to make a pilgrimage to Jerusalem. In March 1522, he went to visit the Benedictine monastery of Santa Maria de Montserrat. After praying long hours at the shrine of the statue of the Virgin Mary, he offered his sword and dagger to the Virgin and officially gave up his military career. Before he left Montserrat, he changed his clothes, giving away his Spanish noble clothes to a beggar and dressing himself as a beggar instead (Mossa, 2012, 7). He continued his journey to Manresa, where he deepened his spiritual experience and laid a foundation for constructing the *Spiritual Exercises*, a spiritual programme for a thirty-day retreat. Within the structure of the *Spiritual Exercises*, the Examination of Conscience or Daily Examen plays one of the most important roles in helping Christians to deepen their experience of God. Much as Tran's *Six-Period Rituals of Repentance* have helped transform the lives of numerous Vietnamese Buddhist followers, so too the Ignatian Daily Examen has transformed the lives of millions of Christians in the last five centuries. In what respects these two methods of prayer share significant similarities is the focus of the next section.

Truc Lam's Six Senses Repentance Rituals

Tran Thai Tong's *Six-Period Rituals of Repentance* helped the practitioner begin with Zen and develop a sense of awareness and purification through examining the six human senses six times a day (Thich, Q.H. 2015).[5] At 5.00 am, one examines the sense of seeing; at noon, the sense of hearing; at 6.00 pm, the sense of smell; at 9.00 pm, the sense of taste; at midnight, touch; and at 3:00 am, thinking or perception (Tran, 2015). To popularize his method, he embedded these rituals in poems so that people could memorize them easily. It is significant to note that poetry has been used as one of the effective methods for religious education in Vietnam. Christian and Buddhist educators have translated religious teachings into poems so that common people, especially children, can more easily memorize the Bible, the catechism, Buddhist teachings and other religious lessons. Realizing that many common people were not ready or well prepared for hour-long meditation, Tran designed this shorter and simpler method of reflection to encourage their ongoing attention to their interior life (Thich, T.T. 2015, 467-468). Although Tran's initial intention was to provide a simple method of meditation for beginners, it has become an essential component of the Truc Lam Zen tradition as a whole and is practised by monks, nuns and lay Buddhists (Thich, T.T. 2015, 467-468). Tran argued that repentance is the prerequisite for advancing in meditation (Thich, T.T. 2015, 266). He also compared repentance with transportation vehicles. Like cars or boats that transfer passengers from one place to the other, repentance helps purify previous karma and prevents new karma. Tran explained that if someone wants his or her mind to be purified, he or she has to repent (Thich, T.T. 2015, 466-468).

---

5   Repentance is a common practice in the Buddhist tradition. What is new in Tran Thai Tong's method is examining the six senses regularly so that the practitioner becomes more aware of external influences as well as more focussed on meditation (Thich, T.T. 2015). In addition, after Tran had studied the Buddha's teachings on how the human senses could cause one to sin, Tran took this teaching seriously and developed a formula of repentance suitable for Vietnamese practitioners (Thich, Q.H, 2015).

Structure and Content

In each examination period, the practitioner first confesses his or her sins to the Buddha by chanting this poem:

> From time eternal
> We have let our true selves stray.
> We have ignored the Truth and caused suffering
> Because of enjoying our false senses.
> Without repentance of old sins
> It is impossible to avoid new sins. (Thich, T.T. 2013, 14)

Then, the practitioner begins to examine each of his or her senses. For example, at dawn, the practitioner confesses to the Buddha the many sins he or she has committed through the eyes and by turning away from the truth:

> I have focussed on evil things
> But ignored good karma
> I enjoyed fake flowers
> But ignored the true moon.
> I searched for impermanent beauty
> And let my eyes be deceived...
> Right views are blocked
> When seeing wealthy ones
> Eyes are attracted
> When seeing the poor
> I ignored them totally. (Thich, T.T. 2013, 14-16)

After confessing sins associated with the sense of seeing, the practitioner reminds himself or herself that sins that have been committed through the eyes will lead to condemnation and that it will take many life-times to be born as another imperfect human being.

Then at noon, the practitioner again puts himself or herself in the presence of the Buddha and begins an entrance formula as presented above: 'From eternal time, we have let our true selves astray. We have ignored the Truth and caused suffering...' Then the practitioner again confesses to the Buddha how she or he committed sins through the ears:

> Hate to hear the Dharma
> Love to hear evil words
> Ignore the truth
> Pursue delusion
> Passion with noisy music
> Ignore temple bell sounds
> Fall in love with meaningless folk poems
> Ignore Buddhist chanting
> Love flattery complements
> True words refused. (Thich, T.T. 2013, 14-16)[6]

Having lived through the day, the practitioner next examines the sense of smell. Before bedtime, he or she examines what has been done through the sense of taste, and at midnight, through touch. One might ask why Tran placed the examination of the sense of sight at dawn after a long night of sleep without seeing anything. He would explain that this helps one to prepare to enter a new day with a pure mind (Nguyễn, H.H. 1996, 92-93).

Understanding that the eyes will have contact with the world all day long and that one is vulnerable to temptation, a meditation on seeing helps one to channel one's thoughts (Nguyễn, H.H. 1996, 92-93). Moreover, he argued that after a long night of sleep, when the mind is not yet fully alert, it is easy for the soul to get excited. Therefore, this practice orients practitioners not only to control their sense of sight but also to channel it to see things without being influenced by what they see.

These examinations serve multiple purposes. First, they help practitioners to be aware of the danger of the human senses and the need to control them. Second, they remind them that the human senses can disturb interior tranquillity, preventing them from having neutral judgement. As it is the tendency of humans to become easily upset, judgemental, worried, greedy or over-emotional, it is helpful to filter what has been seen or heard by being in touch with reality through the senses. Therefore, purifying the senses

---

6   The complete list of forty-two verses for this examination can also be found at the Buddhist online library at *https://thuvienhoasen.org/a6705/13-tua-khoa-nghi-sau-thoi-sam-hoi.*

by examining how they connect with the world will liberate practitioners from disordered attachments and give them freedom. In other words, the repentance rituals offer the practitioner both an experience of conversion and a path towards a deeper experience of transformation through developing joy, freedom and love for all living beings (Thich, Q.H. 2016). More importantly, these rituals help the practitioner develop an habitual ability of discerning multiple impulses that can distract a person from his or her true self (Chan 2014).

Reflecting on his past life as an emperor who was surrounded by worldly affairs, material gains, power, temptation and competition, Tran concluded that those worldly things foster hatred and imprison people (Thich, T.T. 2015). The Repentance Rituals have become a spiritual treasure for the Truc Lam Zen tradition since they were established. For daily practice, some lay Buddhists join the monks and nuns at monasteries, others practise at home on their own at their Buddhist altar. In the second half of the twentieth century, the practice was modified by Master Thich Thanh Từ – a renowned reformer of the Truc Lam tradition. Master Thich Thanh Từ reduced the six periods of repentance to one longer period each day, but the examination of six senses is still traditionally kept. For example, it is conducted at every Truc Lam monastery at 6.00 pm daily (Thich, Q.H. 2015, 714).

Having presented the Truc Lam Repentance Rituals in history and practice, I turn now to the Ignatian examination of conscience.

Ignatian Examination of Conscience

Examination of Conscience or Daily Examen is one of the most important practices in the Ignatian tradition in particular and in the Christian tradition in general. The term 'examination of conscience' is originally found in the Spiritual Exercises text, a thirty-day retreat programme, composed by Ignatius of Loyola (Ganss 1992, 38). Saint Ignatius urged his companions to practise the Examen twice a day (Tetlow 2008, 50). Even if for some reason they had to skip daily prayers or other forms of devotion, they were required to do the Examen daily. The Daily Examen was not constructed merely for Ignatius's companions (the Jesuits), but for lay men and women whose daily lives necessarily involved them in affairs of the world (Tetlow 2008, 50).

The structure of the Examination of Conscience has five steps: gratitude, awareness, examination of conscience, repentance and resolution for the following day. The five-step formula aims to help the practitioner review his or her day 'hour by hour' or from one period of time to another to develop a sense of self-awareness and an awareness of the presence of God (Ganss 1992, 38). As Aloysius Pieris states, 'the very first thing to remember is that no formal prayer begins without an *explicit act of awareness of being in God's presence*. One must *consciously* enter into a "God-atmosphere"…It is after this preliminary act of awareness of being in God's presence that the Exercise begins' (Pieris 2000, 112).

The very first step of the examen locates the practitioner in the presence of God. It is the awareness of God's presence that leads to reconciliation and repentance. St. Ignatius's approach is quite different from the Catholic Eucharist liturgy or Mass that invites Christians to reconcile with God first through an act of penitence, followed by words of thanksgiving (The Roman Missal). Ignatius probably thought that if one is not aware of God's presence, reconciliation and repentance can become mechanical. In other words, reconciliation and repentance are the fruits of awareness of God and not its cause.

As in the Buddhist tradition, the reviewing process in this Jesuit/Christian Examen also has to do with the senses. For example, the first step of the Examen — gratitude — is to review the gifts one has received. By reviewing the gifts, a person truly 'sees', 'hears' or 'feels' the gifts. One cannot give thanks to God for gifts received in the imagination, but gifts such as life, food, shelter, health, weather or family are relatively simple to bring to mind. In other words, all the faculties of a person such as seeing, hearing, feeling, touching and thinking are called upon in the Examen. Roccasalvo explains:

> It was the Daily Examen which put all things in their proper
> perspective of the day. Ignatius exhorts busy people [that] 'they
> should practice the seeking of God's presence in all things, in
> their conversation, their walks, in all that they see, taste hear,
> understand, in all actions, since his Divine Majesty is truly in all
> things by his presence, power and essence. (Roccasalvo 1988,
> 315)

In addition, one can see an interesting similarity between the Ignatian Examination of Conscience and the Truc Lam Repentance
Rituals in that both traditions place the practitioner in the position
of a sinner who needs to convert. Steps three to five of the Examen
invite the practitioner to review his or her life to see how he or she
has failed to live up to Christian values. Pieris explains that, '[t]he
Examination of Consciousness is an exercise that belongs to this
same kind of *confession.* Therefore, the third step—the examination proper—is a way of seeing how one has responded to such
a wonderful Friend and of acknowledging one's failures before
an accommodating Partner in a mood of grace-filled thanksgiving' (Pieris 2000, 123). Although the examination of conscience
is not morally oriented in a strict sense, repentance and conversion play an important role in reminding the practitioner of the
human tendency to be sinful and inviting him or her to return. In
other words, calling for a continual conversion is one of the main
components of the Ignatian Examen. As Roccasalvo explains:

> The Daily Examen provides a framework for prayer that allows
> a person to go back over each day, hour by hour, to evaluate how
> he or she acted or omitted to act, and the underlying reasons for
> such responses and reactions. It is necessary to discover one's
> faults in the context of prayer and to resolve anew to imitate Je-
> sus tomorrow, and the next day. (Roccasalvo 1988, 314)

With this understanding, reviewing and recognizing one's failures is one of the important components of the Examen. Ignatius invites the practitioner to review the day and ask the Lord
to point out the moments of failure in big ways or small. It is
looking at the mistakes one has made during the day that opens

one up for forgiveness and healing. While Ignatius suggested that the Examination of Conscience should be done twice a day, he himself actually practised it more frequently during the day. It became his spiritual habit. As Roccasalvo states, 'He has always kept this habit of examining his conscience every hour and of asking himself with careful attention how he had passed the hour' (Roccasalvo 1988, 163). Stanley also notes that, 'St. Ignatius had a profound sense of the value of repentance as an aid to advancing in that "sense of family" towards God or Father, which he considers in the Constitutions as the hallmark of the Jesuits' (Stanley 1994, 72). Emphasizing the dynamic of conversion through a development of self-awareness in the Ignatian spirituality, Paul Robb, SJ, states, 'We need, therefore, to explore the meaning and implications of this kind of self-awareness so essential for deeper covenant conversion' (Robb 1982, 16).

This kind of self-awareness allows one to recognize and acknowledge human weakness that is vulnerable to external influences. Human life, according to the Ignatian tradition, is a conflict between opposites: light and dark; freedom and unfreedom; life and death (Robb 1982, 20-21). This interior conflicting dynamic puts the Christian in a constant situation of choosing between opposites. Therefore, the Examen helps the practitioner keep in touch with both the 'weeds and [the] wheat' growing together in the field of a person's life. In addition, the Ignatian examination of conscience reminds the practitioner to turn away from disordered thoughts, perceptions, affections, wronged actions or self-centred attitudes and towards a transformed way of life characterized by freedom, love, charity and detachment. In so doing, the practitioner channels his or her life towards the authentic truth in the light of the Christian God. As Tetlow explains:

> The examen is less about our sin than about our growth in Christ-life. At any given moment, every living thing is either growing or dying. Which are we doing now?...Guided by the Spirit, we decide to take responsibility for ourselves in one or more of the five areas of human experience by doing what we need to do more fully alive in Christ. (Tetlow 2008, 50)

Taking responsibility for one's acts becomes an important component of the Ignatian Examen, because this attitude helps one make progress in the spiritual life. This sense of responsibility encourages the practitioner to look toward the following hours or days with a new attitude. It is clear that the fifth step of the Examen gives the practitioner a sense of hope and encouragement as she or he enters the next moments of life. Tetlow explains, 'It is true that we cannot control the future, but we shape the present by how we envision the future. So we take the time to imagine how well we can do without some unholy habit we have chosen to shake, or how we will grow beyond a prejudice we feel' (Tetlow 2008, 52).

The Examen becomes a habitual practice that helps the Christian discern different movements taking place in his or her daily life. While not many Christians have the opportunity to make formal confession or practise penitent acts in the Eucharistic liturgy, the daily Examination of Conscience provides a convenient and effective tool for many Christians to grow in their spiritual lives. Therefore, it is understandable that one of the main intentions of Ignatius was to help the Christian to keep in touch with his or her interior life through a habitual practice (Gallagher 2006, 163). In so doing, practitioners can identify their interior experience of anxieties, fears, resistance, attraction, and disordered desires or inclinations. In addition, our interior, mental feelings are accompanied with a range of thoughts and they occur in the context of constantly changing activity such as work, travel, interactions with others, planning or decision-making. The Examen aims to help a person filter or identify false feelings and disordered desires or inclinations so that he or she can experience joy, consolation, peace and freedom.

Significant Parallels and Differences

Having presented the Ignatian Examen and the *Six-Period Ritu-als of Repentance* in the Truc Lam Zen tradition, I now analyze these two methods of prayer and show the commonalities between them. First, the founders of these two traditions appropriated the existing practices and then modified or intensified some of their elements to help a new generation of followers to practise more easily. For example, while the examination of conscience was for many centuries a practice in the church and had ancient roots (Traub 2008, 106), Tran Thai Tong also appropriated the Buddhist teachings on *āyatana*s (sense bases) and how to channel senses to avoid sins. Second, these two methods have served as a prayer formula that is practised daily. Religious, monks, nuns, lay men and lay women have practised them regularly. Because these two methods are simple but effective, more and more people have engaged in this spiritual practice. For example, lay Buddhist men and women regularly gather at Truc Lam monastery in Da Lat, Vietnam, at 6:00 p.m. each day to do the examination with the monks in the main temple. Third, both methods provide important tools to help practitioners make good choices each day. What choices have I made, and how have those choices affected my life? In other words, developing a strong sense of discernment is one of the important goals of these exercises. Fourth, these methods similarly orient the practitioner to grow in a life of ongoing spiritual conversion, detachment and balance. Fifth, developing a sense of self-awareness in relationship with the surrounding environment is one of the striking similarities between these two traditions. Sixth, reverence to the presence of the Buddha, Bodhisattvas and the Dharma in the Truc Lam tradition, and reverence to God in the Ignatian tradition in each period of examination shows a significant similarity. Seventh, these two traditions both emphasize spiritual conversion quite strongly. According to the Truc Lam tradition, conversion means to move away from one's false-self towards a more authentic one guided by the Dharma. This process of conversion means growing in a deep awareness and recognition of the multiple external and internal forces dominated by the senses. This kind of self-awareness both helps channel one's distorted senses and frees one from being caught in a constant train of disillusioned thoughts. Similarly, the Ignatian Examen is always linked to the discernment of the spirits through which the Christian gradually grows into an awareness of good and bad spirits that constantly operate in a person's life. The authentic self, according to the Ignatian understanding, should be grounded in the life of Christ and guided by good spirits. Finally, these two methods prepare practitioners to enter the immediate future with a positive attitude and a deeper sense of awareness of the multiple external influences that will confront them. With this awareness, one is prepared to respond and to interact with reality.

Distinctions between the Two Methods of Reflection

Besides these similarities, it is important to address some differences between these two methods of reflection. First, while the *Six-Period Rituals of Repentance* are normally conducted in community with verbal chanting, the Ignatian Examen is normally practised individually and typically silently. Second, belief in God's grace is strongly emphasized in the Ignatian Examen and the prayer is located in a larger context of human existence, for example, the presence of the Transcendent, while the Truc Lam Repentance Ritual is more to do with personal effort and is self-focussed, and self-critically oriented. In this sense, developing a relationship with the Transcendent over the course of the day or during the moments of prayer is the ultimate goal of the Ignatian Examen, while the aim of the Truc Lam Repentance Rituals is to develop a strong sense of morality in relation to the self and the surrounding world. One can also see that a major difference between these two rituals is that, while the original texts of the Truc Lam Repentance Rituals are elaborate and descriptive, the Ignatian Examen is short and simple, and invites each individual to imagine and elaborate his or her consciousness of daily life. Finally, while the Truc Lam Repentance Rituals begin with the human senses and deepen a sense of awareness or consciouness, the Ignatian Examen looks first at the interior life and reflects on both internal and external movements including the senses.

Interreligious Applications

This article has explored the historical development, structures, content and methods of the Six-Period Rituals of Repentance and the Ignatian Examination of Concience. It has discussed the signficant similarities and differences between these methods of reflection. In addition, it has analyzed how these methods have contributed to transforming the spiritual lives of millions of Buddhist and Christian followers in Vietnam and in the West respectively. My hope is that it will not only offer a better understanding of interreligious spirituality but also enrich spiritual practices between the Truc Lam Zen and Ignatian traditions. Although fundamental differences between Buddhist and Christian theologies are present and should be recognized (Schmidt-Leukel 2017, 11-18), I would argue that searching for common ground in spiritual practices and insights between the two traditions will open the door for mutual understanding and appreciation. Moreover, as the Truc Lam Zen and Ignatian traditions share some significant insights into the spiritual characteristics of human consciousness and awareness, Christian and Buddhist practitioners can enrich their daily examination of consciouness and their awareness of how they are using their senses by appropriating useful elements from the other tradition.

To take the Christian side first, applying the Truc Lam Zen's method of examining the six human senses – seeing, hearing, smelling, tasting, touching and thinking – first of all could help the Christian develop a deeper sense of gratitude for the free gifts of physical, sensual and mental faculties that have been given by God. The examiner will gradually discover the gift-giver through the gifts received. This discovery on the one hand enables the Christian to praise God as the primary source of life and to experience deeply the presence of God, not only through his or her senses but also through the outside world perceived and experienced by the human senses. In addition, in order to grow into a mature Christian life, she or he needs to develop a capacity of discernment of the spirits that operate in our lives during the day. In other words, the Christian needs to be able to distinguish the multiple influences that either draw a person to God or drive him or her away. In this sense, channelling the human senses in accordance with God's designed plans for him or her will help the person keep in touch with his or her authentic self and experience peace or consolation at the end of the day. Besides, one of the important components of the Ignatian Examen is to orient the practitioner towards a near future, that is, how one will respond to God in a particular situation in the day to come. Therefore, employing the Truc Lam Zen's examinations of the human senses can help the Christian to become more aware of how she or he uses senses to be in touch with Transcendence in each moment of life.

If the Truc Lam Zen's examination of the human senses could help the Christian grow in a more intimate relationship with God and with self, the Ignatian Examen could probably also provide great insights for Buddhist spirituality. One of the most profound components of Ignatian spirituality is to help the Christian grow in a life of gratitude. This is clearly laid out in the daily Ignatian Examen. While the Truc Lam Zen's method of examination is more focussed on individual sins, developing a sense of gratitude for their human senses and for the gifts received during the day would help Truc Lam's Buddhist practitioners experience a new dimension of spirituality shared by Christians and Buddhists.

Another aspect of Ignatian spirituality that can be shared with the Truc Lam Zen's approach to daily reflection is the discernment of spirits. Although Buddhists do not believe in God the creator, many do believe in the spirits. From this belief, in addition to identifying the internal and external influences channelled through senses mentioned above, Truc Lam's Buddhist practitioners might want to look at the stimulus in life through Ignatian lenses, that is, to develop an awareness of the spirits that often influence human emotions and our ways of responding to life circumstances as well as making daily choices. In so doing, both traditions would enrich each other, on the one hand, and open the door for further spiritual conversations, on the other.

Bibliography

Aschenbrener, George, 1972. 'Consciousness Examen,' *Review for Religious* 31: 14-21.

Chan, Hien Tam, 2014. 'Khoa Nghi Luc Thoi Sam Hoi.' *Giac Ngo Magazine*, 24 November 2014.

Dao, Duy Anh, 2005. *Nghien Cuu Van Hoa va Ngu Van* [Research on Culture and Language]. Ha Noi: Nha Xuat Ban Giao Duc.

Dao, Duy Anh, 2010. *Lich Su Viet Nam* [A History of Vietnam]. Ha Noi: Nha Xuat Ban Van Hoa Thong Tin.

Gallagher, Timothy, 2006. *The Examen Prayer: Ignatian Wisdom for Our Lives Today*. New York: Crossroad.

Ganss, George, 1992. *The Spiritual Exercises of Saint Ignatius*. Saint Louis: The Institute of Jesuit Sources.

Modras, Ronald, 2014. *Ignatian Humanism: A Dynamic Spirituality for the Twenty-First Century*. Chicago: Loyola Press.

Mossa, Mark, 2012. *Saint Ignatius of Loyola: The Spiritual Writings*. Nashville: Sky Light Paths Publishing.

Nguyễn, Hùng Hậu, 1996. *Góp Phần Tìm Hiểu Tư Tưởng Triết Học Phật Giáo Trần Thái Tông* [A Contribution to Studying Tran Thai Tong's Buddhist Philosophy]. Hà Nội: Nhà Xuất Bản Khoa Học Xã Hội.

Nguyen, Tai Thu, ed., 2008. *The History of Buddhism in Vietnam*. Washington: The Council for Research in Values and Philosophy.

Pieris S.J., Aloysius, 2000. *Mysticism of Service: A Short Treatise on Spirituality with a Pauline-Ignatian Focus on The Prayer-Life of Christian Activists*. Gonawala-Kelaniya: Tulana Research Center.

Robb S.J., Paul V., 1982. 'Conversion as a Human Experience.' *Studies in the Spirituality of Jesuits*. XIV.3: 1-47.

Roccasalvo, Joan L., 1988. 'The Daily Examen'. In *The Christian Ministry of Spiritual Direction*, ed. David L. Fleming SJ, St Louis: *Review for Religious*: 312-317.

Schmidt-Leukel, Perry, 2017. *Buddhist-Christian Relations in Asia*. Munich: EOS.

Stanley S.J., David, 1994. *A Modern Scriptural Approach to The Spiritual Exercises*. Saint Louis: The Institute of Jesuit Sources.

Tetlow, Joseph, 2008. *Making Choices in Christ: The Foundation of Ignatian Spirituality*. Chicago: Loyola Press.

Thich, Dat Ma Quan Hien, 2015. *Thiền Tông Việt Nam Trên Đường Phục Hưng* [A Rebirth of Vietnamese Zen Tradition]. Ho Chi Minh: Nhà Xuât Bản Tôn Giáo.

Thich, Dat Ma Quan Hien, 2016. Personal Interview (Spiritual Experience in Meditation), 15 July 2016.

Thich, Thanh Từ, 2013. *Nghi Thuc Sám Hối Sáu Căn* [Six Senses Rituals of Repentance]. Ho Chi Minh: Nha Xuat Ban Ton Giao.

Thich, Thanh Từ, 2015a. *Khoa Hu Luc Giang Giai* [A Commentary on the Discourse on the Void]. Ho Chi Minh: Van Hoa-Van Nghe.

Thich, Thanh Từ, 2015b. *Thiền Việt Nam Cuối Thế Kỷ Hai Mươi* [Vietnamese Zen Tradition in the Twentieth Century]. Ho Chi Minh: Phuong Dong.

Thich, Thien An, 1975. *Buddhism and Zen in Vietnam*. Vermont: Charles E. Tuttle Company.

Tran, Thai Tong, 2015. 'Khoa Nghi Lục Thời Sám Hối' [Six Period Rituals of Repentance]. In *Khoa Nghi Lục Thời Sám Hối Giảng Giải*, ed. Thich Thanh Từ. Ho Chi Minh: Nha Xuat Bản Tôn Giáo. The complete list of forty-two verses for this examination can be found at the Buddhist online library at *https://thuvienhoasen.org/a6705/13-tua-khoa-nghi-sau-thoi-sam-hoi.*

Traub, George, ed., 2008. *An Ignatian Spirituality Reader*. Chicago: Loyola Press.

CONTRIBUTORS AND EDITORS

Ursula Baatz gained her PhD at the University of Vienna and has lectured at different universities in ethics and intercultural philosophy. She is an Associate of the Herbert C. Kelman Institute for Interactive Conflict Transformation (Vienna-Jerusalem) and co-founder and co-editor of *Polylog: Zeitschrift für Interkulturelles Philosophieren*. She has been involved in the practice and theory of Christian - Zen-Buddhist Dialogue for many years. Her publications include: *Erleuchtung trifft Auferstehung. Zen-Buddhismus und Christentum. Eine Orientierung* (Berlin 2009); *Hugo M. Enomiya-Lassalle. Leben zwischen den Welten. Eine Biographie* (Zürich 1998); *Hugo M. Enomiya-Lassalle. Una vida entre mundos, Biografía* (Bilbao 2001); *Buddhismus* (München 2002; in Polish 2004, in Hungarian 2006).

Karl Baier studied cultural anthropology, philosophy and Catholic theology. He holds a doctorate in philosophy and works as a Professor within the Department for the Study of Religions at Vienna University, Austria. His publications include a history of yoga's reception in the West and a two-volume study on meditation and modernity, *Meditation und Moderne: Zur Genese eines Kernbereichs moderner Spiritualität in der Wechselwirkung zwischen Westeuropa, Nordamerika und Asien* (Würzburg 2009). His present research interests include new forms of religiosity in the nineteenth and twentieth centuries, mesmerism, occultism, modern yoga research and psychedelics.

Thomas Cattoi is Associate Professor of Christology and Cultures at the Jesuit School of Theology at Santa Clara University, which is part of the Graduate Theological Union in Berkeley, California. He also holds the Dwan Family Chair in Ecumenical and Interreligious Dialogue. He is the author of *Divine Contingency: Theologies of Divine Embodiment in Maximos the Confessor and Tsong kha pa* (Gorgias Press 2009); *Theodore the Studite: Writings on Iconoclasm* (Paulist Press 2014); *Theologies of the Sacred Image in Theodore the Studite and Bokar Rinpoche* (forthcoming). He has published articles in early Christian theology and Buddhist-Christian dialogue. He co-edits the journal *Buddhist-Christian Studies* from the University of Hawaiʻi and is the editor of *Perceiving the Divine Through the Human Body: Mystical Sensuality* (Palgrave Macmillan 2011); *Death, Dying and Mysticism: The Ecstasy of the End* (Palgrave Macmillan 2015); and *Depth Psychology and Mystical Phenomena* (Palgrave Macmillan, 2018). He has been visiting professor at a number of Chinese universities through the Malatesta initiative of the California province of the Society of Jesus. Professor Cattoi is also a licensed psychotherapist (LMFT) in the state of California.

Elise Anne DeVido received her doctorate in History and Asian Languages from Harvard University. She has published works on: women and gender in Chinese and in Vietnamese Buddhism; the transnational Buddhist revivals of the early twentieth century; and Engaged Buddhism. Currently she is the Sheng Yen Foundation Visiting Fellow in Chinese Buddhism at the Graduate Institute for Religious Studies, National Chengchi University, Taiwan.

Sybille Fritsch-Oppermann did an MA in theology in Germany and then spent time in Japan as a postgraduate in Intercultural Studies at ICU, Tokyo. Here she became familiar with Japanese Buddhism, spending several months in a Buddhist monastery and starting research within Buddhist Studies. Her doctorate surveyed Christian existence in a Buddhist context, namely Japan. Since then, she has organized international think-tanks and conferences related to Buddhist-Christian studies in countries such as Germany, Czech Republic, Turkey, Russia and Malaysia, and has conducted seminars and lectures in this field, for example as a junior professor at Hamburg University from 1988-1991, at the Ecumenical Institute, Bossey, and at various other German universities. She is currently the Representative for Tourism, Culture and Public Relations of the Church of Lower Saxony/Upper Harz Region and a Part Time Lecturer at Clausthal University of Technology, Germany.

Elizabeth Harris holds an Honorary Senior Research Fellowship within the Edward Cadbury Centre for the Public Understanding of Religion at Birmingham University (UK). Previous to this, she was an Associate Professor in Religious Studies at Liverpool Hope University (UK), specializing in Buddhist Studies. She is an International Adviser to the Society for Buddhist-Christian Relations and is currently President of the European Network of Buddhist-Christian Studies. Her publications include: *What Buddhists Believe* (Oneworld 1998); *Theravāda Buddhism and the British Encounter: Religious, missionary and colonial experience in nineteenth century Sri Lanka* (Routledge 2006); *Buddhism for a Violent World: A Christian Reflection* (Epworth 2010/now published by SCM); *Religion, Space and Conflict in Sri Lanka: colonial and postcolonial contexts* (Routledge 2018).

Leo D. Lefebure is the Matteo Ricci, S.J., Professor of Theology at Georgetown University. He is the author of *True and Holy: Christian Scripture and Other Religions* and the co-author of *The Path of Wisdom: A Christian Commentary on the Dhammapada*. He is also the author of *The Buddha and the Christ* and of *Revelation, the Religions, and Violence*. He is Vice-President of the Society for Buddhist-Christian Studies, Research Fellow of the Chinese University of Hong Kong, and Trustee Emeritus of the Council for a Parliament of the World's Religions.

John Makransky is Associate Professor of Buddhism and Comparative Theology at Boston College, past President of the Society of Buddhist-Christian Studies, and co-founder of the *Foundation for Active Compassion* and *Courage of Care Coalition*.

John's research focusses on connections between wisdom, compassion and devotion in Indo-Tibetan Buddhism, theoretical bases for Buddhist interreligious learning, and issues in the current adaptation of Buddhist meditation practices. John is the developer of *Sustainable Compassion Training*, which aims to help people cultivate inclusive compassion for action while avoiding empathy fatigue and burnout.

Andreas Nehring is Professor of Religious Studies and Mission Studies at the Friedrich Alexander Universität, Erlangen. His fields of research are: Theories of Religious and Cultural Studies, Postcolonial Theologies, Transcultural Processes of Exchange and Communication between Europe and India, History of Missions. His publications include: *Orientalismus und Mission – Die Repräsentation südindischer Religion durch deutsche Missionare* (Wiesbaden: Harrassowitz 2003); *Religious Turns – Turning Religions: Veränderte kulturelle Diskurse – neue religiöse Wissensformen* (ed. with Joachim Valentin, Stuttgart: Kohlhammer 2008); *Fundamentalism and Secularism: the Indian Predicament* (ed., Chennai: Navashakti 1994); *Postkoloniale Theologie* (ed. with Simon Tielesch, Stuttgart 2011).

Thao Nguyen is a faculty member of the Religious Studies Department at Santa Clara University, California. His research interests focus on Asian religions, interreligious dialogue, comparative spirituality and Christianity in Asia. His current research focusses on Buddhist and Christian popular devotion and meditation. Nguyen teaches courses on Jesus Across Cultures, Asian Religious Traditions, Mary and Guan-yin: Buddhism and Christianity, and Interreligious Studies at Santa Clara University.

John O'Grady is a teacher and part-time lecturer in the School of Religion, Trinity College Dublin. His doctorate is in Buddhist-Christian dialogue. He is Vice-President elect of the European Network of Buddhist-Christian Studies.

Robert Sharf is D. H. Chen Distinguished Professor of Buddhist Studies in the Department of East Asian Languages and Cultures, and Chair of the Center for Buddhist Studies, at the University of California, Berkeley. He works primarily in the area of medieval Chinese Buddhism (especially Chan), but has also published on Japanese Buddhism, Buddhist art, Buddhist modernism, ritual studies, and methodological issues in the study of religion.

Sarah Shaw read Greek and English at Manchester University, where she did her doctorate in English Literature. After studying Pāli and Sanskrit at Oxford, she now writes and lectures on Buddhist subjects. She has written several books on Buddhist meditation and related narratives. She is a fellow of the Oxford Centre for Buddhist Studies, and a member of the Faculty of Oriental Studies and Wolfson College (University of Oxford).

Elizabete Taivane is an Assistant Professor at the Faculty of Theology, University of Latvia, teaching modern world religions, Buddhism, interreligious dialogue, the phenomenology of religion and Christian mysticism. She is a Visiting Lecturer at the Academy of Art in Riga, specializing in Eastern Art. The field of her research is comparative hagiography, comparative mysticism and the comparative analysis of Christianity and Buddhism. She is interested also in the reception of Eastern religious ideas in the Western world and in modified Latvian animistic cults.

Nicholas Alan Worssam SSF studied Theology and Religious Studies at the University of Cambridge, and Buddhism at the University of Bristol in England, and taught for three years in Seoul, South Korea. In 1995 he joined the Anglican religious community, The Society of Saint Francis. Since 2002 he has lived at Glasshampton Monastery in Worcestershire, for the last twelve years serving as Guardian. He was ordained priest in 2007 after further studies at the University of Birmingham, and is an honorary canon of Worcester Cathedral. He is a regular visitor to Amaravati Buddhist Monastery, where he co-leads Buddhist-Christian retreats.

THE EUROPEAN NETWORK
OF BUDDHIST CHRISTIAN STUDIES

The European Network of Buddhist Christian Studies was established 1996 in Hamburg at the Academy of Mission, University of Hamburg. At this time its title was 'European Network for Christian Studies of Buddhism'. At the conference of 1997, which was held at the Benedictine Archabbey of St. Ottilien near Munich, the name was changed to the 'European Network of Buddhist Christian Studies' so that both Buddhists and Christians could be involved on an equal footing. The administrative home of the Network also changed to the Archabbey of St. Ottilien in Bavaria, Germany, because of the Archabbey's strong support for inter-monastic dialogue. The Network is an association of scholars in Europe involved in Buddhist-Christian Studies. Its main activity is to hold a bi-annual international conference on a theme important to Buddhist-Christian Studies. Since 1997, the following conferences have been held:

1999   Buddhist Perceptions of Jesus (St. Ottilien)

2001   Christian Perceptions of the Buddha (Lund, Sweden)

2003   Buddhism, Christianity and the Question of Creation (Scotland)

2005   Conversion and Belonging in Buddhism and Christianity (St. Ottilien)

2007   Buddhist Attitudes to Other Religions (Salzburg)

2009   Sources of Authority in Buddhism and Christianity (St. Ottilien)

2011   Hope: A Form of Delusion? Buddhist and Christian Perspectives (Liverpool)

2013   History as a Challenge to Buddhism and Christianity (In association with the Catholic University of Leuven and held in Drongen, near Leuven)

2015   Buddhist-Christian Relations in Asia (St Ottilien)

2017   Meditation in Buddhist-Christian Encounter: A Critical Analysis (Montserrat, near Barcelona, in cooperation with the Universitat Pompeu Fabra)

2019   Buddhist-Christian Encounter – A Visionary Approach. A Conference inspired by Lynn A. de Silva (St Ottilien, in partnership with the World Council of Churches)

High profile academics have been invited from around the world to contribute to these conferences. The conference papers of each have been published, either as a book or in a special edition of an academic journal.

The first President of the Network was Professor Aasulv Lande, (University of Lund, Sweden). The second was Professor John D'Arcy May, (Irish School of Ecumenics, Dublin, Ireland). The current President is Dr. Elizabeth Harris (Birmingham University, United Kingdom) and the current Secretary is Dr. Martin Rötting (Freising, Germany). In June 2019 she will be succeeded by Professor Perry Schmidt-Leukel (Münster University) as President and Dr John O'Grady as Vice-President.

More information about the Network and its conferences can be found on the Network's website: http://www.buddhist-christian-studies-europe.net/